"Adam-Troy Castro's stories are haunting, visionary, hilarious, demented, acerbic, strange, terrifying, and as full-tilt, whacked-out gonzo as anything I've ever seen."

—ALLEN STEELE, author of *Orbital Decay*

"His plots make you shake your head and wonder why nobody thought of this before. His characters are refreshingly real. His prose is readable without sacrificing complexity. He is, quite simply, one of the finest writers working today."

—KEITH R. A. DECANDIDO, author of *Venom's Wrath*

"Adam-Troy Castro provides some extra brain stimulation. Heavy energy sparks across the synapses in reaction to his brain-tickling prose. Neurons may well overheat. It's good to see a writer who jumps on the back of wild ideas, gives them a taste of his spurs, hangs on for dear life, and lets the ideas take him—and the reader—into new territory."

—ERNEST HOGAN, *Science Fiction Weekly*

"Castro's vivid ideas and accomplished storytelling are a pleasure to read."

—CATHERINE ASARO, Hugo-nominated author of *The Phoenix Code*

ALSO BY ADAM-TROY CASTRO

Lost in Booth Nine

X-Men/Spider-Man: Time's Arrow Book 2, The Present
(with Tom DeFalco)

Spider-Man: The Gathering of the Sinister Six

An Alien Darkness

A Desperate Decaying Darkness

Spider-Man: The Revenge of the Sinister Six

Spider-Man: The Secret of the Sinister Six

*Vossoff and Nimmitz: Just a Couple of Idiots
Reupholstering Space and Time*

Tangled Strings

With the Stars in their Eyes
(with Jerry Oltion)

The Shallow End of the Pool

"MY OX IS BROKEN!"

Adam-Troy Castro

Roadblocks, Detours, Fast Forwards, and Other Great Moments from TV's *The Amazing Race*

BENBELLA

BENBELLA BOOKS, INC.
Dallas, Texas

BENBELLA

BenBella Books, Inc.
10440 N. Central Expy., Suite 800
Dallas, TX 75231
www.benbellabooks.com
Send feedback to feedback@benbellabooks.com
BenBella is a federally registered trademark.

Printed in the United States of America

Library of Congress Cataloging-in-Publication Data

Castro, Adam-Troy.
   My ox is broken! : roadblocks, detours, fast forwards, and other great moments from TV's The amazing race / Adam-Troy Castro.
      p. cm.
   ISBN 1-932100-91-1
   1. Amazing race (Television program) I. Title.

PN1992.77.A5533C37 2006
791.45'72—dc22

                                                                2006014200

Proofreading by Rebecca Green, Jennifer Thomason, and Stacia Seaman
Cover design by Todd Michael Bushman
Text design and composition by John Reinhardt Book Design

Distributed to the trade by Two Rivers Distribution, an Ingram brand
(www.tworiversdistribution.com)

Special discounts for bulk sales are available. Please contact
bulkorders@benbellabooks.com.

This one's for Bill Wilson,
who's run an amazing race.

CONTENTS

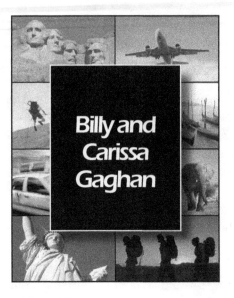

What We Did on Our Summer Vacation

BILLY

The Amazing Race is such a great show because it brings people all around the world to learn about other peoples culture and how they live their life. Also, it is a very competitive game and so you work harder and also learn about different attributes that you never knew you had before. But since the game is so competitive, you never really get to look around to see how truly amazing the place that you're in is. The places that you go to on The Amazing Race all have something in common, that they are famous like the Delaware River or cool like the WORLD'S BIGGEST OFFICE CHAIR (in Alabama). The Amazing Race is a great show and if you think you can do it and you want to do it, do it.

I like The Amazing Race because it is a reality TV show and so the game is not a fixed race and so they don't pick a team and let them win. In The Amazing Race you have to work hard or you're not going to make it that far. Also the people behind the scenes, like the security guys, were really great guys. And the camera and sound guys were really friendly too. The Amazing Race is a truly amazing show that takes people around the world and those people realize how good they have it in America. Also, all of the other people on The Amazing Race 8 were really great people even though some looked bad on the show.

Being a kid on The Amazing Race was awesome because a kid has a different perspective than an adult and because you have more energy to use than an adult. In Costa Rica, at the time I did not sleep for the past three days and I wasn't tired, but some of the others were dead asleep and me and my sister Carissa had a lot of caffeine and adrenaline running through us so we were able to run one mile at 2 o'clock in the morning. But in the Race that we were on, there were no kid challenges or specifically challenges meant for kids. When we went on the show, we though that there would be families with kids, but it was just us and the Black Family. I had a great time any way.

CARISSA

Kids being on The Amazing Race was a very good idea. The Amazing Race can help people learn about other people's culture and language. Also, it helps people go to other places that they would never go to. Being a kid on The Amazing Race was awesome! When you are on The Amazing Race, you can do things that you could never do before in your life! Amazing Race is one of the best reality shows on TV because on The Amazing Race you can learn something new every day until your time is up.

Also the challenges (Roadblocks, Detours and Route Info) were awesome because after you finish one you never know what you are going to go to next, like a Pitstop.

Pitstops can be scary (if you are last) or they can be very exciting (if you are first)! If you are lucky, you may not be eliminated. If you see a Fast Forward and no one took it and you are last, then you should take it. The only problem about taking the Fast Forward is that you can only use it once and that you could come in last place (if you get lost). If you are on The Amazing Race, you get to have camera and sound guys follow you around. They are fun to do things with. You can do fun things like play cards with other teams and camera and sound guys.

In Detours, you can switch them if you can not do them (like the first one is the mud bog and you can't do it, then you can go to another one like de-heading shrimp). In Roadblocks, only one person can do it (two people for the Family Edition). The bad thing about Roadblocks is that you can't switch people and if you decide to do a penalty (decide to quit) then you will have to wait 4 hours. Route Info's are when you have to go some place else. Like if you are in Washington and you might get a Route Info to make you go to Florida. Some Route Info can make you go farther than other Route Info.

Phil is the official eliminator; he doesn't like to eliminate people but he loves to say, "You are Team number One!". And when he says you are number one, he might also say "for being the winners of this Leg of the race" you will get something like a trip from Travelocity or you could actually win something like a car! I wish we won something!

I had a lot of fun on The Amazing Race and I want to do it again when I get older!

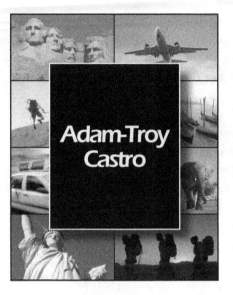

Adam-Troy
Castro

Introduction

'M GONNA CLUE YOU IN on a secret, here.

I hate reality television.

I loathe the concocted situations, vapid contestants, and sniggering sexuality of the many series that hinge on speed dating, cruel pranks, staged conflicts, and the ubiquitous hunger for fifteen minutes of fame.

I hate the television news segments that headline the developments of these shows on days that should be dominated by information of greater import.

I hate shows built on stunts, where people scramble for prizes by humiliating themselves in the most appalling ways possible.

I especially despise the bickering-celebs-at-home subgenre: fine entertainment for those who like being locked in a room with the kind of dysfunctional personalities most sane people would cross the street to avoid.

It therefore follows that I avoid the genre when I can.

And yet I follow *The Amazing Race*, that splendid creation of Bertram van Munster and Elise Doganieri, with awestruck, envious devotion.

This show makes me a panting, unreserved fanboy.

Why?

In part, because I just love the set.

The frantic contestants racing around the world in desperate search of that million-dollar check have their eyes on more than the prize. They're confronting the very diversity of the human experience on this planet, testing not only their speed and skill but also their ability to function in places where their language, their appearance, and their expectations render them alien.

Anybody who's ever run for a plane at the last minute, anybody who's ever come face to face with the poverty of the third world, and everybody who's ever left an overseas resort to explore the countryside and meet the locals, has been on an Amazing Race.

And if some contestants behave badly, then that's interesting too, because anybody who's ever suffered the frustrations of travel has run the risk of doing the same thing. We all know what it's like to drive down strange roads, in places unknown to us, and argue with companions who insist on blaming us for being lost. We've all fought over whether she should have taken that left instead of that right. And we've all found unsuspected prejudices revealed when locals speaking in strange tongues fail to understand what we've said to them very, very slowly.

This is hard enough when we're just trying to find our way to the next major highway.

Imagine how much more difficult it must be when a million dollars rides on getting there first.

Imagine that the road between you and that million dollars has been rendered a minefield of challenges capable of testing your courage, your dedication, and your ability to adapt to strange customs in faraway lands.

Imagine having to travel the route at such a punishing speed that the barriers between you and victory include hunger, thirst, jet lag, exhaustion, and sleep deprivation.

Imagine, finally, that your every waking moment is filmed, and that people will be judging you by your attitude as well as your skill.

Some reality-TV contestants whine and moan because they're locked in a luxury apartment for a few weeks. *The Amazing Race* contestants plow fields in Thailand, hang glide in Brazil, climb mountains in Canada, make bricks in India, descend into catacombs in Egypt, and ascend pyramids in Mexico. Along the way, they struggle with their fears and find themselves accomplishing things that many among them would have considered impossible. A few push themselves to the limits of their endurance, and beyond; others make mistakes they never could have imagined. They laugh, they weep, they break down, they argue, they declare that they can't go on, and then they go on anyway. Some learn about themselves, and some, just as pointedly, don't.

Players learn about their partners, too. Some couples have broken up, forever, on-screen. Others have cemented their relationships and gone on to successful marriages. Racers partnered with their family members have found unsuspected reserves of strength in their fathers and mothers and siblings. They have also demonstrated superhuman patience in the face of partners about as useful as dead cats.

The Amazing Race is, in short, a show rich with comedy, drama, and agonizing twists of fate. It boasts the virtues that so many of its reality-show competitors lack: humanity, a broad canvas relevant to the world we live in, a premise that celebrates human diversity, and a structure that measures the character of its contestants in ways that go beyond willingness to embarrass themselves for fame and glory. It helps, too, that its contestants have shown as much warmth, humor, and nobility as the far more typical fame-whore brattiness.

Is it entirely immune from the geek-show antics that have afflicted so many programs of its type? No, it's not. It has its own questionable elements. Among them: the food challenges that sometimes require contestants to eat until they gag. It's perfectly acceptable to confront Racers with food distasteful to the Western palate, less so to make them eat so much that the sheer volume renders them ill. And, though it's perfectly acceptable to force contestants to live within a very strict budget, and deal with the consequences if they run out of money, it's less so to deliberately take their money away in impoverished foreign countries, and therefore make a game out of forcing them to beg for money in places where many less fortunate people beg just to stay alive. Also, the unpleasantness between teams, and between teammates, sometimes goes beyond the merely stressed into the realm of the downright un-pleasant—a factor that especially afflicted Race 6, in which a number of the more congenial teams fell out early, leaving the field to folks who screamed their way from continent to continent. Elements like these provide some of the show's worst moments, pushing it over the line from international adventure to international freak show.

Against that, we have the classic moments, ranging from comedy to tragedy, with everything in between. Chip and Kim, stopping to spend a few moments with an African family in Race 5; Joyce, weeping as her head was shaved in Race 7; Billy and Carissa Gaghan serenading the Aiello family with "She'll Be Coming 'Round the Mountain" in Race 8. And even if you ignore the drama in the foreground, you still have those marvelous locations in the background: from great natural wonders like "the cloud that thunders," to the glimpses of life in other places. Write off the antics of every single contestant and you still have the glories of our world, featuring sights rarely seen in any conventional travelogue or documentary. It's all here, on one show, along with vivid personali-ties, hair-breadth cliff-hangers, and infuriating twists of fate.

Is it "reality"? Some embittered participants say, not at all. They claim fabricated story lines and producer interference favoring some teams at the expense of others. It's hard not to see some of their complaints as sour grapes, but it's also hard to miss the moments when the seams show. (see p. 27 "Is the Race Real?") The practical difficulties involved in just mounting a show on this scale are so enormous that it's amaz-ing any of the proceedings feel spontaneous at all. But it's not exactly a scripted drama, either. From the moment that first mob of players leaves the starting point to the moment the three final teams converge on the finish line, their journey is up to them.

A few words about the format of this book.

First, our *Amazing Race* episode synopses are brief and fragmentary compared to some of the obsessive recaps available online. A book at-tempting to cover the events of the series in that kind of detail would need to be five times the length of this one. Readers who wish that kind of coverage are hereby encouraged to check the host of blogs and recap sites available. The very best of the summary sites, televisionwithoutpi-ty.com, recaps the adventures of our hustling Americans in exhaustive detail, and with the snarkiest of all possible wit. The shows are also discussed on bulletin boards, whose denizens write literally hundreds of posts debating every last detail of every episode. Television Without Pity has such an extensive board, often visited by Racers, but there's another worth mentioning at www.tarflies.com, another place where Racers hang out and shoot the breeze with some of their most dedicated fans.

At their best, these places provide warm, inclusive communities for fans dedicated to the show and the people who run it. Racers are correct in noting that some of the more obsessive posts cross the line past mere fascination into the realm of the mad. (This can be a good or a bad thing. You can usually tell the difference.) But rather than duplicate that material, this book will zip past it as quickly as possible before moving on to explore other aspects of the show and its attendant issues.

Second, this book must examine the personalities involved, sometimes critically, but cautions readers to exercise extreme skepticism when applying any such observations to the lives any of these people live outside the show. In the past, some overwrought viewers, angered by what they've seen, have gone beyond calling individual Racers assholes (which several have been, at least on the air). They've called for the dissolution of marriages, made assumptions about the intricacies of Racers' sex lives, and even, once or twice, hoped for Racers to experience physical harm. In the sixth Race alone, one Racer was, based on the impression he left on-screen, widely and almost universally assumed to be a wife-beater. Another, though traveling with a girlfriend, was declared a closeted homosexual. A third was branded a racist.[1]

At press time, all three charges have been repeated against various Racers from the ninth competition, on the basis of a single aired episode, viewers happily making the wildest of assumptions on the basis of the most limited exposure. We've even had, from some, the even more distasteful added judgment that the two senior citizens in that competition were "senile."[2]

---

[1] The racist charge against Kendra is, alas, the hardest to refute, and I won't even try, but for the observation that there is a qualitative difference between racist comments made in passing and racist behavior representing the whole of an individual's lifetime. We believe we heard the first. We don't know her well enough to make claims about the latter.

[2] Lest we forget Terri Schiavo, long-distance medical diagnoses, based on images on television, are notoriously unreliable. And in this case, obnoxious as well.

Even the children appearing in Race 8 endured such sweeping criticisms by viewers who should have known better. Three episodes into the competition, the youngest scion of the Black family, 8-year-old Austin, had already been called "useless," and the Gaghan kids, 9-year-old Carissa and 12-year-old Billy, "creepy."

(Of that last extremity, I can only say: there are few people more useless and creepy than grown adults capable of spending their Internet hours writing hateful things about children competing on reality shows. I can understand targeting, or even hating, the adults. They placed themselves in the crosshairs. Their behavior is fine grist for abuse. I'll even give a pass to those who heaped scorn on Race 8's teens, since I'll be doing some of the same. But targeting the kids makes me queasy. Do you really want to be sitting before your computer at 3:00 A.M. telling people across the country about how much you "hate" a 9-year-old girl? If you do, I don't want to know you. Get a grip.)

The thing is, I know where blather like this comes from. Reality shows follow many of the same rules as conventional dramas, in that we're invited to form opinions on the character of individuals presented to us at moments of crisis or stress. We have no problem judging Hamlet or Tom Joad or Gilligan or Bobby Ewing, after similar exposure, so why not judge Colin Guinn or Jonathan Baker or Flo Pesenti the same way?

The answer, of course, is that fictional characters are designed, by their creators, to create a given impression, and that even when the nature of that impression is open to debate, the entirety of the relevant evidence is provided for us. Had Stanley Kowalski, male lead of *A Streetcar Named Desire*, donated a tenth of his salary, every week, to local widows and orphans, there would have been a line to that effect in the play. So it's pretty safe to assume he doesn't. We enjoy the same freedom to assume with every other fictional character. By contrast, when we watch Colin or Jonathan or Flo, or any of the people who create lasting impressions on a show like *The Amazing Race*, we are only getting the smallest part of their individual stories.

I know I sure as hell wouldn't want to be judged, forever, by people who know me only by my behavior during a certain awful weekend in New Orleans, more than a decade ago. It was a bad couple of days, ruined by upsetting conflict with my traveling companions, and it led me to fits of hysteria almost as bad as anything you've ever seen from the most hysterical Racer discussed here. If I can maintain, now, that the "me" people witnessed during that weekend was a skewed sample, then I must concede the same is likely true for the Colin and Jonathan and Flo visible in the edited sequences available to viewers.

Even the most contentious personalities here have been captured during what may have been one of the most frenetic, stressful, and exhausting times of their lives. Imagine the worst things you say in any given month, let alone one crazy month, all edited together, and you might feel a little more kindly disposed toward the show's villains. Imagine your very best moments, given the same treatment, and you might find yourself skeptical about the show's heroes. This book will talk about what these people do on-screen, discuss their behavior, and call them names, but anything in that vein deals *only* with the personalities they display in the course of the show, and is an extremely unreliable way to judge the kind of people they are once the cameras stop rolling.

Third, I have for the most part decided to ignore any other TV or reality-show experience enjoyed by the Racers. Yes, it's fun to know that Chip McAllister, an actor in his younger days, appeared as the young Muhammad Ali in *The Greatest*; or that one member of The Bouncer Brothers also appeared on *Fear Factor*; or that any number of Racers have parlayed the notoriety they received here into later gigs on *Mad TV*, *Kill Reality*, *Battle of the Network Reality Stars*, *Dr. Phil*, the Travel Channel, and low-budget movies. But none of that has any relevance to their performances on *The Amazing Race*, and will largely not be discussed here. The only exceptions to that rule: Alison Irwin, from Race 5, whose contentious relationship with her boyfriend Donny Patrick was foreshadowed by her actions on *Big Brother*; and Rob Mariano and Amber Brkich ("Team Truman Show"), whose notoriety from *Survivor* and *Survivor: All-Stars* had a lot to do with the hostile reception they received from some of their competitors during Race 7.

Fourth, I have taken the liberty of declaring certain teams, usually three per Race, as "Season Superstars." These are not necessarily the final three, or the ones I liked most, but the ones who (by my estimation, at least) made the most compelling television. Season Superstars are teams that came off as one of the show's protagonists or antagonists, *even if* they were among the first teams to go. To my mind, some teams that make it to the final three, and even some teams that win, are not nearly as prominent or as memorable until process of elimination leads the editors with nobody else to show. The decision is, of course, entirely arbitrary, and authors of any other *Amazing Race* books will no doubt come up with entirely different names. But what the hell.

Fifth, I will not dwell on the subsidiary prizes that many Racers win, starting with the second Race, during the many legs that lead up to the finale. Sometimes they win cameras, sometimes money, sometimes automobiles, and (often) free vacations. This is all very nice but repetitive to write about in the course of nine Races; I make exceptions only when the prize is directly involved in the game play, or (as in one memorable Race 8 award) when it's so over-the-top spectacular that it rivals the million-dollar prize for potential value.

Sixth, the interviews here have been edited down to approximately one-third of their duration in the real world, in part because of space considerations, but also to reduce the redundancy and fumfuhing you get from any human beings answering questions without a script. (A few sentences that went nowhere were either cleaned up or excised, and I'm not saying this of the Racers alone—as the recordings testify, I can out-fumfuh any man in the room.) As some of these interviews often doubled back on themselves, and covered subjects in an arbitrary order, the order of questions have often been shuffled to provide some semblance of organization. Some of the very worst comments Racers made about competitors they fought with on-screen have been excised. Some have been kept to reflect the politics that affect the Race. With all that said, I have preserved the words and intent of these interview subjects to the absolute best of my ability.

Seventh—yes, we're heading for a record—the majority of the discussion here is dedicated to the first eight Races, all of which aired before my official deadline. Comments of the almanac type, to wit, the only Racer ever to do this, or the only Racer ever to do that, the first time this ever happened, the last time that ever happened, the most endearing moves ever made by Racers, the most jaw-dropping mistakes ever made by Racers, etcetera, cover only those eight Races. I write these words with no idea what's gonna happen in Race 9. The forbearance of my publisher allowed the addition of one section, dealing with the insertion of commentary about that Race. But production limitations prevented me from then poring over the entire manuscript, changing references to Race records in order to accommodate developments from the latest Race. If any readers find this a serious problem, I gently suggest that they go over the published volume with a pencil, inserting asterisks and parenthetical corrections where needed.

Finally: I will refrain from using the word "Philimination." It's a cool neologism, coined by Racers and embraced by fans, which refers to the sad duty host Phil Keoghan performs every time he tells a late-arriving team that they've been eliminated from the competition. It's also a task he performs extraordinarily well, as witnessed by the sheer number of *Race* fans who have approached him, off-season, to request their own, personal Philimination. (Oddly, he reports, nobody asks to be told they've just won a million dollars.) I avoid the word only because the format of this book will require me to use it more than eighty times, in episode synopses alone, and I suspect its humor value will start to pall by number forty or fifty.

Some acknowledgments before we proceed. This is the part that nobody ever reads unless he has some reason to find his own name listed here. It's authorial indulgence, nothing more. The rest of you can skip it.

The beauteous Judi Goodman, a longtime fan of the show who got me hooked midway through Race 4—one service of many, and not the primary reason I later persuaded her to change her name to Judi Castro, but certainly a point in her favor.

Harlan and Susan Ellison manned their VCR in California when Hurricane Wilma knocked out my power in Florida. Thanks to Harlan, Andrew Fox, and Jack McDevitt, among several colleagues from the fantasy/science fiction community who stepped forward with (unnecessary, but certainly appreciated) offers of shelter during that difficult time.

Thanks, too, to the denizens of my newsgroup on www.sff.net, who indulged my *Amazing Race* mania and, in some cases, refrained from watching the show out of concern that it would "ruin" their appreciation of my weekly commentary. (Yeah, I know that's odd. I think so, too. I'm talking to you, Michael Burstein.) Thanks to Glenn Yeffeth and Shanna Caughey, at BenBella Books, who offered me the chance to work on this labor of love, and showed tremendous patience as the book grew like a fungus. Thanks also to my editor, Jennifer Thomason.

Thanks to my Webmaster, Dina Pearlman of pearlsofwebdom.com, who manages to make me look almost adequate.

One of the more controversial Racers, Jonathan Baker, agreed to a lengthy interview even after I told him that it (and this book) would be critical of some of his more upsetting actions during the show. His co-operation, and his help in contacting other contestants, show a level of good sportsmanship not often credited to him by people who know him only as the screaming meemie from Race 6. It was impossible to write about that competition without taking him to task, and saying some un-kind things, but he made it difficult.

Marshall Hudes, from Race 5, was also terrific to talk to, and a great help when it came to communicating with fellow contestants. I look for-ward to someday enjoying a slice of pizza at his restaurant, Café Nostra.

Similar shoutouts go to Jon and Al, the Clowns from Race 4, among the warmest of the Racers I spoke to, and two of the most delightful I got to meet; also Brennan Swain, the lovely Gaghan family, and the Gui-dos (I got to hear the inspirational dog bark, which was, all by itself, a little bonus).

Special thanks and apologies go out to the charming and funny Don and Mary Jean, whose eleventh-hour interview had to be cut due to space considerations: you guys were great, but you fell victim to harsh realities about the number of available pages. Hellos also to the large number of Racers I encountered, either online or in person, who did not make it into this volume for reasons that have everything to do with the finite amount of time I had to write it: you're all good folks, map-throwing and all.

Thanks to the members of my writer's workshop for their input on sections of this manuscript: George Peterson, Chris Negelein, Wade Brown, Mitch Silverman, and Terri Wells.

And thanks to y'all. As Phil says, "Travel safe."

The Rules

TEAMS WHOSE MEMBERS HAVE A preexisting relationship are transported to the starting line, somewhere in America.

None of these teams know each other beforehand. Nor are they allowed to speak to each other until the Race begins.

They have not been allowed to pack cell phones, GPS equipment, credit cards, or cash. They are responsible for their own clothing, toiletries, prescriptions, and any tools, such as flashlights, space blankets, and sleeping bags, they choose to bring along. The show may provide certain specialty items for use in unusual environments (i.e., wet suits, snowshoes, parkas, protective equipment, etc.), but the contestants remain responsible for everything else.

Every team is accompanied by its crew, comprising one cameraman and one sound guy. Teams are responsible for the travel arrangements of their crews. They must treat their crews as children who cannot be left behind. If they cannot take their crews along, they cannot proceed. Teams that experience unavoidable production delays are often, but not always, given time credits at the close of each *leg*.

Teams are provided a certain amount of cash at the onset of each leg of the Race. This amount can be anything from nothing to hundreds of dollars. It is, in theory, enough to carry teams to the *Pit Stop* that ends each leg of the Race. Teams must use this money to pay for ground transportation, food, tickets to any attractions visited in the course of the Race, shelter when necessary, and any other items they might be required to purchase. There is some room for discretionary spending, but not much. Sometimes, teams have enough extra money to pay for overnight hotel stays. Sometimes they can pick up a souvenir or two. Just as often, they find themselves bankrupted and stranded without carfare. Teams low on cash, or wishing to curry additional advantage, do have the option of begging for money, though teams that do are subject to local laws. For instance: when the issue came up in Race 7, it turned out that teams are now prohibited from begging in any U.S. airports. Any money the team manages to save is added to the money provided on the next leg, so economy is important.

The one major expense paid for by the show is air transportation. Teams are provided with special credit cards that can only be used to purchase tourist-class airline tickets. Teams can *only* buy tourist-class tickets, though sufficiently glib teams have been known to talk airlines into giving them free upgrades to first class. Teams that accidentally buy the wrong kind of ticket must change their tickets, leave their respective planes, or risk penalties that may include disqualification. In Race 8, the credit cards were valid for gasoline purchases as well.

Following instructions provided in their first *clue envelope*, teams must make their way to a specific location, often a country hundreds or even thousands of miles away, to reach the next set of instructions. Getting to that location means the purchase of airplane tickets at the last minute, requiring teams to brave airport crowds in a hustle for the most advantageous arrival times. This is a ritual that Racers will have to go through many times on the course of their respective journeys. Teams have to deal with overbooked flights, dicey connections, weather and scheduling delays, and all airport- security regulations. Teams not strong at this have been known to arrive at their destinations hours or days behind all other players (see p. 116 The Gutsy Grannies, Race 2). In practice, any advantage can be crucial. Even a delay getting off a plane can knock teams out of the Race. The canniest teams try to get seats near the front of their planes.

The same wisdom applies when teams travel by bus, train, cable car, or ferry. As with air travel, local schedules remain paramount throughout. It does teams little good to arrive at a location fifteen minutes after a crucial bus has left when there's a ten-hour wait for the next one. Teams traveling by *taxi* must pay any fare required by the driver. Teams that run out of money must either get the driver to forgive or lower their debt (see p. 238 The Enthusiastic Tourists, Race 5), or somehow obtain enough money to cover the fare (see p. 328 Team Enron, Race 7). Teams that stiff their cabbies are subject to all local laws (see p. 238 Team Extreme, Race 5).

Teams are sometimes expected to travel from place to place using *vehicles* provided by the show, at the show's expense: rental cars or boats. They are responsible for the upkeep of their vehicles. *Flat tires* are considered a reasonable risk, which they must fix themselves or with any local aid they manage to obtain. Sometimes teams suffer more catastrophic failures. If the problem is not the team's fault, then the show will provide a replacement vehicle as soon as one can be delivered. Teams still have to suffer the consequences of any delay. If the problem *is* the fault of the team (i.e., negligence, or outright sabotage like pumping regular gas into a diesel engine), then teams are forced to make do, by any means within the rules.

Following these instructions will often mean performing certain difficult *tasks* before being provided the next *clue envelope*. Tasks are designed to test teams in a variety of different ways. Some reward strength, endurance, and athletic ability. Others test courage in the face of frightening (though rigorously safety-tested) challenges dealing with heights. Still others test manual dexterity, or patience, or the stomach to ingest bizarre local foods, or just plain luck. The variety offered is enough to ensure that smart teams of below-average physical fitness can last as long as dimmer teams comprised of extreme-sports fanatics. And even teams that excel in all areas can be undone by the first poorly timed traffic jam. It happens.

Tasks also follow different formats. Most legs feature both a *Roadblock* and a *Detour*.

A Roadblock is a task that can be performed by only one team member. (In Race 8, sometimes both team members.) The team member initiating the Roadblock must complete it in order to proceed. The other team member is not permitted to help, or take over. During the first four Races, there was no limit to how many Roadblocks any individual team member could perform, a criterion that permitted some strong players to perform every single Roadblock, while their partners merely cheered them on from the sidelines. Starting with the sixth Race, a change in the rules prohibited any one player from completing more than six Roadblocks for the team, thus forcing weaker or more recalcitrant team members to step up as much as possible, lest they find themselves trapped, at the end of the game, by tasks beyond their own ability to perform.

A Detour is a choice between two tasks, each with their own pros and cons. One may be simple but time-consuming, while the other is complicated but fast for teams that manage to finish quickly. One memorable Detour, in Race 4, required teams to choose between loading a pallet with cheese and digging with their bare hands through a fifteen-foot-high pile of manure. Some teams just couldn't fathom the manure. Others were downright excited at the opportunity. Whatever floats your boat, and gets you to the finish line quickly. Teams that find one option difficult or impossible may switch tasks mid-Detour, an option that may be necessary but often costs time traveling between the two locations. (It's often called Bald-Snarking, a reference to Race 3's brothers Ken and Gerard, who made it an art.) On more than one occasion, teams have switched tasks in mid-Detour, found the other option even worse, and switched back. This is not necessarily fatal, but it can be time-consuming, and anything time-consuming in the Race is risky.

Teams unable to complete a given task may elect to *pass*, in which case they will be assessed a *penalty* at the discretion of the show's producers. Penalties have been known to range from half an hour to a full day. For some teams (see p. 329 Race 7's Team Truman Show), taking the penalty qualifies as brilliant strategy. For others (see p. 64 Race 1's Team Oh, Mom), it's a direct path to elimination.

Some legs also have a *Fast Forward*. This is a task that can only be performed by the first team to claim it. Completing it allows teams to proceed directly to the Pit Stop, bypassing the rest of the leg. It is a powerful tool for teams near the end of the pack who need to avoid coming in last. But there are drawbacks: each team is only allowed one Fast Forward in the entire Race, and teams that waste theirs early on cannot choose the option later. Also, teams can easily travel far out of their way to the location of that leg's Fast Forward, only to find out that another team has arrived and completed the task before them. Failing to complete a Fast Forward, or refusing to complete one out of fear, distaste, or preference, can be fatal.

The first four Races featured one Fast Forward for every leg of the Race, except the final round. Many teams had a chance to choose this option. Starting with the fifth Race, a rule change limited the total number of Fast Forwards to three or less. The Fast Forward is not as critical a factor as it once was. But it ought to be.

The fifth Race introduced one final feature, the *Yield*. The first team to reach this signpost has the option of naming a team, somewhere behind them, that upon reaching the same point will have to stop in place for a predetermined period of time. As with the Fast Forward, no team can use the Yield more than once. In practice, most teams virtuously avoid using the Yield. But a Yield claimed at the most advantageous moment can cement an advantage and trap a dangerous team at the rear of the pack.

Meeting all of these challenges, teams eventually reach the Pit Stop for that leg of the Race, often a site with significant local history. Upon their arrival, they are greeted by a native in traditional local garb, and (starting with Race 2) host Phil Keoghan, who milks every possible dramatic pause, often to the point of ridiculousness, while telling them how well they've done. The first team to arrive there often wins an incentive prize, which can be anything from a digital camera to a luxury vacation. (Or better: Race 8's Bransens won a prize with a cash value in the hundreds of thousands.)

The last team to arrive is most often *eliminated*, with Phil's abject apology, leaving a narrower field for Racers proceeding to the next leg. For most of the Race, arriving *first* is nice, but not nearly as important as not arriving *last*.

Teams may arrive at the Pit Stop last and find out that they're still in the game, as a fixed number of *non-elimination legs*, their placement determined in advance, are built into the rules. Players in this position often react with joy or (when they're really tired) resignation. During the first four Races, teams lucky enough to be saved by a non-elimination leg proceeded to the next leg without penalty. Starting with the fifth Race, it got nastier: teams had all their cash confiscated, and had to beg for what they needed to proceed to the next leg. This proved a small impediment for teams that often had little difficulty raising the cash they needed, so the seventh Race tightened the screws still further, divesting teams of everything but their passports and the clothes on their backs. Teams have been known to recover from these handicaps and still compete in the final three. One team has actually won. So it's not fatal. It's still a nasty thing to go through in a country like (picking one example at random) Senegal.

All teams arriving at the Pit Stop without being eliminated are given a *mandatory rest period* of at least twelve hours. Here, they will be allowed to eat, sleep, and mingle with the other teams. These activities are as subject to filming as anything that happens during active legs, a factor which allows home audiences tantalizing glimpses of inter-team conflict, and sometimes inter-team flirting. Pit Stops can last longer than twelve hours, when production requires. Some last as long as thirty-six hours. However long these rest stops last, remaining teams begin the next leg at a time of day corresponding to twelve hours since their respective arrivals. A team that arrives at 5:07 P.M. will leave at 5:07 A.M., and so on. Penalties and time-bonuses left over from the previous legs may well affect their departure times. Bunching points may render the departure point moot, or may not. But it's best to be safe.

The elimination process continues until the *final leg*, at which time the three remaining teams compete for the *million-dollar prize*. The final leg, which is often among the most grueling, can involve several different airplane flights and stops in a number of different countries. It always ends at some location within the continental United States, and has often been close enough to hinge on a final mad dash for the finish line. The previously eliminated teams, including some that fell so early that viewers may have trouble remembering them, are always on hand to cheer the exhausted winners as they run up to the mat.

Everything ends with hugs.

The Real Rules

1. Feel free to make friends with your competitors, socialize with them when not racing, and treat them with all the respect and consideration you'd like to receive from fellow travelers, but don't, for even one tenth of a second, believe that you can trust any of them. Any alliances you form to get from point A to point B can and will be abandoned at the first moment this becomes at all convenient. This may include everything from refusing to share information to downright lying, as in telling you there's no flag over there when in fact they're returning from that flag with the clue that will enable them to beat you.

2. Understand that there's nothing at all personal about this unless you make it that way. Be a sport about it, and the very same people who betrayed you yesterday will happily work with you again to gain a mutual advantage. Be nasty, or vengeful, about it,

and they will say, "To hell with you," even when it costs them nothing. Fighting about it is especially stupid. You're not only making yourself look like an idiot in front of them, but you're also probably doing it on national television. There will be thousands of people on the Internet talking about how stupid you are and how much they want you to lose.

3. Respect your partner. You chose to compete alongside this person. You may come to regret it in the course of the Race, but making an issue about it is a sure way to make your journey more difficult, and miserable, than it truly has to be. Calling your partner stupid, or worthless, or a loser, or an idiot, or worse will not get your team to the finish line one moment earlier. It will, however, give your partner fair excuse to say even worse things to you, and possibly even sabotage your chances out of sheer disgust at your behavior. Be patient, be understanding, be forgiving, and even if you lose, you have the consolation of still wanting to talk to each other afterward.

4. Don't get physical. The shoving incident in Berlin was so ugly that Jonathan Baker briefly became the most hated man on reality television.[3] It's hard to think of a context that would excuse his behavior at that moment, but even if you concede his love for his wife, the pressure-cooker environment of the Race, and the show's ability to create exaggerated "story lines" via editing—as this writer is happy to do—his hotheaded behavior remains the overwhelming impression he left with the general public. You don't want to find yourself in the same position.

5. It's also low-class to harp on the physical fitness of your competitors. Some of them will be athletes, compared to you. Others will be comparatively out of shape. Showing scorn for them, either on the grounds that they're "pretty people" chosen for their matinee-idol looks, or on the grounds that they're "weak" competitors who don't "deserve" their place in the Race, is another good way to look like an idiot, especially if (like Ray, of Race 7's The Bottom Feeders) you make a big deal about your own superiority and then

---

[3] "Briefly" because new reality shows always produce new villains, pushing the old into the forgotten past. At press time, the current jackass du jour is *The Apprentice*'s Brent.

wind up being outlasted several legs by that couple in their sixties. Everybody brings strengths and weaknesses to the table, and you may not be nearly as invincible as you think. Live with it.

6. Read each new set of instructions carefully. If they instruct you to travel by foot, don't take a cab. If they instruct you to take your rental car, don't take a taxi. If they instruct you to perform an entire series of tasks alone, before returning to your partner, don't return to her after the first task and drag her along while you bounce around the city performing the rest of them together. Failing to follow the instructions will not only cause millions of viewers to consider you an illiterate idiot, but may also subject you to time-penalties which will affect your standing and possibly knock you out of the Race.

7. Some Detours are best defined as "Scary but Fast" versus "Unthreatening but Time-Consuming," to wit: tandem skydiving with an instructor, or riding a donkey cart seven miles. Pick the scary options when possible, even if they terrify you. The show's producers aren't interested in seeing you die a spectacular death on camera. To that end they've safety-tested all of these tasks to make sure that they can be completed, with low risk, by contestants of minimal physical fitness. Teams that chicken out of the scary option in favor of the unthreatening but more time-consuming one, especially when they know they're already near the rear of the pack and fighting elimination, may find themselves going home faster than they expected. Also, avoiding the scary tasks is yet another way of looking stupid on television: after all, you *wanted* to be on this show, and should have watched at least one previous Race to know just what kind of activities you would be expected to perform. Don't moan.

8. It's not entirely necessary to speak a foreign language. Indeed, several past winners have been monolingual. However, players who don't know the local tongue should keep the following principles in mind, as they will be helpful not only for the Race itself, but for any other foreign travel they might someday experience. First: locals who have difficulty understanding you are not, by definition, stupid. Second: talking about them as if they are stupid only makes you look stupid. Third: doing it in their

presence might be even stupider, as some understand more than you might initially assume and may be irritated enough to direct you miles out of your way out of sheer pique. Fourth: they won't understand you any better if you scream at them. Fifth: you can't translate English nouns into any indigenous tongue by adding the idiot suffix "-o," and any attempt to employ that technique will just make you look ignorant and clueless. Sixth: hand gestures and other forms of mime are just as unhelpful, unless you're one of a talented few. Fluttering your hands through the air while making vooming noises will not induce any cabbie to take you to the airport, though he may think you're imitating one of the Three Stooges. Seven: most foreign-speaking peoples are confused by the phrase "choo-choo" and will not respond with a lift to the train station. And eight: "Andale! Rapido!" is an obnoxious thing to say to your cab driver even in Spanish-speaking countries. It is downright brain-damaged to say it in Dubai or Korea.

9. Appreciate the trip. If you see something beautiful, allow yourself a moment to feel the awe. If you're treated kindly by a local, take a moment to express thanks and show your own capacity for charm. If you encounter scenes of horrifying poverty, reflect on your own blessings and appreciate the dignity of other human beings in difficult circumstances. In all these cases, understand that you're just one person scurrying about the surface of a great, big world, with differing aesthetic standards and indigenous customs: take the differences you witness as profound testaments to human diversity, capable of teaching you more than you could ever guess about your own provincial assumptions and unsuspected prejudices. Do this and, win or lose, you'll not only enjoy the trip but earn the affections of the millions of people watching you on television. It's certainly preferable to keeping your head down and your eyes focused on the road ahead, thinking of nothing but the Race, the Race, the Race, and about 1,000 times better than complaining bitterly about the conditions, the sanitary standards, the smells, and the people in "ghetto Africa" who "keep breeding and breeding." And, by the way—when you return to a prosperous country again, ratchet down your relief at

driving past all the same stores you frequent in the malls back home. Benetton is not a sign of paradise, and applauding the homogenization of our global culture makes you look like a shallow twit incapable of appreciating everything else you've seen since leaving your driveway.

10. Learn when to shut up. Seriously. If your partner is doing something unpleasant and frustrating, it doesn't exactly help to say, "Come on, honey! Hurry hurry hurry hurry!" Even the calmest players have been known to blow up when offered such unhelpful encouragement.

11. Most importantly, if a million-dollar prize rides on your boyfriend successfully completing a giant bowl of spicy soup, and he seems to be stomaching it well, it is a spectacularly bad idea to call his attention to the puddles of barf left behind by other players.

Is the Race Real?

THE MOST FREQUENTLY ASKED QUESTION about reality television is whether it's a put-on. Are these real people? Are those crazy statements really coming out of their mouths? Are they really as nuts as they pretend?

The answer, as close as we can determine, is...sort of.

The Amazing Race is not a documentary. It's a reality show. Its contestants are cast according to their potential for creating good television, and its dramatic high points are edited for extra punch. It is very much a real race, in that the contestants are vying for that elusive million dollars...but not all of what we see reflects strict journalistic integrity.

For instance: the Race has cast several couples "dating on and off," who we're told go on this show to determine if they still have a future. Sometimes these people fight bitterly. Sometimes they don't. Sometimes, they seem like distant strangers. Which is true? Well, consider that some have been cast months and months after they filled out their applications. In at least two cases known to me, the couples were not couples anymore. But the individuals had been selected as a pair, by producers who wanted their peculiar chemistry. They therefore had to get back together for the duration of the show, pretending a relationship that, strictly speaking, no longer existed. It's no wonder that some of their spats sound like the kind you hear from divorced people, arguing their assets in court; they're very much rehashing old ground. But it's a rerun, not a drama. They're in it for the million.

Second: the editors select the moments that present the people in a unified manner. If the story line goes that such-and-such Racer is a total jackass, then moments of him being thoughtful, or charming, or kind, or self-effacing, are much less likely to get on the air. This is not the same thing as saying that all bad moments are created by editing (the common complaint of Racers horrified by their portrayals), but it does determine what kind of moments are accentuated, and what kind are left on the editing room floor.[4]

Third: reality-show editors are not above total fabrication. Sarah Kozer, who appeared on *Joe Millionaire*, complained in *Time* magazine that producers inserted sexual noises into a scene where she took the titular hunk behind a tree. She even claims they added a line, "It's better if we're lying down," spoken earlier in the day in another context entirely. Some unhappy *Amazing Race* contestants have accused the show of fabricating arguments from bits and pieces of dialogue, manipulating Racers into saying things that don't accurately reflect their personalities, and moving dialogue so their words refer to other things entirely. *The Amazing Race* does not seem to be as guilty of this sin as some other shows we can name, but it is something for a discerning viewer to keep in mind.

I have said this before and I will say it again. *We don't know these people.* It is possible to tell what's real. Extended scenes, where you can actually see the Racers relating to one another, and speaking words that match their lip movements, are safe. It's easy to tell, for instance, that Flo really was having that bad a day in Vietnam. Or that Colin really was acting the

---

[4] Which is, in and of itself, an antiquated notion, as these days deleted scenes are not so much left on the floor as moved to another file on the hard drive. But anyway.

ugly American in that Tanzanian police station. Or that Gretchen really did fall down and bloody her face. Or, for that matter, that Uchenna really did show that much empathy during Joyce's bad hair day. All those moments, while streamlined by editing, provide more than enough visual and auditory information to establish that the events depicted did indeed go down as shown.

Is it just as possible to determine what's fishy?

Well, here are some things to look for:

1. The Wordless Reaction Shot

Take the moment in Race 6 when, during a day-long train ride, Hellboy attempts to amuse his fellow Racers with an ill-advised quip referencing his partner, Rebecca, as a "bitch." The shot cuts to Rebecca, looking pissed off. The implication is that he just shocked her. The thing is: everybody involved in that scene shared that train compartment for quite some time. She displayed any number of facial expressions during that period. Without a look at the uncut footage, there's no way to know that his statement and her facial expression actually went together as portrayed. For all we know, they might have taken place hours apart. She might have taken his gibe with good humor and returned the jab with some equally mischievous remark about his frequently mentioned mother. For all we know she flashed that disbelieving expression later, at something that Race's sweethearts, Jon and Kris, said. *The Amazing Race* features hundreds of these reaction shots, many of which depict tension between teams, or teammates, which may or may not, in fact, have existed. Sometimes they're inserted just to shorten longer "takes" that, seen in their entirety, would give viewers completely different impressions about who these people are and how they're reacting to one another.

2. Constant Repetition

Some Racers seem to have one-track minds. Sometimes they repeat the same bullet points so often that they establish themselves as truly ridiculous people. Well, guess what. Even if they are truly ridiculous people, which some of them seem to be, repetition should not be construed as evidence. For instance: a running gag, in Race 7, is POW Ron's tendency to relate every locale he visits to Baghdad. After a while, viewers wonder, "Can't this guy talk about anything but Baghdad?" Answer: he absolutely can. But he also traveled with a production crew, who constantly asked him, wherever he went, how the places he visited reminded him of Baghdad. So he obliged. He told them, well, that lightning over there reminds me of the bombing of Baghdad, and these crowded streets over here remind me of streets in Baghdad. And these comments were all inserted into the show, one after another, not only bolstering his real-life persona as a Gulf War POW, but also giving the impression that the dude was incapable of talking about anything else. Bill and Joe, of Team Guido, report something similar of their constant harping on the two years they lived in Paris. Remember: the Racers know that only a fraction of what they do will end up on the air. They know they have to answer the same questions again and again and again. They don't necessarily expect the answers to be used over and over again.

3. Frankenbiting

This is not a scene from the sex life of Al Franken, but the practice of taking speech recorded in three or four different installments, and stitching it together to form a shorter whole. Sometimes this reflects Racer intent. Like the rest of us, they can ramble on and on for long minutes, circling the point they intend to make, without always reaching it. The fast-edited show cannot afford to give them those minutes. So the editors cut out all the fat and get the essential point on-screen in twenty words instead of 2,000. And that's fine—except in cases when most of those 2,000 words are modifiers. Here's an extreme example. Imagine these words coming out of your mouth: "You know, I really hate George. Not that I, like, really *hate* him hate him, 'cause he's a friend, and a nice guy and all, and he'd give me the shirt off his back and all, but he's so smart, and so strong, and everything is so easy for him that he just glides along while the rest of us have to struggle. Sometimes I watch him race out of the office, all done for the day while I'm still stuck doing all my work, and it just makes me want to scream." Cut that to, "I really hate George. Really *hate* him. It just makes me want to scream." Not the same message at all. And a sure source of trouble when somebody tells George that you said you hated him, and he says, "Well, I don't believe he said that, necessarily, but if he did, to hell with him." Which is itself edited down to "To hell with him." Again, *The Amazing Race* does not seem as guilty of this crime as some other shows, but editors do have a story to tell, and any obviously shortened speech is good cause for suspicion.

4. Walk of Shame

This one's a classic. A Racer does something a little sketchy, and the show italicizes it by showing him pace in slow motion, while dramatic music stings on the soundtrack. This is very similar to what muckraking TV reports do, when profiling somebody they want viewers to condemn. It even has a name: the slow-motion perp walk. And it conveys guilt, or sinister intent, when the actual moment conveys something else entirely. Remember: these people are in those airports and bus stations for hours and hours and hours; that look might be nothing more than mere indigestion. Genuinely sinister people move at the same speed as the rest of us.

5. The Mysterious Omission

The Amazing Race has been known to leave out vital information, sometimes for reasons of time, and sometimes because it's not all that interesting as drama. In any of these cases, the result is an incomplete picture. For instance: Drew's on-screen physical threat to the Guidos was considered so serious by producers that he was forced to apologize on camera. The clip was never shown. As a result, the threat becomes a momentary lapse, never taken seriously; the Guidos keep their reputations as scheming villains. Rob and Amber, who never seem to fight during the Race as aired, actually did have a small tiff as they entered Africa: less than obvious, it seems, because it manifested as Amber's withdrawn silence and was not obvious in the few short clips that made it to the completed program.[5] The simple fact that we don't see the long days of travel that separate the footage of a jet plane taking off in one country and landing in another puts a different spin on some of the irritable things Racers say to one another. In any event, look for changes of clothing between one scene and the next. See if the cars switch drivers. See if the men sprout and lose five o'clock shadows. See if they look more or less awake. See if people are suddenly wearing bandages they

---

[5] Whether or not she fights that way in real life, she's also a reality-show veteran, who knows that shutting her yap when upset may be preferable to saying something that will show up on T-shirts later.

weren't wearing in the previous scene. Sometimes these omissions make sense: as, for instance, the stories behind the bandages suddenly worn by Drew and Heckboy are really not all that interesting. And sometimes the omissions hide entirely surprising layers of causation. For instance, we are never shown that Colin and Christie may have lost the million dollars to a flat tire, or that the Linz family had to return to Toronto's CN Tower more than once in order to spot the critical clue in the skyline. The shows as aired omit entire Detours and Roadblocks for reasons of time. Never assume you know everything. Or even that Racers do.

6. False Synchronicity

Viewers should never assume dramatic synchronicity—i.e., editing that makes two teams look like they're racing toward the Pit Stop at the same time—to be actual synchronicity unless it's supported by footage in which both teams appear on-screen at the same time. The frenetic editing that marks the end of many legs is often directly contradicted by the official departure times that begin the next legs. One extreme example: at one point during Race 6, a team was trudging to the mat when they thought they saw their rivals behind them. There *seemed to be* a footrace to the mat. The very next leg revealed that the two teams arrived half an hour apart. Generally, the times at the beginning of each leg present a much more reliable measurement of team performance than the editing of the leg before it.

Moments We See Again and Again (Part One)

0. The Dramatic Turn-Toward-the-Camera During the Credits

Listed here as "Dramatic Moment Zero" because it arguably happens more than any other repeated moment, this is the turn toward the camera that just about every team performs during the opening credits sequence. Every team gets a clip of its members engaging in some activity that you might or might not ever catch them doing in their everyday lives,[6] and then, more often than not, a shot of them turning their heads toward the camera. Usually they smile, unless their teams have been cast to be intense, in which case they merely scowl menacingly. There's a certain, endearing "pod people" aspect to all of this, along with the image of Racers so clueless they couldn't figure out where the camera was in the first place.

---

[6] For instance, at least one couple shown gaily roller-skating had never done that together until the crew filming the credits suggested that this was the perfect image to define them.

1. Bunching Points

These are the inevitable bottlenecks that slow Racers down for hours at a time and allow teams that have fallen way behind to catch up. Whenever a team with a four-hour advantage shows up at the airport at 3:00 A.M. only to discover that the first flight out is at noon, they're likely doomed to watch in dismay as every remaining team shows up in time to level the playing field in the morning. Other bunching points are bus stations, public buildings, and attractions only open during specified hours. Bunching points are either annoyances or godsends, depending on what teams you're rooting for. Colin of Team Extreme still complains that his team would have arrived days ahead of everybody else, had the bunching points in Race 5 not continually rescued the teams in the rear of the pack. He's right about that. But it's way preferable to a Race where the ultimate winner is a foregone conclusion by Leg #2.

2. Hurry Up for Nothing

This is the flip side of a bunching point: the frantic dash from place to place, involving reckless driving, exhausting chases through city streets, loud demands to pass that other car up ahead, and angry recriminations between teammates over a few wasted seconds, all of which eventually turn out to be entirely irrelevant as the destination turns out to be a place to…sit around and wait. This is most nastily amusing for viewers when we already know the outcome, and get to see the rear-echelon Racers run themselves ragged for no good reason.

3. The We're-Not-Last Woo-Hoo!

Some Racers have had so much difficulty during a particular leg that they know, for a fact, they're about to say bye-bye. Often, they've done better than they thought they have. One of the great pleasures of the game is watching these folks prepare themselves for elimination, and find out that they're only second to last. Their reactions range from quiet amazement to hysterical shrieking to (if the leg has been very, very hard) unhappy resignation. More than once, they're so ebullient they pick up Phil. Sometimes, if the leg has been hard for everybody, we get to see this moment of astonished survival play out with several teams at a time. Among the many who deserve mention: Tramel and Talicia, from Race 3, Leg #1.

4. Airport Shuffle

This is our exclusive term for the hell Racers go through, braving travel agencies and airport reservation desks in search of the one flight that will get them to Blecchistan twenty minutes ahead of their competitors. Airport shuffle, which can be the single most important activity in any given leg, involves endless hours on standby, endless treks from one airline to another, and, often, endless begging for a place on flights that have already wheeled away from the gate. Racers can be prodigies at Detours and Roadblocks, and yet fall so far behind during airport shuffle that they're left on the ground long after their competitors have landed in destination countries. For the sake of simplicity, we will acknowledge airport shuffle, but discuss the specifics only when they prove of special interest.

5. Locals Laughing at the Silly Americans

Let's be clear about this. Americans may be great folks from a country that has pioneered more fields of endeavor than I have the space to enumerate here, but the same qualities that have made us world leaders have also made us awfully full of ourselves, and awfully easy to laugh at when we're made to do something beneath our dignity. So the crowds that form whenever Amazing Racers make fools of themselves in public are laughing not only at the silly people doing silly things, but also, specifically, at the representatives of a stuffed-shirt republic having some of the self-importance taken out of their tires. For many people around the world, there's a deep satisfaction in watching these Americans act like clowns, especially when (with only two exceptions, so far) none of them have actually been clowns. This schadenfreude is even more delicious for folks toiling at their respective places of employment (i.e., brick and sausage factories, among other things), watching Americans attempt the same work and screw up royally.

6. The Really Bad Cab Driver

The Racer definition of a really bad cab driver is not necessarily the same as the real world's. After all, real-world passengers don't get screwed out of a million dollars if their cabbie slows down at yellow lights. Racers have been known to scream at cab drivers for allowing other cabs to pass them, and for having insufficient command of English in countries where that is not an official language. But these are merely frustrating cab drivers. (And they can be frustrating. Even Kris, of Race 6's The Long-Distance Smileys, who never lost her patience at any other moment, once told a dawdling cabbie that he really sucked.) A genuinely really bad cab driver is one who tells you he knows where he's going, takes your money, and then drops you a zillion miles out of your way at a destination with no even coincidental resemblance to the one you asked for. Cabbies have driven Amazing Racers in the wrong direction, to the wrong airport, on the wrong side of the street, to restricted areas where they will be detained, and (in one memorable case) into the Demilitarized Zone that separates North and South Korea. This can be more than fatal to the outcome of the contest. This can be downright dangerous.

7. The Really Good Cab Driver

On the other hand, cabbies gifted at shortcuts and creative at interpreting local traffic laws come in for more than their share of extravagant praise from Racers who, in expressing their appreciation, do everything but offer to bear their children. Cabbies of this stripe are often assured that they're "the man."

8. Repetition as a Tool for Dealing with Cab Drivers

Never say anything once. Seriously. If you want your cab driver to go, say, "Go Go Go Go Go Go Go Go." If you want your cab driver to stop, say, "Stop Stop Stop Stop Stop Stop Stop Stop." If you want him to go faster, say, "Fast Fast Fast Fast Fast Fast Fast." And so on. Cab drivers in foreign countries really adore this kind of treatment.

9. Bad Vocabularies

Racers have shown some odd gaps in their vocabularies. Among the words printed in clue envelopes that have completely stymied one or more players (in extreme cases, all of them) include "skivvies," "vertigo," "stein," "scarab," "gnome," "dervish," "silo," "relic," and "hangar."[7]

---

[7] Also—in a private conversation with one Racer—"Sympatico."

10. Bad Geography

Racers have also shown some gaps in geographical knowledge. Brandon didn't know anything about the Philippines except that it was "an island." Jonathan Baker (in an outtake) once forgot what country he was in and complimented a native greeter in France by telling him how much he liked Italy. Mom Weaver seemed unclear on whether Pennsylvania was a state, and later identified Ponchartrain as one of the Great Lakes. Several teams from the first Race appeared to have never heard of the world-famous Arc de Triomphe. It's no great insult to these folks to say that nobody ever said participation in the Race required them to be rocket scientists. On the other hand, a few Racers of exceptional erudition have often made the dumbest, most teeth-rattling mistakes, so it evens out. By the way, it's also pretty fun to watch Racers stumble over place names, especially those with too many syllables and a paucity of vowels. Quick, take a taxi to Gzfgwigty!

11. Vomiting

Most in evidence during eating challenges, and never more harrowing than Race 6's soup-eating challenge in Budapest. Discussed, at sadder length, in the Vomit Chapter. (And you know your writing career has reached a new height when you have written one of those. It's, you should only excuse the expression, coming up next.)

To be continued....

The Vomit Chapter

THIS IS AN ANNOYING, AND somewhat disgusting, phenomenon.

We cannot discuss it without being at least a little bit vulgar. But we have to deal with it sooner or later.

This is a show about the rigors of travel.

Travelers get airsick, and seasick, and carsick.

They pick up strange local bugs.

They eat strange foods.

They overexert themselves.

They vomit.

Thus, at least part of the show will be spent acknowledging that travelers vomit.

Is it the main focus of the show? Hell no. Is it even prevalent? Not even close.

Are there close-ups? And slow-motion reenactments?

No.

Are the moments revisited again and again during the clip shows?

No more than absolutely necessary.

But still.

It doesn't take all that much of this to create the wrong impression.

It works this way. If you love any TV show, and use all the persuasive abilities at your disposal to get a skeptical friend to try it, just once, that friend will inevitably give in and watch what will inevitably turn out to be the single worst episode ever aired. That friend will subsequently look at you like you're crazy for ever regarding your favorite show with such over-the-top enthusiasm.

This is commonly known as "The Spock's Brain Factor" because of all the science fiction fans who begged and cajoled their friends to try just one episode of the original *Star Trek*, insisting that it was a smart, intelligently written series, only to have their friends finally give in the same week the show aired the astonishingly awful episode "Spock's Brain." But it's true of any series. Whatever the show, your non-enthusiast friend will break down only to watch the one episode you don't want representing it.

Get that friend to watch another episode and one of two things will happen. Either it will turn out to be a replay of the same episode that turned him off the first time, or another just as bad.

In the case of *The Amazing Race*, you can wax rhapsodic about all the great foreign locales, all the terrific emotional moments, all the fascinating challenges and all the last-minute races to the finish, and all the moments of Racers rising to the occasion with unexpected courage and character, and your friends will tune in only to see Racers vomiting.

Amie vomiting in the Sahara during Race 1.

Peach gagging on the tea during Race 2.

Colin vomiting his ostrich egg during Race 5.

Everybody vomiting in the Hungarian restaurant during Race 6.

You tell your friends that this is not typical and that they should watch the show again. They oblige. And once again see a contestant performing the wide-screen Technicolor yawn. If they somehow miss that, they see the worst of the show's many tantrums...but that's a minor risk; it's the vomit moments that form the strongest and most lasting impression, and folks who drop in only occasionally have an unerring instinct for finding those specific weeks when Racers play bungee with breakfast. As relatively rare as the phenomenon is, the selective sampling is so bad that, on those relatively rare occasions when a Racer does leave an abstract painting on the sidewalk in front of the Louvre, those of us who love the show find ourselves putting our hands in front of our faces and thinking, not, *Gee, I hope that contestant recovers*, but instead, *Oh, God, I bet Bill's watching this.*

This book is dedicated to a good friend named Bill, who has followed my recommendations to watch *The Amazing Race*, not once, not twice, not even thrice, but four times, over a couple of years, and has each time found the travelogue elements of the show far more esophogal than he would have liked. He has therefore formed the conclusion that, for himself at least, this is a show about a succession of Americans engaged in their own personal food drops abroad. Given the random sample available to him, it's even a reasonable conclusion.

But it ain't so, Bill.

Really. It's not.

And I would argue the case further, but—urp—I must be running.

Racers, We Hardly Knew Ye

THE FLIP SIDE OF THE annoying team that lasts leg after leg, trying viewer patience as we all wait for it to go down in flames, is the especially likeable team that breaks our hearts by getting eliminated right away.

Here, our favorites among the also-rans. I use the third leg as a cut-off point and include both Sacrificial Lambs and teams that might have done better if not for some maddening twist of fate.

For instance, Race 2's mother-daughter team Deidre and Hillary. Dang, but those scenes of Hillary consoling her mom were so emotional that we wanted a recount. We want them cast again!

In Race 3, we had Soccer Moms Gina and Sylvia, eliminated just as we were getting to know them. Would have been nice if they'd stuck around longer. Ditto with Tramel and Talicia. Sorry you had to go.

Race 4 begins with Debra and Steve, who struggle so mightily to complete a hike through mountainous terrain that it seems mean to call them by their designated sobriquet for this book, Team Doomed. They were never gonna go the distance, but it would have been nice to see them make it at least a couple of additional legs.

Race 5 begins with the elimination of Dennis and Erika, who fall because Dennis needs to prove he's not a scumbag. We buy it. But we wish The Not-Scumbags had stuck around longer. It also would have been nice to see more of the father-daughter team Jim and Marsha McCoy, who earned a place in our hearts when Jim shrugged off a serious knee injury suffered within a few short steps of the starting line.

In Race 6, we lost Avi and Joe, the New York Jews in Iceland, right away, a major blow to lovers of yiddische wit. Damn it. And how could we forget one of the most tragic losses in the show's history: Lena and Kristy, victims of those damn hay bales?

In Race 7, we lost Ryan and Chuck, The New Stooges, providing proof positive that you can't be funny and charming and vivid in the first leg without also being toast. But Debbie and Bianca, who lost due to the mother of all wrong turns, were the greatest heartbreak.

In Race 8, we lost the Black family, and thus got to see poor Austin's thousand-yard stare. Dang. That must have been one hard elimination for Phil.

Forget the much-discussed hypothetical "All-Star Edition." How about a No-Star Edition?

Bring back all these folks and let them try again!

Who's the Boss?

THERE ARE SO MANY EQUALIZERS built into the very structure of *The Amazing Race* that it seems foolhardy to single out individual teams as exceptional. After all, some of the most talented folks fall by the wayside, not out of any obvious weakness on their parts, but from delayed flights, bad cab drivers, and the ever-present, and ever-annoying, luck-based challenges. For all we know, only that damned hay bale prevented Lena and Kristy from being a million dollars richer today. That said, some teams appear to have had more inherent potential, from that initial "The world is waiting," than others. Here, in no particular order, the best of the best.

Rob and Brennan. The Young Lawyers were athletic, smart, even-tempered, patient in the face of adversity, and personable, gaining the trust of their fellow Racers even as they forged their way to the finish line. Even so, their single most formidable attribute may have been their willingness to cede control when out of their element—a factor that proved pivotal when they found themselves competing in the hometown of their only serious competitors, **Frank and Margarita**, who also kicked serious ass.

Derek and Drew. Any team other teams immediately obsess about is a threat. The Wonder Twins attracted mass emnity right away, and proved as formidable as they looked, falling, at long last, to a clever ruse on the part of their closest allies, **Ken and Gerard**, a pair of seriously unlikely champions.

Chip and Reichen. Another highly athletic team, even if not always a highly rational one; they engaged in some silly cross-fighting before buckling down to nail the finish. **Jon and Al**, The Clowns, and **Jon and Kelly**, The Mockingbirds, were also major teams to watch that Race.

Colin and Christie. For my money, the single best team of two in the show's entire history, whose incredible record—finishing first or second for an unmatched seven straight legs—reflects a competitive spirit that came back to bite them more than once. You know how feared they were if you watch the penultimate leg, in Thailand, where teams that had managed to get ahead of them nervously watched the horizon for signs of their imminent arrival. Even in the final leg, when **Chip and Kim** surged to the finish line, Colin and Christie made the most of every advantage, working with an efficiency that almost brought them back to first place.

Rob and Amber. The *Survivor* stars proved just as formidable on *The Amazing Race*, using trickery and guile to gain every slightest advantage. Their tactics bit them in the butt in India, when Rob's jocular reference to a supposedly nonexistent "faster flight" led two teams to take another look at flight schedules. Like many top-ranked teams who failed to go home with the million, they were ultimately knocked out by a bad taxi ride. In the Race, that's often all it takes.

The Single Best Racer
in the Show's History

ZACH.

This is not a debate, people. This is the final word. After this, no other arguments will be accepted. So you in the back, shut up.

Zach made it around the world with a partner who spent much of the Race falling apart. He spent some lags dragging her from place to place, enduring her abuse, calming her during her frequent fits of hysteria, keeping her on her feet even when she repeatedly declared her refusal to continue, showing (mild) pique only briefly, and ultimately dragging her across the finish line to claim his half of the million-dollar prize. He did this without raising his voice to her. Nobody else has ever managed a feat anything like it. To accomplish it, he must have been approximately twice as good as his next closest competitor.

Does it follow, then, that Flo was the "worst" Racer in the entire history of the show?

No, it doesn't, in part for reasons elucidated in her own chapter, and in part because she had plenty of competition for that dubious distinction: among them folks who threw tantrums, threw maps, seemed surprised that people in foreign countries spoke foreign languages, walked instead of ran, took breaks when they should have hustled, misread clues, called their partners nasty names, and in all other ways zigged when they should have zagged. There were other people so ill-suited for the demands of the competition that you almost wonder if they had the slightest idea what they were getting into. Some got knocked out early. Some lasted leg after leg out of sheer luck.

But the bottom line, Dear Reader, is that some of them would still have beaten *you*.

A Taxonomy of Players

R ACING AROUND THE WORLD with minimal sleep, irreg-
ular meals, spotty opportunities for personal hygiene, constant uncertainty over where you're going next, and constant
pressure to avoid elimination, can take its toll on even the
most centered human beings, and somebody who might be perfectly charming in a café, drinking her daily double latte, can easily turn
into a raging harpy if forced to spend a month camping out in airports.
Those caveats noted, the playing field is level, and there must be a reason, beyond conspiracy on the part of the producers, why some teams
playing this game suffered ugly (and permanent) breakups on camera,
while others forgave nasty things said in the heat of the moment; why
some constantly argued, while others rarely dropped their smiles; why
some moaned and whined about every discomfort, while others rev-
eled in the adventure of their lives; why some shrieked at every mo-

mentary setback while others giggled madly at the sheer absurdity of their situations.

For lack of a better word, we might as well call it character. And win or lose, it's what leaves folks who spent their month abroad clawing at each other like ferrets sewn inside a paper sack looking awfully bad next to those who refused to be riled for any reason.

The Sacrificial Lambs

These are the teams that seem so less than formidable, at the onset, that their elimination seems a matter of time. They are often judged on their age, their weight, their apparent degree of physical fitness, and their lack of "intensity." One of the wonderful things about the show is that Sacrificial Lambs often turn out to be nothing of the kind. In Race 3, two of the Sacrificial Lamb teams (Ken and Gerard, and to a lesser degree Teri and Ian) made it to the finals, losing to a team whose problems were significantly worse than theirs. Race 5's Bowling Moms Linda and Karen, and Race 7's Team Energizer Bunny Gretchen and Meredith, both looked like Sacrificial Lambs, and both met their defeats just short of the finals. Gus, of Race 6, seemed so less than formidable at the beginning that my original name for his team was Team Doomed. (Sorry, Gus.) Let's make the rule that any team still around after, oh, the fourth leg, deserves better than Sacrificial Lamb status. Other Sacrificial Lambs that managed it: Nancy and Emily, Charla and Mirna, Don and Mary Jean.

The Old Folks

The Amazing Race makes a point of including older teams, which in this case means folks who have entered their sixties. Some have been prepared for the rigors of the Race; some have not. At their worst, they make you worried that they're going to fall down and break a hip or something. At their best, they astonish with their tenacity. It's all too easy to mistake them for Sacrificial Lambs.

The Gays

The Amazing Race has featured a number of homosexual couples, of varying effectiveness as teams. (It has also featured a number of gay Racers alongside straight teammates, an interesting dynamic all by itself that has never proven a decisive factor in game play.) These players represent diverse personality types, as should be expected, and are grouped here only because their orientation sometimes proves an issue with other Racers.

The Smilies

Exemplified by Michael and Kathy, Kris and Jon, and John Vito and Jill, these couples express delight with just about everything that happens to them, and remain enthused and affectionate throughout. These folks hug each other constantly. It makes them likeable on-screen, if sometimes a little bland. Some viewers hate these teams beyond all measure, which says more about the viewers than it does about the teams.

Funny, Fat, and/or Bald Guys

For some reason, teams made up of fat guys or bald guys show a snarky humor that renders them incredibly likeable. They're even more dependable if they're bald fat guys. I know this from personal experience.

The Identical Twins

The casting directors just love casting folks like Kami and Karli or Derek and Drew just to screw with our heads and make sure we can't tell who's doing what. Oddly enough, there have not been any identical twins since the institution of the six-Roadblocks-per-Racer rule. Maybe the producers fear being taken in by a fast one.

Men with Whiny Women

These teams feature men who drag their partners all over creation, often doing the majority of the work, while the ladies moan at length about how uncomfortable and stressed and put-upon they are. See: p. 154 Zach and Flo, p. 287 Hayden and Aaron.

Women with Whiny Men

It's a much rarer dynamic, but it happens. See p. 287 Team Hellboy.

Women with Whiny Women

That happens too. See Mary and Peach.

Couples Who (On-Screen, At Least) Can Hardly Stand One Another

This goes for both romantic couples (Alison and Donny) and estranged couples (Wil and Tara). It makes for an uneasy trip.

The Focused to the Point of Arrogance

"This is a race, dammit! Suck it up!"

The Clueless

These are the folks who seem to have wandered onto the set by accident and are actually surprised to find out that some of the stuff they're being asked to do is hard. How did they pick this reality show, anyway? With a dartboard?

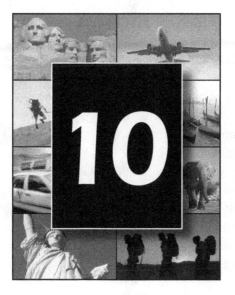

Through Strangers' Eyes

"Everybody laughs at stupid Americans."
—DREW, RACE 1

*"Actually, I think they're just laughing at you. Me, I fit right in.
I meld right into the culture."*
—KEVIN, RACE 1

IT HAPPENS DURING RACE 5. Marshall, of the team I call The Pizza Brothers, calls Russians the most miserable people on the planet. He bases this on the shared demeanor he spies on the commuter train: an entire car filled with people whose expressions seem fixed at grim, and who seem less like people heading out on their daily errands than prisoners, glumly facing another day of shared hell.

Regarding that comment today, Marshall denies any cultural chauvinism. He says it's what he saw. He further says that he has heard the same thing from a number of people who have been to Russia.

It's still an unpleasant thing to say, of course. And one that flies in the face of much we already know about the Russian people. They might not always be overwhelmed with things to celebrate, but when they want to party, look out. Everybody gets swept up in the singing, drinking, and dancing.

And yet his perceptions are not entirely wrong.

This is not true about all Russians, of course. It's a big country, with a number of different regions and ethnic groups. But read the guidebooks. You will find out that a certain hotel offers excellent, "if unsmiling," service. You will find out that an airline is reliable, "if less than warm in matters of customer contact." You will further find out that while the cabbies will get you wherever you want to go, they're "less than friendly."

Are they the most miserable people on the planet?

No. Simply among the most polite.

Some guidebooks also warn visitors against smiling in public. It's considered an invasion of personal space. So people keep a tight rein on their facial expressions, except when with their friends and family, at which point they can smile as broadly and as often as they feel appropriate. Those dour people on the train may have been downright ebullient. They just didn't let Marshall and Lance know.

"Just scream at the people and they seem to respond very, very well."
—AARON, RACE 3

If there's one thing the Race makes clear, it's that the world is not just an exotic obstacle course for American adventures. It's a polyglot of diverse humanity, filled with people who have grown accustomed to wildly different standards of courtesy, service, sanitation, and what to expect from one another.

Racers are yanked from place to place, without orientation, and without warning that the tactics appropriate for one place might well be downright rude in another.

We mention the horrifically crowded trains in India—a factor that often pushes Racers to the breaking point—elsewhere, but here's another one from that country. Many Racers are aggravated by the stupidity of cab drivers who immediately need to stop for gas before they are riding on fumes. Why would any cab driver let his tank get down that low? Answer: because it's standard operating procedure there. They don't want to leave any gas in their tank at the end of the day for somebody to steal, so they replenish their fuel a little at a time throughout their work shift. Any locals flush enough to patronize taxis are well aware of this custom, and come to expect such a stop at the beginning of any major trip. Screeching Americans, who expect a straight line from point A to point B, and especially our heroes, who have a million dollars riding on the journey, just think they're dealing with a bunch of idiots—an impression furthered by the natural impulse to perceive limited intelligence in those on the other side of the language barrier.

> "Why doesn't anybody speak English here? It's driving me nuts."
> —EMILY, RACE 1

Most viewers of *The Amazing Race* tend to remember the outrageous stunts, like bungee jumping, rappeling, rock climbing, and dives into icy water.

But there's an entirely different class of task, rarely cited in any compendium of the show's most challenging moments. These are the occasional tasks that require Racers to perform unpleasant and arduous labor in third-world conditions. This would include building huts, handwashing filthy clothes, making bricks out of mud and straw, and gathering salt—all things that are distasteful indeed for privileged Americans, but which are pointedly things the locals do every single day of their lives. Racers do not provide an ideal advertisement for their own country when they react to these challenges by calling them "retarded" or "stupid," especially when they don't know the full context.

For instance, take that brick-making task that made Colin fume in India.

He didn't know that at many such factories, and quite possibly the very one where his own labor took up only a small portion of one afternoon, the work force represents generational labor. The people making bricks now are the children, grandchildren, and great-grandchildren of other people who made bricks before them. Many have to pay such exorbitant fees to the factory owners that they just fall deeper and deeper into debt, eventually mortgaging the futures of their own offspring to the same profession. By the time their kids start work, sometimes at what we would consider preschool age, they have nothing to look forward to, for the rest of their lives, but mashing mud and straw into those molds.

It's nasty. Debt slavery is still slavery.

I'm not speaking ill of Colin, in particular, when I say he probably doesn't have a clue about any of this. He sees them from an American perspective, certainly as poor manual laborers, but definitely as people who own their own lives. If you had stopped him in the middle of the task to inform him of what was really going on around him, he probably would have wept. And then he would have moved on. Because he had to. This was not his place.

"I could never have been prepared for what I'm looking at right now."
—Reichen, Race 4

The cultural clash issues affect every Racer, to different extremes, at different times. Some react with scorn. Kendra, of This Year's Models, didn't make any friends among viewers with her infamous "They keep breeding and breeding" comment. Others retreat to the comforts of their various religious principles. Blake, of Race 2's Smiley Siblings, had this to say while making an offering in Thailand: "May God save all these people. They're so lost and so confused." Still others seem unfazed. Don and Mary Jean just loved the life they saw all around them in Senegal. Others sympathized with, if not precisely understood, the deep reverence felt by the worshippers at the Rat Temple.

Sometimes, they just have to laugh. One of the funniest moments has Drew trying to communicate with a ticket clerk at the train station. The guy didn't speak English. So Drew asked around to find out if anybody else did. The guy who volunteered obliged by asking the same question Drew just had, also in English. Drew's startled grin was one of the highlights of the first Race.

Sometimes, they make friends. Racers enduring long train rides play cards with locals, or struggle to find common ground with fellow passengers despite a language barrier that (even assuming a common command of English) may include thick, impenetrable accents.

Sometimes, they just get scared.

We have to be honest about this. Sometimes they're right to be scared. On more than one occasion, we witness locals trying to shake the Racers down for more money. On other occasions, Racers wander into dicey areas and wonder if they're about to be mugged or worse. (Kendra's infamous comments about "ghetto Africa" began with just that feeling of helplessness.) Race 5's Brandon had to question one bus driver's trustworthiness. Race 6's Bolo physically threatened another local to get him to back off. Several Racers have felt panicked just by the press of unfamiliar foreign faces in unfamiliar foreign places, sometimes because they felt helpless in the face of poverty, and sometimes because they doubted the intentions of the crowds around them. Remember Emily freaking out in the back of that van, as she tried to find out where the Taj Khema Hotel was. Several of the locals were audibly telling her, "Agra," which just happens to be the answer she needed. But they were also shaking their heads. She thought they didn't understand her. She thought they were stupid. Her inability to understand may have had them thinking the same of her.

> *"How do you live here and not know [where to go]?*
> *I mean, what planet are you on?"*
> —AMIE, RACE 1

One of the most instructive cultural clash moments took place during Race 2, during the show's first visit to South Africa. Teams had to find the Paradise Hair Salon in Zone 23 of Langa Township, a very poor section of Cape Town, notable for dirt streets, corrugated metal shacks, and barefoot children. It's a sad place, in that people live under extreme deprivation, but it is also a vibrant place, filled with energy and life and hope.

As Mary and Peach of Team Cobbler traveled there on a commuter train, a well-dressed local woman warned them, "If you go there, there's a lot of criminals. They will take [your belongings] and will kill you." Another rider advised, "The only thing I can tell you is if you like to be alive, don't go there."

Mary and Peach, not the most fearless team in the show's history, were naturally disturbed by this.

Guess what. They arrived. They had no trouble. And as they interacted with local children, they were driven to tears by unexpected moments of connection.

Now, the township is clearly a poverty-stricken area, which means by definition that it's also a high-crime area. It may simply be that the Americans were walking around with cameras and sound men, and who knows what kind of security men and women were walking around just out of range; certainly, it's hard to believe that the show would expose its cast to such places without addressing concerns over their safety. But it's also true that even this big-budget show did not have the resources to bring an army. The explanation is simple. The locals are not monsters. They're people. Most of them just want to live out their daily lives with a minimum of unpleasantness and fuss. They're perfectly willing to treat others with respect as long as they're treated with respect in return.

Oswald says, "People are people everywhere. If you go and extend your hand in friendship, they'll be helpful." And indeed, he had one of his own best moments sharing details of his life with a local who wanted to know why he left Cuba. Explaining that it was because of the government, he then asked the man about his job. And the guy said, "I'm not working." None of this is deep communication, by any means, but it is human intercourse between two people from wildly different worlds, who, for that one moment, shared peeks at their respective lives. Without fear of hyperbole, it's that, rather than bungee jumping or searches through mounds of poo, that reflects the Race at its absolute best.

> "You need to respect your fellow human beings. You send that into
> the universe, it comes right back at you."
> —OSWALD, RACE 2

People who fly to distant locations only to stay in comfortable hotels and poke around tamed tourist areas don't get a feel for the places they visit. They're reducing the world to a theme park, where the local attractions might as well be pavilions at Epcot. Meeting the people, and sitting down with them (as, for instance, Chip and Kim did, while accepting that African family's hospitality during Race 5), is the true education. Racers speed past so many of the cultures they visit that they don't often get the full taste. And much of what they do get is so fragmentary, so rushed by the constant need to *get somewhere, NOW*, that some of what they do get is reduced to mere obstacle. They therefore struggle against the natural tendency to judge everything by their own, familiar standards.

But here's the surprise: they're not alone.

We can malign Race 8 because of its overcrowded cast, its smaller canvas, its sometimes uninteresting locations and often spoon-fed tasks, but it did bring one fact into strong relief: that cultural clash isn't something we experience only far from home. We get it at home too. We got it, during that Race, from Racers who derided the southern families as stupid, from the several Racers who couldn't believe the yelling they heard from the Paolo family, from the several Racers who derided the Weavers for being born-again Christians, and from the Weavers for the evil they thought they saw in "those people." About the only thing that might have made the mix more potent than that would be a nontraditional family, with gay parents...an unaccountable omission, if only for drama's sake. It might have been fun to see what the religiously conservative Rogers and Weaver families would have had to say about that.

Even as it stands, the clashes that marked Race 8 were not just clashes of personality, but clashes of culture, emphasizing (a small taste of) the diversity within our own polyglot society. They may have been a little more prominent in this Race, because the Racers didn't have all those strange foreign countries to deal with, but they were factors in other Races as well: witness, for instance, the way Race 2's Pastors reacted to Wil's drunken antics, or the way Race 4's Virgins reacted when they found that Reichen and Chip are married.

And this comes from the inhabitants of one country. Just one.

It's worth noting, too, that one of the strongest teams in the history of the show, Race 7's Rob and Amber, ultimately went down due to the language barrier in that most American city, Miami.

Imagine how much more difficult it becomes when plopped down into a society where all the assumptions and expectations are different. And where you're the oddity. The outsider.

At its absolute best, *The Amazing Race* illustrates just how difficult that is. And just how important.

Race 1,
the Expensive Cup of Tea

T HE FIRST *AMAZING RACE* WAS the only one filmed before 9/11. Airing not long after that terrible day, it joined several other debuting shows, like the terrorism drama *24*, in suffering from resonances that were never intended by its producers. In New York, city buses bearing the ad for the show were covered with layers of ash from the World Trade Center. When the show aired, many viewers were less than motivated to watch carefree romps in foreign locales. As a result, it struggled in the ratings throughout its first few seasons, coming close to cancellation several times before its accumulated Emmys and good word of mouth firmly established it as the phenomenon it has become.

There was a fun sense, during this shakedown cruise, that this complicated and unwieldy process had not been fully perfected. A number of "production delays" lead to several teams being reimbursed for time bled by the crews following them around, the subtitles weren't always sufficient to clarify the respective positions of the Racers, and Phil Keoghan failed to join the native greeters at the mat, instead only showing up to tell the various last-arriving whether they'd been eliminated or not. He took a more visible role in events starting in Race 2.

The *Amazing Race* flag, which alerts players to show locations, was for Race 1, and Race 1 only, yellow and white.

The opening narration, dropped after Race 1, follows: "It's the most daring competition ever attempted. Eleven two-person teams, bound by friendship, love, or family, will race around the world. They have no idea where they're going, what dangers they may encounter, or how the journey will affect their lives. Most of the teams will be eliminated, but the team that reaches the finish line first will win a cash prize of one million dollars. This is a race like no other in history. This...is *The Amazing Race*."

For all its relative crudity, this Race remains one of the best. For all the attractive people on display, there's a very real sense that these people were chosen for their diversity, not for their matinee-idol looks. There was arguing, both within teams and between teams, but none of the knock-down, drag-out wild screaming that afflicted some later Races. Even the designated villains, the Guidos, who cut a couple of ethical corners and ultimately went down because of an act of almost incomprehensible hubris, are likeable enough by the standards of some others we've come to meet in subsequent Races. There's a very real sense that they turned their fellow players off with their racing tactics and not with their personalities.

DRAMATIS PERSONAE

1. Team First Out

Married couple Matt and Ana Robar, who earn their title by being the first team ever to suffer elimination, aren't around long enough to establish their strengths. Their weaknesses seem to include dealing with locals and reading maps.

2. The Young Lawyers

Best friends Rob Frisbee, who resembles the able-bodied Christopher

Reeve, and Brennan Swain, who doesn't, may not have the best luck with taxi drivers, but they're cheerful, athletic players who don't indulge in a single serious fight during this Race. The editors love Rob and use his comments so much more than they use Brennan's that the latter sometimes comes off as a bit of an invisible man, but don't be fooled. They're equal partners, one of the most tightly knit teams in the history of the show. SEASON SUPERSTARS

3. Team Guido

Life partners Joe Baldassare and Bill Bartek are one of the few teams ever to bring their own nickname and make it stick. (It's a tribute to their dog.) Though other teams delight in calling them "Bert and Ernie," instead, Guidos they are and forever will be. Tougher than they look, experienced travelers, and ruthless competitors (who once or twice engage in acts of outright villainy that accomplish nothing but alienating other teams), they're not half as bad as their reputation among Race fans suggests, since they display a few moments of good sportsmanship as well. Their biggest weakness, overconfidence, is directly responsible for one of the most jaw-dropping errors in the history of the show. SEASON SUPERSTARS

4. Team Puss

Couple Paul J. Alessi and Amie Barsky earn their nickname when Paul calls himself a "puss" during the gorge plunge that tests his own extreme fear of heights. They are most weakened by Amie's frequent tears and Paul's frequently stated desire to quit the Race when he sees her crying. (He reports on-screen, more than once, that he never wanted to apply in the first place.) Despite plenty of competition, it's this pair that finds the worst place to get lost, in the entire history of the show. I'm serious. It ain't even close to funny.

5. The Fat Bastards

I need to establish right away that the nickname I've given Kevin O'Connor and Drew Feinberg in this book has absolutely nothing to do with their character or body type, but everything to do with all the verbal abuse they shower upon each other in a certain kind of American male's preferred form of bonding. They're constantly calling each other dumb, referring to each other as "fat bastids," and speculating on who's a Big Mac shy of 240. Their interaction, but for a rough spot at the very beginning, is effortlessly, inherently funny. One of the all-time favorites among viewers. **SEASON SUPERSTARS**

6. Team Oh, Mom

Nancy Hoyt and her daughter Emily Hoyt may not be among this Race's stronger teams, either physically or emotionally, but they're contenders. Nancy, in particular, is a sweet, upbeat lady more than a little taken aback by the nastiness she hears and witnesses during the Race—especially, it must be said, when it comes from her daughter, who shows a regrettable tendency to turn her anger at locals in moments of extreme stress. (It's never nice to call natives "stupid" or snap, "Screw you!" at a guy whose biggest crime is an inability to provide helpful directions.) Their biggest weakness: giving up when they think they've lost.

7. The Old Folks

Married seniors David and Margaretta Groark are upbeat, positive, and if not up to the physical standards of some of the more athletic youngsters, certainly game to try. Witness their exhausting hike when they go for the first leg's Fast Forward. Not all of the show's senior-citizen teams will be this formidable. When this team finally falls behind, it's not due to any failure of physical or mental preparedness on their part, but a simple dispute over changing currency. Don't count them out too early.

8. Team Monument

On-again, off-again couple Lenny Hudson and Karyn Jefferson are one of this Race's more troubled teams, in large part due to the disconnect between Karyn's competitiveness and Lenny's more laid-back, sometimes even disinterested, approach to the Race. Her reaction, when he takes an aggressively half-assed approach to a task in Paris, is one of the Race's more uncomfortable moments. It's just as pointedly a moment they recover from.

9. The Schoolmarms

Schoolteachers Kim Smith and Leslie Kellner don't last very long, in large part because they overlook the route marker at the Eiffel Tower challenge. While that error could have been made by anybody, they are not exceptionally fast at recovering from it, and they compound the problem with a wrong turn on their way to the Arc de Triomphe. A little more care, a little more zig when they elect to zag, and they could have been contenders.

10. The Working Moms

Best friends Patricia Pierce and Brenda Mehta enjoy a strong early showing, thanks to a Fast Forward that at one early point sends them to Paris with a two-hour lead. A deliberate ambiguity built into the next leg's Detour soon takes care of that. They might have recovered had they been faster to realize that something was wrong. But I'm not sure you could call that a weakness, either.

11. Team Diesel

One of the strongest teams this time out, separated parents Frank and Margarita Mesa put their differences aside to run a determined, and for the most part angst-free, scramble across four continents. Frank is one of this Race's loudest and most physically fit, while Margarita is one of the stronger strategists. But once the Race returns to America and passes within blocks of their own neighborhood, the home-court advantage jumps up and bites them on the ass. SEASON SUPERSTARS

THE GAME PLAY

Leg #1: "Swing, You Fat Bastard, Swing!"

Departing from Manhattan's Central Park, teams receive ninety dollars and directions to take one of three available flights to Johannesburg, South Africa. There they will have to make their way to Lanseria Airport and book seats on a chartered flight. The clue envelope, here called an information packet, doesn't specify which New York City airport, a deliberate ambiguity which increases the opening confusion level until the mad scramble for tickets begins.

The Guidos, Team Diesel, and the Lawyers are first to Zambia's Livingstone Airport, where they must claim marked cars and make their way to a location identified only as "The Knife's Edge" on "The Smoke that Thunders." Team Oh, Mom, on the second charter, is one of several that hit the road without first determining that "The Smoke that Thunders" references the mist rising over Victoria Falls, and "The Knife's Edge" is a soggy pedestrian bridge overlooking the view, but they get directions and find their way there in short order. One by one, every team receives instructions to find Batoka Gorge.

The Lawyers and The Old Folks compete for the first Fast Forward, a punishing hike to the bottom of the canyon and a location known as the Boiling Pot. The Lawyers make it there first, declaring the trek one of the hardest things they've ever done, and expressing doubt that any of the other teams could do the same. They move on to the Pit Stop at remote Songwe Village. The Old Folks, who push themselves to the edge of exhaustion descending, find the Fast Forward gone and need a rest before climbing back up.

The Fat Bastards have their only serious fight of the entire Race, with Kevin blowing his stack when Drew takes his time getting directions from locals. "This is not New York," Drew protests. "You have to be amicable." The instructions, which include a provision to look for a big tree, are less than helpful.

Batoka Gorge offers the first Detour in the form of "Air" and "Land," the two ways to reach the route marker at the bottom. Nobody takes the time-consuming hike, "Land." Everybody else must ride a zip line and then swing on a flexible line to the bottom of the gorge. This latter option is often misreported as a bungee line. It's not. It's a swing. And as it's one of the scariest tasks of its kind in Race history, many perform it hyperventilating, or crying, or screaming. The most frightened seems to be Paul, the self-described "big puss," who jumps despite what seems to be overwhelming physical terror. But Nancy is no happier watching her daughter go. (It's a dynamic many parents experience, partnering their kids in the Race.) And when The Fat Bastards finally arrive, Kevin cheers on his friend with: "Swing, you fat bastard, swing!"

All teams arrive at Songwe Village by late afternoon, except for First Out, which arrives after nightfall, and achieves the dubious honor of being the first team ever eliminated.

1. Rob and Brennan (The Young Lawyers) 11:23 A.M.
2. Joe and Bill (Team Guido) 11:37 A.M.
3. Frank and Margarita (Team Diesel) 12:05 P.M.

4. Lenny and Karyn (Team Monument) 1:52 P.M.
5. Pat and Brenda (The Working Moms) 3:35 P.M.
6. Kim and Leslie (The Schoolmarms) 5:33 P.M.
7. David and Margaretta (The Old Folks) 5:50 P.M.
8. Paul and Amie (Team Puss) 6:24 P.M.
9. Kevin and Drew (The Fat Bastards) 7:09 P.M.[8]
10. Nancy and Emily (Team Oh, Mom) 7:26 P.M.
11. Matt and Ana (Team First Out) ELIMINATED

Leg #2: Searching for the Arc de Whatever

After a Pit Stop spent in Songwe Village, a sleepy Zambian village of grass huts and modest wooden houses, teams receive instructions to find the Songwe Museum. Many Racers start driving. Few realize that the Songwe Museum is a small unmarked one-room hut less than a hundred yards from where they've spent the last twelve hours. All they had to do was ask somebody.

The Young Lawyers and Team Guido follow Team Diesel on one pointless drive out of town, based on Margarita's vague impression that she'd seen a sign advertising the museum, somewhere or another. (She hadn't.)

White-water rafting earns The Working Moms a Fast Forward, with instructions to proceed 6,000 miles to the Arc de Triomphe in Paris, France.

Teams that find the museum discover cameras and a Detour, "Near" or "Far." "Near" requires teams to drive to nearby Mosi-oa-Tunya nature preserve in order to photograph three hard-to-spot animals. "Far" sends them to a more distant location to find and photograph one elephant. Everybody sees the wisdom of "Near."[9]

---

[8] Watch carefully and you'll note that Kevin exits the charter plane carrying two plastic bottles filled with yellow water. The liquid is exactly what it looks like. It was a small plane and a long flight. You may also note that when Drew arrives at the Pit Stop, his shirt is covered with yellow stains. This is not the same liquid, thank goodness. It's egg yolk. A Roadblock requiring players to consume an ostrich egg was cut from the episode for time considerations. *The Amazing Race* finally aired another ostrich egg competition in Race 5.

[9] Cut footage, available on the season one DVD, reveals the teams celebrating the completion of the Detour with the people of the village where they deliver their photographs. Their dance with the locals is warm, joyous, and filled with the shared humanity that exemplifies the show at its absolute best.

At the park, Nancy scares the hell out of daughter Emily by hopping out of the car to take her close-up of a rhino.

The subsequent scramble for last-minute airplane tickets to Paris is a nightmare. There are tears, recriminations, and blown alliances. A little airport lady who looks like Dr. Ruth helps Team Puss and The School-marms. The Guidos, who began this leg pledging an alliance with The Young Lawyers and Team Diesel, decide by mid-leg that both teams are useless and best discarded.

The Working Moms are first to the Pit Stop.

The clue box under the Eiffel Tower offers the others a Roadblock. One team member must climb to the second level and use the coin-operated telescopes there to find the *Amazing Race* flag flying from another Paris monument. Thanks to The Working Moms, we already know it to be the world-famous Arc de Triomphe. Frank calls it "Whatever that Thing Is." The Schoolmarms miss the clue box and bleed precious time with a pointless elevator ride to the top level. Paul, who has already threatened to quit if Amie doesn't stop crying over everything, threatens to quit again when he can't spot the flag. He wins the leg's "Ugly American award" by cursing and kicking the Tower in rage.

But the most upsetting troubles belong to Lenny, who hereby earns his team the nickname Team Monument. He gives up and comes back down the stairs. Karyn angrily sends him back up. Once back up the stairs, he still has no idea, so he asks around and picks a monument at random, choosing Notre Dame even though there's no flag there. He doesn't admit what he's done until the team reaches Notre Dame. Karyn blasts him with the sheer withering force of her disappointment. When they backtrack, find the clue, and miraculously survive the leg, he won't even look at her. It's not exactly a fun family vacation.

The Old Folks arrive sixth, but follow Team Puss to the Pit Stop without properly completing the Roadblock themselves, and are therefore given a time penalty at the start of the next leg, dropping to eighth place.

1. Pat and Brenda (The Working Moms) 9:06 A.M.
2. Joe and Bill (Team Guido) 11:36 A.M.
3. Rob and Brennan (The Young Lawyers) 12:11 P.M.
4. Frank and Margarita (Team Diesel) 12:18 P.M.

5. Kevin and Drew (The Fat Bastards) 12:27 P.M.
6. David and Margaretta (The Old Folks) PENALTY
7. Paul and Amie (Team Puss) 2:18 P.M.
8. Nancy and Emily (Team Oh, Mom) 2:23 P.M.
9. Lenny and Karyn (Team Monument) 3:03 P.M.
10. Kim and Leslie (The Schoolmarms) ELIMINATED

Leg #3: The Guidos Make Friends and Influence People

Departing the Arc de Triomphe, teams are told to find Le Grande Roue, French for "The Big Wheel," a ferris wheel in clear sight. Most teams have to ask around to get the translation. As the ride closes at 12:30 A.M., teams that don't even leave the Pit Stop until after midnight must wait for the ride to open again in the morning, not that this matters, as the upcoming Detour sends teams to attractions that won't open until mid-morning.

The Guidos, who have made a big deal about having lived in Paris for two years, display the first of several eyebrow-raising gaps in their familiarity with the city and the language by needing a policewoman's help to figure out what Le Grande Roue is.

Detour: "Tough Climb," which sends teams to Notre Dame to climb 297 steps to ring Quasimodo's bell, or "Easy Walk," which sends teams to the statue of a cat at Foucault's Pendulum. The twist complicating the second option is that there are two Foucault's Pendulums in Paris. One is at the Museum of Arts and Crafts, but the one beside a statue of a cat is at the Pantheon. The Working Moms will blow their early lead by being the only team delayed by this fatal error.

In the meantime, we're treated to a fine montage of teams sacking out under a chilly French rain, while the Guidos stay warm sipping tea in their old neighborhood hangout.

Watch this tea-drinking habit carefully in future legs. It will be critical.

Waiting overnight outside another tea shop housing this leg's Fast Forward, Drew says he's less than impressed by Paris. "I just don't think the city's anything special. This is just like being in Soho." From there, The Fat Bastards move on to the Pit Stop, at Les Baux de Provence in the South of France.

The Roadblock requires one team member to do the Jean Valjean thing by traveling two blocks through the Paris sewers. In a cut scene, David of The Old Folks exults, "Oh, I feel just wonderful. My whole life's ambition was to come to Paris and walk in the sewer....I don't think my wife's gonna sleep with me tonight, though."

In an attempt to knock out their stronger competition, Team Guido resolves to help the teams they consider weakest. The strategy fails within minutes, when they duck aboard a train, abandoning Team Oh, Mom and Team Puss on the platform. The tally of Guido haters continues to grow.

One critical factor of the train ride to Les Baux involves efficient travel. Most tourists take the train all the way to Marseilles, then take a long cab ride to Les Baux. But much of that taxi ride is backtracking. Passengers who get off at Avignon enjoy a much shorter cab ride to Les Baux, gaining about an hour over passengers who have gone to Marseilles.

Night falls, and a lonely dog watches from a rooftop as The Working Moms trudge toward elimination.

1. Kevin and Drew (The Fat Bastards) 3:53 P.M.
2. Frank and Margarita (Team Diesel) 4:07 P.M.
3. Rob and Brennan (The Young Lawyers) 4:15 P.M.
4. Joe and Bill (Team Guido) 5:04 P.M.
5. David and Margaretta (The Old Folks) 5:47 P.M.
6. Paul and Amie (Team Puss) 6:47 P.M.
7. Lenny and Karyn (Team Monument) 6:48 P.M.
8. Nancy and Emily (Team Oh, Mom) 6:49 P.M.
9. Pat and Brenda (The Working Moms) ELIMINATED

Leg #4: Proof that David Still Carries a Torch for Margaretta

The clue envelope bears a national flag and the photograph of a man wearing a fez. Teams must proceed to the Port of Marseilles and book passage to the country indicated by the flag, where the man awaits under what looks like a smaller version of the Arc de Triomphe.

Further alienation between teams ensues when there are confrontations over the poaching of cabs. Team Diesel has had it with The Young Lawyers, and vice versa. Team Oh, Mom takes the cab ordered by Team Puss, prompting Paul to fling his clue envelope and announce, "I'm done." Nancy, for her part, is taken aback by the "language I'm hearing, the viciousness, the backstabbing...I don't like it, and I can't get away from it."

When the country is identified as Tunisia, the Guidos arrange a group rate for everybody, but so much animosity erupts during the dispensing of tickets that they end up eating by themselves on the cruise, while everybody else pals around at the big table. "I want to rip off their heads and show them their hearts," says Lenny.

The boat docks in Tunisia, where the man at the French Arch hands Racers their next Detour, which requires teams to search for businesses inside a crowded Tunisian marketplace. "Full Body Brew" requires teams to find a coffee shop using only a photograph. Teams that pick "Full Body Massage" are given a map with the proper location circled, but then have to submit to a twenty-minute massage. Team Puss is the only team to go for the massage, where Paul gets the worst of it from a masseur who twists him into knots.

Now receiving a cigarette lighter bearing a likeness of the ancient Roman Coliseum at El Jem, some 200 miles away, teams have to choose whether to go by taxi (fast but expensive), or train (slow but cheap). The Old Folks run into the worst trouble here, when they find themselves stuck at the cab depot among drivers who refuse to take American dollars.

Cut scenes available on the DVD reveal The Fat Bastards, en route to El Jem, plotting the all-night party all the other teams will throw at the Pit Stop, if the Guidos happen to come in last. "If they decided to go for the Turkish bath," Drew says, "it's their own fault. You saw what that was like in *Midnight Express*."

The Roadblock at the El Jem Coliseum requires one team member to light a torch, walk clockwise to find stairs leading underground, travel through darkened passages to the "Pit of Death," retrieve a sword dangling from a rope, and return. Emily has some troubles with the torch, setting fire to a wall. David of The Old Folks walks counterclockwise by mistake and has trouble finding the stairs going down. It's a fatal delay. The Old Folks finish last and are eliminated, receiving applause and warm embraces from fellow players.

Team Puss, arriving in fifth place because of a production delay, are given a time credit, and depart fourth in the next leg.

1. Joe and Bill (Team Guido) 4:02 P.M.
2. Kevin and Drew (The Fat Bastards) 4:31 P.M.
3. Nancy and Emily (Team Oh, Mom) 4:36 P.M.
4. Frank and Margarita (Team Diesel) 5:03 P.M.
5. Paul and Amie (Team Puss) DELAYED
6. Rob and Brennan (The Young Lawyers) 5:22 P.M.
7. Lenny and Karyn (Team Monument) 5:43 P.M.
8. David and Margaretta (The Old Folks) ELIMINATED

Leg #5: You've Gotten Us Lost Again, Artoo

Teams at the El Jem Coliseum are handed a photograph of a monument consisting of a globe on top of a pillar. A handwritten notation on the photo identifies the site as "Tataouine." Though the Guidos leave half an hour earlier, Kevin of The Fat Bastards is the first we see connecting the place's name to the home planet of one Luke Skywalker. The desert scenes were filmed here in Tunisia.

A 300-mile cab ride later, teams converge on the monument, which is surrounded by marked cars for the Racers. Each car comes with a Detour, "Listening" or "Puzzling." "Listening" requires teams to use one walkie-talkie to find another at the easy-to-find *Phantom Menace* movie set, Ksar Hadada. "Puzzling" requires teams to solve a logical puzzle at a hard-to-find location. Everybody takes "Listening" rather than risk getting lost in the desert, a reasonable decision that won't help Paul and Amie all that much later on. She's already running into trouble before the Detour. Sick for reasons the show fails to specify, but which can be anything from motion sickness to a local bug, her contribution this leg consists of making generous use of a vomit bag.

As the Race enters the Sahara, a compass, a map, and a series of yellow stones lining the region's treacherous roads provide most teams with precious little help finding the next route marker. Some wander for hours, trying every available direction, growing more and more frustrated as they encounter other teams, equally lost, headed the other way. Amie grows sicker and paler.

The Fat Bastards are first to find the arrow pointing off-road, and follow it and subsequent markings to the Roadblock—a task requiring one team member to lead the camel being ridden by the other across desert sands in hundred-degree heat. Drew's aggrieved ranting about having to walk while Kevin rides is one of the highlights of the entire series: "I get screwed on every one. I carry the torch, I burn my arm, walk a camel with you sitting on top of it."

Kevin says, "Drew, come on, it's getting hot up here."

Drew mutters, "I'm gonna kill you when you get offa this thing."

Once almost every team makes it to the Ksar Ghilane Oasis, concerns turn to Team Puss. Where the hell are they? And the answer is: dangerously lost. They've left the road and are now off-road in the Sahara, without any idea where they are or where they should go. Amie is getting sicker and sicker and hasn't had any water all day. Things look pretty bad for them until Paul spots a cluster of parked vans on the horizon, and steers toward it. When Team Puss finally drives up to the oasis from the wrong direction, having missed the Roadblock entirely, the other players greet them with relieved hugs. It's a terrible way to leave the game, and the best thing you can say about Amie is that she spent the day sick as a dog but refusing to quit.

1. Kevin and Drew (The Fat Bastards) 2:24 P.M.
2. Joe and Bill (Team Guido) 2:46 P.M.
3. Nancy and Emily (Team Oh, Mom) 3:12 P.M.
4. Rob and Brennan (The Young Lawyers) 3:52 P.M.
5. Frank and Margarita (Team Diesel) 4:42 P.M.
6. Lenny and Karyn (Team Monument) 4:43 P.M.
7. Paul and Amie (Team Puss) ELIMINATED

Leg #6: Nobody Likes the Guidos

Teams would normally spend the night at the Pit Stop, but an impending sandstorm requires an evacuation to the town of Gabes. There aren't a hell of a lot of cabs available in Gabes in the middle of the night, but that proves a surmountable difficulty, and a long night in the back of a cab provides the only real obstacle between everybody, the Palace Hotel in Tunis, and instructions to search for the next clue in the vicinity of the Coliseum in Rome.

Unfortunately, a strike at the Rome Airport limits the number of flights there. Discord begins early, during a confrontation at the airport ticket counter, when Drew suspects the Guidos of trying to enlist the ticket agent against him, and threatens to break some legs. The Guidos emerge the only team to leave the counter with tickets, and watch the increasing desperation of the other teams with smug triumph, until Kevin of The Fat Bastards wangles superior tickets for his team, the Lawyers, and Team Oh, Mom. With minutes to spare, those three teams head for their flight.

At which point Team Guido attempts a questionable tactic that ratchets up the tension level still further. They see the three teams headed for customs and choose that moment to jump ahead of them, doing everything they can to delay the line and prevent their opponents from passing. Though they fail, it is the final straw as far as the other teams are concerned. There is no remaining good will for the Guidos.

Team Monument, which scores the only direct flight, enjoys a healthy lead upon landing in Rome at 7:10 P.M. They're first to the Detour, in which teams must use a photo to locate one of two statues. "Foot," a giant statue of a, er, foot, will be the easiest, as it's a familiar site to locals. "Hoof" is a detail of a man on horseback, harder to identify, but convenient to taxis afterward. Everybody but Team Monument will go for "Hoof." Either way, both sites are closed for the night, a provision which helps those teams still cooling their heels in distant cities to catch up.

At the next morning's bunching point, the Guidos are the number one topic of conversation. Drew warns them, "Don't even think of saying, 'Good morning.'"

The route marker leads teams to travel by train to Castelfranco, and the Pagani Auto Factory, site of this leg's Roadblock. One team member must drive a small Italian car down a series of confusing country roads to a small village some ten miles away. The other player is driven to the Pit Stop in a Sportster going 180 miles an hour. It's a dull ride for one, a wild ride for the other. The last team to arrive, Team Monument, is saved by a non-elimination leg.

Team Diesel and Team Guido both receive time penalties due to inadvertent rule infractions, which will affect their departure times in the next leg. Team Monument receives a time credit due to a production delay. Their exact arrival times are obscured, but the order is unaffected.

1. Frank and Margarita (Team Diesel) PENALTY
2. Joe and Bill (Team Guido) PENALTY
3. Rob and Brennan (The Young Lawyers) 4:13 P.M.

4. Kevin and Drew (The Fat Bastards) 4:36 P.M.
5. Nancy and Emily (Team Oh, Mom) 4:59 P.M.
6. Lenny and Karyn (Team Monument) NOT ELIMINATED

Leg #7: Glide, You Fat Bastard, Glide!

Teams leaving the Pit Stop receive their Detour immediately. "Glide" or "Ride" both take players to a nearby train station. In "Glide," teams will get a ride there after one team member takes a ride in a glider. In "Ride," team members must first complete an eight-kilometer bike ride. Both tasks have early-morning hours of operation. The chief disadvantage of "Ride" is that it's exhausting. The chief disadvantage of "Glide" is that there's only one glider, requiring teams to take turns.

A few reasons teams give for their choices reveal much about player morale. The Fat Bastards find The Young Lawyers already waiting at the glider airfield and decide to stay there, believing the long wait will be more enjoyable with Rob and Brennan than with the Guidos. Team Diesel goes for the Fast Forward, which involves searching the moat at Ferrara Castle, just to "get away from all the negative energy." Emily of Team Oh, Mom seems a little too spent to make a decision right now, and the currently much perkier Nancy can't get her daughter enthused about either choice—even the gliders, which would enable them to "go out with a bang." They pick "Ride" by default.

Team Diesel finds the Fast Forward after a brief search, eliciting a delighted "Oh, boy!" from Frank. They will reach the Pit Stop, the Taj Khema Hotel in Agra, India, many hours before the other teams even arrive in India.

Drew, who has been shortchanged on fun Roadblocks (as opposed to labor-intensive ones), rides the glider for his team. His reactions to the flight, and 76-year-old pilot, are hilarious.

Teams completing this Roadblock must then make their way to the Red Fort Marketplace in Delhi. That entails finding an international airport. The Lawyers and the Guidos take a train to Rome. The remaining teams call ahead to book a flight leaving from Milan, leading to some tense moments as they delay a departing train long enough for Kevin to arrive from the phone booth. The end result of all this strategy? A bunching, as all these teams connect in Copenhagen.

For the very first time, teams leave a prosperous region in Europe only to experience culture shock in India. Dispatchers stop the cabs in the road, demanding additional payment. Bedraggled, imploring children beg during red lights. It's an upsetting contrast, almost worse for those who stay behind than it is for those who perform the Roadblock, a search for a certain enthused shopkeeper in a crowded marketplace. Nancy, who's last to emerge, is left crying from emotional exhaustion. Emily has her own most panicky moment as their cab is surrounded by curious locals. "They're stupid!" she cries. "These people are nuts! Look at them! They're laughing at us!" No, Emily, they're only wondering if the Americans are filming a movie. A weeping Nancy asks her to please, please stop. Both sob as their cab pulls away from the crowd.

The final clue, a replica of the Taj Mahal, provides the final obstacle, with most teams lost in confusion as they search for directions to the monument and the adjacent Taj Khema Hotel. Most arrive in darkness and are stunned to discover themselves still in the game. But Team Monument has the worst luck with cabs. By then, tension has taken its toll. Their relationship faces an uncertain future.

1. Frank and Margarita (Team Diesel) 8:01 A.M.
2. Joe and Bill (Team Guido) 6:48 P.M.
3. Rob and Brennan (The Young Lawyers) 6:54 P.M.
4. Kevin and Drew (The Fat Bastards) 7:44 P.M.
5. Nancy and Emily (Team Oh, Mom) 8:15 P.M.
6. Lenny and Karyn (Team Monument) ELIMINATED

Leg #8: T-t-taj Mahal, Folks![10]

Receiving no money, teams search the forty-two-acre site of the Taj Mahal for the next clue. Team Diesel gets going eleven hours before the closest competition, but the 6:00 A.M. opening time leaves them with a long night to kill, and shrinks their lead to a mere forty-eight minutes. That's gotta be frustrating. Still, they remain in good spirits, and once they find the clue, Frank does offer to build Margarita her very own Taj Mahal out of Legos.

The Guidos continue their tradition of remarkably ineffective villainy

---

[10] Before the start of this leg, players were surprised with letters from their loved ones. The teary and sometimes quite funny reactions are among the cut scenes available on the season one DVD.

by attempting to slip in with a large tour group that has already purchased tickets. A security guard spots them, prompting the Guidos to claim that they thought admission was free.

Next stop is the Palace of the Winds, in Jaipur, 150 miles away. Budgetary concerns will force them to decide whether the best way there is a fast, but expensive, taxi or a slow, but cheap, bus.

On the way, Drew characterizes India's smells. "This has gotta be worse than smokin' twenty cigars at one time."

In one of her own funnier moments, Emily wonders why her team's cabbie kept blowing his horn twenty-nine times a minute. "Maybe it was a status symbol or something. Like, look at me. I have a horn. Da de da."

A search of the Palace produces this leg's Detour, which involves competing routes to holy men. "Elephant" requires the team to ride the titular beast up a steep path to the Amber Fort. The other is accessible by "Row Boat."

Searching the Palace for the clue, Drew astutely notes, "It's like India in here." Kevin follows that up with, "I bet those elephants smell like elephants." Finding the Wise Man, Drew additionally notes, "He's three days older than kerosene, that guy."

Teams completing the Detour must make their way to the Karni Mata Temple, in the town of Deshnoke, a journey that first requires a 200-mile train ride to Bikaner. Critically, the two trains there leave six hours apart. Only The Young Lawyers, The Fat Bastards, and Team Diesel catch the 3:00 P.M. train. In a major culture-shock moment, it takes Team Oh, Mom "an hour and a half" to find a ticket agent willing to sell tickets to women. They're thoroughly creeped out, and relieved when the Guidos join them on the platform.

The Karni Mata Temple, up ahead, serves a sect that considers rats sacred, and is populated by thousands of them. The Roadblock requires one team member to take off his or her shoes, don extra socks, and search the Temple, teeming with locals despite the late hour, for a canister containing the next clue envelope. Players feel appropriately skeevy as they wander chambers covered with droppings and squirming with sacred rodents. Players are not enthused by this prospect. Drew says he ain't gonna do it. Margarita, who does go on, offers the best cultural perspective. "You look down," she interviews, "and there's hundreds of rats crawling everywhere.... You feel really bad because you want to be respectful, because (the people) are so unafraid and so happy to be there. And you stick out like a sore thumb because you're terrified."

A quick taxi race leads the first three teams to the luxury American hotel in Bikaner. The sun rises before Teams Guido and Oh, Mom arrive to compete for last place.

1. Kevin and Drew (The Fat Bastards) 4:50 A.M.
2. Frank and Margarita (Team Diesel) 5:08 A.M.
3. Rob and Brennan (The Young Lawyers) 5:10 A.M.
4. Joe and Bill (Team Guido) 8:35 A.M.
5. Nancy and Emily (Team Oh, Mom) 8:37 A.M. NOT ELIMINATED

Leg #9: The Expensive Cup of Tea

Two teams torpedo their chances with a pair of the most jaw-dropping errors in Race history.

Teams must take a bus or train 300 miles to the airport in New Delhi, and from there approximately 2,000 miles to the Temple of Dawn of Bangkok, Thailand. They are not told that while the train moves faster, buses take less time to reach Delhi. The Fat Bastards find this out and get to the Delhi Airport an hour ahead of the other teams. Of course, the hours of operation at Bangkok's Temple of Dawn (7:00 A.M.–6:00 P.M.) render this moot as teams have to wait outside for it to open up in the morning.

Team Guido and Team Oh, Mom go for the Fast Forward at Bangkok's Reclining Buddha shrine. Although only one team can claim the Fast Forward, and Emily believes the Guidos never lose anything, Team Oh, Mom decides to stay and compete. It's a major risk. But it's not the fatal error, even when they subsequently lose the luck-based challenge and have to rush to the Temple of Dawn, following a quick route kindly provided by the Guidos.

The Detour at the Temple offers two ways of getting to Kanchanaburi, some three hours away. Teams can go by bus. Or they can search the neighborhood for parked private cars. Buses leave every twenty minutes. Cars can only be identified by their license plates. It seems obvious to viewers that the search for a chillin' ride will likely eat up time, but several teams decide to look. Critically, Team Diesel finds their car within minutes. Just as critically, The Fat Bastards waste more than two hours looking. Late-arriving Team Oh, Mom, who should also go straight to the bus station, searches for the car until Nancy is exhausted and Emily is hysterical. But even that's not their fatal error, which is so completely succumbing to despair that they take a taxi, rather than the required bus.

Meanwhile, flush with victory at the Fast Forward, the Guidos do something even more baffling. They could proceed to the Pit Stop 500 miles away at the Tiger Cave Temple in Krabi. They have enough for a taxi, as their subsequent use for the money establishes. But the Guidos are so certain that the Fast Forward guarantees them victory that they elect to *wait* for a bus leaving eight hours later, spending the day at a hotel where they can "sip ice tea and sit in air-conditioned splendor." Yes. They actually do that.

Everybody else makes it to the Buddhist monastery in Kanchanaburi, site of a Roadblock requiring one team member to take a long walk across the pit housing that establishment's pet tigers. Frank is swatted by one. Drew is sniffed by another. Nervous mom Nancy dies a little watching her daughter take the stroll. All teams move on to Krabi.

The Guidos, who should have arrived hours before anybody else, arrive at the Pit Stop at the Tiger Cave Temple eight hours late because of their dawdling. This error will drive them increasingly behind in the legs that remain. But it's Team Oh, Mom that cannot overcome the twenty-four-hour penalty they receive for failing to complete the Detour.

1. Rob and Brennan (The Young Lawyers) 10:12 P.M.
2. Frank and Margarita (Team Diesel) 11:06 P.M.
3. Kevin and Drew (The Fat Bastards) 3:03 A.M.
4. Nancy and Emily (Team Oh, Mom) ELIMINATED
5. Joe and Bill (Team Guido) 6:31 A.M.

Leg #10: A Visit to the King

The hours of operation provided by two of this leg's locations prove disastrous for the two trailing teams.

All teams need to ride a taxi and a boat to reach "The King" at Thailand's Raile Beach. It's the name locals have given a local adventure-climbing company, and the site of this leg's "Climb" or "Walk" Detour.

(Everybody throughout the day will climb the sheer rock face, rather than hike up the much easier trail.) It's only open from 8:00 A.M. to 5:30 P.M., which is no great inconvenience for Team Diesel and The Young Lawyers, both of whom leave the Pit Stop early in the morning.

Critically, the clue found after the arduous climb sends these first two teams thirty miles away to another site with limited hours of operation: the boat rental establishment Sea, Land, and Trek in Ao Luk, which closes at 5:00 P.M. Only Team Diesel and The Young Lawyers leave the Pit Stop early enough to not only complete the Detour, but reach Sea, Land, and Trek by closing.

Rob breaks a knuckle rappeling down the cliff, but he wraps his fingers in a homemade splint and continues.

Sea, Land, and Trek provides teams with the leg's Roadblock. One team member must paddle the kayak containing his team and their luggage to a cave containing a clue box and snorkeling equipment. This clue directs teams to return their kayaks, hire a boat, and travel some four miles to the waters near Chicken Island, named that because it actually does, no kidding, look like a chicken. (Spooky. I mean, that island's about to lay an egg.) A buoy offshore marks the spot where they dive to find the clue that directs them back to the Pit Stop on the mainland.

The Young Lawyers and Team Diesel are both celebrating at the Pit Stop by sunset.

Things are less certain for The Fat Bastards, who depart the previous Pit Stop at 3:03 P.M., but are able to make it to the King in time to complete the climb. Receiving the clue by a quarter to five, they cannot possibly descend the cliff, rappel to the boat, and travel the thirty miles to Sea, Land, and Trek in the fifteen minutes before that business closes for the night. The delay adds nine hours to their completion time. By the time they complete the kayaking and the snorkeling (Drew adding to this leg's injuries when he steps on a sea urchin), they may have won third place, but no longer enjoy a comfortable lead over the Guidos.

The Guidos, who don't even get to leave the previous Pit Stop until after The Young Lawyers and Team Diesel are celebrating at this one, are also driven farther behind the leads. They need to wait a long night before the King even opens for business. They're downright admirable during the next morning's climb, supporting each other with patience and understanding even as they reach and exceed their physical limits. When done, they're downright proud of what a couple of "old farts" have accomplished. And we should give them that. But look at those arrival times now.

1. Rob and Brennan (The Young Lawyers) 6:03 P.M.
2. Frank and Margarita (Team Diesel) 6:15 P.M.
3. Kevin and Drew (The Fat Bastards) 11:35 A.M.
4. Joe and Bill (Team Guido) 1:30 P.M. NOT ELIMINATED

Leg #11: "Eat, You Fat Bastard!"

Teams must now travel 2,500 miles to the Top Pavilion at Jingshan Park in Beijing, China.

The Young Lawyers and Team Diesel travel to Phuket Airport, arriving minutes too late to catch an 8:20 A.M. flight that, with Bangkok connection, would have placed them in Beijing by late afternoon. As a result, they don't arrive until early the next day.

The Detour is "Volley" or "Rally." "Volley" requires one Racer to score five points against a local Ping-Pong champion. "Rally" requires teams to travel Beijing's streets via bus, motorcycle taxi, and bicycle taxi. The Ping-Pong is clearly the faster choice, even for teams who suck at it: it may take an hour or more to score five points against a champion, but the transportation rally through city traffic can take even longer. Wisely, both The Young Lawyers and Team Diesel go for "Volley," despite worries over China's notorious excellence at the national sport.

On the way, Rob laughs at what both teams expect to be a humiliating experience. "We're underestimating this Ping-Pong dude. Three hours later, [you'll have] balls bouncing off your forehead." But the champion is a young boy. And while the kid is pretty good, he's not an impossible obstacle. Frank finishes quickly, but the kid scores thirteen points before Brennan even scores his first. (Rob steps in to nail the final four points, despite his splinted hand.) But in both cases the game takes far less time than zigging back and forth across the city would have.

Teams completing that task must proceed to a market to buy local delicacies off a shopping list. That list is written entirely in Chinese, so they need to appeal to local shoppers to obtain the necessary five beetle larvae, one squid, and two chicken feet.

In the taxi to the next destination, Rob says, "I think I know what the Roadblock is gonna be."

And, yes, one player must have a local restaurant cook the items, and thereafter eat it all.

Minor emotional complications ensue when Frank and Margarita fight over who's going to do the Roadblock. Margarita takes it because Frank has a stomachache, then opens the envelope and turns green. Frank laughs at her for being a "moron," which she doesn't take well at all. "I do appreciate that she's trying to help me out," he interviews, "but I'm just a little impatient and stubborn and stupid sometimes. So I guess I need to apologize." Which he does.

Brennan eats. "Is it curry?" Rob asks. Brennan replies, "No, it's just...feet." Rob says, "At least you're having lunch."

Both teams reach the Pit Stop at the South Gate of Tiantan Park before the Guidos and Fat Bastards arrive in China.

Those trailing teams land after 4:00 P.M. and choose "Rally" as their Detour option. The motorcycle taxi prompts Kevin to sing the Batman theme and Drew to suppose that his left testicle is rolling around the streets of Beijing. There's a fun bicycle taxi chase through the streets as both teams jockey for position, passing each other several times.

But they don't arrive at the next route marker until the market has closed for the night.

And though they remain neck-and-neck the next morning, it's The Fat Bastards who lose the race to the mat. Poor Drew looks as devastated as any eliminated Racer ever has.

Team Guido, who gets to stay in the Race, is now just a few minutes shy of twenty-four hours behind.

1. Frank and Margarita (Team Diesel) 11:14 A.M.
2. Rob and Brennan (The Young Lawyers) 11:25 A.M.
3. Joe and Bill (Team Guido) 10:51 A.M. (the next day)
4. Kevin and Drew (The Fat Bastards) ELIMINATED

Leg #12: Hitting the Wall

The first task, searching for clues attached to kites at Beijing's Tiantan Park, comes complete with hours of operation that force all teams to find lodging before starting anew the next morning.

Kite clues direct teams to the Juyong Pass at the Great Wall of China. Team Diesel arrives at the Wall first, but nowhere near the specified entrance, requiring desperate improvisation that includes hopping fences and climbing over locked admission gates. But as a result they have quite a bit of trouble finding the route marker. The Young Lawyers have better luck and find the Detour: "Steep" or "Flat." Both options lead teams to one of the pavillions that separate sections of the Wall. "Steep" involves climbing a long, exhausting set of stairs to a pavillion at the top of a mountain; "Flat" heads in the opposite direction and is, predictably, a level walk over a much greater distance.

The Lawyers take "Steep" and drag themselves up the stairs, finding the next route marker while Team Diesel is still hopping fences. The clue reads: "You're expected at North Country Bed and Breakfast. Scotty Lake, Alaska (near Talkeetna)." Getting there requires a 4,000-mile flight from Beijing to Anchorage, and then a two-hour drive to Scotty Lake. When a quick glance at the clue box establishes that Team Diesel's envelope remains unclaimed, The Young Lawyers hope to get to the airport and into the air before Team Diesel can catch up.

It seems possible. Team Diesel is wasting a lot of time. Margarita wants to call a cab just so they have a place to dump their luggage before performing the Detour. Frank ratchets up the sarcasm: "If [you've made a] mistake," he says, putting all the responsibility on her, "we're done." For her part, Margarita can't help wondering, "How did this all break apart, at the end?"

It's all noise. Both lead teams wind up flying the same Beijing-San Francisco-Seattle-Anchorage itinerary. They're in the sky by 1:45 P.M.

Nine hours later, at 10:51 P.M., the Guidos leave the Beijing Pit Stop and are immediately faced with the same hours of operation barrier that bunched the lead teams twenty-four hours earlier. This only preserves the distance separating them from the lead teams. They're on the Great Wall, receiving their instructions to fly to Alaska, at about the same time the lead teams arrive in Anchorage. They can only book the identical itinerary and hope that the teams ahead of them start making huge mistakes.

Meanwhile, the others arrive at the North Country Bed and Breakfast, spending the night in the same tiny cabin before embarking upon the next morning's tasks, which include a Native American blanket toss, and a hundred-mile drive to the Roadblock, and an ice climb at Matanuska Glacier. The final clue of the leg directs those teams to get back on the road, find mile marker 131 on the Parks Highway, hop aboard one of the provided snowmobiles, and make their way to the Pit Stop, a musher's lodge a short ride away.

Team Guido perseveres and makes it to Alaska this leg. But they don't reach the Pit Stop. They only make it as far as the bed and breakfast, still hoping for an unlikely come-from-behind victory.

Are you beginning to understand the cost of that cup of tea?

1. Rob and Brennan (The Young Lawyers) 4:17 P.M.
2. Frank and Margarita (Team Diesel) 5:03 P.M.
3. Joe and Bill (Team Guido) INCOMPLETE—STILL TRAVELING

Leg #13: Trust the Cabbie, Luke

The top two teams must don snowshoes and follow a marked path to Takosha Lodge. The Young Lawyers discover as they leave the Pit Stop that the cold has drained their flashlight batteries of power. Rather than wander off into the Alaskan wilderness in pitch darkness and risk, you know, death by freezing—pointless since the clue also specifies that the hours of operation for the next task don't start until 8:00 A.M.—they elect to hang around for forty-five minutes and wait for the next team.

Frank interviews, "They're afraid of doing anything by themselves, because they're scared... [so] they started following us, of course, as they normally do."

Morning comes after four hours spent warming up in the lodge. We catch up with Team Guido (just beginning the last leg's blanket toss) before we rejoin The Young Lawyers and Team Diesel for the Detour: "Dog Power" or "Horsepower," which involves a choice of eleven miles by dogsled, or thirty miles by snowmobile. Both teams take the former choice, leading to a memorable chase through the countryside capped when the trailing Young Lawyers push their own dog teams to pass the much slower-moving Frank and Margarita.

Teams then take provided cars to Fish Lake, site of the final Roadblock: a masochistic dip in a frigid Alaskan lake. Players must submerge their heads before being allowed to grab the clue envelope attached to a post. Brennan is so shocked by the cold that he climbs out without the next clue and must return. "Shrinkage!" he shouts as he bounds out the second time.

Receiving the clue, teams learn that they must fly to New York and catch a cab to Vincent Daniels Square at 51st and Roosevelt in Queens. Team Diesel howls in premature triumph. They live only six blocks from there!

Meanwhile, the Guidos have reached the ice climb from the last leg. "We're gonna zoom right past 'em and not even look back," Joe predicts. But when they arrive at the eleventh-leg Pit Stop, they're still almost exactly twenty-four hours behind.

Airport shuffle leads to both teams sharing the same flight, which lands in Newark at 6:30 A.M. In New York, the home-court advantage actually works against Team Diesel when Frank insists on giving his cabbie a complicated series of directions intended to bypass Manhattan entirely.

The Young Lawyers merely tell their cabbie to take the fastest possible route. As a result, they're first to the last route marker, and first to take the elevated train to the Shea Stadium stop, where they will have to proceed on foot to Flushing Meadows Park.

Missing that same train by minutes, Team Diesel must now endure a wait for the next one. Still imagining themselves far ahead, their biggest concern is that The Young Lawyers won't show up before it leaves. When the train finally pulls in, with no sign of Rob and Brennan, Margarita is ebullient, literally jumping up and down in giddy premature celebration. Frank is confident, but far from certain.

Up ahead, the Lawyers are greeted by the cheers of their erstwhile rivals and Phil's trademark "nine countries, four continents, 35,000 miles" congratulations.

Team Diesel dashes up a while later, still certain of victory, mistaking the cheers up ahead for those that greet first-place winners. Frank is the one to spot Rob and Brennan up ahead. Margarita falters, devastated for all of two seconds, but then pulls herself together to run the rest of the way.

We follow with a fiendish cut back to Alaska, where the Guidos arrive at the dogsledding task, and receive, instead of a clue, written notification that The Young Lawyers have crossed the mat in New York. Yep, that was sure one expensive cup of tea.

1. Rob and Brennan (The Young Lawyers) WIN
2. Frank and Margarita (Team Diesel) PLACE
3. Joe and Bill (Team Guido) SHOW

The Guidos are the first of only two teams, in the entire history of the Race, to make it into the finals and yet end the Race so far behind that the producers shut them down rather than force them to go through the motions. But the only other team to find themselves in such a predicament, Team Strategic in Race 4, didn't make its own fatal error until the final leg. The Guidos fell irretrievably behind five—count 'em, five—legs from the finish line, surviving until the end only by defeating two other teams and completing two non-eliminations. All jokes about expensive cups of tea aside, everything they did after that one unbelievable miscalculation showed a level of confidence, competitiveness, and spirit that many later Racers would have done well to emulate. Guidos, take a bow.

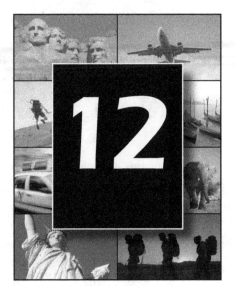

The Guidos Take a Bow

HMMM. THAT DIDN'T TAKE LONG.

Life partners Joe Baldassare and Bill Bartek, who named themselves Team Guido as a tribute to their dog, were the show's first "villains," destined by editing and a series of conflicts with other teams to be remembered as among the Race's most dedicated schemers. As villains go, they're rather mild. Compare them to the "villains" from some later Races and they no longer come off as all that bad. Their disastrous tactical error, late in the competition, also rendered them legends in the annals of Racer overconfidence.

Q: *You got onto the show before it was a phenomenon, during the "shake-down cruise," as it were. How did that come about?*

BILL: This was before the first big wave of reality shows. There had been *Survivor*, one summer of *Big Brother*, and MTV's *The Real World*. We're talking waaaay in the beginning, when there was nothing else. We didn't know what to expect from the show as a game, or what to expect from being the first gay couple to receive such exposure on national television, or how the way we played the game would be portrayed. There was a lot of this stuff going on in our heads.

Q: *So you had concerns about this at the time.*

BILL: We did. Joe and I talked about it before we left. We agreed that our relationship was the most important thing to us no matter what, a million dollars, whatever. We had seen enough reality TV to know that there were emotional scenes. That's what sells. So if this wasn't working out, if we felt we were having a bad time of it, we had a phrase we used, "'Nuff said." We would back off and talk about it later. But we never went there, so it obviously wasn't all that important.

Q: *They never actually tell you to fight.*

BILL: No, no…well, not in our case. They put you in situations where you're bound to. [You're making] life or death decisions, jumping off things, out of planes, doing things that you ordinarily wouldn't do, or couldn't afford. Going to Africa, India, doing chores and performing tasks way out of your normal space. Plus, you're gonna get jet lagged, tired, hungry, and at the [end] of your rope.[11]

Q: *What did the interview process entail?*

JOE: Bill had wanted to be on *Survivor: Australia*, so he downloaded the application, made an incredibly boring [audition] tape and never got an interview. Afterward, he was searching the CBS Web site and came across something called "The CBS Global Adventure Series." It was teams of two traveling around the world. It suited both of us. Neither one of us would be left at home, baby-sitting the dog, while the other had his life changed, or whatever.

The interview process started around November of 2000. We

---

[11] He actually said, "edge of your rope," which would no doubt be even more uncomfortable.

sent in a little tape narrated by Guido asking CBS to take us because he needed a little vacation from us. Bill was the cameraman, I was the voice of Guido, and we cut back and forth between us telling lies and Guido telling the truth. We sent it in, and were probably the second tape they ever received. They had this big, giant blackboard at World Race Productions where they color coded the tiniest, smallest Post-its depending on how much they liked [the applicants]. If they liked you a lot you [went] to the top of the board, and as more tapes came in, you fell down closer to the bottom of the board and didn't get an interview. The lady who received our tape [said] we went into the upper left-hand corner of the board and never moved. So, eventually, mid-December, we got a call asking us to come up to Santa Monica for a personal interview of between five and forty-five minutes, depending on how much they liked us. We went up and lasted forty minutes. On the way out we were told to get approval from our next of kin, medical exams, and [asked] whether we had ever been to Israel. This [last question] indicated to us that we might be going to Arab countries [as we did end up going to Tunisia].

At the end of January we had our second interview, [which involved] being sequestered for between seven and fourteen days. [We were sequestered for ten.] You couldn't talk to any other contestant teams at all. You didn't know anybody else's names. You were only allowed to speak to people on the production staff, and the casting crew, who were interviewing you. You couldn't leave the hotel without permission. We eventually got permission to go out one day and go to a gym to get a little exercise, and stopped at a Costco on the way back for a couple of cases of wine to have with dinner,[12] so we got nicknamed the "Wine Guys," as we were always drinking a bottle of wine at dinner. By the end of ten days [we'd] gone through ten days of psychological exams, a couple of days of not doing anything but sitting around waiting to be called, and then half of us were put through some medical exams. Then we were sent home, and about five days after that, we got the phone call: you're on the show, and you have to be ready in three weeks.

---

[12] Presumably for the rest of their stay, not just for that night's dinner.

Q: *Those psychological tests were evidently not foolproof, as evidenced by some Racers who have fallen apart [on the show].*

BILL: It happened during the interview process. One couple was sent home on the second or third day. We saw people crying, breaking down, kicking tables, and nearly getting into fights with their team-mates or some other team out of some perceived slight, which is incredible since you can't even talk to one another. I think it was just one of those things, especially when you go through days of people telling you to go back to your room, we're going to call you in an hour and a half, and then you go back to your room and wait *all day long* and nobody calls. That's testing your patience, your stamina, and your mental stability to see if you can handle stress. We handled that by playing the whole interview process as a game. We knew that all this hurry-up-and-wait was a preview of the Race, so we did everything in our power to know when the producers were in the building, what car [producer] Bertram van Munster drove, who was up on the penthouse floor, who was being interviewed, and who was not getting called at all. We kept track of other teams with nicknames. If you remember Pat and Brenda—everybody thought they were lesbians, which they're not—they were "Thelma and Louise." We also knew who the top three teams were likely to be: us, Rob and Brennan (who we called "The Studmuffins"), and Frank and Margarita (who we called "The Athletic Black Couple").

Q: *What percentage of these teams ended up in your Race?*

BILL: There were twenty-four teams of two at the beginning of sequestration. One got sent home early. We were told that nine teams would be selected, and it ended up being eleven.

Q: *Did you know what to expect as the Race grew closer?*

BILL: We didn't get the rules until the morning the Race started. [We] were in bed in the middle of the night, and a phone call [came, instructing us] to come down to hear all the little things we needed to know. So [that's] when they explained the Roadblock, the Detour, the Fast Forward. We had one chance to ask questions, and that was it.

Q: *So now it starts. You go off to Africa, where you face that crazy swing into the gorge....Was this your first indication of how crazy things were to become?*

BILL: Joe and I looked at each other at the end of that day and said, if this is what's going to happen, this Race is not for forty- or fifty-somethings. We were literally dead in our bed, and we knew we had to get up in four hours and race again: how were we going to do that every day?

JOE: Bill leans up on the pillow and looks at me and says, "If the rest of the Race is gonna be like this, I don't know if I can do it." I say you better damn well do it. We're gonna win this thing, and we've got another forty days of this stuff. You're not wimping out on me now!

BILL: We had no idea what to expect. It's different now. Racers have watched other seasons and have seen jet lag, sleeping on planes....We didn't have a clue. Season one teams really went through hell, figuring out the game from day one.

JOE: The production staff didn't know what to expect either. They were figuring out a lot of it as we went along. At one point in time, around India or Thailand, the staff shared with us that we were three days ahead of where the production staff had been when they did the Race. They were having a hard time keeping up with us. We got to the Eiffel Tower before the clue box was there. When we first got to JFK, South African Airlines wasn't set up yet. We didn't know whether we were doing something right or wrong. There was no one there to give us a clue, nobody to greet us, or anything.

BILL: The first season was a real nightmare. I don't think they planned on having thirty-six hour Pit Stops, but they began having them right away, in Paris, because production people got sick, locations weren't ready for us, we weren't supposed to arrive places for two or three days later....

Q: *Tell me about the hardships of the Race. Sleep deprivation, hygiene...*

BILL: I don't remember sleep deprivation being much of a problem. We washed our clothes every time we were in a hotel. That's how we got the nickname "The Magic Backpack." We always managed to have clean clothes, rolled not folded. We wanted the other teams to think we were in better shape, even when we were dying.

JOE: The other thing is you really are not eating very well—a lot of sandwiches, coffee. I had never seen Bill drink a Coca-Cola in the fourteen years I had known him, and suddenly he's living on Coca-Cola and tuna-salad sandwiches. You're eating out of gas stations.

Q: *What about your camera crew, your silent partners in all this?*

JOE: Oh, you can't deprive the camera crew of food or bathroom breaks along the way. These guys have the right to stop and have a meal, a right to stop and get eight hours of sleep. You can't just say, "We're gonna drive in a taxicab all day and skip two meals," because you can't make that decision for them.

BILL: We would give them half our food, the Powerbars we were carrying in our backpack, just so we could keep going rather than have them forcing us to stop. We treated them as if we were a family of four and they were our children and we'd tried to keep them happy and content and be aware of their needs. We always explained to them what we were going to do or what we thought we'd do next, where we were going and how we were going to get there. If you don't work with them, if you don't get along with your camera team, it's the kiss of death. We had one guy with the camera who couldn't run. He was younger than we were but fat and out of shape. He didn't run! So you can't go running away, because he's not going to follow you, and he can't catch up to you, and he will make your life miserable.

JOE: He would have us film things two or three times when it wasn't crucial to our racing. He wouldn't do that if we were going to miss a plane or something. . . .

BILL: . . . but you have to get along with them. The ultimate way they control you is by getting releases from all the other people on film, which can take fifteen minutes of explaining in different languages.

Q: *How quiet are they on the ride?*

BILL: They're the eyes and ears of production and are prepared with questions, everyday. You don't know this until after the Race, but they've been told what to ask you by the story editor. We can look back now and see the ways we were set up. The biggest example is we lived in Paris for two years. They asked us about it a couple of times in one day, and we couldn't figure out why. Then in the episode we say it five times in a period of two minutes, as if we're bragging.

JOE: The one thing we were noted for was we never rested in a cab. We were always strategizing, talking about the Race, constantly going back and forth trying to figure out what we were doing. Versus, we heard from our camera crews that certain teams were dozing off in the back of their cabs, some weren't getting along well, or they wanted to go sightseeing. We said, we'll come *back* to these places if we see something we like!

Q: *You guys were the first team to have serious conflicts with other teams, like on the boat to Tunisia.*

BILL: That was really about Joe and I getting a cabin when the boat was oversold. So I knew I had to step up and help because I speak French. In addition, we did it as a group so we got everybody a group discount. The computers went down, and it took so much time to hand out the tickets that everybody thought I was screwing them in some way.

JOE: One team, Lenny and Karyn, did get screwed out of a cabin, but we made an arrangement with the production staff that Lenny and Karyn could come into our cabin, which slept four, rather than have our production crew sleep with us. Once we got under way, [the producers] rearranged some people so Lenny and Karyn could have their own cabin and wouldn't have to share with us. So they never had to show Joe and Bill being nice to anybody!

Q: *Then there's the airport body block incident.*

BILL: There's the Guido side of the story and the Kevin and Drew side of the story. The bottom line is we were never reprimanded by production for anything: pushing, shoving, anything. Maybe people say we were dirty players because we stood in front of them, but all we did was stand in a line. This was not a line to get on the plane, but a security entrance. I was meaning to slow them down, but we never broke a rule. And we never pushed anybody, because we were in front. How could we push anyone?

JOE: Drew was made to apologize to Bill, on camera, for threatening to break his legs. You can't touch another contestant aggressively; you can't threaten another contestant verbally. This isn't real life. This is playing a game with rules.

BILL: I didn't like the way Drew treated me, honestly. I was not gonna have a big guy sort of push a gay guy around. That was really my gut feeling. So I was going to do something to show that I can play a tough game too. To me, it was a gay/straight issue. I'm not proud of the way I reacted; I probably should have turned the other cheek, but I didn't. I reacted the way you've seen. Because of this, we came off as very evil, and the gay movement shunned us.

Q: *It's also true that every season, Racers have picked a team to hate.*

JOE: And you don't get mad at a weak team. A weak team is inconsequential. You get mad at the team you think is gonna win. You do everything you can to push them down and get them eliminated. There's only a couple of ways fellow contestants can manipulate the game. One of them is to pick a weaker team, [help them], and push everybody down a notch, hopefully knocking out that stronger team you think is gonna win. And then you can knock off that weaker team later. Everybody tried to do that with Nancy and Emily. We all caught on to that real early.

Q: *Now I'm gonna ask you about the most interesting thing that happens to your team. I think you already know what it is, but the title I give your season is "The Expensive Cup of Tea."*

(*Bill and Joe laugh.*)

Q: *You guys were very smart. Even the people who thought you were villainous agreed that you were very smart Racers. And then we come to this point where you lose a tremendous advantage with this jaw-dropping error. What was going through your mind on that day?*

BILL: We make it to the bus station, we've just won the Fast Forward, and the clue says you can take a bus, a train, or a taxicab. First thing we see is Kevin and Drew. Now, we know they haven't won the Fast Forward. We know they're doing something else on the bus. [They haven't even done the tigers yet.] So we get on line and we need to go to this place 1,000 kilometers away, 660 miles, and I get to the ticket window, and we have just missed the morning bus by half an hour. The next one doesn't leave till 5:30 in the afternoon. The lady behind us in line speaks perfect English, and she says, I'm going to the next town south [of where you're going], you need to take that 5:30 bus. She tells us, and the lady behind the window tells us, you can't take a cab, it's a thousand kilometers away. And we're thinking, she speaks English so well, she knows where we're going, and she's really being so helpful. We just took our eyes off the ball for a second and believed what she told us. "You can *never* take a cab 600 miles in Thailand." The thing is, we had enough money and we could have. The cabs were on the other side of the sliding glass door.

JOE: Every other time in the Race, our mode was ask three people and get it verified three times.

BILL: It was a compounding effect. We'd been up all night, sleeping on a concrete floor, getting chewed up by mosquitos, ebullient about winning the Fast Forward, now we've got this lady helping us, and we just accepted it without checking out a taxicab. We had the money. We just took our eyes off the ball and got stupid for a split second.

JOE: We were also thinking that the Fast Forwards were getting more valuable. The last one Frank and Margarita got was worth fourteen hours! So we figured, even if we waste some time, we're still coming in first. So we rented a cheap hotel room, we washed our clothes, we sunbathed, and then, believe it or not, we almost missed the bus!

(In the background, Guido goes nuts with barking. First time he's audible, entire interview. He must be reliving the trauma. No gold-plated supper dish for you, young man.)

Q: *This happened five legs from the end. Because you had two non-elimination legs, and one team competing with you for last place, you spent the rest of the Race twenty-four hours behind everybody else.*

BILL: That night we had to decide whether to go on or give up. [We knew] anybody could make an error; anybody could get caught up in an airport for twenty-four hours. We could be neck-and-neck again.

JOE: And the most important thing was we wanted to make it to the final three. We wanted to make it through the entire Race. We didn't want to be eliminated along the way. We were going to be at least third. And that meant we had to knock out Drew and Kevin. Which we did.

Q: *But after Thailand, with the exception of Kevin and Drew, you never saw the other Racers again.*

JOE: This is a funny little point. In Beijing, we [accidentally] picked the Pit Stop hotel as a place to spend the night. We weren't supposed to. We just needed a place to stay [waiting for the food market to open in the morning]. So we're in the lobby, looking at them, and they're looking at us, and Margarita's thinking, "Holy shit! How did they catch up?"

Q: *They must have thought you'd taken the SST.*

Brennan Swain
(of The Young Lawyers)
Makes His Case

BRENNAN SWAIN AND HIS GOOD friend Rob Frisbee went down in history as the winners of the first *Amazing Race* (and the first happy beneficiaries of the show's now-infamous hometown curse).

Q: *You were the very first team ever to take the Fast Forward, which I understand you came to regret when you found out what you had missed* [the gorge swing].

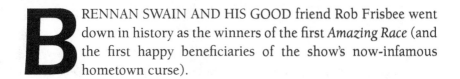

BRENNAN: *(laughs)* I guess there are two things to say about taking that first Fast Forward. The first is, as you said before, we didn't know what to expect. We learned the rules on how this giant worldwide Race was going to work two days before it even started. We didn't know what a Detour was. We didn't know what a Roadblock was. We didn't know what the Fast Forward was. So we heard about this Fast Forward pass, how it allowed you to skip all the tasks, and theoretically vault the team in last all the way up to the front. Rob and I were the first team to get to it. And we knew that the last-place teams were about six hours behind us. So we thought, if this could take them and put them in the lead, what kind of huge lead could it give us? This was gonna be able to sustain us for a few days. Never knowing that they were going to have bunching points almost every leg for the entire Race. So we decided to go for it, and, at the time, thought it was a good choice. In the end I certainly don't regret it; I wouldn't change a thing, because we won. But, yes, when we got to the Pit Stop and Team Guido came in, and I asked them what they got to do, and they described that crazy swing into the gorge, I regretted missing that.

Q: *I confess I want to fly over there just to do it myself.*

BRENNAN: The funny thing is that's one of the things I've talked about. Gee, I won half a million dollars. I should just fly over there and do it.

Q: *In the second leg, you were one of the teams that failed to realize that the Songwe Museum was only a hundred yards away from the Pit Stop. How long were you wandering?*

BRENNAN: Two hours. I must say, that's one of the drawbacks to what we call alliances on *The Amazing Race*. It's not *Survivor*. It's a different game. I remember my first inclination was, "Songwe Village, Songwe Museum. It's got to be close by." But we decided to form an alliance with the other teams, and Margarita [of Team Diesel] said that she'd seen a sign out on the road. So we got into our cars and followed her based on what she thought was the case, and in the end it turned out not to be. So we were lost, probably a good two hours. But the game reserve we had to go to, that the next clue led us to, didn't open till six in the morning. And we were lost from midnight to about two. So it didn't hurt us, but it certainly was a frustrating night.

Q: *The Race has been described like war in a way. Moments of sheer terror punctuated by long periods of boredom. These were periods when you were stuck someplace and had no idea when you'd next be running. Can you tell me about those?*

BRENNAN: Some of those were very welcome, to get a rest. But at the same time, you have your adrenaline going, and you just want to move. But certainly there were times when it was a long and boring wait. I remember, in the second leg, when we got to Johannesburg before catching our flights to Paris, Frank and Margarita and Team Guido were able to get some sleep. But my hiking boots were soaked from being at Victoria Falls, so I just stood in the bathroom, under the automatic hand dryer, trying to dry my boots for an hour or so. People watching on TV see all this craziness in about an hour, over what happened in a couple of days. But there were lots of times when you were doing some mundane things, like trying to dry out your boots.

Q: *The third leg included a long night killing time on the streets of Paris, waiting for sites to open.*

BRENNAN: We spent that night wandering around. We had gotten to the Big Wheel [before it closed], but couldn't do the Detour clue, which was either go to Notre Dame, or go to Pantheon. So we checked out Notre Dame, checked out the Pantheon, figured out which one we wanted to do, and went back to the barge on the Seine River that was our Pit Stop that time, and went to sleep. So that night wasn't too bad. Probably our most difficult overnight, waiting for something to open, was in India. When we got to the Rat Temple, it was eleven at night. It didn't open until four in the morning. And we were just beat down after a twelve-hour train ride, and we got into this little town square where the Rat Temple was, and there were a lot of locals around. And in India, we stuck out like sore thumbs. So they would come over and stare at us as we were laying there trying to sleep. And that was a little bit unsettling. I actually had a pocket knife with me that I got out and kind of held close. I was lying on a concrete bench...that really was the lowest point in the Race. So there's certainly times when your adrenaline's going, because you know there's something happening in the morning, where the Race is gonna start up again. You're trying to sleep; you're being harassed by locals. You're tired at the same time. It's a mix of all those different emotions that play into it.

Q: *India has always taken the position, in the Race, of the country that shoves your face in reality after you've been relatively comfortable in Europe, and a lot of Racers from various seasons react to it with extreme emotion. How was it for you?*

BRENNAN: I'm the kind of guy who's not afraid of much, can handle pretty much anything, and is usually pretty practical and logical. We had been to Tunisia, which was a difficult country. But when we got to India, it was like nothing I'd ever experienced, and the culture shock was so great that all I thought to myself, at one point, was, "I want to go home. I've had enough of this." It was right when we got to India. The first thing we did was a [crowded and confusing marketplace] Roadblock. All the teams were there at the same time. We got done with this, got lost for about forty-five minutes, and were on our way to the Taj Mahal, and it was about a full hour drive. And at that point, we thought we were in last place, because we were lost for about forty-five minutes. In other points in the Race, if you got lost for that long, you probably were the team that was going to get eliminated.

Q: *But this was the leg where everybody got lost on the way to the Taj Mahal.*

BRENNAN: It was actually to the Taj Khema Hotel, which is near the Taj Mahal. Yeah, everybody got lost. But we didn't know that. We thought we were the only team that had. And so...here I am in this foreign country, with extreme culture shock. The driving in India is just absolutely insane; it's like nothing you've ever seen. People ask me about the most dangerous thing I did on the Race. They expect me to say bungee jumping or skydiving, and I always say it was driving in India. You're on those roads, and there are cars and trucks and buses, bikes and rickshaws and elephants and camels, and everybody's honking and you're going all over the place, so all that, together with the culture shock, and the fact that we thought we were going to be eliminated...I just thought to myself, "You know what? I'm ready for this to be over. I'm ready to go home."

Q: *But then you found out otherwise.*

BRENNAN: And then we found out we were in third place, and I went, "Okay. Bring the next leg on." (*laughs*)

Q: *You mentioned Tunisia. Tunisia was one of the scarier moments of the Race. It must have been scarier to experience. That was the one where Paul and Amie got very badly lost in the Sahara Desert. I think it's fair to say that they got more disastrously lost than anybody else in the history of the show.*

BRENNAN: It is absolutely fair to say that, and the reason it's fair to say that is it is a production; even though you're out there racing around the world, you're not alone. When you're in a cab in the middle of Tunisia, you're with a camera crew, they're filming you, and that's all there is. However, that camera crew still has contact with the producers. And that was the one time on the Race that the camera crew lost contact with the producers. I don't remember whether their cell phone ran out of batteries, or we were so far out in the middle of the desert that their satellite phone couldn't get a signal, but whatever it was, they were lost; production didn't know where they were. The producer of the show, Bertram van Munster, is so well traveled. He's been all over the world. Nothing fazes him. But I could see in his eyes that he was a little bit scared at that point. They came in, probably, about four hours behind the rest of the teams, so it was a long time they were out there lost, and we didn't know what was going to happen.

Q: *So that was very real. Everybody was getting scared for them at that point.*

BRENNAN: It was real. Of course, it is reality TV, so it's edited, a lot of times, for something to look more dramatic than it is. But this one really was a scary moment.

Q: *I've already talked to the Guidos about their big so-called "villainous" moment....*

BRENNAN: Yes. (*laughs*) I know where you're going.

Q: *In real life, it strikes me as just a kinda dumb thing to do, and not really "villainous." But it was a big deal at the time.*

BRENNAN: We were right there. We were the third team behind them in line. Nancy and Emily were first, Kevin and Drew were second, and we were bringing up the rear. It was just one of those moments where, *at the time*, it just kind of ticked us off. We'd been trying all morning to get on flights. At some points we were down like seventy people on the standby list, so there was just no getting out that day. But we'd managed to talk ourselves onto this flight. All of a sudden, they say, "You can get on this flight, but it's leaving in about five minutes," so the girl's gonna walk us through security and get us through as fast as she can, and we get up, and here's a team we've already had some animosity toward trying to hold us up as we're hurrying through. It really pissed us off. I didn't like it. But when I look back on it, I realize their thoughts were, "We're going to do anything we can to hold these guys up." All they intended to do was try to pretend they lost their tickets, so we would have had to stand in line way behind them. But the fact that we were being escorted past them just created this big hubbub. One of the things is when you've always got these giant backpacks on, you kind of forget that they're there. The big to-do on that was everybody saying that one of the Guidos pushed Nancy. And I don't think he did that. He never pushed her. He never physically put his hands on her. All that happened was she ended up running into his backpack because he kind of moved it in the way. It ended up being blown way out of proportion. But at the time, we were pissed. And afterwards, we just wanted nothing to do with them.

Q: *But after the Race, it all became water under the bridge.*

BRENNAN: I think we all realized, afterward, that everybody's doing what they can to win. When I watched those episodes for the DVD, and it was the first time I watched them for a long time, it sort of brings back those feelings, and I realize how much, during the Race, I just couldn't stand those guys. Afterwards, we became friends with them, and I think it's because we realized that we had this amazing experience together. We may have been enemies on that experience, but we had this amazing experience together. What I always find really interesting is that there's a quote in the third episode, after something goes down at the Pantheon, where Joe says they're not on the Race to make lifelong friends. And what I find interesting is we *are* still friends with those guys.

Q: *Let's talk about a couple of other things you did. You mentioned the walk through the Rat Temple.*

BRENNAN: What was odd to me was the way they were revered. That just seemed so odd to me, that we could walk into this, and [the worshippers] were chanting and singing, and feeding them. In one area that was cordoned off, there was a 10-year-old crippled boy, and we found out later that they wanted the rats to walk over him because if the rats touch you, that's blessing you. So they just took him into this area and laid him on the floor and hoped that the rats would walk over him in the hopes that he'd be blessed. It was so foreign to anything that I know.

Q: *It was certainly one of the more exotic places you went.*

BRENNAN: Another small example of what makes India so different is nodding your head and shaking your head. That's pretty universal. In most countries you go to, you nod your head, that means yes, you shake your head, that means no. Not in India. In India, they have this kind of strange head-bob thing where they kind of move their heads off to the side, and boy, did that cause problems. When [Nancy and Emily] were trying to figure out how to get to the Taj Khema Hotel, Nancy was asking a woman if she knew where this place was, and the woman was just kind of bobbing her head, and Nancy couldn't figure out if the woman understood her or not.

Q: *Now, let's move on to Thailand, and the Expensive Cup of Tea. What did that look like, from the perspective of someone watching the other teams come in?*

BRENNAN: It was such a long drive down to southern Thailand that we had no idea what kind of place we were going to come in when we got down there. So we check in and we're the first-place team, and an hour later Frank and Margarita come in. And once our two teams were there, we were getting ready to go down to where they had us staying, and we asked one of the producers, "Where is everybody else?" And he said, "Well, I can't tell you, but just know this: come back in the morning, because there were major tactical mistakes made." We had no idea what he meant, but we were a little excited, because on the Race you like to hear that other people made mistakes.

Q: *It wasn't clear for a while, but that was when it became a two-team Race, because two teams were too far behind to catch up. Even so, there must have been a fair amount of schadenfreude going on.*

BRENNAN: Oh, absolutely.

Q: *You were laughing at the end of the next leg, when you said, "Joe and Bill are leaving the Pit Stop now."*

BRENNAN: That was a pretty short leg. We were able to complete it in one day. We knew what time they'd checked in the morning, and I kept my eye on my watch, because I knew that as much as there were bunching points, I knew that there was a chance those opening hours could do what they did.

Q: *Moving on, you had one of the more exciting climactic episodes beating Frank and Margarita in their hometown.*

BRENNAN: People say it's because they had a bad cab, but I've done a lot of thinking about this. The truth us, that train came as soon as we got there. They came up to that platform about a minute after us. If we'd gotten on the same train, I would have to guess, I'd put good money on it, we'd have to beat them in a footrace. Give them a cab that follows us all the way, put us on the same train, we still win that race. I really think that, once we made no serious mistakes, there's a point where no matter what happened, we were going to be the team that wins a half-mile run in a footrace.

Q: *And then comes what had to be your favorite moment in the Race, as you're running up to the finish line and you realize Frank and Margarita are not there.*

BRENNAN: We're already pretty confident that we're first, but as we're running toward the finish line, we hear one of the crew members say, "Way to go, guys." We come around the bend and hear teams cheering. It all added up. I was probably eighty percent sure, but I really didn't want to believe it until we stepped on the mat and Phil said, "You guys are the official winners of *The Amazing Race*." There are people who say, in sports, when they win the World Series, or the Super Bowl, are asked how they feel and say, "It hasn't sunk in yet." That really is the case. It is such an indescribable moment. There are no words to capture it. And because the Race was so grueling, and so long—it was just thirty days of stress and emotion—it didn't sink in until hours after the Race was over with. It was like a dream.

Q: *You've made the wry observation that Rob got all the long quotes on-screen. There have been jokes online to the effect that you did indeed open your mouth during the Race, but it just wasn't shown that much.*

BRENNAN: You can probably tell from this interview that I tend to be long-winded. The editors told me that it was hard to take a sound-bite from me, because of the way I explain things. Rob is very succinct, and he sums things up in one sentence. So, especially in the first half of the Race, when there were a lot of teams and teams weren't getting much screen time, when they needed one from Rob and Brennan, the better sound bite came from Rob. The thing that really makes that interesting is, in real life, I'm the extrovert, and Rob's the introvert. I'm the one who likes to be out with people, I'm the one that likes to talk, and Rob's the one who likes to stay home and watch TV, read a comic book or something. Halfway through the show, Rob's best friend from law school, who, through Rob, I'd also become friends with, called me up and said, "I don't understand this show at all! It's the complete opposite of real life!" I always say I'm happy with the way we were edited, because we were good guys, we were a well-liked team, and people always say, "For once, nice guys finished first," but at the same time, it was very frustrating for me, because I do go online and read what people have to say. People say, "Why is that Brennan so quiet? He doesn't say anything. He doesn't contribute anything to the team." And, let's be honest, when you're on a TV show, you like to see yourself. So it is frustrating at times.

Q: *I know that keeping quiet about the outcome was part of the deal. What was it like for you, watching the Race with family and friends, experiencing their reactions as the Race went on, and holding this secret to yourself?*

BRENNAN: It would have been a lot more difficult if we'd finished second. And the reason I say that is, here I go through this absolutely amazing experience. I know it's going to make great television. I know my family is going to really enjoy watching it. And I know they're gonna be ecstatic at the end when they see me come home victorious. And so, watching it every week, I never really want to tell them, because I want to see their reaction when that big moment comes. If we'd finished second, I know that they're gonna be excited, they're gonna enjoy watching the whole time, but all of a sudden they're gonna have this big letdown at the end. I might have wanted to tell them, "Don't get too excited. It's not gonna turn out the way you want it to." And so, I honestly never told a single person, and neither did Rob. We held it to ourselves. We had each other to talk to about it. We had the other contestants to talk to about it. And I never had a problem keeping it a secret. And it really was great having my parents at the finale viewing party and getting to see their reaction, along with my brother's.

Q: *And I gather their reaction was what you hoped for.*

BRENNAN: Absolutely. I had my mom in tears, come up to me, hugging me. "Oh, I can't believe you did it!" That was such a great experience for them. They'd had parties every week. They live in New York, whereas I live in L.A., but they'd had all these parties with friends and family. To be able to top it off with a victory, it was just great seeing that surprise, so I had no problem keeping that secret.

Q: *Returning to the finale for a second, you came in first, and greeted Frank and Margarita, but you knew you weren't going to wait there for a full day....*

BRENNAN: No, we knew the Guidos were twenty-four hours behind at that point. But when they came in the next morning, some of the other teams went to the airport to greet them. We were so tired that we'd gone to bed early and did not know the other teams were going to greet them, but I'm actually kind of disappointed that we weren't there. As much as they were our enemies at that point, it was such a special experience to me to have the other teams at the finish line, cheering us on, that I kinda felt bad we hadn't been there to greet them at the airport.

Q: *Any parting thoughts?*

BRENNAN: One cool thing about being on the first season is that you get a chance to meet everybody from all the different seasons. I liken it to a fraternity. We're the seniors, and every year we get to invite new people in.

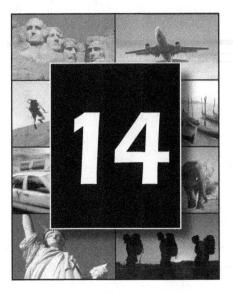

Moments We See Again and Again (Part Two)

12. Phil, Pausing

Phil is a master of the dramatic pause, even if he sometimes goes overboard. Whenever a team arrives, sweaty and flushed, at the Pit Stop, he looks grim and says something like, "Blondie and Dagwood?" Pause, Pause, Pause. Continents rise from the sea. The White House welcomes several newly elected presidents. Dinosaurs come back. "You're the Last Team to Arrive." Pause. Pause. Pause. We use another TV to watch the entirety of *Lawrence of Arabia*. "The good news is that this is a non-elimination leg, and that you're still in the Race." Teams have been known to mock Phil during his pauses, telling him to just spit it out already. It has been noted that if Phil raises his eyebrow before speaking, the team can probably count on racing another day.

13. Phil, Letting the Mask Slip

Phil is supposed to be impartial, but his mask slips from time to time. He's been known to break up at the antics of some teams and get teary-eyed when dismissing others. Once or twice, he's even gone frosty with annoyance. He seemed to dread giving the bad news to the children involved in Race 8. These brief glimpses into the inner Phil are one of the show's enduring teases.

14. Phil, Pointing

Phil usually stands at the mat, projecting calm and gravitas, impassive as any judge as the teams rush toward him. Hotly contested legs sometimes show him pointing, at some indeterminate horizon, presumably at his first sight of contestants coming into view. Only a churl would suggest that some of this pointing may be staged or, thanks to editing, not necessarily connected to the Racers we're supposed to believe he's pointing at.

15. Common-Sense Follies

Contestants asked to share their Race strategy for the benefit of viewers at home often say things that belong in the "duh" category, to wit, things like, "Our strategy this time out is to make sure we don't get lost." That's good. "Our strategy is to perform the tasks as quickly as possible and get to the finish line as soon as we can." That's also good. "As long as there's one other team behind us, we're not last." Gee, that's also good. "We're looking for a farm, so it's probably in farm country." (Yes, somebody actually said that.) Brilliant. Make a drinking game out of taking a shot any time some team member presents something mind-bogglingly obvious as if he just figured it out right now, and you'll likely be three sheets to the wind by the end of a typical leg.

16. The Footrace

These are legs so close that the difference between elimination and staying in the game comes down to a sprint. In extreme cases, Racers quick on their feet can catch up and overcome teams with a substantial advantage.

17. The Woeful Wrong Turn

We all know this one from our everyday lives: missing a critical exit, and driving on obliviously, sometimes for an hour or more, until the sheer unfamiliarity of your surroundings gradually forces you to the conclusion that you've made a serious mistake. The Virginia Girls experienced a particularly awful example of this in Race 7. After coming in first on the previous leg, they set off for the Andes, missed the turn-off quickly found by every team, and were next seen meandering along a beach, wondering when they were going to spot the Andes. Missing one of the world's great mountain ranges may strike you as a particularly embarrassing way to go down, but let's be honest: you've been that lost at least once. You just didn't have a million dollars riding on it, and millions of viewers screeching at you for being stupid.

18. Crowded Trains in India

Some Indian commuter trains are so crowded, requiring passengers to force themselves past dense walls of humanity just to enter and exit, that American contestants often find themselves pushed to the limits of their personal comfort zones. On the several Races where this proved a factor, some Racers had to fight off surges of claustrophobic panic. Several of the women complained of groping and other inappropriate contact. Some ladies who proved exceptionally strong in other circumstances felt genuinely menaced here. In subjecting Racers to this particular obstacle not just once, but several times, the show highlights the differing standards that separate the relatively coddled United States from the more teeming environments elsewhere. It's a challenge less fun, but considerably more enlightening, than the bungee jumps marking the Race at its dizziest.

19. Worst to First

Any team that begins a leg bringing up the rear are under extreme pressure to make up lost ground, lest they find themselves facing elimination. The Fast Forward option, which was much more prominent in Races 1 through 4, provided many such teams a chance to change their luck, and claim whatever first-place prize Phil happened to be handing out. Exceptional navigational skills, and luck with airline reservations, have accomplished much the same. A few teams so far behind that they seemed to be living on borrowed time, have been able to change their luck so completely that they ultimately went on to win the million dollars.

20. First to Worst

Teams that have been riding high go on to have a spectacularly bad day, miss every possible connection, blow the tasks royally, get lost, bicker, make mistakes, and find themselves eliminated at the end of the same day they began prematurely counting their winnings. Ah, fate.

21. We're So Fat

Though the Race favors folks who don't tire easily, players of less-than-ideal physical fitness have been known to make it into the top three. Sometimes, making good decisions is more critical than being able to run a quick mile. That said, older or fatter Racers, of the sort who grow winded climbing steep hills, do note the contrast between themselves and the more athletic types around them. Sometimes they're defiant, sometimes they're despairing, sometimes they're apologetic, and sometimes they're downright amused. The Air-Traffic Controllers and Race 8's Wally Bransen are among the several who bring up the subject at least once a leg. But so did the svelte Amber Brkich, in Race 7 (who at least had the excuse of fretting over her upcoming wedding). And they're not alone. There are also the folks who complain....

22. We're So Stupid

Teams that get lost easily, or have trouble reading instructions, or that make dumbfounding errors in the heat of the moment, tend to realize it, and often point it out, with attitudes ranging from philosophical to furious. Sometimes they're not as dumb as they think they are. As in real life, the most reliable way to measure degrees of dumbness is to note how rarely the truly, profoundly dumb think of themselves that way. (On *The Amazing Race*, the dumbest people don't bemoan their own inability to read street directions in foreign countries. They call the streets stupid instead.) For those who simply make a lot of mistakes, or are too intent on racing to stop and think, calling themselves stupid is just another mark of frustration. One can imagine them, later watching their real or imagined ineptitude from the safety of their couches at home, still shaking their heads and chanting, "Dumb, dumb, dumb."

23. You're So Stupid

The flip side of the downright endearing complaint, "We're so stupid," is the abrasive one, "You're so stupid," or its variant, "You're an idiot!" which frustrated Racers often inflict on their partners. The implication, here, is that the speaker has achieved a much higher level of intellectual development, and should be making all the decisions. Interestingly enough, "You're so stupid!" is most often used by Racers who have abdicated the responsibility for critical decisions. When those decisions fail to work out, or result in outright disaster, the Racer who avoided the decision is then free to assign all blame for the team's bad luck on the other one. You will find much the same technique at work in most presidential administrations. Ditto for the partner-management technique that so often goes hand-in-hand with this one....

24. "You Never **Listen** to Me!"

Several hours ago, you and your partner argued over whether to take the exit north or south. You never came to any satisfactory conclusion, and ended up going north by default. You should have gone south. Now, hours out of your way, struggling to make up time lest you receive the eyebrow of elimination from Phil, you must listen to hours and hours and hours of that whiny voice in the backseat, assuring you that everything would have gone perfectly if you'd just done whatever the hell your smarter partner wanted. Somehow, when things happen the other way around, that voice rarely says, "I'm sorry. You should have gone with your own instincts." No. Somehow, the stridency is always limited to, "You never *listen* to me." This chant, on the Race as in life, is just what you want to experience on a trip around the world, whether it involves a million-dollar prize or not. (Raise your hand if your loved ones have never done this to you. I don't see any hands.)

To be continued....

Race 2,
the Ballad of Wil and Tara

THIS SECOND RACE BENEFITED FROM another "villain": Wil, of The Constant Snipers, who was such an abrasive presence that half the fun was watching him alienate or irritate everybody else around him (including his separated wife, Tara). He spent much of the Race, in every conceivable climate, wearing a crocheted cap that (we can't help think) must have become pretty rank by week three or four. In large part because of his antics, this emerged as the only Race where interaction between teams camped at the Pit Stop became a visible, and critical, part of the proceedings. (There was also a little in Race 5.) It all came down to one of the wildest footraces in the show's history.

Phil now took a more visible role in the proceedings. He no longer showed up only to greet the last team to the Pit Stop, but was there for everyone, ensuring that nobody could be tipped off by his mere absence or presence. Racer interaction with Phil became one of the show's enduring pleasures.

The Amazing Race banner changed colors to yellow and red.

DRAMATIS PERSONAE

1. Team Awesome

Deidre Washington, 51, and daughter Hillary Washington, 23, just getting to know each other after years of relative separation, are sweet folks, who fall behind leaving the first airport and remain near the end of the pack until their early elimination. They lose right away, but their best moment of the Race is the same moment they take their leave. They weep.

2. The Gutsy Grannies

It's churlish to say so, but Peggy Kuhn, 63, and Claire Jinks, 65, who provided their own team nickname, are by far the weakest of the Race's senior-citizen teams. They're game, but in over their heads, unprepared for the pace or the sometimes scary stunts. "We're not tough," Peggy says, "but sometimes we're almost fast." That's not exactly a ringing self-endorsement. It's like saying a movie doesn't quite suck, but is sometimes almost good. That's not a quote for the poster. If they have any strength, it's in their support for one another. Their greatest weakness is planning an itinerary that makes sense.

3. The Bookends

Contractors Shola and Doyin Richards, 27, initiate the show's tradition of casting identical twins, a nightmare for folks like the author who must then figure out who's saying what at any particular moment. They're among the most determinedly identical of any twin pair to come, which is one hell of a statement, so thanks a lot. You can tell them apart because Shola wears an earring. Unless that's Doyin. In any event, one of them. Nice guys, but sheesh. Their strengths include volleyball; their weaknesses include desert navigation and stick shifts. Doyin, by the way, is pronounced as if you were going to say "dweeb" but put an "n" at the end, instead.

4. The Pastors

Married church pastors Russell Kalenberg, 46, and Cyndi Kalenberg, 43, have one of the most no-nonsense approaches on display here. Russell's sometimes stern expression manifests as a resemblance, at certain odd angles, to a scowling Harrison Ford. (The author's wife fails to see it.) Their weaknesses include a lack of travel experience.

5. The Bouncers

Friends Alex Boylan, 24, and Chris Luca, 25, are physically fit, tightly knit pals who excel at physical tasks and are easy to spot as favorites from early on. Their friendship, and Alex's flirtation with Tara of The Constant Snipers, provides some hefty inter-team conflict. **SEASON SUPERSTARS**

6. The Constant Snipers

Separated married couple Wil Steger, 36, and Tara Lynch, 31, both furniture designers, provide the majority of the friction this time out, calling each other stupid and doing whatever they can to make teeth grind worldwide. Wil wears the second of the show's god-awful hats, in this case a rainbow wool cap that elicits almost as much abuse as he does. He's such an irritant that the suspense is less about who's going to win than who's going to beat him. It comes down to the wire. As for Tara, she proves less interested in Wil than she is in Alex, a triangle that doesn't do much for team cohesiveness. **SEASON SUPERSTARS**

7. The Smiley Siblings

Blake Mycoskie, 25, and Paige Mycoskie, 21, are a tightly knit, physically affectionate young brother and sister whose deep warmth for one another leads to some of the more disgusting bulletin board speculations in the history of the show. (Folks who indulged: get a life.) They make some odd strategic decisions along the way, including some that jeopardize their Race longevity early on, but are very much a team to beat.

8. Team Forgettable

I hate to do this to such evidently decent people, but I can't help it. Married couple Norm Davis, 39, and Hope Davis, 38, are not in the Race for very long, and provide precious little drama while they're around, which no doubt speaks well of them. But they create no indelible impression. The best I can say about them is that they seem to be good-natured.

9. Team Fabulous

Oswald Mendez, 31, and Danny Jimenez, 36, "fabulous" gay friends from Miami. Nicknamed "Cha-Cha-Cha" by other teams, their strengths include taking it easy when they can; their weaknesses include heights and, um, taking it easy when they can. **SEASON SUPERSTARS**

10. Team Cobbler

Sisters Peach Krebs, 33, and Mary Lenig, 38. Peach is the more high-maintenance of the two, a fact that will require some heavy lifting on Mary's part. The epitome of First to Worst.

11. The Best Enemies

Former roommates Dave Lepeska, 28, and Gary Rosen, 33, both writers, have a sort of Woody Allen/Tony Roberts thing going on, with Gary trying hard to be Woody and often falling flat. (Some of his wisecracks at the expense of local cultures fall into the offensive category.) By their own admission, they're "best enemies," who at times barely seem to tolerate one another. (You want a glimpse of their true relationship? Check their last scene together. They're pals.) But after a rocky start, prompting them to describe themselves as "stupid," they rally and make it most of the way to the end.

THE GAME PLAY

Leg #1: Kissing Fat Maria

At the starting line, in the desert near Pahrump, Nevada, teams receive $200 and instructions to take one of two available flights to Rio de Janeiro, Brazil.

The first seven teams arrive in Rio at 11:28 A.M. and race to the famous statue of Jesus atop Corcovado Mountain. Peach is the first to get motion sickness on the curvy ride, but the Cobblers are first to the route marker and its instructions to kiss "Fat Maria" on Paquetá Island.

Fat Maria is a tree the locals kiss for luck. The Siblings are the only team to make the mwaah noise. Mwaah. Completing this absurdity earns teams their shot at snagging ferry tickets back to Rio the next morning. Though ferries leave forty-five minutes apart, the first can only carry three teams, so reaching the reservations desk outside the Lido Hotel is critical. The first major conflict, this Race, occurs when Tara finds the reservations desk before Wil, who's inside the adjacent hotel looking in the wrong place. She therefore witnesses The Smiley Siblings and The Bookends snagging tickets before her. Howling, "I was here first!" and whapping another Racer on the back with her clue envelope, she not only begins her team's Race-long feud with the Siblings, but also sets up her first major argument with her ex, as they bicker over who's responsible for screwing up.

Meanwhile, Team Cobbler argues over whether to spend their spare money on food or a bed for the night. The weather is so pleasant that many teams just sleep on the beach, but Peach wants food. And she tells her sister, "I don't even like you," for good measure. Sheesh.

The next morning, teams take their ferries back to Rio, where they will have to take a cable car to find the route marker atop Sugar Loaf Mountain. The 8:00 A.M. ferry carries The Pastors, The Bookends, and the Siblings. The 8:45 A.M. carries the Snipers and Team Forgettable. The 9:30 A.M. carries The Bouncers, The Cobblers, and Team Fabulous. Team Awesome and The Gutsy Grannies bring up the rear at 10:00 A.M.

The route marker atop Sugar Loaf Mountain provides the Detour. "Mountain" requires teams to rappel 590 feet down the face of Sugar Loaf Mountain. "Beach" sends teams back down by gondola and then by taxi to Ipanema Beach, where they must use a provided photograph to identify the woman who inspired the song "The Girl from Ipanema." Most teams gulp and take the fast descent, despite various levels of white-knuckled nervousness. The Grannies, who want no part of it, rush to the Beach and survive another day largely because Team Awesome, their competition for last place, is among the slowest to work the rappel.

Team Awesome's elimination turns out to be their finest hour. Deidre wants to be miserable about ruining things for her daughter, but Hillary is less concerned with her early disappointment than she is about not allowing her mom to feel bad. "You're awesome," she keeps repeating. "You're awesome." And though first out, they definitely are.

1. Wil and Tara (The Constant Snipers) 11:06 A.M.
2. Cyndi and Russell (The Pastors) 11:34 A.M.
3. Shola and Doyin (The Bookends) 11:35 A.M.
4. Blake and Paige (The Smiley Siblings) 12:19 P.M. TIE
5. Hope and Norm (Team Forgettable) 12:19 P.M. TIE
6. Chris and Alex (The Bouncers) 12:20 P.M.
7. Mary and Peach (Team Cobbler) 12:45 P.M.
8. Oswald and Danny (Team Fabulous) 12:46 P.M.
9. Gary and Dave (The Best Enemies) 1:24 P.M.
10. Peggy and Claire (The Gutsy Grannies) 1:32 P.M.[13]
11. Deidre and Hillary (Team Awesome) ELIMINATED

Leg #2: Hope Is the Thing with Feathers

Receiving $200, teams must make their way to a samba club and find the dancer whose headdress matches the feather they've been provided. Gary of The Best Enemies says, "That girl was hot. If I just had a couple more minutes with her, I could have gotten her number."

Along the way, Wil warns Tara not to lose her clue envelope. This is the setup to a punch line that won't pay off for another ten legs. Wait for it.

A route marker at the summit of Pedro Bonita Mountain provides the Detour, "Freak Out" or "Seek Out." In "Freak Out," a local instructor takes Racers on a tandem hang-gliding trip down to Sao Coronado Beach. In "Seek Out," Racers take a taxi to the same beach and use a metal detector to search a mile and a half of sand for their buried clue.

A few teams actually have trouble making this decision.

The Gutsy Grannies go for the Fast Forward, which will require the team to score ten points against two professional Brazilian volleyball players.[14] They wisely back off when they see The Bookends already waiting for the game to start. The Best Enemies also decide to compete, a bad move, as Gary is not exactly an athletic type and his team scores only three points in the time it takes The Bookends to score ten. The Bookends can proceed to a jungle camp near Iguazu Falls, some 900 miles away. The Best Enemies only proceed to the metal detectors, and

---

[13] They wear T-shirts helpfully assuring viewers that the TV camera adds ten pounds.
[14] Watching them compete would have been painful.

soon Gary says, "This is just... this is just... this is like the most... ehh-hhh...." (They eventually glide.)

Meanwhile, other teams atop Pedro Bonita shame the recalcitrant Grannies into hang gliding. Tara tells them that if they don't, they'll have to relinquish the T-shirts labeling their team "Gutsy." The Grannies give in, but Peggy is still nervous, since she "can't run that fast... and I'm just exhausted." Give the old lady credit for eventually taking the plunge, and for joking that she wants to take glider lessons now, but it's only a matter of time before this team falls out.

The bus ride to the village of Foz do Iguacu, 900 miles away, offers an unusual wealth of disasters. The Siblings leave their money in the taxi and have to beg for bus fare. The bus carrying The Bouncers, The Bookends, and the Snipers has a flat, and the driver is so slow to fix the problem that the teams take over. The bus carrying The Best Enemies breaks down entirely. The Grannies are bumped off their connecting bus and forced to take a later one. The plane carrying Phil crashes. Okay, I was kidding about that one.

At Foz do Iguacu, The Bouncers and The Constant Snipers decide to help each other on the road, but Wil pulls out without waiting for the other team, declaring that they can just catch up. Irony ensues when his team's vehicle breaks down, and he must ask The Bouncers for help. Tara calls him "a horrible, evil man." The Bouncers thinks she's great fun. And so it begins.

The Roadblock, a speedboat ride to find the route marker in the vicinity of Iguacu Falls, is fun but less of a factor than all the disasters leading up to it.

1. Shola and Doyin (The Bookends) 10:34 A.M.
2. Chris and Alex (The Bouncers) 10:47 A.M.
3. Wil and Tara (The Constant Snipers) 10:47 A.M.
4. Mary and Peach (Team Cobbler) 12:14 P.M.
5. Gary and Dave (The Best Enemies) 12:17 P.M.
6. Cyndi and Russell (The Pastors) 12:22 P.M.
7. Oswald and Danny (Team Fabulous) 1:14 P.M.
8. Peggy and Claire (The Gutsy Grannies) 2:40 P.M.
9. Blake and Paige (The Smiley Siblings) 3:35 P.M.
10. Hope and Norm (Team Forgettable) ELIMINATED

Like many of the adventurous stunts required of Amazing Racers, this leg's hang-gliding task is a permanent local attraction run by local entrepreneurs. If you want to soar at 2,270 feet (or higher), and even do some loop-de-loops, check out the Web site at http://www.justfly.com.br.

Leg #3: The Wrong Kind of Detour

The Detour and Roadblock are not nearly as critical as one of the most stressful rounds of airport shuffle in the show's history.

Receiving $150, teams must depart Brazil through São Paulo and travel nearly 5,000 miles to Cape Town, South Africa. The next route marker awaits inside the cell where Nelson Mandela was imprisoned for eighteen years.

There's some early intrigue when the Grannies sleep past their 2:40 A.M. scheduled departure time. Blake of The Smiley Siblings, who is already awake, notes that they're still in their tent and suffers a visible crisis of conscience wondering whether to wake them or not. He decides not, and goes back to bed. You really can't blame him for feeling conflicted. It doesn't end up mattering, as the Grannies do rouse themselves by 3:00 A.M., and all nine teams do end up sharing the same couple of early-morning flights to São Paulo. But again, this doesn't bode well for the oldest team's prospects. And things don't improve.

A nightmarish full day of scrambling for flights in São Paulo leaves everybody booking multiple-hop itineraries, which shake out as follows:

5:45 P.M.: The Bookends and The Pastors. London, then Cape Town.

9:40 P.M.: Team Cobbler. Milan, London, then Cape Town.

9:45 P.M.: The Best Enemies. Lisbon, then London, then Cape Town.

11:00 P.M.: Team Fabulous. London, then Cape Town.

11:10 P.M.: The Gutsy Grannies. New York, London, Johannesburg, then Cape Town.

11:25 P.M.: The Bouncers. Frankfurt, then Cape Town.

11:40 P.M.: The Smiley Siblings and The Constant Snipers. London, then Cape Town.

Some of these teams are depending on standby for their later connections. Some will have further headaches. But only one team, the Grannies, fails to cross the Atlantic on its first flight. Doesn't bode well.

Cape Town arrival times shake out at:

7:00 A.M.: The Best Enemies, Team Fabulous, The Constant Snipers. 9:00 A.M.: The Bookends. 9:45 A.M.: Team Cobbler. 10:30 A.M.: The Smiley Siblings. 1:20 P.M.: The Bouncers. 1:30 P.M.: The Pastors.

All but the last two teams reach Mandela's cell (section B, cell number 5) before the Grannies even arrive in London. Ouch. Making matters worse, the Grannies haven't allotted themselves enough time to get through security, and miss their London connection. Double ouch.

The clue hidden on one of the cabinets inside Mandela's tiny cell leads teams to the next route marker at Kalk Bay Harbor, site of a Detour: "Dance" or "Deliver." "Dance" requires teams to earn twenty-five rand (about two dollars) dancing with street performers, and "Deliver" requires teams to transport 125 kilograms of fish. Most teams immediately pick "Dance." (For details on the leg's memorable Roadblock, see p. 53 "Through Strangers' Eyes.")

As for the Grannies, they make it as far as Mandela's cell before being told to skip the rest of the day's tasks and proceed directly to the Pit Stop, Lanzerac Manor, in South Africa's wine country. By then they're a full day behind almost everybody else. Interview segments give representatives of several other teams a chance to express deep affection for these fine ladies, but the Race itself has moved on, as all races must.

1. Oswald and Danny (Team Fabulous) 2:52 P.M.
2. Wil and Tara (The Constant Snipers) 2:52 P.M.
3. Gary and Dave (The Best Enemies) 2:52 P.M.
4. Mary and Peach (Team Cobbler) 5:56 P.M.
5. Blake and Paige (The Smiley Siblings) 6:02 P.M. TIE
6. Shola and Doyin (The Bookends) 6:02 P.M. TIE
7. Chris and Alex (The Bouncers) 8:50 P.M.
8. Cyndi and Russell (The Pastors) 8:51 P.M.
9. Peggy and Claire (The Gutsy Grannies) ELIMINATED

Leg #4: A Dip in the Pool

Partying a little too heartily at the Pit Stop, Wil howls, "I want to party with the hot South African Ladies, Man!" Behavior that doesn't endear him to The Pastors. Meanwhile, Tara abandons Wil to cuddle up with Alex, continuing a flirtation destined to get under Wil's skin.

Teams must grab one of two available charter flights, and travel 800 miles to Walvis Bay, Namibia. Team Fabulous, The Constant Snipers, The Best Enemies, and Team Cobbler snag reservations for the 9:00 A.M. flight, leaving The Bookends, The Smiley Siblings, The Pastors, and The Bouncers tied at noon.

"I don't know what we're doing here," Wil says, when the first flight descends. "It's all sand." And so it is. The landscape is sand swept and desolate, with few pockets of civilization.

Teams must now find their way to Swakopmund Lighthouse on the coast. Interestingly, the clue doesn't specify how, leading some teams to waste time at the car-rental counter. Team Fabulous lucks out when the clerk offers to arrange a lift for two, suggesting only that they pay their driver whatever they feel fair. (The benefits of being nice.) Wil, by contrast, is less than a gentleman about the taxi fare, telling another counter lady, "You're ripping me off, but…karma comes around. I'll deal with it, because I know that when someone rips me off, they'll be ripped off in another way."

The lighthouse offers Racers a view of a parking lot with flagged vehicles. From there teams have to drive to a giant sand dune the locals call the Matterhorn, and climb to the top.

Danny of Team Fabulous is feeling some leg pain, so the team goes for the Fast Forward, which is among the easiest ever. The route marker is in the Swakopmund Hotel's swimming pool. Retrieving the clue involves getting wet. Period. Afterward, exchanging currency, Oswald explains himself to the desk clerk. "Usually, when we walk into a hotel like this, we walk in with our Prada gear, looking fabulous, and look how we're dressed [now]. We feel so inadequate." Thanks. I'm sure she was wondering. Team Fabulous moves on to the Pit Stop, the Amani Lodge outside the capital city of Windhoek.

The top of the Matterhorn offers the Detour "Slide" or "Stride." In "Slide," Racers sled down the front of the dune on sand boards, at speeds approaching fifty miles an hour. Nobody chooses "Stride," a slower descent on foot. After that, teams must drive 125 miles to the village of

Spitzkoppe, where the General Dealer (essentially, local convenience store), provides the next clue in the form of the postcard of the day. The Roadblock requires players to use their dwindling funds to haggle for five carvings at a local marketplace.

Among the Racers on the second flight, The Bouncers take almost a full hour to secure their taxi, and Peach is so weak from illness that she can barely climb the sand dune. But it's The Bookends who get disastrously lost. Asking a local where to find the Matterhorn sand dune, they receive the less-than-helpful answer, "In the desert." Between that, Shola's uncertainty with stick shifts, and getting bogged down in sand, they don't arrive at the Matterhorn until after the Detour shuts down for the night. Say good-bye, twins.

1. Oswald and Danny (Team Fabulous) 7:47 P.M.
2. Gary and Dave (The Best Enemies) 10:03 P.M. PENALTY
3. Wil and Tara (The Constant Snipers) 10:34 P.M.
4. Blake and Paige (The Smiley Siblings) 11:34 P.M.
5. Mary and Peach (Team Cobbler) 11:34 P.M.
6. Cyndi and Russell (The Pastors) 11:44 P.M.
7. Chris and Alex (The Bouncers) 12:17 A.M. PENALTY
8. Shola and Doyin (The Bookends) ELIMINATED

Driving through the desert, all teams have to bring along a local driver, who is required to take the wheel after dark. Even in daylight, roads are so treacherous that all teams are required to drive at twenty kilometers an hour under the speed limit. Both The Best Enemies and The Bouncers drive at the speed limit instead and receive forty-two-minute penalties that affect their departure times at the start of the next leg.

Leg #5: Butch in the Bat Cave

At the Pit Stop, the Siblings tell The Bouncers they want to take Wil and Tara down. The Bouncers bring this to Wil and Tara. "I'll feed him to the tigers," responds Wil.

Team Cobbler is also upset at the Siblings for using a shortcut last time to get past them on the way to the mat. To make peace, the Siblings let them leave the Pit Stop first. "Welcome to the world of being human," snaps Mary.

Receiving eighty dollars, teams must book an itinerary to Bangkok, Thailand, where the next clue awaits at Siam Center. The Constant Snipers are elated, as their shared business takes them to Bangkok three times a year...and they stay at Siam Center. Familiarity breeds advantage. Just ask Gary: "My parents always took me to Thai restaurants....I know the culture." Ho, ho, ho.

There's another silly confrontation between Blake and Wil at the Johannesburg airport. Blake says, "Since Paqueta Island, you've done everything in your power to make my life a living hell. I came on this trip to have fun, and it's not fun anymore." Wil responds, "You should be focused on your own game." The encounter fails to help.

Confrontations continue after all the teams land in Bangkok. With the alliance between her team and The Bouncers back on again, Tara wants to wait for Chris and Alex to get through customs. Wil wants to leave them behind, and gets mad when she objects. "Tara, you're stupid. I don't want to play anymore. I'm done." He curls up in the first of many snits to come. Later, Tara makes sure The Bouncers know that Wil wanted to abandon them. Gee, that's helpful.

Both Detour options, "Confusion Now" and "Confusion Later," require Racers to indulge in local rituals. In "Confusion Now," teams must find one specific water taxi out of many along the canals, and take it to a bird market where they'll have to buy (and release) a cageful of sparrows. In "Confusion Later," teams take a taxi to Chinatown, then buy a paper car, which they need to burn at a specific shrine as an offering to their ancestors.

In practice, there's confusion both "Now" and "Later." The Pastors fail to notice a sign pointing toward the bird marketplace and end up climbing a long flight of stairs for no reason. The Siblings and The Best Enemies burn offerings at the wrong shrines. (The Sibs don't get it right until their third try.) The Constant Snipers hire a bad taxi. Conversely, Team Fabulous talks Fern, a local they meet on the bus, into dropping her plans for the day to guide them everywhere they need to go.

The town of Ratchaburi hosts this leg's Roadblock, where one team member must don a protective mask and search for the final clue in a rank cave filled with millions of bats. Oswald takes the task for his team, seeing it as his chance to be "really, really butch." And Cyndi completes the task despite overwhelming terror, impressing her hubbie mightily.

During the last race to the Pit Stop, the Thai river house Ban Plai Pong Pang, Wil promises Tara that if they make it, from this day forward, he will never be anything but humble. He insists: "I'm serious." Let's see how long that lasts.

1. Chris and Alex (The Bouncers) 6:11 P.M.
2. Mary and Peach (Team Cobbler) 6:42 P.M.
3. Wil and Tara (The Constant Snipers) 7:19 P.M.
4. Blake and Paige (The Smiley Siblings) 7:22 P.M.
5. Gary and Dave (The Best Enemies) 7:23 P.M.
6. Oswald and Danny (Team Fabulous) 8:31 P.M.
7. Cyndi and Russell (The Pastors) ELIMINATED

Leg #6: Danny the Butch

Returning to Bangkok with another $120 in their pockets, teams brave another crowded and confusing marketplace to find the next route marker.

Meanwhile, Wil's fresh humility lasts about ten seconds, by Tara's reckoning, as he immediately hectors a slow boat pilot with, "GO! GO! GO! GO!" And Gary's frequent attempts at humor, which are sometimes funny but just as often fall flat, ratchet up the obnoxiousness level. Aside from trash-talking several of the remaining teams in stereotypical terms that in context have more to say about him than anyone else, he holds up a sheet and says, "Look at this. This," indicating a long word, "is one word in the Thai language. I'm upset that the British never [colonized] this place, because nobody speaks English. How can you make anybody go fast when it takes fifteen minutes to write one word?" Not cool, Gary.

Every team must now travel 500 miles by train to the city of Chiang Mai.

Along the way we're treated to one of the great language barrier moments. Team Cobbler tells a cabbie they need the train station. He responds, "Elevator?"

When the next available express train turns out to be several hours away, many teams go shopping. But there's still tension. Tara continues to cuddle with Alex, dismissing Wil with, "[He's] gotta suck it up." And Peach snaps with resentment when Mary stops her from buying a pair of pants.

Everybody's dismayed by the muggy, fourteen-hour train ride. But Oswald comes the closest to breaking. Interviewing, "The Race has made me realize that five-star hotels are worth every penny that you pay for them," he comes close to quitting until sufficient sleep leaves him raring to go again.

The next morning's Detour represents two ways to travel downriver: "Boat" or "Beast." In "Boat," teams use a long pole to navigate a bamboo raft. In "Beast," teams travel by elephant. Everybody picks rafting. On the river, Team Cobbler comes from behind to overtake The Best Enemies. Wil, whose raft-steering expertise flouts Newton's Laws of Motion, deftly navigates Tara's end of the raft (and Tara) into a fallen tree. Danny jumps into the water to clear an obstruction, and congratulates himself on his unexpected butchness.

Teams claim parked four-by-fours and drive thirteen miles to the village of Me Ping, site of the Roadblock, where one team member must scrub the markings off a live elephant painted for religious ceremonies. Peach, Gary, Blake, Oswald, and Alex make short work of this, splashing their animals with water and getting the colors off in minutes. Wil scrubs almost daintily, and falls behind.

Nearby Karen Village provides the next Pit Stop. The Bouncers and The Constant Snipers expect the non-elimination, and walk up side by side, in no particular hurry, the unspoken agreement being that The Bouncers will step on the mat first. At the last second, Wil steps out in front, takes Tara with him, and claims the penultimate spot for his team. He says it's his way of severing ties. Alex concludes, "Screw him. I think I'm just gonna take his girl."

1. Mary and Peach (Team Cobbler) 8:55 A.M.
2. Gary and Dave (The Best Enemies) 8:56 A.M.
3. Blake and Paige (The Smiley Siblings) 9:00 A.M.
4. Oswald and Danny (Team Fabulous) 9:08 A.M.
5. Wil and Tara (The Constant Snipers) 9:22 A.M.
6. Chris and Alex (The Bouncers) 9:23 A.M. NOT ELIMINATED

Leg #7: Peach Fizzes

There's no Pit Stop intrigue, thank goodness.

Receiving $180, teams find the Temple of Seven Spires, where the clue box tells them to make their way to the tallest building in Hong Kong.

The overnight bunching in the Chiang Mai airport is marked by tension between The Best Enemies, when Dave books a flight two hours later than necessary. Gary shouts: "Are you a [bleep]ing idiot or what?" Later, when Dave calmly explains that this is not an effective means of intra-team communication, Gary snots, "We just have to know our strengths, David. From now on I'll talk to people. You'll open clues." Oh, ho, ho, ho.

Meanwhile, Tara continues cuddling with Alex. Assume this for every remaining leg.

Team Cobbler falls behind in Hong Kong, getting the last train from the airport. They get into worse trouble when they mangle the name of the city's tallest building and direct their taxi driver elsewhere. It's tough to miss the tallest building in the damn city, but they manage it…only to fall even further behind when they attempt to go for the Fast Forward and get there ten minutes after The Best Enemies.

Gary says that getting the Fast Forward is like losing your virginity. You can only lose it once, and never come back to it. Plus it makes you scared and giddy. His team does get the Fast Forward in this leg. I don't need to know about the other thing.

The Fast Forward is a face-reading session with fortune-teller Amelia Chow, who tells Gary that he's too smart and doesn't listen to people, and tells Dave he's surrounded by two-faced people who want to use him. I want stock tips from her.

The Detour is "Wishing Tree" or "Herbal Tea." In "Wishing Tree," teams taxi eighteen miles to a Wishing Tree, which they need to feed a wish. "Herbal Tea" is another crowded, confusing maze-of-streets challenge, culminating in a cup of exceedingly nasty herbal tea.

Everybody but Team Fabulous chooses the vile tea, which (I'm sorry to say) does not give off clouds of dry ice vapor. Most soon move on to the Roadblock at the docks, which requires one team member to move a one-ton shipping container with a crane. Danny gets to be butch again.

Continuing the theme of the leg, it's the by-now-far-behind Team Cobbler that has the biggest problems with the tea, as Peach runs outside to decorate the pavement. She weeps, "I'm exhausted. I'm nauseous. I have nothing left. I don't want to be pushed anymore. I don't have a stomach of steel. I don't have legs that just keep going."

They're not the only team feeling that way. Oswald later says his ambition for the day is to throw up on Phil's shoes. That would make an interesting Roadblock all by itself. (I suspect Race 5's Charla would be best at this, as she's closest to the target.)

Recognizing the inevitable, Mary treats Peach to a leisurely meal in a comfortable Hong Kong restaurant. They take their time, decompressing. The elimination, on a junk in Hong Kong Harbor, is no big surprise.

1. Gary and Dave (The Best Enemies) 4:11 P.M.
2. Chris and Alex (The Bouncers) 5:43 P.M.
3. Wil and Tara (The Constant Snipers) 5:50 P.M.
4. Oswald and Danny (Team Fabulous) 6:29 P.M.
5. Blake and Paige (The Smiley Siblings) 6:32 P.M.
6. Mary and Peach (Team Cobbler) ELIMINATED[15]

Leg #8: Wil and Blake Both Feel Stupid

Receiving $100, teams depart the junk and travel by public bus to the town of Repulse Bay, where they must find the statue of Tien Hou, the goddess of the sea. Nobody goes for the Fast Forward at the Po Lin Monastery, though Wil and Tara fight over it, at length, bouncing from bus station to ferry and back again, calling each other stupid and eventually doing exactly what everybody else does. But I'm sure it was a fun couple of hours.

The route marker at Murray House provides the Detour, "Dragon" or "Lion." In "Dragon," teams must paddle a vessel known as a dragon boat (designed for a crew of twelve) 600 meters. In "Lion," teams must put on ceremonial lion garb and parade four times that distance, through a maze of narrow streets and steep stairs. The Best Enemies elect "Dragon" and quickly establish themselves as the last people you'd ever want paddling your lifeboat. Team Fabulous chooses "Lion" and giggles almost nonstop as they navigate dry land.

All teams must travel 4,500 miles to the Opera House in Sydney, Australia. Team Fabulous has the best time obtaining reservations (see p. 418 "The Most Endearing Racer Moments"). At the airport, Gary tells a no doubt bemused ticket clerk, "We would like to get on the same flight

---

[15] Their defeat is a de facto surrender, but they're so far behind by then that it doesn't affect the outcome.

[as] the two deceitful and untrustworthy people [before us on line]."[16] He then demands to know if she can think outside the box. "Can you think outside the box? No?" She was probably wondering about the backstory there all day.

The Roadblock at the Sydney Opera House bounces one team member all over Sydney, following clues written in Australian slang. Players must check out the "surfie in the lairy daks" (the surfer in the loud trousers), get the next clue from an "ankle-biter" (small child) in the park, and proceed from there to find a "sheila in Aussie cozzie" (girl in a bathing suit). The sheila sends players to find a "bushie" (somebody from the countryside), who at last sends players back to their partners. It would be a lot easier, you know, if those Australians just spoke English.

Team Fabulous, The Bouncers, and The Best Enemies all make it through the Roadblock and to the Pit Stop, on the roof of the Museum of Contemporary Art, without incident. But both Wil and Blake screw up royally by assuming the Roadblock over and returning to their respective partners immediately after meeting the "surfie." As a result, they drag Tara and Paige all over creation, in the rain, following the rest of the slang-driven clues, before realizing at task's end that they have done it wrong. Both teams return to the Opera House so the guys can run the same damn course all over again.

Tara and Paige are left on the steps bonding over the reading-comprehension problems of their respective partners. From the expressions on their faces, the guys are damn lucky it's a non-elimination leg. Because this is precisely the kind of thing that gets brought up, in arguments, for the rest of your life.

1. Oswald and Danny (Team Fabulous) 8:26 A.M.
2. Chris and Alex (The Bouncers) 9:10 A.M.
3. Gary and Dave (The Best Enemies) 9:19 A.M.
4. Wil and Tara (The Constant Snipers) 9:59 A.M.
5. Blake and Paige (The Smiley Siblings) 10:06 A.M. NOT ELIMINATED

---

[16] A reference to Tara and Wil.

Leg #9: Golf in Hell

The Bouncers and the Siblings compete for the Fast Forward, which requires both players to eat one of the "famous" meat pies at Harry's Café. (Yeah, I've heard of them. Now.) Eating the pies earns The Bouncers the right to proceed to a certain Aboriginal camp, deep in the Australian Outback. They're on a plane to Melbourne, first stop on the way there, at 11:06 P.M., almost seven hours before the operating hours of the leg's other first option, a climb to the top of the 440-foot Sydney Harbor Bridge. That's one hell of a stress-free leg. And they even get to eat a celebrity.

As it happens, the first charter to Adelaide isn't until 1:00 P.M., a bunching point that brings every team within half an hour of The Bouncers. Of course, The Bouncers won't have to perform this leg's Detour or Roadblock. The Best Enemies, alone on the last charter at 1:30 P.M., are considerably more stressed. They can only conclude, "All we have to do is not screw up."

Good plan.

Meanwhile, temperatures in the Outback are well over a hundred, or, as Tara puts it, "hotter than a well-digger's ass in Texas." How would she know?

The Detour in Coober Pedy is "Cool Down" or "Heat Up." "Cool Down" sends teams into a mine to find an opal in a big mound of dirt. "Heat Up" sends teams to the driest, hottest golf course in the entire world to play three holes. The catch is that, on this course, it's very difficult to tell which tee corresponds to which hole. They'll also be playing in temperatures approximating 130 degrees, giving an unpleasant double meaning to the golf term "stroke."

The Siblings choose golf, reasoning that their dad loves the game and nothing, not even seeing them win the million dollars, would make the old man happier than watching his kids sizzle on the course from hell. They dehydrate quickly, putting balls into the wrong holes.

The mine isn't much easier. The teams bring stones to the surface, only to be informed by the judge, a local with a truly heroic belly, that they've unearthed everyday, garden-variety rocks. Wil screams, "I'm not a miner!" and Tara calls him an idiot again.

The Best Enemies stand within sight of the dirt pile containing the opals, pointlessly digging in the hard stone walls instead. And then they decide to switch tasks, even though neither one of them has ever played golf before. After all, Gary reasons, "How hard can it be?" For guys who don't play golf? In 130-degree heat? A little like sitting on a hot waffle iron while doing the Sunday *Times* crossword puzzle in pen. Oddly, they seem to have better luck golfing than the folks who grew up doing it. But they don't even get to the Roadblock, a boomerang toss at the Breakaways National Park, until after everybody else has moved on to the Pit Stop, a traditional Aborigine camp.

Upon elimination, Gary offers a deadpan: "Phil...I know I haven't been the most thoughtful contestant. But I love this Race. Just give me one more chance...for old time's sake." It doesn't work.

1. Chris and Alex (The Bouncers) 3:35 P.M.
2. Blake and Paige (The Smiley Siblings) 5:01 P.M.
3. Wil and Tara (The Constant Snipers) 5:06 P.M.
4. Oswald and Danny (Team Fabulous) 5:09 P.M.
5. Gary and Dave (The Best Enemies) ELIMINATED

Leg #10: Chris Confides in a Sheep

Receiving $140, teams must now travel 2,000 miles to Queenstown, New Zealand. That involves loading their four-by-fours aboard tandem trailers known as road trains. An experienced driver takes them and their vehicles three and a half hours to the bush community of Glendambo, where they have to sign up for 10:30 A.M. or 11:15 A.M. charter flights to Adelaide. It's from Adelaide that they'll depart for Queenstown.

At a Glendambo service station after a morning of false starts, Tara tells Wil to make up his own mind concerning what he wants to do: go to the airport, book the Adelaide flights first, whatever. He reacts by saying, "I quit!" and plopping himself down on one of the pump-station islands. Tara calls him an idiot again, deals with the reservations herself, and then amuses her friends The Bouncers by shouting out her car window, "Can I please have a new partner!?!"

Sorry, dear. You should have thought of that before you left.

The Siblings fall behind during airport shuffle, but catch up during a long overnight layover in Christchurch. Then they claim not to have bags, and board with the backpacks that every other team has to check. The useful lie steams The Bouncers and Snipers, who accomplish nothing by confronting the gate clerk about discrepancies in rule enforcement. The lady doesn't particularly care. But The Bouncers have a plan (see p. 412 "The Smartest Moves Ever Made by Racers").

The Siblings claim the Fast Forward, a wild ride down a river courtesy of an outfit known as Shotover Jet Boats, finding the route marker after several minutes of speed and spray. That earns them a straight line to the Pit Stop, Inverary Sheep Station, near the town of Canterbury.

For the others, the route marker is on a tiny gondola suspended on a wire over the second-highest bungee jump in the entire world. This Detour offers "Quick Jump," which requires teams to tandem leap 450 feet over a canyon, or "Long Hike," which gives teams the option of returning to solid land and descending a twisty path to the same spot. The "Jump" is the clear choice, though the acrophobes among the remaining players look like they'd much rather walk (see p. 418 "The Most Endearing Racer Moments").

Count Wil among the green. His broad smile at the end of the leap, when he realizes he's still alive, is his best moment in the entire Race. Immediately afterward, he asks Tara if this means they're back together. She says absolutely not, but she is proud of him. Alas, the bickering begins anew on the road. "Who brought us this leg?" he demands. "You? . . .You just drove. How does it feel? Huh? This is what you blame me for, every single time."

Charming guy.

The Roadblock at Inverary Sheep Station involves sheepherding, and requires one team member to separate three black sheep from nineteen white ones, and get them into a corral. The sheep vigorously resist this procedure. They're not, like, sheep, you know. The trick, which all three Roadblock teams have to find out by painful trial and error, turns out to be not chasing the sheep but simply opening the corral, a familiar place sheep are willing to enter of their own accord. After that, just release the whites. But I do give Chris of The Bouncers kudos for his ineffectual alternate method, leaning down to complain into one white sheep's ear: "Why won't you listen to me?"

Many Racers say this to each other, but he is the only one to ever say it to a sheep.

1. Blake and Paige (The Smiley Siblings) 2:13 P.M.
2. Wil and Tara (The Constant Snipers) 3:13 P.M.
3. Chris and Alex (The Bouncers) 3:41 P.M.
4. Oswald and Danny (Team Fabulous) 5:04 P.M. NOT ELIMI-NATED

Leg #11: Taking Out Tara at Mount Terawera

Receiving twenty dollars, teams must board camper vans and drive 500 miles to the Maori Arts and Crafts Institute in Rotorua on New Zealand's northern island. That involves a ferry ride from Picton to Wellington. Catching the 11:30 A.M. ferry seems critical, as the next one doesn't leave for two hours.

The first Constant Sniper to call the other one stupid, during the long drive to Picton, is Wil. But she lets him know he's a jerk, before he calls her an idiot again. Fun, fun, fun for the camera crew. He does apologize to her, later, but only when she's asleep in the backseat and can't hear it.

Meanwhile, Oswald, who got his first driver's license "just before the Race," busts his driver's-side mirror against a barrier on the side of a bridge. Not a big deal.

On the ferry, Tara leaves Wil to pal around with Alex some more. By this point it's hard to blame her. Not that Wil's a bad guy, but the tension level between them is so high that it only makes sense for her to seek out what she calls a "comfort zone."

Later, on the long ride to Rotorua, Wil calls Tara "sunshine." She shakes her head silently. The next shot, demonstrating the splendid sense of irony that so distinguishes the editors of this show, reveals the pair driving through a torrential downpour. Now, that's symbolism.

Bunched at the Maori Arts and Crafts Institute at 7:00 A.M., teams watch a native ceremony before receiving instructions to drive 100 miles to the Waitomo Caves.

After a Race filled with Fast Forwards that have included a refreshing dip in the pool and a nice meal of meat pie, The Constant Snipers pick the one that involves an exhausting nearly vertical run across loose volcanic scree to the bottom of the caldera of Mount Terawera. And once they reach the bottom and get their clue, they still have to hike back out. Think about it. A refreshing dip. A meat pie. Versus a volcano. It's all fate.

Wil's comment to the effect that you can't take out Tara at Mount Ter-awera fails to bring a smile to her lips. Later, when he asks her if she's looking forward to filling his wool cap with money, she says she wants to fill his mouth with a sock so he'll shut the hell up.

It's no wonder that by the leg's end, both Tara and Wil are making sounds to the effect that they're pretty much over as a couple. But there are still two legs left. Stay tuned.

For the others, the Detour is "Drop" or "Climb." In "Drop," teams and their guide descend the world's tallest free rappel, 350 feet to the bottom of the Lost World Cave, very close to the clue box at Jesus Rock. "Climb" allows teams to descend a hundred-foot ladder, only to endure a walk the rest of the way to the clue box at Jesus Rock. Everybody takes "Drop," and then drives a hundred miles to take on the Roadblock, a bumpy ride on an all-terrain vehicle.

The Pit Stop is the Warbirds Hangar at the Ardmore Airfield on the outskirts of Auckland. And then there are three.

1. Wil and Tara (The Constant Snipers) 1:03 P.M.
2. Blake and Paige (The Smiley Siblings) 3:30 P.M.
3. Chris and Alex (The Bouncers) 3:58 P.M.
4. Oswald and Danny (Team Fabulous) ELIMINATED

Leg #12: Maui, Land of All-Inclusive Directions

Teams receive fifty dollars and, thanks to a route marker at the tomb of Sir John Logan Campbell, the Father of Auckland, their next destination is Maui, Hawaii. Naturally enough, the airport becomes an all-night bunching point. Just as naturally, Tara goes over to hug Alex, and just as naturally as that, Wil gets upset at what he sees as her lack of team spirit. It continues: on the flight to Maui, Tara sits and cuddles with Alex while Wil sits alone, reading a guidebook and giving off wavy heat lines. Fun, fun, fun.

Once in Maui, and driving another flagged vehicle, Tara displays the disorienting effects of a month in multiple foreign countries. "We're in America," she wonders. "What side do we drive on?"

Following clues to the water tower at the Pauwela Pineapple Field, teams find the Detour: "Bike" or "Water." In both cases the task involves a search for colored pineapples (or simulacra thereof) in a large pineapple field. In "Bike," teams have to find the only red pineapple hidden in the entire field. In "Walk," teams search on foot for one of only four yellows. Everybody chooses "Walk" and everybody finds the yellow pineapple within a few minutes of one another.

Fifteen miles away, teams take boats from the dock at McGregor Point, traveling another five miles by boat to a route marker floating near the extinct volcano, Molokini Island. The Roadblock requires one team member to don snorkel gear and swim down to a trio of bouyant cases, tethered by cables to the sea bottom. To complete the challenge, players must remove the straps sealing the case and retrieve the clue inside.

Though first to the route marker, Wil has the most trouble working underwater, continuing to struggle with the seals for long minutes after Blake and Alex have already opened their cases, retrieved their clues, and departed. "I can't do it," he reports. Tara shrieks, "SUCK IT UP OR GO QUIT AGAIN! YOU ALWAYS QUIT! GET DOWN THERE AND DO IT! THE OTHER BOATS ALREADY TOOK OFF! HOW CAN YOU NOT DO IT?" He goes back down, comes back up to report failure, goes back down again, and once again says he can't do it. But this time the clue is actually floating in the water beside him. "Idiot," concludes Tara. Fun, fun, fun.

The Pit Stop is Huialoha Church, a remote house of worship only accessible via an unmarked access road. Everybody gets lost, to some degree or another. The Bouncers have the worst luck. At one point, Alex asks directions from a spectacularly unhelpful Hawaiian man whose vague arm gestures, as he gives directions, seem to indicate the world, the universe, and alternate dimensions. Alex asks him how far to go. The old guy says, "A little bit far," but is unable to specify how far. Maybe a mile and a half, the old guy says. Chris grumbles, "Everything's a mile and a half away in this country," forgetting for the moment that he's already back in his homeland.

The Snipers arrive less than a minute after the first-place Siblings, but because of a production delay that delayed them by one minute, are given a one-minute credit and awarded the same trip to London and Paris.

1. Blake and Paige (The Smiley Siblings) 11:12 A.M.
2. Wil and Tara (The Constant Snipers) 11:13 A.M. CREDIT
3. Chris and Alex (The Bouncers) 12:39 P.M. NOT ELIMINATED

Leg #13: Showdown in San Francisco

The last leg becomes a veritable mini-drama, detailing an ongoing melt-down in the contentious relationship between teammates Tara and Wil.

Teams receive one dollar and instructions to find Queen Kaahuma-nu's birthplace at Hana Bay. The route marker there provides instructions to fly 2,800 miles to Anchorage, Alaska, and proceed to Lake Hood Airport, where they must find Rust's Flying Service.

The airport bunching provides the leg's first low comedy when Wil loses the clue envelope and can't remember the destination in Anchorage. (That's the punch line we were talking about.) He is forced to beg for help, in the last leg, from two teams he's been alienating since the first leg. Predictably, The Bouncers and Siblings are not exactly inclined to help. As Paige puts it, with a delighted grin on her face, "They picked the wrong people to be mean to the whole trip if they want favors." And, you know, she has a point.

Alex tells Wil, "You wouldn't give us the clue if we lost it at this point in the Race. There's no way you would." Tara protests that she would. And Alex agrees. But he feels Wil wouldn't. And so he doesn't either.

Wil threatens to quit and calls Tara stupid for believing The Bouncers to be her friends. Her response, that they're striking back at Wil and not her, may not show an excess of team spirit, but seems true enough (more in "The Most Jaw-Dropping Errors Ever Made by Racers" and "The Smartest Moves Ever Made by Racers").

Desperate research gets the Snipers on a charter flight to Trapper's Creek, Alaska, where teams spend the night in igloos and Tara tells Wil that he has the social skills of a gnat. "I'd rather not win the money," she says, "so that you don't get the money."

There's much more in that vein, alas. The next morning, Wil gets on Tara's case for driving her snowcat too slowly, saying he's sick of her and calling her stupid. (His subsequent apology doesn't meet with much enthusiasm.)

Fifty miles later, in Big Lake, teams pick up tools that include hammers, saws, power drills, and a blowtorch, and proceed to Hurricane Gulch, where the Roadblock requires one team member to free the clue frozen in a globe of ice. (The hammer and chisel are by far the most effective.) The Bouncers and the Siblings make short work of the task. Wil threatens to quit, tells Tara to shut up, and channels his anger smashing the globe with a hammer. There's some serious sublimation going on there.

The Race moves on to the final destination city: San Francisco. With the Siblings last to get a taxi, what ensues is one of the two most exciting finales in the show's history, starting with a maddening road race between The Bouncers and The Constant Snipers. Wil, aware that his team cannot beat The Bouncers in a footrace, attempts to throw the others off by having his taxi lead theirs to a dead end on the wrong side of the bridge.

It's a heroic effort. But it doesn't work. Tara yells that Wil's an idiot, and he tells her to shut up. I should put that on a macro.

Wil and Tara are first to Fort Baker, by less than a minute. The footrace that follows ratchets up the suspense still further, with The Bouncers pursuing The Constant Snipers across open ground. (For more details, see p. 141 "Did Tara Throw the Race?")

1. Chris and Alex (The Bouncers) WIN
2. Wil and Tara (The Constant Snipers) PLACE
3. Blake and Paige (The Smiley Siblings) SHOW

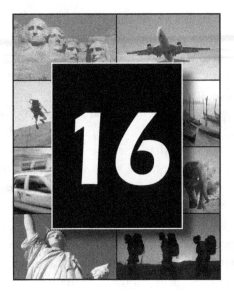

Did Tara Throw the Race?

I CONFESS BEING EMBARRASSED TO EVEN bring up the question. It's piggy, obnoxious, confrontational, and gross. But I can't avoid it. It's been brought up elsewhere, and deserves coverage.

The bottom line: I don't believe it, not in a million years.

I can't credit a woman who has shown so much energy and competitive spirit, involving all manner of hardships all over the world, deciding on a whim to sacrifice her share of a million dollars, just to spite her hubby and show her affection for a guy she's known for only a few weeks.

But I understand why some people would think so.

Here's the circumstantial evidence behind the theory. Wil and Tara are a contentious couple who have been separated for longer than they were together. Their relationship is a rocky one. It's fair to say that they care for each other, but don't always like each other. Their interaction, on the Race at least, was punctuated by shut ups, resentful silences, and mutual accusations of stupidity. At one point, Tara even interviewed that she was treating Wil worse than she ever had when they were to-gether...and that he was treating her better, a sorry statement indeed, given how many fights we'd seen.

We don't know, and have no business knowing, what started this merry-go-round. We only need to observe that it's there.

We also need to observe that, during the Race, Tara increasingly chose the company of her competitors Chris and Alex (and mostly Alex) over her nominal partner Wil. She cuddled with Alex during the Pit Stops, took their side in their disputes with Wil, laughed with them when Wil did something irritating or pigheaded, sat with them on planes, and generally treated them as a welcome (her phrase) "comfort zone." This, by itself, made the tension worse. Whatever feelings of emotion-al cuckoldry Wil might or might not have had, he was nevertheless vo-cal about his conviction that Tara's activities harmed their chances as a competitive team. It became an even greater point of contention be-tween them.

All of this became critical in the final leg, which Wil had rendered even more stressful by losing an all-important clue. The tension be-tween them, throughout this leg, was so thick that even a knife might not have been sufficient to cut it. The Race producers might as well have imported a jackhammer for the purpose. Critically enough, we got an important clue popular among Race fans of the sort who like to formu-late conspiracy theories: Tara's scornful declaration, beside a campfire in Alaska, that Wil didn't deserve his share of the million dollars, and that she'd almost give up her half if that meant he wouldn't win his. (Add-ing still more grist to the rumor mill: Chris and Alex were present and heard her say it.)

The bickering continued. We'll bypass the precise blow-by-blow and say it got so bad that when Wil used a hammer to get inside the ice globe containing the next clue envelope, you could see him mentally picturing the target as Tara's head. (There is no reason to believe he ever struck the real Tara in anger. Indeed, the best thing you can say about him, in this context, is that it's pretty hard to imagine. But he was very angry indeed, at that moment, and the ice sculpture represented a con-venient, socially and morally acceptable Tara substitute.)

The Race moved on San Francisco, scene of one of the tensest, most hotly contested legs ever and, for Wil and Tara, the angriest bickering yet.

All of which brings us to that final footrace. Wil and Tara reached Fort Baker first, by a minute or two. They struck out for the finish line. It was a long run. But though Wil, at least, was able to build on his lead, Tara soon fell behind him, running so slowly that Chris and Alex were able to catch up and overtake her. The boys were first to the finish line and they took home the million dollars.

There you have it. She was fed up with Wil. She liked the other guys a lot. A day or so earlier, she even came out and said she didn't want Wil to win. She ran slowly, and her team lost.

The unavoidable implication is that she threw the Race away, just to spite her husband.

Many Race fans believe it.

But the major problem with the theory is that it requires Tara to make the following conscious decision: *I hate this bastard so much right now that I don't want half a million dollars for myself.*

Granted that she'd said something to that effect a day or so earlier, there's a world of difference between speaking those words in anger and actually putting them into practice.

Throwing the game, just to *start*, requires her to be vindictive, crazy, self-destructive, irrational, flighty, and stupid. All at the same time.

Just to *start*.

And it also ignores the copious exculpatory evidence, starting with the miles Tara and Wil had already run that day, after a month of exhausting travel. Both were no doubt sore and running on fumes. Both expressed skepticism over their chances of defeating Chris and Alex in a footrace. For all her anger, Tara stressed to Wil, and to their cabbie, that she needed a two-hundred-yard head start just to stand a chance. This is not the kind of warning given by a woman who wants to lose. It's the kind of warning given by a woman who knows her physical limitations. Two hundred yards is the length of two football fields: a substantial distance, representing what must have been serious doubts about her ability to run as fast as a formidable competing team. Her pace, when she fell behind Wil, and was subsequently overtaken by Chris and Alex, was much closer to a jog.

Sorry, folks. There's a logical principle known as Occam's razor, which holds that the simplest possible explanation is almost certainly the true one. The simpler, and more reasonable, explanation here is that Tara didn't cheat, and that her reaction upon being overtaken was helplessness, rather than secret satisfaction.

That is what I believe, anyway.

Only Tara knows for sure.

But even that is not necessarily the end of it.

Because there's another factor, affecting all competitions, and that's motivation.

It's where we get the hoariest of all clichés, "giving 110 percent." It means exceeding one's usual limitations: ignoring exhaustion, pain, self-doubt, and defeatism, and pressing on long after a reasonable person would lie down and quit. People who give "110 percent" may lose, but you can never accuse them of not trying to win. You find that statistic apt not only in sports competitions, but also in life-or-death situations, where some people survive long after lesser folks would have just fallen over and died.[17]

And one of the factors that goes into giving "110 percent" is teamwork. People give "110 percent" when they would rather endure the worst than let their partners down.

Did Tara throw the Race?

Not believable for a moment.

Did she give "110 percent"?

That's a fair question, and open to interpretation.

Her relationship with Wil, during the Race, was marked by resentment, frustration, and anger, exacerbated by her affection for their strongest competition. Much as she clearly wanted to win, these are all factors capable of diluting her motivation. That "110 percent" may have likely been closer, in her case, to 105. Or even, taking away all benefit of the doubt, ninety. She no doubt ran as fast as she could at that particular moment, but might not have reached her absolute limits, let alone exceeded them.

---

[17] The author's personal favorite example: the failed Antarctic expedition of explorer Ernest Shackleton. He pushed himself past all reasonable limits and achieved a certain kind of greatness, in failing utterly, that rendered him immortal in a way that actual success would not have. He didn't give 110 percent. He gave several thousand percent. Seriously. Look it up.

In short, she might have run faster had she and Wil not spent so much time, in that last leg, calling each other stupid.

This is something only she knows.

If even she knows.

We can only wonder if she wonders.

Moments We See Again and Again (Part Three)

25. We're the Best Team Ever

This may not be entirely fair to bring up, as all teams are encouraged to tell the cameras why they're the team to beat, and few folks are going to enter this competition saying something like, "Our ultimate plan is to drag our droopy butts across a handful of legs, whining all the way, before expiring in humiliation by Leg #3." Everybody, even the long shots, says they're going to win, even if it's hard to come up with a good reason why they'd think so. But some teams actually take this rah-rah spirit past the realm of reasonable confidence into the realm of entitlement. They'll talk about how they're the only team that knows what they're doing and how all the other teams suck. Few teams that behave in this manner are right. Some, like Team First Out, go down fast. Others, like the Guidos, stumble in some spectacular, jaw-dropping manner. Of all the teams that ever used "we're the best, and everybody else sucks" rhetoric, Race 5's Colin and Christie and Race 7's Rob and Amber came closest to factual accuracy. They were the Teams to Beat. And they both lost.

26. Where Is Everybody?

Imagine you're in a race around the world that regularly takes you through airports and bus stations. Imagine that you've spent the whole day running your own course and have yet to encounter any of the other teams. This may mean you're in the lead. It may also mean that you're hours and hours behind, or on a one-way road to nowhere. Either way, isolation robs you of any meaningful reference point, and fosters an uncertainty that has led some Racers to wildly incorrect assumptions about their own standing in the pack. Feelings of invincibility war, moment by moment, with feelings of imminent doom. It's no wonder Racers express such relief upon spotting their competitors on the road: if they're doing badly, then at least somebody else is in the same boat. This phenomenon is particularly irksome in cases where multiple teams find themselves sitting around at one bunching point or another, for what may be hours, while one much-feared team remains missing in action. Has that team taken the Fast Forward? Have they found a shortcut? Are they already chilling at this leg's Pit Stop, sipping margaritas while they hatch their nefarious schemes? Or are they stuck in traveler hell, somewhere far behind, having misinterpreted their clue or missed the last train out? It's no wonder that, when such folks show up, looking much worse for wear, even their bitterest rivals report a little surge of relief. It may mean the game's still on, but at least…the game's still on.

27. Racers Assuming that the Whole World Is Interested

The insular environment and obsessive competition of the Race leads many Racers to a peculiar form of tunnel vision, manifested by the irrational belief that the ordinary citizens they encounter around the world are themselves deeply invested in the outcome of the contest. This can be a helpful assumption, in certain circumstances (as when Racers enlist the enthusiasm of native guides, or cab drivers), but enters the realm of self-delusion when otherwise sane Racers do things like advise reservation agents in airports not to sell the same tickets to people standing directly behind them in line. This never works, as the clerks can only get in trouble by failing to do their jobs. See also Wil of the The Constant Snipers, in San Francisco, advising a bored airport cop that he had to get the first available taxi in order to win a million dollars. Generally, using the Race to get service people to excel is a good thing; asking the same service people to break the rules or, in extreme cases, the law, is just plain silly.

28. Everything's Hopeless...before the Commercial

A team that suffers a setback in mid-leg will declare themselves doomed or lost or unable to continue, leading to a slow-motion close-up of a Racer succumbing to temporary despair. This moment of pure tragedy is almost always followed, a few short annoying advertisements later, by the Racers in question finding a way out of their predicament, and moving on, often to victory. This phenomenon occurs most frequently in airports, with Racers trying to argue their way aboard overbooked flights. They are told that there are no tickets, look crestfallen and defeated, declare themselves screwed, and then, one dramatic sting and a commercial break later, find out that the ticket agent has managed to get them seats after all. Whew! Rescue from Certain Doom happens so often, in the course of the nine Races aired so far, that it always comes as a little surprise when Racers who declare themselves sunk actually do turn out to be sunk. Generally, a team sunk at the end of the first segment stands a good shot of staying alive, or even coming in first, at the leg's end. And even teams that fall irretrievably far behind, have a chance of catching up to others at a bunching point.

29. "I Can't Read Maps!"

This is a frequent complaint of the Racer in the backseat, who will as often as not go on to claim actual retardation in the field of map reading. The expectation is that the Racer behind the wheel will both drive and read the map at the same time, while the Racer in the backseat complains about all the vital road signs being missed.

30. "I Don't Know How to Use a Compass!"

Pretty much the same phenomenon, though this often leads to somebody providing a mini-explanation of where to point the little needle.

31. Stick Shifts

Several Racers have spent their time on the road stalling out and grinding some poor transmission into gravel. It needs to be said, here, that map reading, compass reading, and using manual transmissions are all necessary curricula for Racers, and that if they're not among your skills when you hear from the producers, you need to hurry up and learn.

32. Map Throwing

Driving on unfamiliar roads (or, in at least one case, navigating unfamiliar waterways), and taking heat for getting the team lost, the navigator gets so fed up with dealing with the driver's attitude that s/he flings the map in a huff. This is not a particularly nice thing to do, but it's the first refuge of the terminally frustrated, and it's not limited to the most combative teams. Even some teams that get along most of the time (The Bowling Moms) are guilty of this particular sin. It's a good thing for them that gas stations don't dispense copies mounted on concrete.

33. Racers Coming to Grief in Their Own Home Cities

Racers who find themselves in places where they've actually lived often believe they have the home-field advantage, but it doesn't often work out that way. In practice, the home field is a minefield: a fine place for Racers to overthink their strategy, fall prey to overconfidence, or run into unexpected gaps in their local knowledge. Sufferers include Team Diesel from Race 1 (who are beaten to the finish line, mere blocks from their home in Queens), The Constant Snipers from Race 2 (who claim the advantage in San Francisco, and promptly lose it), Race 8's Paolos (who live in New Jersey and have trouble navigating in Manhattan), and The Schroeders (who come from New Orleans and fall behind in a leg that culminates in their own hometown).

34. You Lost WHAT?

The best advice for any world traveler is to never leave any location, anywhere in the world, without first taking a moment to inventory your belongings. Haste now leads to heartbreak later when you realize you've lost something vital. But haste now is of course the very point of *The Amazing Race*, and scarcely a Race goes by without some team forgetting something of extreme importance. Racers have left behind their money, their maps, their clue envelopes, their passports, their luggage, their tickets, their paperwork, and (sometimes) their sense of reasonable perspective. They've also lost items the rules required them to bring. In the best-case scenario, the items in question are dispensable, easy to replace, or just sources of contention (Hellboy's sunglasses). In the worst, Racers realize they're missing something important many miles down the road, and have to turn around, hoping that the lost item is still wherever they've left it. It could be worse, though. In the unlikely event the producers follow up the "Family Edition" with experiments involving six-, eight-, or ten-member teams, then the potentially abandoned items could, in theory, include entire family members. ("Where's little Kevin? I haven't seen him since Malaysia. . . .")

35. Hateable Clothing

Racers have limited baggage space and dress for utility rather than aesthetic impression. That means novelty T-shirts, short shorts, baseball caps, sneakers, and the like. Nobody will ever accuse any of them of making eloquent fashion statements, especially since sharp-eyed viewers can spot how often the same items are recycled. That said, several Racers have worn items so woeful they become prominent supporting players in their own right. For some reason, these are most often hats: see the brimmed hats worn by Rob and Brennan of Race 1, Wil's crocheted cap from Race 2, or Ian's foreign-legion special from Race 3. We recognize these most often because we spend so much time looking at Racer faces. If Racers wear embarrassing underwear as well, we don't often get a chance to see it.

To be continued. . . .

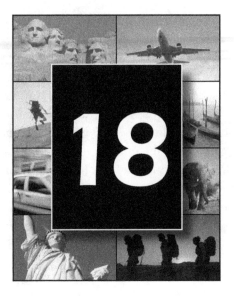

Race 3, Stop the World, She Wants to Get Off

T
HE THIRD RACE FEATURED TWELVE teams instead of the usual eleven, two teams with thematic connections to 9/11, and the most tempest-tossed team until Race 6. It was dominated by the travails of that team, which included both the best Racer of all time and one of the most fragile. But there were other high points: namely a diesel versus unleaded leg that at one point had *half* the teams scrambling to correct a disastrous error.

DRAMATIS PERSONAE

1. Team TNT

Tramel Raggs, 22, and his older sister Talicia Raggs, 29, form the self-described Team TNT, which they say only needs one spark to blow the house down. Among several teams thrown farther behind by a bus crash in the second leg, they never quite catch fire, let alone blow down any houses. But they're good folks.

2. Team Albatross

Platonic college friends Flo Pesenti, 23, who's in public relations, and Zach Behr, 23, a production assistant, have their friendship tested as few teams ever have, as Flo is…shall we say…somewhat less up to the rigors of the game than she initially imagined. Zach, who worries at the onset that Flo might be just a little high-maintenance, gets his answer underlined and italicized, finally running what, for long stretches, amounts to a heroic one-man race. (Giving Flo credit for self-awareness, she has since then shown good-natured incredulity that they remained friends when it was all over.) **SEASON SUPERSTARS**

3. The Soccer Moms

Gina Diggins, 35, and Sylvia Pitt, 34, are homemakers from South Carolina, who enjoy a single leg before dropping out, leaving a pleasant impression but never emerging as a serious threat to anybody. I'm glad they got to enjoy the trip.

4. Team Grumpy

Ian Pollack, 50, a retired private investigator, and his wife Teri Pollack, 49, are the oldest team this time around, and, though not bad folks, among the most abrasive. Ian, in particular, barks orders like a drill sergeant, not only at taxi drivers but at his own wife. ("Teri!" he cries at one point. "*Come!*" He sounds uncannily like a master barking at a dog.) This leads to a somewhat wonderful twist in Vietnam, site of the war Ian fought in as a younger man. Most likeable whenever racing to the mat, when Ian hollers, "I'm coming, Phil!" **SEASON SUPERSTARS**

5. The Long-Distance Daters

Michael Ilacqua, 28, and Kathy Perez, 31, are one of this Race's two Smiley couples, taking satisfaction from the journey as well as the competition. Alas, they're so laid-back that they fail to take timely action when a crisis jeopardizes their standing.

6. Team Oh, Brother

Ken Duphiney, 40, a freelance casting director, and his younger brother Gerard, 35, of this self-titled team, are in many ways a replay of Race 1's Fat Bastards: two balding, roundish men who use humor and drive to stay in the game far longer than many younger and more athletic players. Much is made, early on, about the differences between them: one liberal, one conservative; one gay, one straight—but that's just packaging. They're tight. They recover from an early slow start to become a potent force. **SEASON SUPERSTARS**

7. The Sweetheart Smileys

Another Smiley team, New Yorkers John Vito Pietanza, 28, and Jill Aquilino, 24, became involved after her brother and his best friend, F. T., died on 9/11, on the 105th floor of the World Trade Center. They run this Race in part as a tribute to him, and if you think we're going to say anything cynical about that, you're crazy. Jon Vito and Jill make one of the show's more distinctive couples, and one of the all-time most persistently cheerful.

8. The Law Babes

Recent law school graduates Heather Mahar and Eve Madison, both 25, intend to bring their sex appeal and native intelligence to the Race. They have both. But the combination doesn't work nearly as well as intended. Among their weaknesses: Eve's intense fear of heights. But worse than that: the lawyer's knack of outthinking the simplest of instructions.

9. The Wonder Twins

Identical twins Derek Riker and Drew Riker, both 25, continue the series fascination with players almost impossible to tell apart. Their good looks and athleticism make them an instant object of hate for some other teams, who judge them a serious threat. A team to beat. Possibly one of the best teams ever. But their biggest weakness is the chicanery of others.

10. Team Oh, My Papa

Conservative dad Dennis Hyde, 48, and his gay cheerleader son Andrew Hyde, 21, also hint at some interpersonal conflicts about Andrew's lifestyle, but it doesn't seem to affect their closeness, or their enthusiasm, at any point during their short time on the Race. Airport shuffle proves their downfall, despite a heroic attempt at recovery.

11. The First Responders

It would be nice to report that police officer Andre Plummer, 32, and firefighter Damon Wafer, 33, the second of this Race's 9/11-themed teams, prove equal to every challenge that faces them abroad. Alas, they do not. Though capable of every physical challenge the Race throws at them (Damon, in particular, is the rare Racer who actually rappels for a living), they're most dependent on following other teams. They deserve our respect for putting their lives on the line at home, not so much when it comes to booking travel, or waking up on time. (Only a churl would extrapolate their oversleeping here to worry about their swiftness whenever alarms go off in their respective precincts.) With the sole exception of Race 1's Team Puss, they find one of the show's all-time worst places to get lost.

12. The Twin Haters

Lifelong Friends Aaron Goldschmidt and Arianne Udell, both 27, are among the teams who develop an instant antipathy toward The Wonder Twins, on the grounds that the Twins are good-looking athletic boys who presumably don't need the million dollars as much as the Haters do. Arianne, in particular, is a little bit too vocal on the subject.

THE GAME PLAY

Leg #1: Finding Pablo

Teams lined up at a location on the edge of the Florida Everglades receive $100 and instructions to find the Angel of Independence, a statue adorning a traffic circle in Mexico City.

Zach interviews that Flo is a high-maintenance girl who "may" be trouble on the road. And, by the way—the *Titanic* may experience some delays on its way to New York. But, stay tuned.

The route marker by the statue offers up one of the Race's funnier tasks: find a man named Pablo, somewhere in Mexico City. Gee, that won't take long. Afterward, go to the Bronx and find Tony. The dumbfounded teams soon figure out that the building in the background of Pablo's photograph is a cathedral at Zocalo Square. Pablo's sitting exactly where photographed, which is damn convenient. Had he slept in, or taken an overseas vacation, this might have taken a while. Imagine: maybe that's Pablo, standing next to Waldo.

In any event, Pablo sends teams to the Hotel de Cortés, where players find sign-up sheets for three charter buses leaving two hours apart the next morning. The 8:00 A.M. bus carries The Twin Haters, Team Albatross, The Sweetheart Smileys, and The Long-Distance Daters. The 10:00 A.M. bus carries the Law Babes, Team Oh, My Papa, The First Responders, and the Grumpies. Everybody else gets seats at noon.

The Wonder Twins and Team Oh, Brother both consider themselves in serious trouble if they depend on that last bus, so both get up early and compete for the Fast Forward, a search for a certain street typist at Santo Domingo Plaza. Oh, Brother gets it first but sticks around long enough to tell The Wonder Twins they can call off the search. Might as well be considerate, if it doesn't cost you anything. And the balder brothers will spend that karma, later on.

Meanwhile, everybody else heads for Taquesquitengo Airfield, site of this leg's Detour: "Wings" or "Wheels." "Wings" is tandem skydiving with a divemaster. "Wheels" requires teams to direct a donkey cart, whose driver speaks no English, seven miles through local streets using only a hand-drawn map. "Wings" is clearly the better choice, though teams on the first couple of buses have enough of a head start to nurse their acrophobia by taking "Wheels" instead. This being early in the Race, Flo actually goes ahead with the skydiving despite palpable nervousness, and admits afterward that the experience was kind of cool. Expect that can-do attitude to change.

Eve of the Law Babes, who describes skydiving as her "biggest fear," goes anyway and suffers a screaming, shrieking, sobbing panic attack before, and during, her plunge. The show offers primo footage of her spazzing in mid-air, giving her tandem instructor a hell of a ride. She does it, though, so give her credit. She did it and didn't sue the guy.

Upon completing the Detour, everybody drives marked vans to the Pit Stop, at the Hacienda San Gabriel de las Palmas. But it's The Soccer Moms who miss the goal.

The First Responders, who fail to guide their donkey cart via the correct route, receive a seventy-eight-minute penalty: the first in a series of major errors by this team that should be more formidable than it is.

1. Ken and Gerard (Team Oh, Brother) 10:36 A.M.
2. Flo and Zach (Team Albatross) 1:09 P.M.
3. Aaron and Arianne (The Twin Haters) 1:11 P.M.
4. Michael and Kathy (The Long-Distance Daters) 1:33 P.M.
5. John Vito and Jill (The Sweetheart Smileys) 1:35 P.M.
6. Heather and Eve (The Law Babes) 2:16 P.M.
7. Andre and Damon (The First Responders) 2:52 P.M. PENALTY
8. Dennis and Andrew (Team Oh, My Papa) 3:29 P.M.
9. Teri and Ian (Team Grumpy) 3:33 P.M.
10. Tramel and Talicia (Team TNT) 4:28 P.M.
11. Derek and Drew (The Wonder Twins) 4:37 P.M.
12. Gina and Sylvia (The Soccer Moms) ELIMINATED

Leg #2: TNT Fizzles

Teams must now drive themselves 130 miles to Teotihuacan, where the next route marker awaits atop the Aztec Pyramid of the Sun. A 7:00 A.M. opening time guarantees a mass bunching for any teams that don't get lost. Alas, a number manage to make the 130-mile drive last well into morning.

During this ordeal we learn that Aaron is not exceedingly fond of slow-moving lumber trucks. Well, neither am I. But how else are we to get lumber?

The First Responders, who received a seventy-eight-minute penalty last leg, oversleep their scheduled departure time this leg. It's not the last time they could benefit from the use of an alarm clock. Stay tuned.

The Wonder Twins win the Fast Forward, an acrobatic stunt at Mexico City's Museum of Anthropology that involves swinging around a hundred-foot flagpole with famous performers known as the Voladores. This wins them instructions to the Diamante K Bungalows, fifty-seven miles from Cancún.

The pyramid clue directs teams to travel a thousand miles by bus to the San Marino Marina. That's a twenty-four-hour ride. Among the teams who make the 10:00 A.M. bus: Oh, Brother, The Sweetheart Smileys, The Twin Haters, Team Albatross, The Long-Distance Daters, and

The Law Babes. The First Responders, who miss that bus by minutes, have to wait to ride the 1:30 P.M. bus with Oh, My Papa, Team Grumpy, TNT, and (losing much of their Fast Forward advantage) The Wonder Twins. That second bus suffers a serious collision with a car at 12:15 A.M.; nobody on the bus is seriously hurt, but the passengers all have to wait half an hour for another bus to come by. The spread widens.

The first group arrives in Cancún at 9:42 A.M. (Arianne promptly amuses the cabbie by peeling off her clothes to don her bathing suit in the backseat.) The Detour, a search for a route marker hidden in the water, is between "Man Power" and "Horse Power." The first involves searching a small area in a kayak, the second a large area via WaveRunner.

Somewhere around here we see the first sign of Flo antics yet to come. She says, "Uhhhh, *helllo*!?!" with growing exasperation, when Zach fails to realize he's expected to help her with her backpack. What an inconsiderate lout he must be. Be afraid.

The second bus carries several teams who have less-than-happy experiences with their WaveRunners. Among them, Team TNT putts along at minimal speed, debates accelerating, and wipes out. This prompts Tramel to sputter, "I could walk faster!" Maybe, but not on water. He's more philosophical in the drink after a second wipeout: "At least I get to pee, though." (Yes, he actually says that.)

While he amuses himself grossing out his older sister (that is, assuming he was kidding), the teams ahead of them start arriving at Chankanaab Park, site of a Roadblock requiring one Racer from each team to find one of the clue envelopes at the bottom of a lagoon filled with dolphins. The dolphins show little interest in the proceedings. But they're cool anyway.

Of the three teams hitting the mat after dark, Team TNT arrives last. Tramel shrugs: "You win some, you lose some." Good attitude. But also, good-bye.

1. Derek and Drew (The Wonder Twins) 3:18 P.M.
2. Aaron and Arianne (The Twin Haters) 4:43 P.M.
3. Heather and Eve (The Law Babes) 4:44 P.M.
4. Michael and Kathy (The Long-Distance Daters) 4:45 P.M.
5. Flo and Zach (Team Albatross) 4:49 P.M.

6. Ken and Gerard (Team Oh, Brother) 6:02 P.M.
7. John Vito and Jill (The Sweetheart Smileys) 6:52 P.M.
8. Andre and Damon (The First Responders) 7:45 P.M.
9. Dennis and Andrew (Team Oh, My Papa) 7:46 P.M.
10. Teri and Ian (Team Grumpy) 7:47 P.M.
11. Tramel and Talicia (Team TNT) ELIMINATED

Leg #3: Limo to Oblivion

Receiving $444, teams must now fly 5,500 miles to London, England, making their way to the next route marker outside the Cambridge establishment Scudamore's.

On the way to the airport, Team Oh, Brother notes all the teams fixated on getting rid of The Wonder Twins and exults that their own pudgier physiques free them from such obsessive scheming. They begin to look less like a team destined to fall in the early rounds and more like one that might go the distance. Let's see how that works out for them.

Airport shuffle proves unusually grueling, with teams agonizing over whether to wait for a direct flight from Cancún or go through the larger hub, Mexico City. Nobody flies directly to Miami, which might have been a decent plan, especially since several teams stop there anyway. In any event, the eventual London flights, involving several different airlines and itineraries, arrive at local times ranging from 6:35 A.M. (for The Wonder Twins), throughout the day and evening for the remaining teams, all the way to 9:45 A.M. *the following day* (for Team Oh, My Papa).

The route marker at Scudamore's offers up the Detour: "Punt" or "Bike." In "Punt," teams paddle a boat one mile down the river, collecting clues dangling from a nearby bridge. In "Bike," teams ride a marked six-mile course on tandem bicycles. Ken and Gerard take "Punt" and delight locals by falling into the water (see p. 418 "The Most Endearing Racer Moments"). Team Albatross also tries "Punt," a task which marks another downturn in Flo's enthusiasm, before switching to "Bike."

Eve of The Law Babes complains about the hard wooden seat on the punt, the weight of her backpack, and having to run all the time. And seriously, who could blame her? Did anybody ever say that carrying things and running was involved here?

The Wonder Twins complete the Detour so early they spend most of the day lying around in the sun as they await the 7:30 P.M. charter bus to Aberdeen, Scotland. The delay allows Team Oh, Brother, Team Alba-tross, The Law Babes, The Twin Haters, and The Long-Distance Daters time to catch up, and the Twin Haters a long ride bitching about Derek and Drew's straight teeth. The Sweetheart Smileys make the 10:00 P.M. charter with seconds to spare, leaving The First Responders and the Grumpies to bring up the rear at 1:30 A.M.

That's a pretty impressive spread, but wait. It's not until *eight hours later* that Team Oh, My Papa arrives in London. They rush to the Fast Forward at the Duxford Imperial War Museum, a task which requires Dennis to drive a tank through an obstacle course in less than ninety seconds. He nails this on the first try and earns his team champagne and a long limo ride to the Pit Stop at Dunnottar Castle, in the Scottish town of Stonehaven. Well, at least they're comfortable.

A field near the castle hosts the Roadblock, which requires one mem-ber of each team to compete in three traditional Highland games: the caber toss, the hammer throw, and the shot put. Only Team Oh, My Papa arrives at the Pit Stop after dark. So much for Fast Forwards.

1. Derek and Drew (The Wonder Twins) 10:56 A.M.
2. Ken and Gerard (Team Oh, Brother) 10:58 A.M.
3. Flo and Zach (Team Albatross) 10:59 A.M.
4. Aaron and Arianne (The Twin Haters) 11:00 A.M.
5. Heather and Eve (The Law Babes) 11:01 A.M.
6. Michael and Kathy (The Long-Distance Daters) 11:13 A.M.
7. John Vito and Jill (The Sweetheart Smileys) 1:59 P.M.
8. Andre and Damon (The First Responders) 5:26 P.M.
9. Teri and Ian (Team Grumpy) 5:28 P.M.
10. Dennis and Andrew (Team Oh, My Papa) ELIMINATED

Leg #4: The Law Babes, Passing the Bar in Porto

Receiving $150, the teams must walk a mile and a half to nearby Stone-haven Harbor and retrieve their next clues from bottles dangling by ropes off the edge of the dock.

Mere minutes apart after the last leg, the first six teams march there in a grim parade that Flo characterizes as a "twin hunt." Yes, the twins are still enduring more than their share of hostility, and yes, the only folks palling around them at this point are the other brothers, Ken and

Gerard. Both sets of brothers form an alliance. It's nice to have allies you can depend on. He said, cuing the ominous music.

A thousand miles away, Calem Port Lodge in Portugal offers the leg's Detour, "Old School" versus "New School," representing two different ways of delivering port wine to local restaurants. In "Old School," teams load a ninety-pound barrel of port wine aboard a traditional Portuguese boat, and help the oarsman row across the water to the town of Porto. Teams only have to deliver that one barrel to one restaurant. In "New School," teams load nine crates aboard a truck and make deliveries at three restaurants. The first two teams to the route marker, The Wonder Twins and Team Oh, Brother, both elect "Old School," which subsequent events clearly establish as the choice less subject to the whims of traffic and the less-than-talented truck drivers among the field of competitors.

Among teams performing "New School," The First Responders have the worst troubles. First they smash a crate. Then they deliver to the Majestic Restaurant first, even though the rules of the task specify that it must receive its delivery last. Then they find themselves blocked in behind the truck driven by The Law Babes. Then they're forced to help The Law Babes unload in order to free their own vehicle. Then The Law Babes block them in, a second time, in another narrow street. One would expect The First Responders to be well accustomed to being stuck behind slow-moving vehicles when time is of the essence, but Andre's frustration is palpable. He moans, "She's killing me, D! She can't drive a stick!" Finally squeezing past her in one narrow alley, he sneers, "I have plenty of room. I didn't go to Harvard."

Eve dents her truck on a concrete pole.

A mass bunching ensues in the train station before all teams travel 200 miles by rail to Lisbon, where they must find Gate F of the Estadio do Restelo, a soccer stadium in Lisbon. They arrive at night, and face the Roadblock, which requires one team member to block one penalty kick from a teenage soccer player. This, Phil points out, is not as easy as it sounds in a country where most kids play soccer from early childhood on. And, we should add, most of these Racers don't have the typical American advantage of being extra wide.

Even so, the soccer is evidently not as difficult as the final instruction to *walk* one and a half miles to the 400-year-old fortress known as the

Torre del Belem (see p. 402 "The Most Jaw-Dropping Errors Ever Made by Racers").

1. Heather and Eve (The Law Babes) PENALTY/ELIMINATED
2. Ken and Gerard (Team Oh, Brother) 2:29 A.M.
3. Flo and Zach (Team Albatross) 2:31 A.M.
4. Derek and Drew (The Wonder Twins) 2:32 A.M.
5. Andre and Damon (The First Responders) 2:33 A.M.
6. Teri and Ian (Team Grumpy) 2:34 A.M.
7. John Vito and Jill (The Sweetheart Smileys) 2:36 A.M.
8. Michael and Kathy (The Long-Distance Daters) 2:40 A.M.
9. Aaron and Arianne (The Twin Haters) 2:54 A.M.

Leg #5: Running on Empty

Receiving $500, teams must now make their way to the unnamed and unspecified "westernmost point in continental Europe," figuring out that it's Cabo de Roca, only twenty-two miles away.

The site is accessible by several routes. Buses and commuter trains can be used to travel most of the distance, but taxis are the fastest if not most cost-efficient choice.

The Grumpies are in fine form this particular morning, snapping and sniping with almost every step. They can't even agree on who gets to talk to the taxi driver. "The bottom line," Ian says, "is I'm the pilot; she's the navigator. When I say fly, we need to fly." She rolls her eyes. Talk about airing your issues.

The First Responders catch up with the two brother teams at the train station and offer them a thirty-euro bribe just to let them tag along as far as the correct stop. Yes, they actually do that (see p. 403 "The Most Jaw-Dropping Errors Ever Made by Racers").

The Detour at Cabo de Roca is "Ropes" or "Slopes." In "Ropes," teams take a shuttle bus to the top of the cliff, and rappel 300 feet to a clue box on the beach below. In "Slopes," teams hike down instead.

As always, in tasks involving rappels, the scarier task is clearly the preferred one, and most Racers go for it. For The First Responders, it's almost like a day at work. Teri examines her line and wonders and wonders, "What happens if that undoes?" receiving the honest answer, "You fall." Thank you, Sir Isaac Newton. Gerard tells big old fat Kenny to pretend there are a dozen glazed donuts at the bottom, and Kenny all but runs down the cliff. Good thing Gerard didn't say pizza. Or Kenny might have been pizza, too.

As for Flo, she suffers a shrieking, wailing, helpless panic attack upon beginning her descent, and has to be pulled back up, forcing her team to hike instead. Zach tells her it's okay. It's the team's first really bad moment. But stay tuned.

Teams must now drive marked cars 250 miles to the port city of Algeciras, Spain, where they'll need to book a ferry to Tangier, Morocco. It's a long overnight drive, likely intended to produce a mass bunching aboard that first 7:00 A.M. ferry. But of the several teams stopping for gas, four—half of those remaining in the game—fill their tanks with unleaded instead of diesel, turning the night into an exercise in recovering from self-inflicted disaster (see p. 403 "The Most Jaw-Dropping Errors Ever Made by Racers").

Arriving in Tangier, teams make it to the Viajes Flandria travel agency, where they sign up for charter buses to the city of Fez. There they encounter the Roadblock. One player from each team must navigate the narrow streets of the Old City to find a tannery, where clues are submerged in vats of foul-smelling dye. Cruelly, only three of the twenty-five vats contain any clues at all. Yecch.

Finally, teams claim a marked car and rush to the fortress Borj Nord, where Phil awaits. Arriving many hours after everybody else, The Long-Distance Daters just smile, as Kathy has agreed to join Michael in San Diego. A fine consolation prize at that.

1. Ken and Gerard (Team Oh, Brother) 4:31 P.M.
2. Andre and Damon (The First Responders) 4:37 P.M.
3. Derek and Drew (The Wonder Twins) 4:44 P.M.
4. John Vito and Jill (The Sweetheart Smileys) 5:24 P.M. TIE
5. Flo and Zach (Team Albatross) 5:24 P.M. TIE
6. Teri and Ian (Team Grumpy) 5:28 P.M.
7. Aaron and Arianne (The Twin Haters) 7:04 P.M.
8. Michael and Kathy (The Long-Distance Daters) ELIMINATED

Leg #6: Ian Needs a Rug

Receiving fifty dollars, teams must now drive themselves 100 miles to the Hussan II Mosque in Casablanca.

The Sweetheart Smileys break down thanks to a radiator leak, and lose "about an hour" before their vehicle is replaced.

The route marker at the Mosque advises teams to travel 150 miles by train to Marrakech, and then take a taxi outside the city to the oasis known as the Palmeraie. Only The Wonder Twins, Oh, Brother, and The First Responders make the first train at 9:10 A.M. Team Albatross misses it by minutes and has to ride with the Grumpies and late-arriving Sweethearts at 11:10 A.M. The Twin Haters miss that train and don't get to leave Casablanca until 1:10 P.M. Looks bad for them.

The Detour at the Palmeraie is between "Now You See It" and "Now You Don't." "Now You See It" requires teams to ride horses to a nearby patch of dirt, where they have to dig up pottery etched with the new clue. In "Now You Don't," teams ride a sand bike a greater distance, and make a sand rubbing of the clue. In both cases, the clue is in Arabic and will have to be translated by locals.

Taking "Now You See It," Team Oh, Brother has trouble finding the buried clue, and switches to "Now You Don't." It's a seriously risky move that Oh, Brother will end up making several times in the course of the Race; oddly enough, giving up consistently *works* for them.

All three teams on the second bus want to go for the Fast Forward. Flo and Jill play "rock-paper-scissors" to settle who gets to fight it out with the Grumpies. The Sweethearts win the toss but lose the Fast Forward, a search through a pile of oriental rugs.

After the Fast Forward, Ian points at his heels and shouts: "Teri! *Come!*" Which is not his most endearing moment. But anyway.

Team Albatross arrives at the Palmeraie, where Flo asks the departing Ken what choice her team should take. Ken is incredulous: "You think I'm gonna tell *you?*"

Flo whines. "Oh, come on, Kenny, you rat! I'm, like, four hours behind!"

More like an hour, really. But it fails to persuade Ken.

The route marker on the terrace of the Café Glacier provides the Roadblock, which sends one member of each team down to the street to help a street vendor sell five bowls of escargot. Flo actually shows considerable enthusiasm here. She hates rappeling, but will sell snails.

The Pit Stop is the rooftop of the nearby Riad Catalina guest house. But getting there proves a serious problem for The First Responders, whose bad cabbie takes them out of the city, and deposits them in, for all intents and purposes, Idaho. No, not Idaho. That would be a bit much. But a desolate, isolated location, inhospitable to tourists. No, really. Not Idaho. Questioned by local officialdom, they wisely refuse to give up their passports, are detained, and wind up requiring rescue by the show's security staff. The delay plucks them out of the top tier and returns them to the rank of the bottom feeders. They will need a phenomenal leg, next time, to recover. But guess what isn't fated.

1. Teri and Ian (Team Grumpy) 3:25 P.M.
2. Flo and Zach (Team Albatross) 5:19 P.M.
3. Ken and Gerard (Team Oh, Brother) 5:20 P.M.
4. Derek and Drew (The Wonder Twins) 5:27 P.M.
5. John Vito and Jill (The Sweetheart Smileys) 5:32 P.M.
6. Andre and Damon (The First Responders) 7:04 P.M.
7. Aaron and Arianne (The Twin Haters) ELIMINATED

Leg #7: The Load in Gerard's Pants

Receiving one dollar—that's right, one dollar—teams now head for Munich, Germany.

Airport shuffle proves a bitch. Team Grumpy gets a flight to Zurich first thing in the morning. But just getting out of Morocco is a nightmare for everybody else. Moving on to Casablanca, Team Oh, Brother, The Wonder Twins, and The Sweetheart Smileys finally make a flight to Paris at 11:45 A.M.; Team Albatross gets a flight to Frankfurt at 3:00 P.M.; The First Responders don't get on a Paris flight until 3:15 P.M.

The only Racers to arrive in Munich in daylight, Team Grumpy is first to find Kasperie the really annoying hand puppet, who sends them to the Pillar of St. Anne in Innsbruck, Austria.

One short train ride later, Team Grumpy opens the clue box and finds the Detour: "Sled," which requires teams to ride along with the Austrian bobsled team, or "Skate," which requires teams to run a relay with professional skaters. Both tasks feature 8:30 A.M. opening hours, a delay of twelve hours, which represents a pretty definite bunching guarantee. And, indeed, Oh, Brother, The Wonder Twins, and the Smileys are all able to catch up to the Grumpies during the overnight wait.

Alas, for The First Responders, they miss a vital connection and end up spending the night in the Paris airport. Well, at least they're not detained.

Arriving in Munich late at night, Team Albatross decides to stay in town and take the Fast Forward in the morning. The search for a cheap hotel marks another serious downturn in Flo's morale. "This is so ghetto," she whines, refusing sight-unseen to stay in a youth hostel or any other place that costs less than twenty-five euros, because they're "gross." In the end, they stay in a place called McBed, before taking the Fast Forward, which involves hitting the river and flagging down the surfer riding a stationary wave. This is as stress-free as any activity with Flo has been this trip, and has Team Albatross headed for the Pit Stop, a meadow below Neuschwanstein Castle in Fussen, Germany, by shortly after 7:00 A.M.

At 8:30 A.M., The First Responders finally arrive in Munich. Andre and Damon can only hope that somebody ahead of them makes a serious mistake.

Teams completing the bobsleds take a cable-car ride to the Seegrube Station, where the Roadblock requires one player from each team to put on safety gear, board a gondola, and descend 230 feet to the ground via winching cable. It's a scary task, which leads Ken to yell to his brother from the ground: "Do you have a load in your pants?" The show fails to provide the answer. But that's okay. If affirmative, we really didn't need to know.

Now on the way to the Pit Stop, Team Oh, Brother suffers a flat tire and, rather than stop to change it themselves, drives the rim until the tire shreds. Not the smartest or most capable way to deal with that situation, but it gets them to a service station.

Meanwhile, The First Responders fall asleep on the train to Innsbruck, and miss their station. This is a delay they don't need. But they show grace when eliminated, and tell Phil they have something for him: their one-dollar allowance for this leg. They never needed it.

1. Flo and Zach (Team Albatross) 10:02 A.M.
2. Derek and Drew (The Wonder Twins) 12:44 P.M.

3. John Vito and Jill (The Sweetheart Smileys) 12:45 P.M.
4. Teri and Ian (Team Grumpy) 12:53 P.M.
5. Ken and Gerard (Team Oh, Brother) 2:42 P.M.
6. Andre and Damon (The First Responders) ELIMINATED

Leg #8: Teri's Pants Don't Matter

We have a partial replay of Race 2, as one player (Flo) begins a flirtation with one of her team's strongest competitors (Drew).

Which leads me to one thing I've never personally understood, since it's (alas) outside my own personal experience: how is it, exactly, that anybody develops an infatuation with *one* identical twin and not the other? I can understand if you meet one twin while the other is off in Borneo or something, but if you meet both twins at the same time, under circumstances that require both to act in more or less the same way, just how do you go about deciding that one is incredibly attractive while the other has the kind of good looks you can just take or leave? And for folks who manage that kind of incredibly difficult value judgment, is it ever difficult to remain faithful in dim light?

Anyway. Whatever.

Receiving $240, teams must find a nearby farm and search a giant haystack for clue envelopes.

Team Albatross arrives first. Flo doesn't want to touch the hay, but Zach climbs to the top of the stack and finds the clue envelope within seconds.

Excuse me, but that deserves repetition. *She doesn't want to touch the hay*.

The Smileys and Wonder Twins also find the clue in short order, and encounter the Grumpies as they drive away. When Ian asks directions to the farm, both teams tell him they're lost too, and leave feeling the warm glow of their own naughtiness. "That was so rude," says John Vito. "We're so going to hell," agrees Jill. But the tactic doesn't slow down the Grumpies, who find the clue within two seconds.

Seriously: haystacks are supposed to be tougher than that.

(Wait for Race 6.)

All teams now have to leave Germany and find the Rheinfall, in Switzerland. There's one mass bunching on the 5:45 A.M. ferry to Romanshorn and another on the one-hour train to Schaffhausen. The Smilies fall behind at the taxis, but this hardly matters. You see, the flag is on the outcropping that separates the Rheinfall into two sections. The ferry pilot says, "yah, yah," when asked if he's willing to wait, and "yah, yah," when asked if it's okay to leave backpacks aboard. "Yah, yah" turns out to mean "I have no idea what the hell you're saying." All the lead teams are left stranded when the fellow sails away with all their belongings. Excuse me, can I hit your head with this hammer? "Yah, yah."

The Zurich town square, known as the Lindenhof, hosts the Detour, which offers teams two different ways to obtain a six-digit code capable of opening the safes containing their next clue. In "Count the Money," teams remain next to the safe and count the mixed Swiss currency in a bowl. In "Run the Numbers," teams must obtain the numbers on a metal statue at the corner of Sihl and Bahnhof, the sum of the numbers on the north face of the clock at St. Peter's Church, and the number of trees on the Lindenhof marked with red ribbons. The first choice seems easiest to teams capable of dealing with unfamiliar bills and coinage. But the only team to take that option, Oh, Brother, elects to abort. But those who take to the streets task are bedeviled by their own counting errors.

When Oh, Brother opens its safe, Teri of the Grumpies asks Ken for the combination. She seems aghast at his rudeness when he says no. Well, it was worth a try.

Lovely, mountainous Grindelwald is the site of the leg's Roadblock, a crossbow competition which requires all participating Racers to shoot an apple off a mannequin's head. This ain't easy. (Zach gets it first, another of several reasons to name him the best Racer of all time.) But the true challenge here is an exhausting march across alpine streets to the Pit Stop at the Chalet Arnika. It doesn't exactly help that the teams have no idea where they're going, and for a long time can't find anybody capable of giving directions.

During this interval, Flo needs Zach to carry her backpack. Oh, Brother travels cross-country and gets lost. Teri complains that her pants are falling down. "This is more important than your pants falling down," Ian replies. "You're not modest."

It all comes down to a thrilling footrace between Oh, Brother and the Sweetheart Smileys, who approach the mat from opposite directions. Oh, Brother wins by seconds. But non-elimination reprieves the Smileys. Next time, somebody's in for trouble.

1. Derek and Drew (The Wonder Twins) 4:55 P.M.
2. Flo and Zach (Team Albatross) 4:56 P.M.
3. Teri and Ian (Team Grumpy) 5:03 P.M.
4. Ken and Gerard (Team Oh, Brother) 5:07 P.M.
5. John Vito and Jill (The Sweetheart Smileys) 5:08 P.M. NOT ELIMINATED

Leg #9: A Whine and Cheese Party

This leg, and the one after it, were both aired together as a two-hour episode.

Receiving forty dollars, teams must search the bottom of the gletscher-spalte (a gorge) to find the key that unlocks their cars for the leg.

The 9:00 A.M. opening hour guarantees a tight bunching at the gorge. Teams race up the hiking path, claim their car keys, and drive themselves thirty-six miles to Kandersteg to load their cars aboard the train that will take them through the Alps.

The Sweetheart Smileys take the Fast Forward, a visit to a cheese-making cabin where a huge wheel of cheese has been sliced into cubes. Directions to the next Pit Stop are hidden somewhere underneath all that lactose goodness. All the Sweethearts have to do is eat "slimy" cheese until they expose the clue. They're at their most likeable ever, smiling through their shared misery. But they overcome their nausea, find the clue, and head straight for the Steamship Savoie, floating on Lake Geneva. Yay!

Meanwhile, the Grumpies discover that their destination, the "Red Bridge," is a famous bungee-jumping site. They take great satisfaction in informing Flo.

(Well, so would I. I'm mean that way.)

Not long after that, in a seeming replay of the Wil/Tara ferry dynamic, Flo leaves Zach alone in the car to pal around with Drew.

The Detour at the Red Bridge is between "Extreme Swiss" or "Very Swiss." The first is the highest bungee jump in Europe: a 620-foot plunge into a gorge. In "Very Swiss," teams must drive eight miles to a nearby farm, where the keys to clue boxes hang hidden in a few of the bell collars worn by seventy-five goats. Flo is not the only person too intimidated to bungee. Neither member of Oh, Brother will do it. And Teri won't do it so Ian can't do it. Only The Wonder Twins take the plunge, while everybody else chases goats.

(Incidentally, there's a brief crash course in body language in the way Ian stands with folded arms, watching Teri struggle with the seal on the envelope. There's less tension, envelope-wise, at the Academy Awards. But anyway.)

Before they return to their cars, teams are surprised with mobile phones they can use to call their loved ones at home. The cruel but effective gimmick: they must make the calls brief or risk falling behind. Touching as these teary interludes are, it is amusing to watch Zach use part of his allotted time to make sure his sister paid his credit card bill. And it's downright hilarious when Ken and Gerard, rushing to their car after their own call, urge Flo to take "all day." (The amount of playing with Flo's head that goes on in this leg, and elsewhere, really suggests that the other Racers have gotten her number.)

The Roadblock at the Chateau de Chillon requires one Racer from each team to construct two bicycles capable of passing the stern judgment of the crack safety inspector, before proceeding on those bikes to the Bassett Marina. That's tough. But the ride to the marina, where teams find the paddleboats they take to the Pit Stop, provides the real drama for the two teams bringing up the rear. Teri bangs up her bike, requiring a quick roadside repair. And Flo throws a real snit, first flinging her bicycle helmet into Lake Geneva, then crying and whining all the way to her non-elimination.

1. John Vito and Jill (The Sweetheart Smileys) 12:42 P.M.
2. Ken and Gerard (Team Oh, Brother) 2:00 P.M.
3. Derek and Drew (The Wonder Twins) 2:14 P.M.
4. Teri and Ian (Team Grumpy) 2:35 P.M.
5. Flo and Zach (Team Albatross) 2:41 P.M. NOT ELIMINATED

Leg #10: The Bonfire of the Manatees

The Wonder Twins remember it's their birthday today. Happy, happy, joy, joy.

Teams now return to Geneva and find the tallest fountain in Europe, the 450-foot-tall Jet d'Eau, where a clue box informs them that the next clue will be found in front of the Petronas Towers, in the country represented by "the enclosed flag." (It's Malaysia.)

Flo and Zach already know where the Petronas Towers are, but ev-

erybody else has to ask around, leading to a memorable encounter between Team Grumpy and a local who sadly informs them, "You're on
the wrong continent." Hee hee.

The extremely lame challenge at the Petronas Towers in Kuala Lumpur is a plug for Kodak EasyShare cameras, requiring teams to take their
picture in front of the building. The show was paid for by the product
placement. We haven't been. We therefore skip ahead to the good stuff.

Teams have to go to the National Orchid Garden in Singapore and
find an orchid named after Margaret Thatcher. Naturally, they arrive
only after this attraction has closed for the night, and just as naturally,
Flo is less than enthused about Zach's suggestion that they book rooms
at the YMCA. *She doesn't want to touch the hay.* In the end, they wind
up sharing a room with Derek and Drew, even though Flo is quite clear,
in an interview, that she wishes she were sharing Drew's bed instead of
Zach's. Yes, she actually says that.

The whole trip is starting to read like the buildup to the murder in an
Agatha Christie mystery.

Morning. The 8:30 A.M. bunching at the Orchid Garden, where the
Margaret Thatcher Orchid grows next to the route marker providing this
leg's Detour. "Dry" requires teams to find Singapore's most popular television comedian, who is waiting for them in an apartment complex surrounded by streets named Choa Chu Kang. Making matters worse, the
building he's in has apartment numbers that vary from wing to wing, and
elevators that don't stop on consecutive floors. "Wet" sends teams to the
Singapore Zoological Gardens, where they have to take a dip in the manatee enclosure. Travel time aside, the manatees are by far the easier choice
(and the more attractive; hell, people pay money to do the same thing),
but teams aren't warned in advance how screwed up the addresses are, so
most of them drop in on the annoying TV personality, who acts like he's
making the most of his few seconds of exposure to American audiences.
He should not sit beside his phone waiting for offers.

Only the Grumpies and The Wonder Twins swim with the manatees,
who must be thanking the cetacean gods for pool filters. Along the way
Ian treats us to a discourse on his team's disposable travel underwear,
which is also nice.[18]

---

[18] We should send his phone number to Race 9's Fabulous Furry Freak Brothers, who on one occasion confess to not wearing any.

Meanwhile, at the apartment complex, Flo screams at Zach again, this time for refusing to give their only map to their temporary navigation partners, Team Oh, Brother. Later, in the car, Zach has his one and only moment of seeming to lose his temper, as he asks Flo not to yell at him all the time. It doesn't slow her down. Fun, fun, fun.

Players retrieving the leg's final clue, the Fountain of Wealth at Singapore's Suntec City, get sopping wet as they pass under the arcing water, but also get directions to the Pit Stop atop nearby Mount Faber. The Sweetheart Smileys, who have fallen behind on the roads, don't quite manage to catch up with the Grumpies, and are last to the mat. So it's good-bye, kids. Have a nice life.

1. Derek and Drew (The Wonder Twins) 10:22 A.M.
2. Ken and Gerard (Team Oh, Brother) 10:33 A.M.
3. Flo and Zach (Team Albatross) 10:34 A.M.
4. Teri and Ian (Team Grumpy) 10:45 A.M.
5. John Vito and Jill (The Sweetheart Smileys) ELIMINATED

Leg #11: Oh, Brother Pulls a Fast One

As the Race moves on to Vietnam, the red-and-yellow Race flag is temporarily replaced with an all-yellow flag, to avoid confusion with the national colors of the Vietnam flag.

Receiving eighty dollars, teams now head for Ho Chi Minh City, where they must find the statue of Bac Ho (Ho Chi Minh) in Rex Square.

Only the Oh, Brothers escape an overnight bunching at the Singapore airport, snagging an 11:30 P.M. plane to Kuala Lumpur at the very last minute. This seems a spectacular coup, as it gets Ken and Gerard to the hub airport many hours ahead of the other teams. But all it earns them is a night in the Kuala Lumpur airport, waiting for the same flight that everybody else catches the next morning. Ah, well. Easy come, easy go.

The route marker beside the statue of Bac Ho leads teams to the leg's Detour, on the Mekong Delta, seventy miles from Ho Chi Minh City.

In the cab, Flo suffers her first crying fit of many to come in Vietnam, following an extended whine over Zach's refusal to save time by cutting a customs line at the airport. Heroically holding his temper, as he's been doing for a while now, he points out that she's refused to do other things, like bungee jump, for instance. Bad mistake. Flo cries: "That's so ignorant and obnoxious, when you know there's a thousand physical risks associated with bungee jumping!...I'm tired of having to scream and I'm tired of having to override your decisions!" At his own lowest ebb, Zach mutters, "Okay, if you're tired, let's just stop. Whatever." And this is just the beginning. The team's friction, over this leg and the next one, is so horrific that the rest is by necessity covered elsewhere (see p. 179 "It's Her Party, and She'll Cry if She Wants To"). But let's just say— Zach suffers the torments of Job.

Ian's return to Vietnam is also too interesting to fit within this capsule; see p. 419 "The Most Endearing Racer Moments."

The Detour is "Easy Buy" or "Hard Sell." In "Easy Buy," teams take a sanpan out into the floating marketplace to find the one merchant selling water coconuts. In "Hard Sell," teams take a shoulder basket filled with fruit into the land market, and attempt to earn 40,000 dong (about two and a half dollars). Team Oh, Brother switches Detour options again when a pouring rain complicates their search of the floating marketplace. But again, it works for them. They hit upon the epiphany that allows them to finish the task quickly: namely, that it's not their fruit, that they're not concerned with making a profit, and that they can sell four baskets at the rock-bottom price of 10,000 dong apiece faster than they can sell individual pieces of fruit at the going rate.

Returning to Ho Chi Minh City, teams encounter the Roadblock, which requires them to ride a cyclo bike on a flagged course through the city streets. The course includes a ferry ride across the Saigon River, where the Pit Stop awaits at the Café Thu Thiem. The leaves obscuring the clue box present problems for the trailing teams, Oh, Brother and The Wonder Twins, but Ken and Gerard are able to exploit the situation for their own advantage (see p. 413 "The Smartest Moves Ever Made by Racers" for the detailed rundown; it's a busy leg, for cross-referencing). And so we say good-bye to everybody's toughest competition, The Wonder Twins.

1. Teri and Ian (Team Grumpy) 5:19 P.M.
2. Flo and Zach (Team Albatross) 5:58 P.M.
3. Ken and Gerard (Team Oh, Brother) 6:13 P.M.
4. Derek and Drew (The Wonder Twins) ELIMINATED

Leg #12: Ebbing Flo

This leg, and the next one, aired together as part of a two-hour season finale.

Teams paying attention begin this leg knowing that it must end with a non-elimination, if the finale is to feature the same three teams. That should diminish the stress level. It does not. Flo falls as completely apart as any Racer ever has. It ain't funny, and there's too much of it to discuss in this space (see p. 179 "It's Her Party, and She'll Cry if She Wants To" for further details).

Receiving $162, teams are instructed to travel 400 miles by train to the Imperial Palace in Hue. That's a twenty-four-hour ride from Ho Chi Minh City. Skipping past the angst at the train station, which is covered elsewhere, we move on to the next morning, with the less frazzled teams dazzled by the beauty of the Vietnamese countryside.

Along the way, we're treated to *The Amazing Race* at its most contemplative. The Oh, Brothers, who lost an uncle in Vietnam, and Ian, who fought there, are most touched by the dramatic disconnect between the peaceful vistas they see and the reputation of a country that for so many in the West still remains shorthand for the worst elements of the human experience. "I never would have said I wanted to visit Vietnam," Ken interviews. "Our Uncle Tom was here and died of Agent Orange. So [I] don't know to handle it."

As for Ian, he interviews, "I'm from a generation that lost 58,000 soldiers fighting a war that I believed for a long time was probably the wrong war to fight. But I believe in my country, right or wrong, and the bottom line is these people were fighting for what they believed in. It's very interesting to see what this country is all about without a war going on." And, again, if you think I'm going to make fun of any of that, you're crazy.

The interlude ends in Hue, where teams scramble for the Clue Box inside the Imperial Palace. The Oh, Brothers are the first to the route marker, which sends teams sixty-five miles to the tiny village of Nam O, Da Nang.

The Detour is a choice between two forms of transportation: "Basket Boats" or "Basket Bikes." In "Basket Boats," each team member must paddle a Vietnamese boat resembling a teacup across the river to a route marker on an island. In "Basket Bikes," each team member must ride a bicycle rendered top-heavy with dozens and dozens of locally made shrimp baskets—a huge inverted pyramid of them—down a dirt road to a route marker a mile away. Predictably, the local kids laugh uproariously at the silly Americans having trouble on the bikes...and not so predictably, help (though offers to pay has something to do with it). Zach and Flo have a bit more trouble when they attempt the task; she ends up throwing her second bicycle helmet of the game.

The boat quay at Hoi An is site of the leg's Roadblock. From there it's a quick fifteen-mile cab ride to the Pit Stop at China Beach. Nobody's eliminated. But Zach and Flo are lucky just to have made it through the day.

1. Teri and Ian (Team Grumpy) 5:35 P.M.
2. Ken and Gerard (Team Oh, Brother) 5:52 P.M.
3. Flo and Zach (Team Albatross) 8:02 P.M. NOT ELIMINATED

Leg #13: They freakin' WON!?!?

The obvious winners have all fallen out, leaving the finals to middle-aged marrieds, a pair of balding and out-of-shape brothers, and a platonic couple troubled by the female's extreme mood swings. Flo swears that she won't threaten to quit again. Let's see how long that lasts.

The Buddha at the Quang Minh Temple in Da Nang alerts teams that their next stop is Honolulu, Hawaii, where they must receive a blessing from the Kahuna. No, not Frankie Avalon. The clue specifies that they must depart Vietnam via Hanoi, which involves another seventeen-hour bus trip.

Ian makes himself such a pest to the woman at the Da Nang travel agency, intruding upon her side of the counter, that Ken asks him to give the lady some space. Even Teri says that it might be better to let Gerard do the talking. Ian thinks he and the lady are getting along just fine, insisting: "I'm telling you, before you guys got here, this lady and I were holding hands." Probably the only way to keep her from fleeing out the door. (Here's a tip, as useful in real life as it is in the Race: if everybody in the room tells you you've crossed the line, chances are you've crossed the line. See p. 265 "Colin on the Care and Feeding of Tanzanian Cabbies," too.) Both teams rush to the train station for their journey to Hanoi, holding tickets that will take them to Honolulu via a single stop in Japan.

By the time Team Albatross arrives at the same travel agency, there are no longer any remaining economy class tickets. And, yes, Flo threatens to quit again, telling Zach that if he can't get seats, he should just buy tickets to JFK (see p. 414 "The Smartest Moves Ever Made by Racers" for more details).

Making it to the beach in Hawaii, Flo greets the Brothers with, "Where did you guys go? Mickey D's?"

Ken asks, "Why?"

She moans, "I'm so hunnnngry."

And Ken speaks for viewers. "Oh, you gotta stop whining, already." Hee hee hee.

Teams take another flight to the island of Kauai, where the Detour offers them a choice between "Quick Jump" and "Slow Walk." The first requires Racers to share a 160-foot drop into water via a zip line; the other, to descend via the usual winding path. Flo is predictably pissed off about the jump. But this time she sees that there's no choice, grits her teeth, and slides down in Zach's arms, admitting afterward that the ride was "awesome."

On to the destination city, Seattle, Washington. A taxi race to Kerry Park leads teams to the route marker and instructions to travel on foot to the International Fountain at Seattle Center. It would be nice to report that Flo's fresh can-do attitude lasts, but then Zach makes the mistake of treating the Space Needle as a destination and not a nearby landmark. She shrieks, "You INSIST upon not being honest with me over whether you know where we're going!" Fun, fun, fun.

The Roadblock at Lincoln Park requires one team member to spin the animal faces on a totem pole, in the same order various animals appeared throughout the Race. (The correct order is donkey, dolphin, horse, goat, and manatee.) When Racers hit on the correct combination, the mouth at the bottom of the pole opens and reveals the final clue envelope, with instructions to proceed to Gasworks Park. One breakneck cab ride, and one heartfelt apology, later, the million dollars goes to the one team that came closest to breaking down.

1. Flo and Zach (Team Albatross) WIN
2. Teri and Ian (Team Grumpy) PLACE
3. Ken and Gerard (Team Oh, Brother) SHOW

It's Her Party, and She'll Cry if She Wants To

RACERS HAVE CRIED. RACERS HAVE screamed. Racers have whined. Racers have threatened to quit, and some actually have quit (more than one team, in fact, if you include the de facto surrender of Race 2's Team Cobbler). But nobody, in the history of the show, has ever fallen apart as completely, and as catastrophically, as Flo did during Race 3's stop in Vietnam. Her collapse was so total that only the superhuman patience of her Race partner Zach got her to the end of the leg.

None of this endeared her to fans. And it's not hard to see why. In a show populated by many whiny women, and a couple of even whinier men, she reached heights of whininess that affect the human ear about as beneficially as the average ice pick. She was so very memorable, in all the wrong ways, that when Chris, of the Race 4 team here dubbed the F-Bombs, mocked his lagging girlfriend Amanda by calling her "Flo," every viewer knew exactly what he was talking about. No Racer wants to act like Flo, even if some of them forget themselves and become Flo for short periods.[19]

But what, exactly, was up with Flo?

There's the rub.

The first major thing to remember here is that Zach did not drag Flo into the Race. She wanted to go. From all available accounts, she initiated the application process, and he went along only after *she* invited *him* to be her partner.[20]

This could not have been a blind decision on her part. Race 1's contestants had no idea what they were getting into, and were capable of being surprised by the gorge plunge required of contestants in the show's first leg, but by the time she filled out her application, the series was already a known quantity. Potential Racers already had some idea of the challenges they'd have to face, challenges that were likely to include things like rappeling down cliffs, fighting for plane reservations, enduring long hours on buses and trains, and sleeping in uncomfortable places. Flo, who, from the evidence on the air, may be any number of things but can never be accused of being outright stupid, had to understand that if she got on the show she would be facing these ordeals, as well.

The second big surprise, to longtime viewers who formed their overwhelming impression of the woman on the basis of her behavior during the second half of the Race, and who now watch that season again after the memories have been allowed to settle in concrete, is that for a while Flo actually seemed up to it. Check out the skydiving task in Mexico. It's startling, now, to think of Flo climbing a stepladder, let alone skydiving...but there she was, swallowing her clear terror to do what had to be done. She was not the one who freaked out in the air. That was Eve, of The Law Babes. Flo looked green, and was no doubt just as frightened as Eve, but steeled herself for the inevitable and got on with it. That's not the act of a coward, or a whiner. That's the act of a person who controls her fear...which is about as distant a description of the Flo we think we know from the Race as the English language could possibly produce.

---

[19] Temporary Flos include Race 6's Hayden, and several members of Race 8's Weaver family. But there have been males as well: witness Race 6's Hellboy and Race 7's Heckboy.

[20] Good move.

The third thing to remember is what else had she done by this point in the competition? Answer: along with her partner Zach, she had made it to the airport, booked her flight, landed in Mexico City, found Pablo, claimed a seat on the next morning's shuttle bus, and then enjoyed a restful night in a comfortable hotel. That's it. Seriously, people. If we've traveled at all, in our lives, we've endured more strenuous package tours than that. It's safe to say that when Flo hit this particular Detour, she had endured very little real stress, and little anxiety beyond the standard inner refrain of *can't be last, can't be last, can't be last.* The skydiving represented the first time she'd been asked to do anything hard, and she pulled it off with minimal whining. It's safe to say that this was the Flo Zach met at Vassar, and the Flo he thought he'd be racing with. And it's just as safe to say that when he wondered, in an interview, whether she might turn out to be a little too high-maintenance, he had no real idea of how much that worry would come back to haunt him.

Now contrast that Flo with the irritable and snappish Flo who punted in Cambridge only a couple of legs later. Or, better yet, with the shrieking, sobbing Flo who panicked during the rappeling task in Portugal. Though this was still early on, by Race chronology, this Flo had already missed meals, suffered sleepless nights, endured a number of long airplane rides, and tasted the Race as a difficult endurance test rather than a theoretical romp around the world. It does little good to say that many Racers endured the same challenges, for much longer, without losing their cool. That's entirely true, and it's very much one of the more mysterious phenomena visible on the show. The issue here is less what enables some people to endure than what makes other people break, less whether Flo should rappel than just what changed between Leg #1 and Leg #5. And the answer is Flo herself. The stress was getting to her. It was already deforming who she was, and changing her Race persona from who she wanted to be on this trip to who she was going to become.[21]

---

[21] It's worth noting, here, that only a few hours separated this incident from her team's serious car problems in Spain—and her very first whines to the effect that it was useless even trying and that they might as well quit. It's also worth noting that when a mechanic succeeded in fixing the problem, she bounced out of her funk a lot more quickly than she would have later in the Race. It's certainly a landmark, marking another way station in her descent into the abyss. But it's not the bottom floor. And her quick recovery is enough to establish just where she was in the degenerative process that was taking place.

The rest of the legs leading up to Flo's colossal freak-out in Vietnam provide successive snapshots of a Racer in the process of unraveling. She became whinier, of course—witness, for instance, her attitude as Zach searched for a cheap hotel room in Munich (Leg #7), her emotional outbursts when she thought her team had lost in Lake Geneva (Leg #9), and yet another sobbing fit as the Race entered Vietnam (Leg #11). Giving her all due credit, Flo didn't leave the Race without recognizing that all of this made her a pain in the ass, but the question remains: what kind of pain in the ass? And the answer is: one who was progressively worse as the Race went on. If you want another example, contrast the Flo from Marrakech (Leg #6), who had a great time selling escargot in one open-air market, with the Flo who wailed and begged and seemed nothing but frantic as she tried to sell baskets of fruit in another (Leg #11). But for the particulars, these were nearly identical challenges. But the earlier Flo performed the task with a smile on her face, and the latter Flo kept snapping with anxiety and irritation.

Once again, they're barely even recognizable as the same woman. That latter Flo described herself as "emotionally and physically exhausted. Wet and cold and miserable." It's far from helpful to snap that she was in the same boat as everybody else, and that other Racers had been and remained cheerful from the first "Go!" the very last leg. The more relevant point is that Flo was the only person inside her own skin. She was the only person who could feel how hard this was all hitting her. And subsequent events proved that her self-diagnosis was as accurate as anybody could ever expect.

We now face Flo's worst hour, which was simultaneously Zach's greatest: simultaneously some of the most regrettable behavior we'd ever seen from a Racer, and some of the best.

As the twelfth leg began, the first thing we noticed was a serious, and I mean serious, further step in Flo's deterioration. She must have had one hell of a bad night, after everything else she'd been through, because the girl was dragging. As she put it, in an interview, her body was crying out for food and sleep. She didn't even *look* good anymore. Her face was slack, and her eyes were bleary. Almost at the onset, she said, "I wish we'd been eliminated."

Zach, who showed signs of being thoroughly fed up with her last leg, now tried to cheer her up. "Come on, Flo, be happy about it."

"I'm done being happy about it," she muttered. "This is misery."

She continued to drop anchor at the train station in Ho Chi Minh City, where teams had to book a train to the city of Hue. That was a twenty-four-hour ride. Flo wouldn't even consider it. She said, "I'm not doing this. I'm not."

Why not, asked Zach.

"Because it's torture...twenty-four hours on a non-air-conditioned train? You're out of your mind."

He pointed out that they didn't know the train wasn't air-conditioned.

She said, "I don't even *want* to do it, so let's just forget it." This came off as highly unattractive petulance, to say the least, but her next major speech made the stakes as clear as they could possibly be. "I'm gonna have a breakdown on this train. Do you want to watch it happen? I'm sorry, Zach, I just don't want to do this anymore."

Most Race viewers took all this as just another annoying tantrum from a woman who'd been acting like a spoiled brat, but let's take another look at what she said: she was tired, she was miserable, she was suffering, and she thought she was going to have a breakdown on the train. What if she was not merely acting like a drama queen? What if she meant the words literally? What if she felt how frayed she was and knew a breakdown to be a very real possibility?[22]

In any event, Flo did manage to catch some sleep at the train station. Everybody noticed that something was happening to her. Gerard asked Zach, "Is everything all right?" And a frazzled Zach, betraying the tension he had not allowed himself to show his teammate that day, responded with a grim, "Define all right."

Even grimmer irony ensued as handling Flo prevented Zach from booking passage until all the sleeper cabins were taken. As a result, Flo had to endure the next twenty-four hours in a hard train seat. This

---

[22] I am not a medical professional, and am not qualified to use that word in any clinical sense. Neither is Flo. But it is the word she used before she hit bottom, and the word she uses in retrospect. With the proviso that the term carries no medical weight, it seems a reasonable self-diagnosis. And people present at the time seem to agree. I can't be sure what was in Ian's mind, but when he observed, "I think Flo's having a major . . . incident," the hesitation seems easy to peg as a moment of disconnect between the first word that came to mind and the word he decided he'd better use instead.

was a major blow. It's quite possible that, had Flo been able to lie on a soft mattress for the next eight or twelve hours, and sleep off whatever the hell she was going through then, she would have arrived at Hue relatively refreshed, and the rest of the leg would have played out quite differently. Instead, she suffered a "horrible night," and woke up still looking like hell. By her own admission, she felt "trapped." Again—and I honestly cannot repeat this enough—many Race fans hated her by this point, reading all of her complaints as the rantings of a self-pitying drama queen. But it's all too easy to sit at home, with our fat asses firmly planted on our sofas, and ignore what we're really seeing, while simultaneously forgetting that we've been through it ourselves.[23]

We moved on to the taxi ride to Hue's Imperial Palace. Flo looked drawn, sick, and despairing that the whole merry-go-round was starting up again. She said she was sick and wanted to throw up. She only barely went along with the search for the clue box, promising, "I'm not gonna get involved, but how do you know this is the right way?" She snapped at Ian, complaining that there was "no point" in running.

She fortunately got a little sleep in the subsequent cab to Nam O, Da Nang, but not enough to prepare her for the leg's Roadblock, "Basket Boats" or "Basket Bikes." The first involved paddling boats that resembled teacups to a clue box on a small island across the river. Flo, who admitted in an interview that her brain had "shut down" by this point, had reached a state of total helplessness, and could not or would not apply herself enough to master the unfamiliar vessels. She moaned, "Let me hold on to your boat. You know I can't get there by myself...you need to help me. I can't do it." Before long she was sobbing and weeping again. She cried, "I can't . . ." and vowed, "I want out of this game."

---

[23] Another travel tale from personal experience: A few years ago, my future wife and I flew cross-country, from Miami to Los Angeles, so I could introduce her to my future best man and his wife. Between the rigors of travel and a very early flight, I had slept maybe two hours in the previous forty-eight. I arrived exhausted and jet-lagged, didn't sleep the rest of that day, and had trouble keeping my eyes open as our hosts took us to the Magic Castle, a private club for magicians I'd wanted to visit for thirty years. Sitting mere feet from one sleight-of-hand artist giving what I can only describe as a brilliant performance, my greatest concern was not insulting the man by falling asleep in front of him. I'm not entirely sure I managed it. By the time we left, I was not fully coherent. And that's just after one rough night. If you're like most people, you have similar stories. Now multiply that jet lag by a couple of dozen flights, that one night of limited sleep by weeks, that feeling of imminent collapse by however much worse Flo had it, at the time...and put a million dollars on me getting up and doing something difficult, at right that very moment. I might have been as indefatigable as Colin, Reichen, either Chip, or any of the Smileys...or I might have whined as badly as Flo.

It got worse as an error in navigation took the team to the wrong island. She curled into a little ball of misery and said again that she wanted to quit.

There's no doubt: she wasn't putting this on. She was fragile as hell right then. And yes, it was damn difficult to watch. Annoying, even. But is there any real doubt that Flo's collapse is somewhat more extreme than anything we've seen on the show, before or since? Race 1's Amie had crying jags like this and didn't become infamous. Race 1's Emily had emotional lows like this and didn't become infamous. Race 2's Peach broke down like this and didn't become infamous. Race 8's Weaver family had entire legs like this, and—well, there the argument falters. But Flo became infamous. Is it because she was a bigger bitch than anybody in the history of the show? Or because what was happening to her was harder to watch?

In any event, Zach deserves a medal for what happened next. They were back where they'd started, having failed miserably at the boat task. She didn't even want to talk to him at that moment. But he talked slowly and calmly. "If you're gonna quit the game, we should at least talk about it, because I don't think you should just throw the game. We should talk about it, because it's my game too. Why don't we just walk over to the bikes and see if that's any easier. If we quit we're out of the game for sure. . . . If we come in seven hours later, we can still cross the finish line and have a good Race." The show has rarely displayed a better, more tactful way of talking sense to a person who was, at that point, not ready to hear it. And so she agreed to move on, to "Basket Bikes."

Alas, that task was even tougher, even more frustrating at a point when she couldn't handle frustration. Suffice it to say she threw her second bicycle helmet of the game (the first one, of course, going into Lake Geneva), and again curled into a weeping ball, wanting nothing but escape.

Zach got them out of the situation by paying locals to paddle the boats for them. It stretched the rules, and debate still rages on whether he should have been permitted to do this, but he needed to do something. The remarkable thing is that he hadn't even raised his voice. He had shown his frustration in previous legs (notably earlier in Vietnam, when for a moment he seemed ready to quit himself) but had been nothing but gentle and understanding toward her today. How did he manage it? His on-screen interview may be a little inconsistent in its use of past and present tense, but is otherwise succinct. "I have no idea how I maintained cool during these situations. I don't know what's going on. But there has to be someone who remained stable. I just shower Flo with positive thoughts and hope something good comes out of it."

Flo looked even worse in the cab to the leg's Roadblock: she was red-eyed, red-nosed, and visibly nodding: she was literally having trouble keeping her head up. (If you need proof that her emotions reflected actual physical distress, this shot presented it.) But something happened during the relatively stress-free sanpan ride: she reacted to the relative peace of her surroundings and started to pull it together. Her mood lifted. She noted her "first smile of the day." Zach said he was "happy to see it." If his own mask slipped at all, it was during the subsequent cab ride to China Beach, when she clutched her soda and said, "The only thing keeping me sane is this Diet Coke, bringing back memories of real life." He didn't quite look at her when he said, "Good." And at that point, frankly, he could be forgiven.

There's no doubt that the Flo of Leg #12 was the most difficult partner any Racer has ever had to deal with, before or since. And it's debatable just how much we should blame her. After all, while it's true that everybody has a different breaking point, it's also true that many people do find the inner strength they need to exceed theirs. Taking the argument to its logical extreme, there's absolutely no doubt that what this Race's Ian experienced during the Vietnam War, and certainly what Race 7's Ron experienced in Iraq, were far tougher and far more painful, by many orders of magnitude, than anything Flo experienced here.

That said, there is a significant difference between the sobbing wreckage Flo was in Vietnam and the woman she was in the final leg. Oh, she was still fragile. She still threatened to quit, at least once. She still whined, multiple times. She still threw tantrums, multiple times. And she still bit Zach's head off for much of the final sprint through Seattle. None of this was a big surprise. After all, one would not expect anybody to recover from the quivering ball of jello she was, all the way to Wonder Woman, in the space of a couple of days. It was remarkable enough that the process had been reversed at all.

But she also did something she would not have done only a short time before. She participated in the zip line Detour, despite her terror of heights . . . and afterward admitted that she'd enjoyed herself.

And at the end of the Race, she did something even more important. She admitted that she'd been a colossal pain in the ass (see p. 420 "The Most Endearing Racer Moments").

Many fans were not willing to forgive her, by that point. They were too irritated that the prize money went to somebody they saw as patently useless.

And, yeah, that is annoying. Especially if you credit her for having any responsibility for her own actions. People have risen to tougher occasions.

That said, it's worth noting two more things.

One: if you listen to her, she and Zach are still speaking.

Two: knowing the opinion many fans have of her, Flo has shown up at several of the TARcon fan gatherings . . . and those who meet her there describe her as a genuine sweetie, with a real sense of humor about the appalling impression she left on-screen.

So, there are basically two ways of reading Flo's character arc. Keeping in mind that this is not a fictional construct but the edited experiences of a real woman living on this planet in our lifetime, those two arcs are:

A useless whining bitch treats her partner like dirt, pisses and moans, and allows herself to be dragged all over the world until she wins her share of a million-dollar prize she doesn't even come close to deserving.

Or,

A young woman goes on a long and difficult journey, finds out that she's not nearly as strong as she believed herself to be, suffers extreme mood swings exacerbated by stress, tries to get off the ride, ultimately cracks, and with her friend's patient support finds the hope and strength she needs to carry on. Afterward, she shows remarkable grace in victory despite a reputation that, for some, will always be stained by the things she said and did at her worst moments.

I don't know about you.

But I sure know what interpretation I prefer.

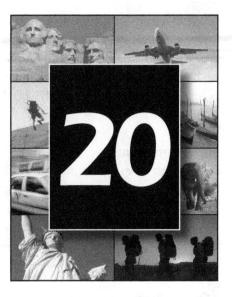

Moments We See
Again and Again
(Conclusion)

36. If You Only Heard

Producers encourage teams to talk about their "least favorite" competitors, a game that some players have resisted. At the same time, others have participated with gusto. Sometimes, teams don't need any special encouragement. And sometimes the feelings, whether better or worse, are not reciprocated. This leads to a favorite editing trick which contrasts Team A, on the road, talking about their vast affection for Team B and how "nice" they are, with Team B, "simultaneously" trash-talking Team A with all the rhetorical skills at their disposal. The message, that the Race encourages backstabbing behavior, is accurate enough, but not always as simultaneous as the editors like to pretend.

37. And Late Into the Night

This happens when the vagaries of luck or connection times separate teams by many, many hours. All the successful teams finish the leg in broad daylight, or even morning, and sad music starts to play as we fade to pitch darkness, when the last team arrives sweaty, exhausted, and aware that the jig is probably up. Usually the aftermath of disastrous navigation, it can be hard to take when it happens to a team you like, or a downright hoot when it happens to somebody you don't.

38. Threats to Give Up

Some players react to bad moments by, more or less, throwing up their arms and saying the hell with it, let's go home. The decision rarely sticks, but there's no doubting that the players mean what they're saying at the time. Among the Racers who declare finito at least once, sometimes to fatal effect: Paul (Team Puss, Race 1); Nancy (Team Oh, Mom, Race 1); Flo (Team Albatross, Race 3); Marshall (The Pizza Brothers, Race 5[24]); and Adam (Team Hellboy, Race 6).

39. Crowded and Confusing Marketplaces

Americans are used to spacious, brightly lit indoor shopping malls, with name-brand stores and conveniently placed maps equipped with arrows that remind the weary shoppers where they are. *The Amazing Race* regularly sends its contestants into crowded and confusing marketplaces, which Phil often describes as "mazes," comprising hundreds of tiny, minimally marked alcoves at either side of streets that seem barely wide enough to walk in single-file. Often, players will have to comb these narrow avenues for one specific merchant, selling one specific item; sometimes, they have to manage this trick without so much as a simple address. Players have encountered crowded and confusing marketplaces on numerous continents, and have yet to run across a food court with an Orange Julius.

40. Our Big Buddy in the Sky

This one's a little sensitive, so I'll do my best to be politically correct here. There's nothing wrong with praying for guidance, or strength, or patience, or understanding. There's nothing wrong with being bolstered by your faith, especially in an endeavor as fraught with stress as *The Amazing Race*.

---

[24] I'm referring to a few comments Marshall passed during the chocolate-eating task in South America, not his team's later decision to concede defeat in Africa. Their decision to stop, based on Marshall's knee injury and clear evidence that they had probably already lost, may have been controversial, and the only clear-cut surrender in Race history (there having been a couple of debatable ones), but you can't call it a tantrum or a snit. They had good reason.

Far from it. That's all admirable. But saying that God wants you in the Race, or that He's responsible for every stroke of luck you experience, is a little more questionable, and any comments to the effect that He supports your team over another are arrogant in the extreme. Whatever else you can say about the Supreme Being, it's a bit much to believe He cares much about the results of reality television. Were He really proactive about such things, then all the entrants who invoke Him during their *American Idol* auditions would be able to carry a note. They aren't. So He's not. Besides, if I really credited God for (picking one example at random) helping Brandon and Nicole in the mud pit, I would also have to credit Him for any bad luck that's afflicted other teams. And I really find it hard to picture Him sitting up there in His Heaven, snickering for hours and hours while Lena and Kristy dealt with those hay bales. Because that, Lord, was just plain mean.

41. Racers Congratulating Themselves on Their Own Moral Superiority

As with the rest of us, in our own everyday lives, Racers are the stars of their own personal movies, seeing their own wants and needs and mo-tivations and making their judgments of others based on what may be only fragmentary knowledge. Sometimes this leads to Racers talking about the high moral principles they bring to the Race while condemn-ing the actions of other Racers, often just as admirable, who have the temerity to play as if they want to win. Any careful observation of the Race reveals several serious disputes that start only because one team attributes open malice to the, at worst, unthinking actions of another. Even in the pressure-cooker environment of the Race, some of these fights could have been avoided if only an omniscient observer capable of seeing both sides (like a producer) sat down both teams and caught them up on the he-said, she-said. (Not that the producer would want to.) What we get instead is the frequent spectacle of teams presenting themselves as paragons of virtue surrounded by foul villainy, even in cases where the offense is merely playing the game to win.[25]

42. Grown Men Weeping with Love for Their Wonderful Ladies

This particular tradition is more common with older Racers, who may have forgotten the core of strength in the ladies they fell in love with,

---

[25] See, for instance, the moral revulsion Colin and Christie and Brandon and Nicole shower on Chip and Kim, for the horrid crime of playing within the rules, in Race 5, Legs #11–12 (pp. 258–261).

way back when. They see their sweeties pushing themselves to their limits, and lose it. Among the folks this happens to: Russell of Race 2's Pastors, interviewed after elimination at the leg where Cyndi braved the terrors of the bat cave; Don of Race 6's Team Spry, unable to believe Mary Jean's endurance hauling salt from Senegal's Pink Lake; and Uchenna of Race 7's Team Enron, suffering the husbandly torments of the damned as Joyce sacrifices her hair to the cause. Folks who like to include *The Amazing Race* in the truism that reality TV celebrates only the worst of the human spirit have to ignore such moments to make their thesis fly. Prone to such moments myself, I've been known to weep with empathy. And I'm not about to make fun of it.

43. Women Weeping Because They Can

Ladies, on the other hand, don't face the same cultural imperatives against tears, and will often weep just because that's how they're wired. It can be a sign of weakness: the actual indication that a Racer has had all she can stand (see Race 2's Peach and Race 3's Flo). But often, on the show as in life, it's just something they have to get past before they're ready to fight again. Big criers include Race 1's Amie and Race 8's Christine Godlewski.

44. The Most Important Leg Ever

Being on *The Amazing Race* breeds a certain kind of unavoidable tunnel vision, where catching the next subway, or hopping aboard the next tuk-tuk, seems the most critical moment you have faced so far. Certainly there have been a number of moments where Racers turned toward the camera and solemnly described whatever was about to happen as the single most important moment of the Race. And such moments don't all happen in the last leg. The Expensive Cup of Tea happened to be one. And the Yielding of Colin and Christie was another. But the Race hinges on so many unpredictable travel connections, so many bunching points, and so many twists of fate that there's no real way for players to tell for sure. The same teams who excitedly announce the crossing of the Rubicon are often the very same teams who get lost in marketplaces one leg later. The urge to invest random left turns as the most important moment ever is most absurd in the early legs, when teams who snag a half-hour lead feel confident enough to declare the Race as a whole all but won. Seriously, how can they think that?

45. Will They **Ever** Leave?

This is the opposite of the Sacrificial Lamb: the horrifically annoying team that stymies fans by refusing to go down, leg after leg. Fans tend to get worked up, rooting against them, often bemoaning that the abrasive but tenacious Racers have "ruined our show." This is, after all, the primary function of a good villain, whether genuine or created by editing, but it's such a pervasive event that it becomes a character all by itself. It becomes especially dramatic in the final leg, when the finalists include two teams, one of which is likeable or at least acceptable as the winner, and one that viewers fervently don't want handed a check for a million dollars. And it becomes even more dramatic when grudges enter the game play. In Race 8, some members of the Linzes echoed the sentiments of a large number of viewers, when they said they would be happy if the winners were "anybody but the Weavers."

46. Alpha Males versus Beta Ladies

This is less an often-observed scene than a Race trend. Teams composed of strong, athletic guys tend to last the longest, and are most likely to make it into the final three. Teams composed of women tend to fall early. Now, there are exceptions to both halves of the rule. Certainly, Tian and Jaree made it a long way, as did Kami and Karli. But so far (as of Race 8), no all-female team has ever made it into the final three. Not one. Only two have even made it into the final four: The Bowling Moms, and the Godlewski sisters. This has been such a Race truism that it's reached the status of an itch. Where are the Amazons when you need them?

47. The Overconfidence Rule

With the exception of Rob and Brennan in the first Race, no team that won the first leg has ever won the Race. Kind of an object lesson in peaking early, ain't it?

48. Hellboy Threatening to Throw Himself Hither and Yon

And then we enter the realm of players who do the same thing so often that their own idiosyncrasies become Race mainstays. Hellboy, who on at least three occasions threatened to toss himself off bridges and conveyances, joined the ranks of the immortals.

Race 4,
Not the Usual Bunch
of Clowns

RACE 4 WAS THE LAST one where the late, lamented Fast Forward played a specific, ongoing strategic role. It was also one of the few without any obvious "villains." Chip and Reichen seemed to qualify, in the early running, but by the end they had taken such ribbing from their erstwhile friends The Mockingbirds that they stepped into the protagonist position. Not that any of this matters, really. It was a fun Race, marked by one of the gooiest and yet most triumphant Detour options in the show's history, and a final leg that saw one leading team make one of the most unfortunate navigation errors of all time.

DRAMATIS PERSONAE

1. The Adrenaline Junkies

Models Tian Kitchen, 30, and Jaree Poteet, 33. A team of strong, adventurous women, handicapped only by the ugly bickering that drives them apart at moments of extreme stress. (It gets woefully nasty in Amsterdam.)

2. The Air-Traffic Controllers

Self-described "old, fat, middle-aged guys who don't look like they can do much of anything," Dave Cottingham, 43, and Steve Meitz, 46, are an early source of concern among some players who believe that their profession will lend them an uncanny advantage booking reservations in airports. That assumption turns out to be flawed. Air-traffic controllers are good at guiding airplanes, not necessarily at booking tickets for them. The team survives as long as it does by timely use of the Fast Forward, and by critical errors on the part of a couple of stronger teams. Their biggest strength: their determination and their refusal to give up.

3. The Chippendales

Pilot Reichen Lehmkuhl, 28, and consultant Chip Arndt, 36. An athletic married couple from California. Their strengths are legion. Not a team to underestimate. Named by their fellow players, their major weakness is Korean food. **SEASON SUPERSTARS**

4. The Virgins

Millie Smith, 29, an environmental teacher at an aquarium, and self-employed Chuck Shankles, 28. Dating twelve years, and still not past that particular threshold. A consummate (sorry) team, most amusing when the slug line repeatedly identifies them as virgins on-screen. Millie's mole becomes the subject of much discussion from other teams. Greatest weakness: Millie's asthma, which kicks up at moments of stress and sleep deprivation.

5. Team Santini

Corrections officer Steve Cottingham, 47, and his 21-year-old son Josh Cottingham, a computer technician. Strengths: a certain ruthlessness.

Weaknesses: the stubborn Josh makes some awfully poor decisions, but it's not that which dooms them.

6. Team Gmunden

Another Russell and Cindy, this one is model-actor Russell Brown, 32, and Cindy Duck, 39, an investor. They're a solid if not wholly memorable team, who fall due to the kind of mistake than anybody could have made. Weaknesses: the letters E and N.

7. The NFL Wives

Monica Ambrose, 29, and Sheree Buchanan, 31, spouses of players on the Atlanta Falcons, get their own chance to compete, and do quite well, despite a certain weakness with navigation.

8. Team Strategic

Best friends David Dean, 32, who owns a marketing agency, and Jeff Strand, 37, a real estate broker, are one of this Race's absolute strongest teams, able in both athletic and cerebral challenges. Their fatal weakness: airports in Australia.

9. Team F-Bomb

Dating couple Amanda Adams, 25, a medical technician, and Chris Garry, 28, a graphic designer, earn their sobriquet in this book when so much of Amanda's early dialogue is bleeped.

10. The Mockingbirds

Engaged couple Kelly Parks, 30, a model, and Jon Corso, 28, are both type A personalities, and one of this Race's strongest, if most frequently bickering teams. We name them after Kelly's sometimes nasty wit, which most famously manifests in her enthusiasm for picking on Millie's mole—verbally, you understand, as the other thing would be just plain disgusting. A team to watch. **SEASON SUPERSTARS**

11. Team Doomed

Married parents Debra and Steve Carmody, 49 and 40, respectively, are another pair of self-described fat, middle-aged but pleasant people, who seem a little out of their depth from step one. Nobody's choice for front-runner, they hit the wall right away when required to deal with alpine elevations.

12. The Clowns

Yay, The Clowns! Jon Weiss, 40, a professional human cannonball (no, really), and Al Rios, 34, a clown on a cruise ship, initially irritated some viewers because of their constant mugging, which is easy to mistake for hogging the camera. Guess what: it's just who they are. They become one of the most likeable, and most even-tempered, teams in the show's history, earning points with their enthusiastic beeline for a great big pile of poo. **SEASON SUPERSTARS**

THE GAME PLAY

Leg #1: Don't Call Your Girlfriend Flo

Teams gathered in L.A.'s Dodgers Stadium receive $200 and instructions to fly to Milan, Italy, where they must search through the Galleria for charter bus tickets leaving at 2:00 A.M., 4:00 A.M., and 6:00 A.M., respectively. The tickets are hidden in various places around the mall. Once a team has opened a ticket, they may not exchange it for another. Obviously, teams that arrive here first, on the earliest plane from America, have a potential advantage in the scramble for best departure times, but that advantage is not ironclad, as the first three teams, The Mockingbirds, Team Gmunden, and The Clowns, all hastily claim seats on the middle bus.

It's a frigid night, so most teams want to find lodging at the Hotel Nuovo. Team Doomed dithers about the price, wanders off, and returns to find all the rooms taken. The Chippendales generously volunteer to share, rather than force the older couple into the streets. But Steve weeps about his error, and requires serious consolation from the missus.

The Virgins, Team F-Bomb, Team Santini, and The Air-Traffic Controllers depart at 2:00 A.M. Team Gmunden, The Mockingbirds, The Clowns, and The NFL Wives depart at 4:00 A.M. The remaining teams bring up the rear at 6:00 A.M.

The teams are unaware that they're headed into the frigid Dolomite Mountains, where they must make their way to the base of Cinque Torri, ride chairlifts to the top of the mountain, and find the route marker that provides this leg's Detour: "Search" or "Rescue." None of the twelve teams take "Search," which obliges teams to use a handheld locator beacon to search a 160-acre snow field for a signal emanating from under the snow. The signal leads to a key they can use to start up a snowmobile that can take them to their next clue. The task's main drawback: it might take forever. In "Rescue," teams must climb a slope, cross an alpine rescue bridge consisting of four steel cables, and ride a 250-foot zip line across a ravine.

The real challenge after "Rescue" turns out to be the grueling hike back to the chairlifts, where a clue box will send them to the Hotel Lajadira at the base of the Italian Alps. This exhausts almost everybody. (When Amanda of the F-Bombs falls behind, Chris calls her "Flo.") But the two most physically challenged teams run into the worst problems. Dave of The Air-Traffic Controllers hurts his knee so badly that Steve has to lead him out, one step at a time, at one point even using his own feet to carve stairs in the snow. It's a genuinely touching triumph of friendship and endurance. Team Doomed, which arrives on the last bus, among a group of younger and fitter teams, falls fatally behind.

The NFL Wives take the Fast Forward, a snowshoe hike up a steep hill, which doesn't seem to provide much of an advantage over the other options.

1. Millie and Chuck (The Virgins) 11:52 A.M. TIE
2. Steve and Josh (Team Santini) 11:52 A.M. TIE
3. Amanda and Chris (Team F-Bomb) 11:52 A.M. TIE
4. Monica and Sheree (The NFL Wives) 12:49 P.M.
5. Steve and Dave (The Air-Traffic Controllers) 1:05 P.M.
6. Kelly and Jon (The Mockingbirds) 1:16 P.M.
7. Jon and Al (The Clowns) 1:22 P.M.
8. Russell and Cindy (Team Gmunden) 1:44 P.M.
9. Reichen and Chip (The Chippendales) 2:29 P.M.
10. David and Jeff (Team Strategic) 3:08 P.M.
11. Tian and Jaree (The Adrenaline Junkies) 3:43 P.M.
12. Debra and Steve (Team Doomed) ELIMINATED

Leg #2: Venice on Seven Dollars a Day

Receiving seven dollars, teams are directed to snow-raft down the ski jump known as the Trampolino Olimpico, leading to a memorably reckless improvisation when Mockingbirds Kelly and Jon inadvertently make it to the top without their required inflatable raft. The fastest way to get to the bottom, where the rafts are, is to slide down on their butts. Kelly screeches in an "I-can't-believe-I'm-doing-this" way all the way down, while Steve and Dave, of The Air-Traffic Controllers, watch in aghast horror.

From there, teams must make their way to the Ponte della Guglia Bridge in Venice, starting at one of two possible train stations. There's an odd confrontation at the onset, outside the locked terminal of the Calalzo train station, when The Chippendales arrive late and seize the door handles to hijack first place in line. "It was a really childish thing to do," Reichen admits in a subsequent interview, "but I thought it would help." The silly tactic is revealed as even more pointless when a bus to the much preferable Alpi train station arrives, and everybody hops aboard.

All teams but The Mockingbirds and The Adrenaline Junkies, who arrive at the Calalzo station after this mini-drama is over, board the first train from Alpi. That train arrives in Venice at 8:18 A.M., giving its contingent first crack at this leg's Detour, which offers teams two different routes to the same plaza. In "Waterway," teams must navigate a gondola using only a map, and are prohibited from asking any locals for directions. In "Pathway," teams are allowed to ask locals for directions, but must travel confusing Venetian streets on foot. Both the arrival time in Venice and the completion time of this particular Detour turn out more or less irrelevant, as the next route marker leads teams to a party at the Palazzo da Mosto, not even set to begin until 5:00 P.M.

The Air-Traffic Controllers, who are already exhausted and achey, take the Fast Forward, an appearance with a local troupe performing a form of street theatre known as commedia dell'arte. It would have been interesting cross-cultural pollination for the American clowns to take that.

The Roadblock rewards pattern recognition, as teams search a dark, spooky party filled with masked revelers for the masks that match the photos they're provided at the door. Players who guess wrong must return outside to the back of the line. Some teams require several attempts to get it right. Those who make it face a footrace across town to the deck of the motor launch, Citta di Padova, where every team but the first arrives within a tight fifteen-minute spread.

1. Steve and Dave (The Air-Traffic Controllers) 2:45 P.M.
2. Reichen and Chip (The Chippendales) 5:20 P.M.
3. Kelly and Jon (The Mockingbirds) 5:21 P.M.
4. Tian and Jaree (The Adrenaline Junkies) 5:22 P.M.
5. David and Jeff (Team Strategic) 5:23 P.M.
6. Jon and Al (The Clowns) 5:24 P.M.
7. Russell and Cindy (Team Gmunden) 5:25 P.M.
8. Millie and Chuck (The Virgins) 5:26 P.M.
9. Steve and Josh (Team Santini) 5:27 P.M.
10. Monica and Sheree (The NFL Wives) 5:31 P.M.
11. Amanda and Chris (Team F-Bomb) ELIMINATED

Leg #3: Screwed by the Critical "-en"

Receiving $480, teams must travel by train approximately 300 miles to Vienna, Austria, where a marked path through the city sewers will lead to the next clue.

The strong lead enjoyed by The Air-Traffic Controllers gives them a great chance to catch an early train. They blow it by going to the Padua station, which has no convenient trains to Vienna. Two other teams are delayed by medical issues as Millie of The Virgins suffers a serious asthma attack and is attended by her fellow virgin Chuck and The Clowns.

But none of this matters much, as the earliest bunch of teams arrive in Vienna at 6:37 P.M., and the sewer task isn't available until 8:00 A.M. The result is a mega-bunch, tightening everybody together.

In the morning, teams emerging from the sewers must grab a horse-drawn carriage known as a fiacre, and ride six miles to Schonbrunn Palace. The tricky part here is the fiacres arrive in groups of three, thirty minutes apart, and the rules require teams to claim their seats by grabbing passes first. This provision allows attentive players an opportunity to evict those who merely hop on without looking. At 8:30 A.M., The Clowns evict The Chippendales, and The Adrenaline Junkies evict The Mockingbirds. The 9:00 A.M. dash for the second group of fiacres leads to a collision between Chip and Millie, and a bloody lip for Chip.

Detour: "Mozart" versus "Beethoven." In "Mozart," teams must carry a string bass six miles to Figarohaus, where Mozart wrote *The Marriage of Figaro*. The bass is heavy, but Figarohaus is a famous location, so finding it should be easy. In "Beethoven," teams must carry sheet music eleven miles to one of Beethoven's lesser-known residences.

The Mockingbirds take the sheet music and promptly demonstrate one of the chief dangers of calling your teammate stupid. Jon wants to make sure they're headed for the right place, asking, "What if there are a few places where Beethoven wrote music?" Kelly can't believe this: "What are you, stupid? How many Beethovens do you think there are?" He asks the right question; she leads the team to the wrong place. At least she admits it, afterward.

Teams completing either task must make their way to the base of the Donaturm, a 1,150-foot tower overlooking the Danube, where the Roadblock awaits. It's a 450-foot bungee jump, the single highest tower drop in all of Europe. Whee! When Steve of The Air-Traffic Controllers goes, Dave cracks, "It was like an eclipse. . . . Greenpeace called and said, would you please stop throwing whales from the tower." Gee, I like these guys.

Team Santini takes the Fast Forward, which requires teams to don formal attire and deliver a tray of champagne flutes across a ballroom filled with waltzing couples. Spillage ensues. But they complete the task and are able to take the first available train 185 miles to the the Pit Stop at the 400-year-old castle Seeschloss Orth in Gmunden, Austria.

The Air-Traffic Controllers know they're in last place again, and can only hope that somebody gets lost on the way to Gmunden. A helpful ticket agent obliges, by issuing Team Gmunden tickets for Gmund, instead. Whoops.

1. Steve and Josh (Team Santini) 2:57 P.M.
2. Monica and Sheree (The NFL Wives) 3:51 P.M.
3. Reichen and Chip (The Chippendales) 3:53 P.M.
4. Tian and Jaree (The Adrenaline Junkies) 3:57 P.M.
5. Millie and Chuck (The Virgins) 4:43 P.M.
6. Jon and Al (The Clowns) 4:47 P.M.
7. David and Jeff (Team Strategic) 4:57 P.M.
8. Kelly and Jon (The Mockingbirds) 5:00 P.M.
9. Steve and Dave (The Air-Traffic Controllers) 6:04 P.M.
10. Russell and Cindy (Team Gmunden) ELIMINATED

Leg #4: A Roadblock to a Better Orgasm

Receiving $444, teams must fly 800 miles to Paris, France, and from there make their way to the racetrack in the town of Le Mans.

A memorable feud begins as The Virgins, who believe the Munich airport more likely to have early flights, withhold this information from The Mockingbirds. Kelly says, "[Millie] is like one of those little cheerleaders in school. I used to throw spitballs in their hair when they were out there cheering. She's too happy."

The Chippendales have to get off the connecting flight in Frankfurt when they realize their seats are business class (a Race no-no). Getting another flight costs them an hour.

The Roadblock at Le Mans requires one team member to change all four tires of a race car, then ride one lap with a professional driver at the wheel. Kelly, who has made Jon promise to give her the next Roadblock, whatever it is, is not happy when it turns out to involve changing tires. Jon compares the Roadblock to a woman's orgasm: "They bitch about it, they're hard to come by, and when they finally get it, they're good for about a week." Now, that's the kind of quote you want your fiancée's parents to hear when they watch the show.

Teams completing this task must choose a marked car and drive 500 miles to the port of Marseilles, where the next clue awaits at the lighthouse on port number four. A 9:00 A.M. opening time virtually guarantees a mass bunching, though rancor ensues when teams arriving early are asked to line up by the side of the road, and attendants direct the late-arriving Chippendales and Adrenaline Junkies to the very front of the line. Every team gets upset at this. Steve of The Air-Traffic Controllers even channels his inner Corleone: "Hey, girls, check your tires when you pull out, because (oh, God) you never know what'll happen." Whoo.

The route marker at the lighthouse directs teams to drive ninety-three miles to a mountain range known as the Gorges du Blavet. The Chippendales drive to the wrong place and take an aimless, time-consuming walk in the woods before realizing their error. The Adrenaline Junkies fall behind and take the Fast Forward at the Musee des Tapisseries, which requires them to assemble the pieces of a mural depicting the Pit Stop at the Chateau des Alpilles.

Detour: "Ropes" or "Slopes." In "Ropes," teams rappel 230 feet down a cliff to a route marker at the cliff's base. In "Slopes," teams travel to the same route marker via a long, sloping path. "Ropes" is clearly the better choice, which is why every team ends up doing it. From there it's just a 150-mile drive to the last Pit Stop, at the Chateau des Alpilles, where quite a nasty little windstorm is starting to pick up. Though Kelly and Jon lose half an hour from bad directions, it's Team Santini that gets so lost on the way to the cliffs that they arrive at the Pit Stop in darkness. "I got what I wanted out of this [Race]," says Josh. Steve claps his son on the back and says, "I always had what I wanted."

1. Tian and Jaree (The Adrenaline Junkies) 2:26 P.M.
2. Jon and Al (The Clowns) 2:41 P.M. TIE
3. Millie and Chuck (The Virgins) 2:41 P.M. TIE
4. Monica and Sheree (The NFL Wives) 2:45 P.M.
5. Reichen and Chip (The Chippendales) 2:54 P.M.
6. David and Jeff (Team Strategic) 2:57 P.M.
7. Kelly and Jon (The Mockingbirds) 3:00 P.M.
8. Steve and Dave (The Air-Traffic Controllers) 4:19 P.M.
9. Steve and Josh (Team Santini) ELIMINATED

Leg #5: That's One Big Mound of Poo

Receiving ninety dollars, teams have to fly 1,000 miles to Amsterdam, Holland, where the next route marker awaits at the skinny white bridge known as the Magere Brug.

Team Strategic and The Air-Traffic Controllers take the biggest risk. Their itinerary connects in Paris, but at two different airports, requiring them to land at Orly, grab taxis, and reach Charles de Gaulle in less than thirty minutes. Bumper-to-bumper traffic between the two airports renders this impossible and obliges both teams to scramble for alternate passage that takes them to Amsterdam almost two hours after everybody else.

The clue at the bridge instructs teams to take a metal boat and travel by water to the Scheepvart Museum. Many teams get lost or confused navigating Amsterdam's waterways. Many bicker, though it's The Adrenaline Junkies that hit their snippiest, angriest low of the entire Race, fighting over the map and generally being nasty to each other. This only gets worse as the day wears on. (They get better in subsequent legs.)

We also hear the first of many usages of The Mockingbirds' nicknames for Millie and Chuck: "Millie the Mole" and "The Werewolf," respectively. Though Racers have often given each other nicknames, ranging from amusing to nasty, these particular sobriquets are fated to become especially prominent as the Race goes on.

The route marker in front of the museum offers a Detour: "500 Kilograms" or "15 Feet." In "500 Kilograms," teams drive thirty miles to an outdoor market, don wooden clogs, and use a traditional stretcher to load a scale with exactly 500 kilograms of cheese, no more, and no less. In "15 Feet," teams drive twelve miles to a ranch which processes cow manure for local farms, and find their next clue by searching a fifteen-foot-tall pile of cow manure with their bare hands.

The Clowns earn our respect for all time by excitedly shouting, "Manure!" at the very prospect, then enthusiastically flinging it at each other at the site, like the party animals they are. The Mockingbirds also go for poo, confront "poo quicksand," and exchange a pooey high five, before gagging in comic unison. The NFL Wives take poo as well, reasoning that it's just more of what they're used to dealing with in diapers. Among the teams who decide they'd rather not, The Chippendales have the best brain-fart moment when Reichen has to remind Chip how tall he is, and how small he'd be next to a fifteen-foot mound.

"500 Kilograms" emerges as a dull task by comparison, though it does take place in full view of many locals who enjoy laughing at the silly Americans.

The Virgins take the Fast Forward. Amusingly enough, given Millie's brand-new nickname, it turns out to be ten revolutions strapped to the sails of the Molen van Sloten Windmill in North Amsterdam. Once done, they proceed to the Pit Stop at Kasteel Muiderslot.

A final Roadblock requiring one Racer from each team to count and contain twenty-five live eels takes less time as the day wears on and the eels look less "live." Kelly asks Jon what they feel like. He responds, "a slippery penis." She immediately shows interest in touching one.

1. Millie and Chuck (The Virgins) 2:25 P.M.
2. Jon and Al (The Clowns) 3:15 P.M.
3. Kelly and Jon (The Mockingbirds) 3:34 P.M.
4. Reichen and Chip (The Chippendales) 4:26 P.M.

5. Monica and Sheree (The NFL Wives) 4:43 P.M.
6. David and Jeff (Team Strategic) 5:05 P.M.
7. Tian and Jaree (The Adrenaline Junkies) 5:42 P.M.
8. Steve and Dave (The Air-Traffic Controllers) ELIMINATED

Leg #6: Stinky Smelly

Receiving $110, teams must now fly 4,700 miles to Mumbai, India, and find gate number one at Bollywood's Film City. They don't know that the leg to come is among the most unpleasant of this Race. It's a good thing that The Adrenaline Junkies have recovered from their bickering of the last leg, and achieved a détente that they maintain almost without interruption for the rest of their time as a team. Pretty good for a pair that seemed about to come to blows.

The usual round of airport shuffle comes to naught, as everybody arrives between 10:55 P.M. and 11:30 P.M., and the film studio doesn't open until 9:30 A.M. So there's a mega-bunching as all Racers bed down outside the studio gates. On the way, many players are taken aback by the poverty and crowded conditions of Mumbai. Reichen and Millie are among those moved to tears. Chuck spots the biggest rat he's ever seen, scurrying across the city streets. In the morning, teams watch pigs rooting in garbage and barefoot children leaving a filthy shantytown on their way to school. Everybody seems just a little bit somber. But then it's time to race again.

A bike ride to Studio 10 leads Racers to a musical in production, and a Detour: "Suds" or "Duds." In "Suds," teams must find an outdoor Laundromat and wash one bundle of filthy, muddy and manure-encrusted clothing until the next clue emerges on the fabric. In "Duds," teams must locate a hard-to-find clothing shop (P. Amarlal) and search thousands of saris to find the one with their clue printed on it. As usual, the labor-intensive, and more unpleasant, task seems the faster choice.

In both cases, just getting there on India's intensely crowded trains is an ordeal. Boarding the already packed cars requires teams to physically force their bodies into the already sardine-like conditions. This is harder on the women. The usually confident Kelly gets claustrophobic under the press of bodies. The Adrenaline Junkies are fondled. Jaree cries. The NFL Wives, who don't even reach the train until after some of their competitors have completed the Detour up ahead, just grit their teeth in discomfort, and remain last for the rest of the leg.

The Virgins make the worst mistake, at "Suds." Instead of taking the bundle of clothes marked for Racers, Millie grabs a bundle of clean clothing completed by the Laundromat and dumps the contents into the filthy wash water. This is not taken well by the locals who actually had to clean these clothes for a living. Whoops.

Teams who complete either task proceed to the Sassoon Docks, where the route marker provides a Roadblock. One team member must enter a fish market, find one vendor who has compiled a huge pile of dead fish, and search that pile for twenty Palai fish, which must then be loaded into baskets and delivered to a market manager who will only provide the final clue upon being given twenty fish of the correct species. Some require several trips. Players who do "Suds" *and* this, after the crowded trains, are pretty ripe by the end of the day.

Team Strategic just barely beats The Chippendales in a footrace to the Pit Stop at the arch known as the Gateway of India.

1. David and Jeff (Team Strategic) 12:51 P.M.
2. Reichen and Chip (The Chippendales) 12:52 P.M.
3. Kelly and Jon (The Mockingbirds) 1:19 P.M.
4. Millie and Chuck (The Virgins) 1:34 P.M.
5. Tian and Jaree (The Adrenaline Junkies) 1:36 P.M.
6. Jon and Al (The Clowns) 1:37 P.M.
7. Monica and Sheree (The NFL Wives) ELIMINATED

Leg #7: Facedown in Odiferous Glop

Receiving seventy dollars, teams now face another mass bunching as they await the morning and a 860-mile train ride from Panvel to Ernakulam.

On the way to the train station, Tian and Jaree experience a harrowing brush with mortality as their cabbie races down the wrong side of the highway with his headlights off. This is not a good safety policy in any culture. Bad cabbie. *Bad* cabbie. *On* the paper!

The train itself is a major endurance test; the stench is described as next to unbearable, leading most teams to pay the additional sixteen dollars per person for seats in the stinks-slightly-less zone. Only The

Virgins decide to tough it out, a decision which leaves them safely out of earshot as The Mockingbirds entertain The Chippendales by riffing on Millie's mole. "Say it!" Kelly sings. "Moley-moley-moley-mole...." The Chippendales are scandalized and amused and no doubt happy that they haven't been targeted themselves. (For that, they're gonna have to wait a couple of legs.)

Later, as teams search for the billboard bearing their next clue, The Mockingbirds are scandalized themselves when they wave at The Virgins and The Virgins refuse to wave back. Jon can only wonder why, with a plaintive, "All I did was call her Moley-Moley-Moley-Moley-Mole." The ways of Virgins are mysterious, my son.

The billboard directs teams twenty-five miles to a sports field in Alleppey, site of the one of the most disgusting Roadblocks ever. Each participating player must lie down in a swamp composed of mud and other suspect substances, and hold on to a tow bar while being dragged through the glop by a bull. Every team notes the bulls continuously adding to this soup, if you know what I mean, and several teams note that it's almost impossible not to swallow some. Yuck, yuck, yuck. This bull-surfing is evidently a popular sport among the locals, who should be sent a supply of handheld video games immediately, as they've found at least one adventure sport that being a couch potato is significantly healthier than. Among the Racers who immerse themselves, kudos are most owed Tian, who loses her grip twice and has to perform the task three times before she's allowed to move on, looking adorably vile. Jaree tells Tian she looks "sexy as shit," a sentence that can be taken both ways and, in this context, should be.

The Detour is "Baskets" and "Trunks." In the first, teams load ten live chickens aboard a bicycle wagon, and drive it themselves to a farm that's circled on a map. In the second, they use an elephant to deliver two bales of fabric to another location. The Clowns know elephants, of course, so they take that option. So do most of the others, with only The Chippendales hitting the bicycles. It's worth noting, therefore, that several Racers find the pachyderm spine downright painful to the groin. Jon says he'd rather spend two hours being dragged through the bull poop than be on that elephant for another five minutes. And Kelly complains that her "cookie" is killing her. Every joke that comes to mind is X-rated.

For Racers who finish, it's just a short hop to the Pit Stop, appropriately enough at a place called the Finishing Point. In the end, it's a race between The Chippendales and The Adrenaline Junkies for last place.

1. David and Jeff (Team Strategic) 4:02 P.M.
2. Jon and Al (The Clowns) 4:06 P.M.
3. Kelly and Jon (The Mockingbirds) 4:16 P.M.
4. Millie and Chuck (The Virgins) 4:16 P.M.
5. Reichen and Chip (The Chippendales) 4:17 P.M.
6. Tian and Jaree (The Adrenaline Junkies) ELIMINATED

Leg #8: An Editor Cackles in Darkness

During the Pit Stop, Reichen and Chip out themselves to their competitors. The revelation could not have come as the greatest possible surprise to anybody who's been paying sufficient attention, but does not please The Virgins.

As long as everybody's sharing confidences, The Virgins tell their competitors (who have not had the benefit of on-screen labeling these past few weeks) that they've been dating twelve years and have not had sex yet. The Mockingbirds then take great pleasure in announcing that they're living in sin and had sex the very first week. Millie and Chuck are less than thrilled by this. Until Race 8, it's the ultimate Red State/ Blue State moment.

Teams receive $120 and instructions to head for Malaysia, which leads to a lovely game of airport shuffle involving the ethics of horning in on another team's action, the many irritations inherent in butting into a long line, closed doors, and risky, but potentially advantageous, flights connecting through Madras. The Chippendales actually leave the airport when a roaming travel agent horns in offering a better flight as long as they follow him to his office an hour's drive away. Now, that's a major risk. And even as The Clowns, The Virgins, The Mockingbirds, and Team Strategic all depart on an 8:30 A.M. flight that connects through Mumbai, The Chippendales are at the distant boarded-up travel agency discovering that their magic flight is all booked. But there is a direct flight, which might be even better.

There's even more intrigue in Singapore, where The Virgins spend the night searching for better flights even as The Mockingbirds merely curl up on the floor to catch some z's. So airport shuffle continues.

How does it all shake down? The Chippendales and Clowns and Virgins are first to Malaysia, where they receive a blessing at a "cultural village" and then move on to the Kota Kinabalu boat jetty, site, at last, of this epic leg's Detour. It's "Net" or "Trap." The first requires teams to use a pole net to snag fifteen fish from a pen. In "Trap," they have to haul a heavy lobster trap out of the water. The Virgins take "Net" and get up to eight before Millie spills 'em back into the water and has to start all over again. Even for folks who like the team, it's a perversely satisfying moment: like watching Laurel and Hardy try to put up a roof aerial.

Onward to Manukan Island, where the Roadblock requires the participating Racer from each team to prove proficiency hitting three different targets with three different traditional Malaysian weapons (a bow and arrow, a blowpipe, and a spear). Chuck of The Virgins has some of the worst trouble with this, leading Millie to note, I kid you not, "I was so scared he was going to get in that downward spiral, and not be able to perform." Later, as he tosses the spear, she cries, "It has to stick in, Chuck!" You kinda know there's at least one *Amazing Race* editor who's having entirely too much fun with this couple.

The Pit Stop is just a short jog down the beach, where the late-arriving Mockingbirds are saved by a non-elimination leg.

1. Jon and Al (The Clowns) 2:05 P.M. TIE
2. Reichen and Chip (The Chippendales) 2:05 P.M. TIE
3. Millie and Chuck (The Virgins) 2:19 P.M.
4. David and Jeff (Team Strategic) 2:50 P.M.
5. Kelly and Jon (The Mockingbirds) 3:36 P.M. NOT ELIMINATED

Leg #9: The Long Sleepless Night of The Virgins

Receiving $130, teams must travel seventy-eight miles to Poring Hot Springs and navigate a series of rope bridges 100 feet off the ground to reach their next route marker.

The 6:30 A.M. opening time creates a bunching that affects everybody but The Mockingbirds, who don't arrive until all the other teams are ready to leave. Kelly is not pleased when Jon, bursting from two cups of coffee, delays them further to water the bushes. "Are you *kidding* me?" she screeches. (She wants to run the leg, and he doesn't want it running down his leg, if you catch my drift.) They bleed even more time when they get lost on the grounds. It looks pretty final for them. But wait. The Virgins managed no sleep the night before and are so exhausted that both have trouble just staying awake. Maybe that will be enough.

With all the leading teams already driving 145 miles to the next route marker, The Mockingbirds realize that their only chance is to go for the Fast Forward, 140 miles away in Sepilok. It's the site of the Orang-utan Rehabilitation Center, home to the last wild orangutans in northern Borneo. Once there, the team will have to hike deep into the forest, find a feeding station, and hand-feed four pieces of fruit to these furry cousins of Dr. Zaius.

Unknown to The Mockingbirds, another team has headed for the Fast Forward by mistake. Rather than turn back, The Chippendales proceed, and find themselves unexpectedly moved as the gentle great apes approach and accept the fruit from their hands. It's a genuinely cool moment. But The Mockingbirds also endure that long drive only to discover that they're screwed. "That's it, babe," says Kelly. "We're out." Jon, frustrated beyond all endurance, tells her to do something anatomically impossible. But wait.

Elsewhere, the Trushidup Palm Oil Plantation hosts a Detour, "Chop" or "Haul." "Chop" requires teams to use long-poled blades to chop down palm nut bunches until they find one with a clue envelope attached. It's difficult, requires expert use of the blade, and every envelope with a clue is outnumbered by three empty ones. "Haul" requires teams to use numbered wheelbarrows to load correspondingly numbered trucks with twenty-five nut bunches, not receiving their clue until their truck rolls off the envelope. This task is difficult, too, as the trucks are already so full that the thorny, sticky nut bunches have a tendency to roll off the trucks when tossed. The Clowns finish "Haul" first. Team Strategic has trouble just finding the clue envelope. The logy Virgins get lost on the way and are so frustrated (sorry) by both tasks that they give up on "Haul," switch to "Chop," then return to "Haul." The Mockingbirds, arriving long after everyone has left, stand next to the truck marked "5" and argue about which truck it is. Looks bad for them. But wait.

A final Roadblock at the Gomantong Caves requires one team member to climb a crude rattan ladder and retrieve a clue envelope fifty feet above the cave floor. Despite a substantial lead over The Mockingbirds, the exhausted Virgins squander their advantage and become the least likely team ever to go down from sleep deprivation.

1. Chip and Reichen (The Chippendales) 10:26 A.M.
2. Jon and Al (The Clowns) 12:56 P.M.
3. David and Jeff (Team Strategic) 1:11 P.M.
4. Kelly and Jon (The Mockingbirds) 2:42 P.M.
5. Millie and Chuck (The Virgins) ELIMINATED

Leg #10: Squirming, Resentful Spaghetti

Receiving $400 and completing a minor task at a Buddhist temple, teams receive instructions to travel 4,000 miles to Seoul, South Korea, where the next route marker awaits at the base of the Seoul Tower.

Arriving first, Team Strategic and The Clowns discover that the next task requires a three-hour taxi ride to the Sundam Valley. Both teams decide to squeeze into one cab. As a result, they share the pants-wetting moment when their cabbie takes them over "the bridge we're not supposed to cross," into the Demilitarized Zone separating North and South Korea. Yow.

The Roadblock takes place at a frozen river, and requires one player to jump through a hole in the ice, swim along a guide wire against river current, and emerge upstream. Even if that player completes the task quickly, he will not be certified to receive his clue and leave with his partner until his body temperature returns to normal and a doctor certifies him healthy enough to leave. There are divers stationed under the ice, in case the swimmers run into trouble, and a bank of heaters to warm the successful participants up as soon as possible, but this is still a formidable, punishing, and frightening task, not for the timid. Al speaks for everybody when he moans, "I don't wanna do this...." And then he does it anyway.

Teams that complete this return to Seoul and search for a route marker on subway station 228 (Seoul University). Traffic back into the city is so horrendous that several teams hop from their taxis to proceed the rest of the way by train. It's a costly decision for some, including Team Strategic, which is directed to the wrong line by a local woman who insists, "I'm right." Meanwhile, The Mockingbirds bicker over strategy, leading Kelly to tell Jon, "I want you to lose, just to prove that assholes never win. And lucky me, I'm engaged to the asshole. Yay."

The Detour is "Strong Hands" or "Strong Stomach." In "Strong Hands," teams find a local martial-arts center, where, after a few minutes of instruction, each team member must use Tae Kwan Do to shatter three sets of wooden planks. "Strong Stomach" sends teams to a local restaurant where they must eat a bowl of a Korean delicacy that, they don't discover until they get there, is live octopus. (Even chopped up for easier eating, the pieces continue moving on the plate and inside the diner's mouth.) When The Chippendales go for this latter option, Reichen looks like a deer caught in headlights. In a voice-over recorded later, Chip captures what the experience was like. "[With] the first octopus I put in my mouth, I tried to swallow the head of it, but by that time its tentacles had all attached themselves to my teeth, so I had this web of octopus in my throat." Imagine squirming, resentful spaghetti. Reichen asks the proprietor if he's allowed to throw up. (Given the choice, she demurs.) Chip saves the day by remembering how they got through the oyster shooters at their wedding. Arriving later, Team Strategic takes one look at the plate and decides to go for "Strong Hands" instead. Meanwhile, across town, Kelly injures her knuckles on the planks, and manages the last set only by channeling her irritation at Jon.

It all comes down to a final cab ride to the Pit Stop at Gyeongbok-gung[26] Palace, where one team is saved by non-elimination.

1. Kelly and Jon (The Mockingbirds) 3:46 P.M.
2. Reichen and Chip (The Chippendales) 3:55 P.M.
3. Jon and Al (The Clowns) 4:04 P.M.
4. David and Jeff (Team Strategic) NOT ELIMINATED

Leg #11: Send Home the Clowns

Teams make their way to Hanggang Park, on Yeouido Island, where tugging on kite strings makes clues fall from the sky. (Not all the time, just today.) Said clues advise teams to travel 7,000 miles to Brisbane, Australia, where the next route marker awaits at a hotel penthouse.

Every team wants to get to Singapore as early as possible, so they can arrange the best connecting flight to Brisbane. The Singapore Airlines flight carrying three teams leaves promptly at 2:00 P.M. Alas, The

---

[26] Gesundheit.

Clowns have booked passage on a Korean Air flight which is delayed by two hours. An eleventh-hour attempt to book seats on the same flight as the others fails, leaving The Clowns in serious trouble. "I can feel the blood going right to my head," stresses Jon, as he paces through the airport wearing his clown nose. The team does manage to find a direct flight to Brisbane that might well get them to Australia in time, but this is still going to be close.

First out of the Brisbane Airport, Team Strategic goes for the Fast Forward, which involves traveling one hour to a nearby beach, boarding surfboards, and paddling through heavy surf to "rescue" a "drowning" swimmer. The task is harder than it sounds, as the lady in question plays "limp" quite well, and offers the pair no help loading her aboard the surfboard. But the team completes the task and receives authorization to proceed to the Pit Stop at the Mooloolaba Yacht Club.

The Detour at the penthouse is "Face First" or "Feet First." "Face First" requires Racers to don safety gear and perform an Australian, or face-first, rappel straight down the 200-foot building. In "Feet First," teams scan the skyline for another building bearing the *Amazing Race* flag, travel down the stairs, run through the streets of Brisbane, and climb thirty stories to find the next route marker. Nobody takes "Feet First," a sure path to elimination.

The Clowns land in Brisbane just as The Chippendales and The Mockingbirds begin suiting up for this task. Kelly is worried about the descent, as her injury from the last leg is still preventing her from making a fist. Jon cries up at her: "You're letting that gay guy beat you!" which makes the still-descending Reichen snap, "Jon, you're such an ass!" Kelly shrieks and hyperventilates, but eventually makes it. Both teams reach the bottom minutes apart, receiving instructions to pick a marked car and drive forty-three miles to a public aquarium called the Underwater World, in Mooloolaba. The Clowns, arriving at the penthouse not long after The Chippendales and Mockingbirds have left, descend quickly despite Al's acrophobia, and move on, still making up lost time. But will it be enough?

The Roadblock task at Underwater World requires one team member to don scuba gear and walk through the shark tank, giving the toothy predators right of way. The final clue envelope lies in a chest on the tank bottom. But the critical factor of this penultimate leg turns out to be the final instruction of the leg, which requires teams to walk to the Yacht Club a kilometer away. The Chippendales misread the clue and drive instead, receiving a thirty-five-minute penalty that comes damn close to allowing The Clowns to catch up. Another fifteen minutes would have done it. But at least the other teams have stuck around to say good-bye.

1. David and Jeff (Team Strategic) 10:41 A.M.
2. Kelly and Jon (The Mockingbirds) 10:59 A.M.
3. Reichen and Chip (The Chippendales) 11:33 A.M.
4. Jon and Al (The Clowns) ELIMINATED

Leg #12: Mishap Central

With the final three already decided, two legs still left to go, and no penalty for coming in last during a non-elimination leg, the results are a foregone conclusion at minute one. We know that the three teams that start will be back next time, their positions somewhat shuffled, but their chances in the final leg still more or less what they are now. Suspense is therefore minimal, except for one tense moment at the midpoint.

Deprived of The Virgins, Kelly and Jon have now firmly established their former moley-mates, The Chippendales, as their current designated targets of mockery. Much is made of The Chippendales' gayness, their preference for sweaters, and their alleged affinity for sheep.

Teams that have been frugal up until now are rewarded, as any leftover funds can now be added to the single dollar they receive for this leg of the Race. Don't spend it all in one place, guys.

A search through giant piles of raw wool at Ferny Hills provides the first bunching, as the facility doesn't open until 6:00 A.M. The second bunching occurs after the clue envelopes buried in the wool advise Racers to return to Brisbane Airport and fly 1,000 miles to Cairns, where their next task awaits at the Wild World Zoo. The bunching continues as everybody makes a 7:45 A.M. flight and continues on the road, with Racers only a few car lengths apart. A task requiring one team member to feed the zoo's fifteen-foot crocodile, while the other takes pictures of the experience (thus providing yet another too-obvious plug for Kodak), offers some tension when Kelly forgets to obtain a camera, but it doesn't separate the teams in any definitive way.

Neither does the subsequent Detour at Wangetti Beach, "Saddle" or "Paddle." "Saddle" requires teams to search for clues on horseback, and "Paddle" sends teams into the surf by inflatable kayak. Though The Mockingbirds overshoot the beach entirely, and The Chippendales begin by searching in the wrong direction, competition remains tight, even as teams receive instructions to move on to an off-roading Roadblock thirty-five miles away. We are still waiting for the critical error, and Chip running over Reichen's foot with the SUV is not it. Though we're sure it hurts.

The Mockingbirds have their worst moment of the Race at the off-road challenge, when Jon flips his buggy and Kelly panics, certain that he's dead. He emerges laughing, and her fear predictably turns to anger. Ever romantic, she screams, "I need you to win the million bucks!"

All in all, it's been a pretty bad day for mistakes. "We cannot have children," Kelly concludes, upon reaching the Pit Stop at Ellis Beach. "We would not want them to inherit our stupidity."

1. David and Jeff (Team Strategic) 1:47 P.M.
2. Reichen and Chip (The Chippendales) 2:14 P.M.
3. Kelly and Jon (The Mockingbirds) 2:38 P.M. NOT ELIMINATED

Leg #13: Look Before You Fly

Receiving only one dollar, teams are bunched by another 6:00 A.M. opening time, this one at the Tjapukai Aboriginal Cultural Park, where they need to watch a native fire ceremony in order to receive their next clue.

Aggressive, motivated driving during the subsequent fifteen-mile road race to Cairns Airport's General Aviation Terminal gets scary as The Chippendales lose control on wet pavement and skid off the road. Luckily, the car doesn't roll and they can get back on the road, unhurt. "We can't do that again," says Reichen. "Nope," says Chip.

The General Aviation Terminal offers an obvious Detour: "Wing It" or "Wander It." In "Wing It," teams tandem-skydive, with their instructors, to the next clue. In "Wander It," teams must drive to a nearby mangrove forest and use boats to find their way out. Nobody is stupid enough to get bogged down in "Wander It." Besides, says the still-shaken Reichen, as the plane reaches the desired altitude, "[It's safer here than] in the back of the car, when Chip is driving." That's perspective for you.

Teams now receive directions to fly 4,700 miles to the "Big Island" of Hawaii, hop into marked cars, and drive themselves to Kaulana Bay, the southernmost point in the United States.

Sydney offers direct flights there. But there are no direct flights out of Sydney until the next day. The Chippendales and The Mockingbirds choose a more roundabout itinerary, connecting through Tokyo. Team Strategic flies to Sydney, booking no further flights beforehand, in the hopes that Sydney's status as a major hub will offer better options. It doesn't. By the time they land, all the useful flights have left. Hours of research at the airport fail to uncover any workable alternatives connecting anywhere in Asia.

Things look just as bad for The Mockingbirds, in Tokyo, when an erroneous dash to the wrong terminal causes them to miss the vital connection by minutes. They are left behind even as The Chippendales take off. The Chippendales enjoy a nice stress-free flight, rendered even nicer when their economy tickets somehow land them in first class. So they stretch out and order champagne.

Jon cheers Kelly up by hoping The Chippendales suffer diarrhea on the plane.

The Chippendales arrive in Hawaii, happy to be ahead of The Mockingbirds but worried about the whereabouts of Team Strategic. (We get an update: they're still in Sydney Airport. Gaaah.) Traffic slows their drive to Kaulana Bay, where a Roadblock requires Chip to swim out into the surf, retrieve a painted stone in the reef, then bring it back to shore and chisel out the clue. That sends them sixty miles to another route marker at Hawaii Volcanoes National Park.

Meanwhile, The Mockingbirds arrive in Hawaii. Kelly euphemistically "can't swim with the sharks today," so Jon takes the Roadblock. Intent on keeping his underwear dry, he chooses to perform the task naked, thus giving the censors something to blur.

The clue at the lava field directs The Chippendales and The Mockingbirds to fly 2,900 miles to Phoenix. They'll find their next clue at a monument bearing the anchor of the *Arizona*. Both teams meet up at the connection point in Honolulu, but by that point The Chippendales have had time to question their fellow passengers and obtain reliable directions. Upon reaching Phoenix, The Chippendales are first to the taxis, first to the route marker at the anchor, first to Sun Devil Stadium, first to complete the logic puzzle that leads to section 214, row 33, seat 11, first to follow the clue found there to Papago Park, first aboard the mountain bikes, first down the bike path, and first to reach the finish line, with The Mockingbirds consistently only minutes behind.

Farther behind than any finalists since the Guidos, Team Strategic gets the news at the lava field in Hawaii. They're only the second pair of finalists, in the entire history of the Race, to be removed from the field out of producer mercy. That was one baaaaaad move in Cairns.

1. Reichen and Chip (The Chippendales) WIN
2. Kelly and Jon (The Mockingbirds) PLACE
3. David and Jeff (Team Strategic) INCOMPLETE

Fixing the Race

ERE'S ONE UNIVERSAL RULE: ANYTHING popular enough to attract a legion of fans also invites criticism that it ain't as good as it used to be. The folks who discover it first delight in telling newbies that it was ten times better in the days of yore, when they were the only folks paying attention to it. Name a Broadway musical, a rock group, a writer, or even a reality TV show that you discovered just now, and somebody will regard you with superior, knowing pity and say, "Yeah. Too bad you weren't around at the beginning."

The Amazing Race is no exception. Many fans have been vocally upset with everything that's happened since its first Race. They considered the show "ruined forever" when the cryptic clues were scaled back in Race 2, when the Yield was introduced in Race 5, when everybody started screaming at each other in Race 6, and when a much-simplified competition suitable for children was scheduled for Race 8. Somehow, every incarnation becomes the apocalypse. Somehow, the fans are still around by the time the next Race comes along, this time bringing friends they want to introduce to this show that sucks so much now.

To be perfectly clear about this: unlike a certain ox, the Race is not broken. At its very worst, it still provides more thrills and laughter and moments of occasional beauty than any other reality show on the air. But it can still be tinkered with a little. Below, this book's prescriptions:

1. More Third-World Destinations

The show is best when it sends competitors to exotic locales, far from familiar comforts, less impressive when it sends them to locales that seem just down the block from Disneyland. Many Racers have reacted to the conditions they found in impoverished places with astonishment, horror, or revulsion, thus establishing that exposure to such conditions can be as clear a character-defining moment as any number of rock-climbing or cliff-rappeling challenges. A little more historical context would be fine, too. All too often, the show requires Racers to zip to and fro without any pause to reflect on any of the places they visit. But one of the finest moments in the show's entire history occurred outside of competition, when Racers were stirred and moved by their visit to the Slave House in Senegal. A pinch more of that would not only reveal even the most frenetic Racers as more than the whooping ninnies they sometimes appear to be on the series, but add some much-appreciated nutritional value.

2. Fewer Passive Tasks

Too many tasks consist of strapping Racers into some kind of vehicle and letting them enjoy (or endure) the ride while somebody else does all the work. Now, a little of this is fine. We can understand the value of a good zip line now and then: it's photogenic, and if it tests the Racers in no other way, at least it challenges their fear of heights. We can use a little of that. But for Racers who have no fear of heights, it's essentially an amusement-park ride. It doesn't ask much of them. Nor do the tasks that send Racers to some distant location just to look at something. Race 8 had all too many of these: from the task that required Racers to receive a clue from (the owner of) famed movie icon Bart the Bear, to the task that required them to sit around waiting for Old Faithful to blow, or the task that required them to get their pictures taken with Buffalo Bill. Tasks like these are transparent delaying actions, useful only in keeping Racers from arriving at more interesting locations before the production staff is ready for them. They challenge the Racers not at all. Please, please, please: let's cut these to an absolute minimum. Let's require Racers to actually do something.

3. Fewer Bunchings

I understand that the Race can be hard to manage, and that you want to keep the competitors close enough to maintain the level of suspense. But wide spreads have a narrative kick just as thrilling as close finishes. There's a genuine thrill that comes from watching a favorite team reach a route marker hours after everybody else, work like hell to catch up, and (if they're lucky) stay in the game to fight another day. Whenever bunchings exceed two per leg (and there were times in Races 6 and 8 when they seemed to arrive with monotonous regularity), it's hard to maintain the sense that all this effort matters, and that Racers have a reason to proceed from place to place at more than a slow walk. Please, as much as possible, limit the phenomenon to airports and monuments.

4. No More Binges

It's perfectly okay to challenge Racers with food unfamiliar to them: live octopi, chicken feet, or some of the Argentinean meats offered in Race 7. Stomaching unfamiliar food is, after all, one of the challenges of world travel. But challenges that require Racers to vomit or eat to the point of physical pain are seriously uncool: even if there were any entertainment value in watching sickened contestants puking their guts out, requiring it of them is cruel, and possibly dangerous. We've had all we can take of this. Let's not go there again.

5. No More Muggings

With the major exception of the Race 7 finale, when the money woes of Uchenna and Joyce kept the tension building until the last few seconds, the "mugging," or confiscation of money and luggage as a penalty for coming in last during a non-elimination leg, has never inconvenienced anybody. Every team that's ever been mugged has managed to beg enough funds to continue; indeed, every team that has ever been re-lieved of its luggage has managed to find outfits suitable for subsequent climates. All the mugging has ever done is made a distasteful game out of begging, often in some of the poverty-stricken regions of the world. Seriously: if producers need to penalize Racers for coming in last dur-ing non-elimination legs—as I agree they do—there are alternatives. How about giving them *more* luggage? Telling Racers they have to car-ry a twenty-five-pound weight all the way to the next Pit Stop? Or giv-ing them an extra task they have to complete next leg, before they'll be allowed to check in? Or prohibiting them from getting aboard certain conveyances that other Racers can board with impunity? These penal-ties would handicap late-arriving Racers without forcing them to equate their need to win this competition with the needs of any local poor.

6. Bring Back the Fast Forward

During Races 1 through 4, the Fast Forward was a constant issue, tempt-ing with its promise of easy passage, but providing contention between teams as Racers argued over the best time to use it. It was an invalu-able equalizer, allowing physically weaker teams a chance to stay in the Race, and more ruthless teams something to fight about. Following those early competitions, the Fast Forward was cut down to three, two, or (in the case of Race 8) only one appearance a Race. Reduced to a wild card, its effect on the final outcome is practically nil. We're given to un-derstand that this was at least in part a budgetary decision, made at a time when the show was struggling in the ratings. But the show's a hit now. Can't we bring the Fast Forward back and restore some unpredict-ability to the proceedings?

7. Either Eliminate the Yield, or Provide Alternatives

The Yield, which gives teams the ability to force the Racers behind them to stop, has never been a popular innovation. All it does is foment fight-ing between Racers. This is not entirely a bad thing, as it can be amus-ing to watch Racers use this serious weapon to pursue petty grudges. But, you know, as long as you're providing a weapon of that kind, let's provide Racers with some additional options. For instance: the Anchor, which would give trailing Racers a chance to slow down the teams al-ready ahead of them. ("We just got a phone call. Sorry, you've just been

Anchored. You can't get on the plane.") Or, as an alternative, the moral opposite of the Yield: the Lifeline, which allows Racers to give a half-hour bonus to another team of their choice. Why would any team ever want to use such a thing? Well, aside from making alliances meaningful in a way they aren't now, imagine yourself racing against a team of triathletes and a team of overweight accountants. You may not like the accountants very much. But you would certainly prefer to Race against them, next leg, than give yourself a heart attack competing against folks you know to be faster than you. Adding the Anchor and the Lifeline to the Yield (in, let's say, alternating legs), and telling each team that they can only use one option, ever, ratchets up the strategy and the politics. Alternatively: just get rid of the whole idea.

8. More Interaction with Locals

The most interesting thing Racers ever have to do is interact with locals. Indeed, that's the very point of the "crowded and confusing marketplace" challenge, as well as the challenges that require Racers to shine shoes or sell escargot. But why not go further? The very next time there's a major overnight bunching point at some distant locale, why not arrange for each team to attend a separate friendly family dinner with people who live there—thus enjoying the hospitality and the culture of the people they're visiting—with, perhaps, the next day's clue handed them as a surprise dessert? There are any number of families, around the world, who would leap at the chance to meet "famous" Americans and appear on American television. And any number of Racers who would find this the most rewarding part of their trip. It wouldn't take much effort to work out any number of ways for Racers to meet, and get to know, the actual inhabitants of their global obstacle course. And any number of ways the show would be improved as a result.

9. More Diversity among Contestants

The show has done quite well in this area, featuring many folks of different ethnic, religious, and educational backgrounds; it's certainly done quite well by its gay contestants, and was one of few major reality shows to feature a little person. It's still hard to avoid noticing how many of the Racers have been actors or models or showbiz fringies. Why not cast the net just a little bit wider? How about a hearing-impaired contestant? How about openly gay women instead of men for a change?[27] How about some more folks who look like they could be working in the cubicle next to you?

10. The Flo and Hellboy Amendments

If you threaten to quit more than five times, you *have to*. And if you threaten to throw yourself off bridges more than three times, you *have to*.

11. Fix Phil's Syntax

Why, exactly, does Phil say, "I'm sorry to tell you that you've *both* been eliminated from the Race?" Doesn't the *both* go without saying? Is there any circumstance where he would say, for instance, "Colin, you've been eliminated; Christie, you get to continue alone"?

---

[27] There actually have been, their names withheld here because I don't have their permission to reveal information they kept private during the Race. So no correction is necessary. I'm talking about willingly outed ladies as open about it, on the air, as several male couples have been.

When the World
Is Your Big Top

AL RIOS, A TEACHER WHO, off-season, performs as a clown on cruise ships, and Jon Weiss, a human cannonball for the Ringling Brothers Circus, made up one of the show's more congenial and amusing teams that could often be spotted juggling rubber balls or sporting rubber noses while waiting for various flights to leave.

Q: *Were there any difficulties to the Race that we didn't see on the air?*

JON: From the first episode, Al and I had no idea what the hell we were doing. We were the least educated about *The Amazing Race* of any other team. We were afraid to spend money. We didn't know if we didn't have money to get to the next Pit Stop, we'd be eliminated. We split a hamburger and a coffee for an hour and a half at McDonald's, at two o'clock in the morning.

AL: No, it was longer. It was like three hours. We were in Milan, and we just wanted to sit someplace where it wasn't cold outside. I said to Jon, "Go and get the cheapest thing. We'll sit at this table and split it." For me, one of the most difficult things was how exhausting the Race is, at the pace you're running at. A lot of people tell me, "Well, you just did that one thing, you finish one leg of the Race, and then you get to the first Pit Stop, and then you get to sleep for twelve hours." I try to explain to them that it looks like one day, but I think that first leg of the Race lasted for three days. They don't give you a place to sleep. They don't give you food. You only get food at the Pit Stop, and a place to sleep that isn't a five-star hotel. The twelve hours are broken up into interviewing time, eating time, washing your clothes time, preplanning for whatever you might think is ahead time. The Race gets so exhausting by the fifth week that it's amazing that you're mentally and physically able to keep it up.

Q: *A lot of people have talked about the killer fatigue that makes people do stupid things or fall down emotionally by the end of the show.*

JON: There's no question that you're physically and emotionally drained. Al, how much sleep did we get in that first three days? Ten hours?

AL: If that.

JON: You've got to remember. When we got to the Pit Stop, we were trying to figure out where the cabs were, where the airport was, where we were going next, and we were strategizing the whole time. So we spent many, many hours at the Pit Stop doing that. Al, where was it, we were strategizing, before we had to go beneath the ground, the sewers?

AL: In Austria.

JON: Yeah, it was you, me, Chuck, and Millie.

AL: We sat up until four o'clock in the morning until we just passed out, exhausted, trying to figure out, "I wonder what they're going to have us do. Let's just look at the whole town and figure it out on paper. Blah, blah, blah." None of it really came to anything.

JON: And I wasn't much help because I was falling asleep by that time.

AL: One other thing, Adam, if you don't mind me saying, one thing I noticed with Jon and myself was, when you're away and cut off from your family, your children, your parents ('cause we don't get to talk to them, we don't get to give them a call and say, "How's everything going at home?"), it plays a little game on your mind as well.

Q: *I think there was one Race where they allowed people to make one phone call.*

AL: That wasn't on our Race. I think that was on *Amazing Race* 3.[28]

JON: Oh, I definitely would have been making that phone call. That's for sure. The thing is I'm around my kids and my wife for twenty-four hours a day. So the hardest part for me was being detached from them with no communication. The first time I called home when the Race was over, my wife said, "Who's this?" She didn't recognize my voice. Emotionally you're just crying, and then you can't wait to see one another. And it's healthy. I'm trying to think of this other part, Al, when we were in Malaysia. You remember Malaysia?

AL: Yeah.

JON: When we had the blessing ceremony. There are moments like that when you really wonder where you are in the world and what you're doing. As far as I'm concerned, the poignant moments like that were probably the most troubled things for us in the whole Race. I remember reflecting on that after the Race.

AL: We did a lot of that. We were thankful and so appreciative of the opportunity we were having. We were out there, we wanted to race, but we were thankful and appreciative. We would stop and say, "Holy cow, look at this, we're on a gondola in the middle of Venice. This is amazing."

Q: *One of the things you said at the beginning is that you were not very aware of the show before you were on it, at least not as much as some teams. Not long ago, I attended a mass casting call in Orlando, and by my estimation maybe seventy-five percent of the people didn't know the show and didn't know what would be required of them. Did it really take you by surprise?*

---

[28] It was.

AL: I started watching with *Amazing Race* 3, once we knew we were going to apply for it. What we found out is that the other teams watched from the beginning. Some of them knew where the past Races went, how the travel was. They knew who the people were, the different teams. I was vaguely familiar with it.

Q: *Whose idea was it to apply?*

AL: It was my idea. I saw it online. My cousin said, "Hey, you should check this out." I got the application, printed it out, sent it to Jon, and said, "Jon, you've got to fill this out." A couple of days later, I called him and said, "Jon, did you fill this out?" "Yeah, yeah, I'm working on it." A couple of days later, "Jon, did you fill it out?" "Yeah, yeah." Finally, I called his wife. I said, "Laura, is Jon gonna finish that application?" She said, "He hasn't even started it."

JON: (*laughing*) I procrastinate all the time!

AL: I had to light a little fire under his butt to get it going.

JON: But, you know, Al, I'm forever in your debt for giving us the opportunity to do this Race, believe me.

Q: *One of the things that always stands out for me is when the Race goes to India, because Racers are always having the extreme poverty shoved in their faces. Some Racers have very emotional reactions to that.*

AL: That was probably one of the most humbling moments in the entire Race for Jon and me. I'll never forget arriving in India at about eleven at night, eventually finding a cab that would bring us to Bollywood, and as we were driving through the streets seeing mounds of garbage—I'm not kidding—fifteen to twenty feet high. Digging through those mounds were packs of dogs, wild pigs, rats, and little children. This was like twelve o'clock midnight. You'd see 6-year-olds digging through that. It's very strange, a surreal experience. You'd say, "Here we are, racing around the world for a million dollars, yet I'm looking out my taxi window to see 5- and 6-year-olds digging through garbage to survive."

JON: [During the subsequent Detour] we went to deal with the sari shop to get our clue while everyone else went to wash the clothes. But I remember when we finally got the clue, we were all excited and having fun with the locals. I remember leaving, when we were going down that street. Al, do you remember seeing that little baby on that piece of cardboard?

AL: (*fervently*) Oh, yes.

JON: It was a very young baby, maybe, what? Three months old?

AL: Three to six months old. We were walking down, and on a piece of cardboard there was this naked baby, just lying on the sidewalk. And Jon pointed it out, and I was like, "What's going on here?" So, later on, once we got to the Pit Stop, we asked somebody, and they said, "Oh, it was probably some mother who left her baby there so she could go out and work and make money. And she'll come back and pick him up at the end of the day."

Q: *That's rough.*

AL: That's really rough. And there's also one clip of Jon. I remember, we went back to the hotel, because we had a couple of hours before taking a train—the twenty-six-hour train—and in the hotel they gave free coffee and donuts. And we were walking, and I remember Jon in the train station, and seeing this older gentleman, just begging. And then he looked at the donut and went down and just handed it to him.

JON: Another hour later we were looking at him. We were standing there. I was saying to myself, and I think I said to you, "I wonder why he's looking at it like that? Why doesn't he eat it?" And then finally, [we thought] maybe because he's never seen a donut before.

Q: *Maybe it took him a while to recognize it as food.*

JON: And then he finally started eating it. You remember spending the night at gate ten, and seeing the kids going to school the next morning? Coming from those houses made out of nothing, and they were all in uniform. And they had nothing down there, but they were in uniform. Al and I were really taken aback by that.

Q: *Jon, that must have affected you as a parent.*

JON: Yes.

Q: *If I have any personal objection to the show, in recent seasons, it's the way it makes these well-off Americans beg in countries where people are begging to live.*

JON: People can't afford to give us money! I mean it's kind of ridiculous.

AL: I don't like it.

JON: I don't like it either. Al and I have talked about it before.

AL: I understand why they do it, because a lot of people don't like that if you come in last during a non-elimination round, nothing happens. So I think, and this is totally just me thinking out loud, is that they were, like, "Okay, what can we do? We can take all their money away from them. They can beg." Not even taking into consideration that we're running around trying to race for a million dollars, begging people who have *nothing* to give us money. I don't like that either. I know that now, what they do, they added that they take their backpack and the clothes off their back.[29] I don't know. I guess the producers could think of a better way.

Q: *There is an "ugly American" aspect that some of the Racers display. They get stressed out and get rude to locals. They sometimes condescend to the things they're seeing. . . .*

JON: You know, Adam, I met people who were in the military in Korea. They watch the show through their network, with the Korean people among their friends. The Koreans absolutely loved Al and I because of how we treated the Korean people. We didn't judge anybody. We went into their culture, their society, and carried ourselves as Americans properly. I think that's the least we could do. A lot of times the Racers say, "Why don't they speak English? What's the matter with these people? Are they stupid?" I wouldn't want people treating us like that.

AL: We are visiting their country. We are guests in their country. We don't know their language, and [as Racers] we don't know where we're going, but we can try to pick up a couple of phrases, like "Excuse me." Why do we insist that they speak our language?

---

[29] This is his verbatim quote, which is *clearly* not what he meant. Racers are not left to wander the third world completely naked. Fun as that might be to watch.

Maybe we learned it through our experiences with the Circus—just embracing other cultures, and learning from other cultures, and trying to be a part of another country, whether it's Italy, or Malaysia, or Korea, instead of expecting them to bend to us. It's like Jon said, we had been in touch with this lady. She does things for the Army. She would use the episode from when we were in Korea, and show U.S. soldiers a clip of Jon and I when we were talking to the taxicab driver and how we got through Korea, and then they used a clip of, I think, Chip and Reichen, when one of them said, "I shouldn't even pay you because you didn't even speak English," or something like that. She said, "The same situation there, under the same stress. They just handled the situation differently." It blew me away, because I never thought about it that way. I thought it was a great point she brought up.

Q: *It is one of the things I find most educational about the show. You get a concentrated version of the people who do behave like ugly Americans, and what you're getting is a hothouse version of the way many of us do behave in foreign countries when we're not racing, have full bellies, and clean clothes on. Al, you had mentioned to me that you used these experiences in your own classes when you teach.*

AL: Absolutely. I'm a special-ed and regular-ed teacher, and I sometimes talk about my experiences on *The Amazing Race*. And I'll talk about being respectful, not only of other cultures, but of other people in our society. I see so much of people not respecting other people for who they are and what they are. It doesn't matter if this kid isn't wearing the best, brand-new sneakers or the best jacket. He's still a human being. He's still a person. And I try to instill that in my students. I try to explain that and give them an example of how I did it, when I was on the Race. Yes, I was running. Yes, I was in a rush. Sometimes people didn't understand what I was saying. So it's also my responsibility to slow down, respect them, speak slowly, and see if they can help me. And they really get it. It really rings through to them, and it rings through to other people in the classroom. A lot of the kids I work with are emotionally disabled, and they'll say something derogatory to another student, or something, and I'll just say, "Why would you say that? Why would you do that?" And it really rings true, especially since I used it in real life on the Race.

Q: *We'll return a little bit to the Race itself. How did you spend time at bunching points, where you had seven hours to kill before you were able to get in someplace?*

AL: One of the most memorable times was in Venice, Italy. We were one of the first ones to the route marker. [The masque party] didn't open until 5:30 P.M., and we were there at 11:00. So we said, let's go look around. And we spent the whole day walking through Venice with our backpacks. We visited some of the churches. We went down to St. Mark's Square. We just had a great time. And it was raining, it was cold. By the time we got back to that house, about 4:00, every Racer sat there and waited the entire day in front of that door, and we were the last ones on line!

JON: Whenever we waited for a couple of teams, the smart-mouthed teams, to show up to verify that we were there first, there were all these arguments and disagreements. There was always a problem, on our Race, where people would get there first and other people wouldn't respect the fact that they were there first. There used to be so many arguments on our Race. A lot of the stuff, you didn't see. Eventually, what happened, like for example with the bungee jumping, was that before you went up, you had to take a number, so they started doing the number thing, which worked out a lot better. We were number ten to go into [the masque party], remember, Al? And we just looked at each other and said, "Don't worry about it, we'll be fine." We didn't know that after you got that you had to run to the Pit Stop.

AL: We were laughing about it. We looked into the camera and said, (*weepy voice*) "Ooooh, we're the last ones! What are we doing to do!?!" We came in sixth out of ten, so we beat a lot of other teams.

Q: *During the Pit Stops, you're not allowed to wander and learn your way around.*

JON: In India we had a thirty-six-hour rest period, but we had to sleep on that boat, with no electricity.

AL: Oh, that was horrible. Uccch.

JON: That was horrible.

AL: It was full of mosquitos, we had to sleep under nets, and by ten o'clock at night, they shut all the electricity off.

JON: On the way to India, Al was sick on the plane ride for twelve hours. He had some kind of stomach flu.

AL: I got sick during the downtime in Amsterdam. We got something to eat, and I was so sick the next day that I told Jon, "I don't know if I'm gonna be able to do this." He said, "Don't let the other teams know you're sick!"

JON: Al was so sick that leg. We just wanted to complete that leg and get to the Pit Stop.

Q: *One of the very last stunts you did was the face-first rappel. And it was Al who had the most trouble with that.*

AL: Jon did his thing, zipped down. I am deathly afraid of heights, and they edited it to look like I was stalling. But there was a mandatory four-to-six-minute downtime it takes them to set everything up again. But they made it look like I was stalling. I'm always asked, "You were behind in the Race, and you held your team up." But the minute I had the opportunity, I went and did it. I was walking down the side of the building going, "This isn't so bad. It's like walking on sand." And then we had the shark cage....

JON: And that was funny, too, because Al goes to walk through the tank, and I'm sent to this particular area to watch him, and I don't know that they told him the sharks have the right of way. Or not to move his hands around, because the sharks might mistake it for a fish. So I'm yelling, "Al! Go under the shark! What is your problem!?" So I look like an idiot yelling at him, and Al's standing there with his arms folded and this dumb look on his face....

Q: *Not long after that, you were eliminated. How far were you behind Chip and Reichen?*

JON: (Shouting, pure shtick) They cheated! They drove to the Pit Stop [when they were supposed to run]! They're two cheaters! (*Jon and Al laugh.*)

AL: At the airport we were about an hour and forty minutes behind all the teams. But when we got to the Pit Stop we were only fifty-two minutes behind. They had a thirty-minute penalty, so it was only about twenty-two minutes. The Race is a race, and what happened happened, but all I say is, I wish [Phil] had said to them, "You didn't follow that last clue correctly. Read it, and follow it correctly." They would have had to jump into a car, drive back, park, and then run.

Q: *It's been done inconsistently. There have been memorable times when they did send people back.*

JON: Oh, really.

AL: Yeah. They learned from our season. You know, when we were eliminated was one of the more memorable things for us. I couldn't believe this happened. Usually what happens when somebody is eliminated is the producers take that team and the team disappears. They're gone. When we started walking away, the three teams that beat us started applauding us and gave us hugs. And I think the producer, Bert van Munster, was blown away by this. He's like, *"Get the cameras over here! Get this!"*

Q: *Any final anecdotes?*

JON: I'd like to tell you about the time we were on the train. Can I tell them about that one, Al?

AL: Sure. Which train?

JON: With the cheese.

AL: (*wryly*) Go ahead.

JON: We're on the train, and we decide to change compartments, so we have to go and let our crew guys know. So I went down to the dining car. And they're not supposed to offer us any food, but they had some cheese they weren't eating, and they urge me to take it. So I take a piece of cheese, and it's Limburger. Horrible tasting. And I say, "Thanks, guys. I have to do this to Al. If this thing even touches Al's tongue, he's gonna have a heart attack." So I get Al and tell him we're in trouble [for moving], and they start asking, "Where were you?" and like that. And they offer him the piece of cheese. Al, take it from here.

AL: First I was like, "No, no, I don't want any." And they say, "Go ahead, go ahead." And finally, I say, "Okay, I'll have a little piece."

And I take this cheese, and I swear to you, I put it on my tongue, and I'm like, "BLEEEURERRGGHH!" And I run and start throwing up in the bathroom. And meanwhile, they have their cameras out, and they're videotaping me as I try to get the stuff off my tongue....

(*Jon giggles madly.*)

AL: I was surprised it didn't make the air.

JON: We were all on the ground laughing. There were five crew guys on the ground laughing as hard as they could, two filming Al in the toilet.

Q: *Any last thoughts?*

AL: I still can't believe that we got through the whole audition/application process, and that with our busy schedules, and always traveling, that we were able to accomplish all that. But, overall, it was just the opportunity of a lifetime for us. I think what it shows is that anybody can do anything they want, as long as they put their minds to it and focus on it, whether it's with a team, or a husband, or wife, whatever. Anybody can do anything they want. I really believe that. We look forward to the next opportunity to do *Amazing Race All-Stars*, or a reunion Race, and we hope that comes about.

JON: There's a lot of families and kids that watch the show, and we try to tell them that when you play a game, you don't always win, but you can walk away with your head held high.

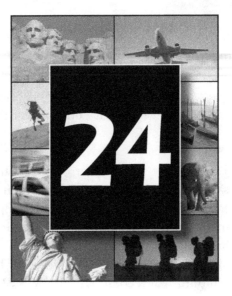

Race 5,
"My Ox is BROKEN!"

I N AN ATTEMPT TO CUT costs and offer new complications, the producers began Race 5 by cutting down on the available Fast Forwards (waaah!), introducing the controversial Yield (which I'm fifty-fifty on), and bankrupting teams who showed up last during non-elimination legs (a questionable measure which has only been a major factor once). None of these measures detracted from one of the show's more satisfactory competitions, which included among other attractions the strongest team of all time (Colin and Christie), and one that survived well past its expected expiration date (Linda and Karen). The drama included the most serious international incident to date.

DRAMATIS PERSONAE

1. The Not-Scumbags

Dennis Frentsos, 27, mortgage broker, and Erika Shay, 25, wedding planner. This young, energetic couple wastes no time proving that you can be handicapped by worrying too much about what other people think of you.

2. Team Extreme

Colin Guinn, 24, cell phone store owner, and Christie Woods, 26, in pharmaceutical sales. The single most formidable team in the show's entire history, adept at both physical and mental challenges, substantially less impressive in tasks involving food or the handling of recalcitrant farm animals. Christie is a former Miss Teen USA. Major weakness: Colin's anger-control problem, most clearly manifested by his open defiance of police officers in third-world countries. **SEASON SUPERSTARS**

3. Team Internet

Bob Barron, 61, retired, and Joyce Nicolo, 54, medical practice administrator. The oldest team this time found love online, after losing their previous partners. Their relative weakness in physical challenges is offset by their confidence and mutual affection. Expect big troubles in airports.

4. The Enthusiastic Tourists

Chip McAllister, 46, Web company employee, and Kim McAllister, 44, recruiting company employee. This pair of married parents entered the Race deeply in debt, confident of emerging in first place. Physically outclassed by the younger and stronger teams, and prone to serious errors in the early legs, they are nevertheless powerful competitors delighted by just about every foreign locale they visit. Critical weaknesses include Chip's fear of heights, his tendency to squander limited cash reserves on overtipping, and his personal agenda of hugging everybody. Critical strengths: Chip's bottomless stomach and Kim's hidden cunning. **SEASON SUPERSTARS**

5. Team Divine Intervention

Models Brandon Davidson, 25, and Nicole O'Brian, 21. It's hard to tell which of these two people is prettier. Their strengths include their vitality and their love for one another, coupled with a religious faith that manifests here in at least one moment of unnerving divine intervention. But at a key moment, it's vanity that threatens to put them down for good.

6. The Clueless Barbies

Kami French, 26, café manager, and Karli French, 26, student. Another of the show's pairs of twins, Kami and Karli have a serious map-reading problem coupled with a tendency to do things the hard way. Their worst moment is an outrageously wrong-headed ploy attempted in an Asian airport.

7. The Pizza Brothers

Restauranteurs Marshall Hudes, 31, and Lance Hudes, 26. Early foes of Charla and Mirna, their greatest enemy seems to be blind chance, until Marshall hears from his knees.

8. Team Habibi

Named for the Arabic word for "friend," which they used to distraction in Egypt, this team features Charla Faddoul, 27, store manager, and Mirna Hindoyan, 27, lawyer. These cousins present the most distinctive team this time out, mostly thanks to the presence of Charla, a little person determined to prove she is as formidable as any of the Racers of average size. This she certainly does. Though she can't run fast, she can carry more than her share of the load. Among the team's weaknesses: she often has to. Another: Mirna takes the lead in initiating, and pursuing, pointless feuds. **SEASON SUPERSTARS**

9. The Bowling Moms

Linda Ruiz, 45, tennis teacher, and Karen Heins, 41, homemaker. One of the weakest teams physically is also among the most tightly knit. Supportive of each other, even when things go badly, even if they do engage in one moment of irritated map-throwing. The most successful all-woman team in the show's history, matched only by Race 8's Godlewskis. **SEASON SUPERSTARS**

10. Team Just a Flesh Wound

Jim McCoy, 53, helicopter pilot, and daughter Marsha McCoy, 26, law student. This team set a record, for shortest distance covered before running into serious trouble (maybe half a dozen steps), that is likely to remain unbroken.

11. Team Big Brother

Dating couple Alison Irwin, 23, and Donny Patrick, 21, earn their name from Alison's prior TV appearance as one of the memorable "villains" on *Big Brother*, where among other things she reportedly complained at length about Donny. They are one of many pairs who claim to join the Race to "see if they have a future." The on-screen evidence looks bleak, especially since Donny ends their brief appearance declaring how much he hates her. Yow. Not one of the more enjoyable teams, to say the least. But they go quickly.

THE GAME PLAY

Leg #1: I'm No Scumbag

In this two-hour episode, Jim of Team Just a Flesh Wound is one of several players who tangle and fall as the Racers bolt from the Santa Monica Pier. The accident drives a nail into his knee and soaks his pant leg with blood.

Meanwhile, establishing a theme, Mirna of Team Habibi says, "Come on, Charla, run! Run, Charla, run!" The little lady is running, just not very fast, and if she needs reminding at this point, she shouldn't be here.

The clue envelopes placed on their luggage advise Racers to drive a provided vehicle to LAX, where they will take one of two permitted flights to Uruguay, the trick being that the second flight to take off arrives earlier thanks to a shorter layover.

Every team manages to get on the road quickly except for Team Habibi, with its slower running speed, and Team Internet, which can't figure out how to open the trunk of the rental car.

At the airport, Dennis of The Not-Scumbags tries to hold a place in line for Team Big Brother and The Clueless Barbies. This pisses off a number of other teams, including The Pizza Brothers and The Enthusiastic Tourists, who are on the same line vying for the same limited number of seats. Somebody calls Dennis a scumbag, an insult which will have fateful consequences.

Meanwhile, Team Just a Flesh Wound is told that the team cannot get on either flight with the oozing gash on Jim's leg, and must endure a time-consuming trip to the airport clinic before being allowed to board. Tensions rise as this requires a shuttle ride through heavy airport traffic. Making the second flight with three minutes to spare, Jim says, "It probably would have been faster to amputate the leg." Marsha suggests a cutoff point at about the collarbone.

Their flight, arriving at 12:35 P.M., also carries Team Big Brother, The Clueless Barbies, Team Divine Intervention, Team Internet, Team Habibi, and The Bowling Moms. The earlier, and slower, flight, which catches up enough to arrive at 1:00 P.M., carries The Not-Scumbags, Team Extreme, The Pizza Brothers, and The Enthusiastic Tourists.

Now in Uruguay, the teams have to take a bus seventy-five miles to a beach bearing a huge statue of a hand, protruding from the sand. The fingers represent a drowning swimmer going under for the last time. That would make me want to take a dip. What about you?

The clue box leads to Gorriti Island, where they have to search a hundred marked trees for the earliest tickets to leave the island the next day. 8:00 A.M., 8:30 A.M., and 9:00 A.M. tickets are available. During that search, Team Habibi tries to team up with Team Just a Flesh Wound, but Marsha will have none of it, thus prompting the first of Charla's many, many complaints that no other team will help them.

Team Internet, Team Big Brother, and The Bowling Moms get an 8:00 A.M. ferry. The Clueless Barbies, Team Just a Flesh Wound, and Team Habibi 8:30 A.M. The Pizza Brothers, Team Divine Intervention, The Not-Scumbags, and The Enthusiastic Tourists bring up the rear at 9:00 A.M.

One night of camping out later, The Clueless Barbies gush about the island's natural beauty. Cut to The Pizza Brothers grumbling that it is a hellhole and that they can't wait to leave. Ah, well.

The clue box on the mainland directs teams to the Jose Francisco Gonzales Meat Warehouse in the suburb of Maldonado. First, of course, they have to find that clue, and some prove less than observant. The Clueless Barbies walk right by it twice, each time noting that they must be walking right by it. Teams that actually find the clue and make it to the warehouse by bus or taxi will have to carry a fifty-five-pound side of beef a half mile to the La Rosada Carniceria butcher shop.

Team Big Brother and Team Habibi are the first to obtain oozing sides of beef. Carrying theirs through the neighborhood, Team Big Brother finds itself followed by a hungry dog. Team Habibi has bigger problems. At first, Charla tries carrying both backpacks so Mirna can carry the meat, but Mirna is still not strong enough, dropping it twice and fretting about mad cow disease. They end up drafting locals to carry the backpacks, while Charla drapes the meat around her own shoulders. But even then they walk four blocks past the butcher shop.

Imagine being a pedestrian, just happening to walk down the street, and spotting a party that consists of the diminutive Charla with a side of beef around her shoulders, the much taller Mirna telling her how strong she is, a pair of bemused locals carrying their backpacks for them, and a camera crew filming their every move. You'd probably wonder about that all day.

Teams that actually arrive at the butcher shop learn they have to make their way to the Blue and White Hotel, several miles away, where the next clue awaits in a box across the street. Jim slips on the blood on the floor of the butcher shop and goes right down. He's really not having a good upright Race so far.

Teams bunched up outside the butcher shop take turns taking the few available taxis, leaving Team Extreme and The Not-Scumbags to scramble for the last one. Dennis lets Team Extreme have it "as a good faith gesture," irritating Erika but explaining in a voice-over that he hopes it proves he isn't a scumbag.

The clue box across the street from the Blue and White Hotel, which is blue and white, offers a Detour: "Zips" or "Chips." In "Zips" team members must pull themselves hand-over-hand across a line between the hotel's two towers, 210 feet above the street, before riding a zip line down to the pool. In "Chips," teams head to the hotel's casino, where they're provided twenty chips to bet one at a time. If they fail at "Chips," they must proceed to "Zips." "Zips" is clearly the preferred choice, as most teams recognize, but the biggest barrier here turns out to be simple reading comprehension, as two teams, The Clueless Barbies and The Enthusiastic Tourists, completely miss the "across the street" part of the clue, and find the casino task without first obtaining their clue envelopes. When both teams win at roulette, they are handed clue envelopes directing them to travel ten miles by taxi to the Pit Stop, a "one-of-a-kind homestead" called Casa Pueblo. Though the first and second teams to arrive, they must go back and pick up that envelope before being permitted to check out. "We're so dead," Chip frets.

Meanwhile, at the hotel, Charla and Mirna win at roulette. Mirna wants to stay to play one hand of blackjack, but Charla says no. They depart the hotel for the Pit Stop, just before The Not-Scumbags arrive. Jim, riding the zip line down to the pool, grimaces that this really isn't the best thing to be doing one day after receiving twenty-four stitches.

1. Alison and Donny (Team Big Brother) 12:48 P.M.
2. Marshall and Lance (The Pizza Brothers) 12:51 P.M.
3. Linda and Karen (The Bowling Moms) 12:54 P.M.
4. Bob and Joyce (Team Internet) 1:05 P.M.
5. Charla and Mirna (Team Habibi) 1:08 P.M.
6. Brandon and Nicole (Team Divine Intervention) 1:13 P.M.
7. Colin and Christie (Team Extreme) 1:27 P.M.
8. Chip and Kim (The Enthusiastic Tourists) 1:28 P.M.
9. Kami and Karli (The Clueless Barbies) 1:29 P.M.
10. Jim and Marsha (Team Just a Flesh Wound) 1:39 P.M.
11. Dennis and Erika (The Not-Scumbags) ELIMINATED

Erika philosophizes, "Well, at least we lost by being nice." And they're both nice about losing, too. At least they're not scumbags.

Leg #2: I Don't Love Big Brother

Receiving $136 for this leg, teams must take their provided cars seventy miles to Montevideo and find the Shake Mega Disco, where they will have to search a crowded dance floor, covered with foam, for inflated balls painted to look like globes. Some of the globes contain clue envelopes; some do not.

At the disco, all teams receive instructions to drive 100 miles and catch a ferry to Buenos Aires. Though Team Habibi gets lost and arrives at the last minute, they are able to leverage Charla's size into an "emergencia" that holds the ferry long enough for that team to board. "My size is an advantage," she confides, "because most people think I can't do anything."

The clue to this leg's Detour is hidden at Recoleta Cemetery, at the grave of former first lady Eva Perón. Now, that's respect for a national figure. In "Perro," teams must walk eight dogs past three checkpoints, one mile to the statue La Flor. In "Tango," teams must first travel one and a half miles through crowded streets to a darkened tango theatre, where they will have to search among many similar tango-dancing men on stage for the one pictured in a printed program. Only the correct dancer will give them the clue.

Tango turns out the easier choice, as teams that go for the dogs by and large...go to the dogs. Team Big Brother falls apart under the pressure, as Donny can't find the checkpoints on the map, and Alison gets tangled in leashed mutts. The dogs don't help by mounting each other whenever Donny stops to study the map. Electing to jettison the dogs and go for "Tango," Alison rages: "If I see a friggin' checkpoint on this way, I'm gonna flip out." Donny is more than fed up by this point: "That's nothing new, and you're not gonna scare me. You're an embarrassment." She replies, "You're a loser." Later, on a bus, she says, "I was wrong because I didn't control you more." He mutters, "Psycho."

Teams finishing either "Perro" or "Tango" must travel seventy miles by bus or taxi to La Invernada, a traditional Argentine ranch where a Roadblock directs one team member to engage in the Argentinian sport of ribbon roping. This involves chasing a herd around a corral until you manage to snatch one of the kerchiefs the cows wear.

Team Habibi gets there first. It's clearly safer for Mirna to enter the corral, rather than subjecting Charla to animals that tower over her, but Charla gives her pause with one of the greatest lapses of logic ever displayed by any Racer. "You might have to stick your hand in the cow's ass." Mirna, incredibly enough, takes this at face value: "Charla, can you stick your hand in the cow's ass?"

Meanwhile, behind them, the early friendship between The Clueless Barbies and The Enthusiastic Tourists is threatened as both refuse to cede a taxi to the other. For Chip, it's just part of the game. But the Barbies think things have just gotten ugly.

1. Brandon and Nicole (Team Divine Intervention) 11:50 A.M.
2. Charla and Mirna (Team Habibi) 11:51 A.M.
3. Jim and Marsha (Team Just a Flesh Wound) 12:21 P.M.
4. Linda and Karen (The Bowling Moms) 12:28 P.M.

5. Bob and Joyce (Team Internet) 12:31 P.M.
6. Colin and Christie (Team Extreme) 12:32 P.M.
7. Marshall and Lance (The Pizza Brothers) 12:41 P.M.
8. Chip and Kim (The Enthusiastic Tourists) 1:08 P.M.
9. Kami and Karli (The Clueless Barbies) 1:13 P.M.
10. Alison and Donny (Team Big Brother) ELIMINATED

At the end, Donny says, "Dealing with Alison was the hardest part of the Race for me.... in the Race, I hate her. I'd rather change partners than be with her."

Leg #3: Oh, Fudge[30]

Receiving eleven dollars, teams must now drive themselves sixty miles back to Buenos Aires and fly 1,000 miles to San Carlos de Bariloche, in Patagonia, where the mayor will give them their next clue.

All teams get to the airport while the ticket counters are still closed for the night. The Pizza Brothers find out one airline has a flight that leaves at 9:40 A.M. An eavesdropping Charla gets on that line first, ahead of Marshall and Lance. When Marshall tries to find out if they're buying tickets for anybody else, Mirna not only tells him to mind his own business but tries to stop Team Divine Intervention from answering the simple question. Marshall strides away muttering, "I hate her so much I can't even tell you."

In a great editing moment, Nicole of Team Divine Intervention gazes heavenward, while her voice-over talks about asking the Lord to calm her down. She's staring at a departures monitor.

The 9:10 A.M. flight leaves with Team Extreme and Team Habibi. The 9:40 A.M. leaves with The Pizza Brothers and Team Divine Intervention. Every other team, except for Just a Flesh Wound, gets on the 10:30 A.M. flight. Just a Flesh Wound doesn't take off until 11:30 A.M.

Teams who reach the mayor are given directions to the Del Turisto Chocolate Factory, two blocks away, and site of a particularly nasty Roadblock, in the form of a table bearing almost 11,000 chocolate candies. Only twenty of these candies have white centers. One team mem-

---

[30] Some fans immediately dubbed this leg, "Charla and the Chocolate Factory." And here I thought I was clever when I came up with it independently. Hmmph.

ber will have to find one of those twenty by biting into candies one at a time. A little man about Charla's size stands by as Oompa-Loompa and dispenser of clues.

The Pizza Brothers arrive at the Factory just as Charla and Mirna are leaving. Lance amuses himself by yelling, "Bitch!" out the car window. Then karma strikes. As Marshall begins biting into chocolate, Team Internet, The Bowling Moms, The Clueless Barbies, and The Enthusiastic Tourists all arrive, find the white center, and move on before him.

Teams finding the chocolate race to a nearby ski resort, Villa Catedral, and find a Detour with a choice between "Smooth Sailing" (paragliding 5,000 feet in tandem with an instructor) or "Rough Riding" (mountain biking six miles down the same mountain). Nobody will be foolish enough to take the bikes. Chasing Charla and Mirna up the mountain, Colin declares, "I am so serious. We have to beat the midget."

The Pit Stop is fourteen miles away on a tiny island a few short steps from the shoreline of a resort called Bahia Lopez. Most players wade there across the shallows. Only The Clueless Barbies swim across deep water, making the child greeters giggle. Limping up to the mat, Marshall notes for the first time that his knees are killing him: the first stirrings of a problem that will prove critical in the days to come.

1. Colin and Christie (Team Extreme) 3:15 P.M.
2. Charla and Mirna (Team Habibi) 3:21 P.M.
3. Brandon and Nicole (Team Divine Intervention) 3:54 P.M.
4. Bob and Joyce (Team Internet) 4:22 P.M.
5. Kami and Karli (The Clueless Barbies) 5:04 P.M.
6. Linda and Karen (The Bowling Moms) 5:15 P.M.
7. Chip and Kim (The Enthusiastic Tourists) 5:17 P.M.
8. Marshall and Lance (The Pizza Brothers) 5:34 P.M.
9. Jim and Marsha (Team Just a Flesh Wound) ELIMINATED

Leg #4: Tears and Caviar

Charla and Mirna, not sufficiently engaged by their antipathy toward The Pizza Brothers, find themselves in an even more rancorous feud with Team Extreme.

Receiving $241, teams have to take secure bus tickets for a twenty-hour ride to Buenos Aires, where they will take off for St. Petersburg, Russia. Once in Russia they will have to find the battleship *Aurora*, famous for firing the first shot of the Russian Revolution. That, people, is just to find their first clue. Something like two days of travel. What a serious schlep.

Colin's previous comments about being "so serious, we have to beat the midget" aside, the actual war between the two teams begins when Mirna barges into his conversation with a bus-station employee. Colin points out, quite rightly, that the next bus doesn't leave for hours, and there's no point in interrupting. "Mirna," he voice-overs over a shot of himself shaking his head in disbelief, "might just be the rudest person I've met in my entire life." Another unnecessary argument on line for a nonstop bus drives the wedge in further, leaving Mirna to complain, "I can't stand criminals." Also a bit much.

Once in Russia, the clue at the battleship *Aurora* leads to a Detour: "Block Five Shots" (of a hockey puck) or "Drink One Shot" (balancing a shot glass on a saber). About all worth special notice, here, is that Brandon elects hockey rather than compromise his religious principles by drinking, and Charla's quite the sight in oversized hockey gear. Meanwhile, Marshall is now limping, in serious pain.

The Bronze Horseman, a monument to Peter the Great, leads teams to the leg's true drama: a Roadblock at the Old Tower Restaurant, in the town of Pushkin. Players have to eat one kilogram, or just over two pounds, of caviar. Christie, who arrives first, gags at her very first mouthful, but once she's begun, has to go through with it. A few spoonfuls later, she's weeping, and fighting through her revulsion. It doesn't help when Brandon and Nicole show up and the just-as-revolted Nicole likens the experience to "swallowing a giant lugie," or when Chip catches up and shovels down his entire bowl.

With Chip and Kim moving on the Pit Stop at Catherine's Palace, and Christie and Nicole getting sicker with every gulp, Charla and Mirna arrive, and the war between teams continues. When Mirna declares, "[Charla] is the strongest woman here," Colin mutters, "I hate [her]." Charla further endears herself to everybody by singing, "It's no big deal," and crowing, "Mmmm-mmm, this is so good." But the taunting has an effect on Christie that Colin's patient support, his most sympathetic moment on the entire Race, has not. She grits her teeth through her tears and begins to force spoonful after spoonful into her mouth. She is nauseated by the time she finishes, but she gets it done. Nicole, meanwhile, is so sick she gets woozy and curls into a ball on the floor. And the remaining teams, which include The Clueless Barbies, The Bowling Moms, and Team Internet, are starting to arrive in Russia.

Nicole needs time to recover. But then, in her finest moment, she gets up and bravely attacks the caviar again....

1. Chip and Kim (The Enthusiastic Tourists) 9:11 P.M.
2. Colin and Christie (Team Extreme) 9:42 P.M.
3. Marshall and Lance (The Pizza Brothers) 10:09 P.M.
4. Charla and Mirna (Team Habibi) 10:13 P.M.
5. Brandon and Nicole (Team Divine Intervention) 11:50 P.M.
6. Linda and Karen (The Bowling Moms) 12:14 A.M.
7. Kami and Karli (The Clueless Barbies) 12:50 A.M.
8. Bob and Joyce (Team Internet) ELIMINATED

Leg #5: Clueless in Cairo

Receiving $123, teams travel twenty miles by train to St. Petersburg, where they must find the Hermitage Museum and search for Rembrandt's *The Return of the Prodigal Son*. The clue awarded there directs teams to fly 2,000 miles to Egypt and search for the Tower of Cairo, a 600-foot observation deck overlooking that city.

Team Extreme books tickets that get into Cairo an hour ahead of everyone else. They extend this lead during their stopover in Paris by booking an even earlier flight that gets them into Cairo thirteen hours ahead of the pack.

A cabbie brings The Bowling Moms to the wrong airport. As a result, they miss their flight out, but are able to catch up with everyone during the layover in Frankfurt.

Team Habibi arranges its own earlier connection in Frankfurt and sneaks away from the pack while everybody else is bedded down for the night.

In Cairo, Team Extreme finds a Fast Forward, extending its lead further. When this task, which involves delivering a sarcophagus to a priest at the Pharaonic Temple, doesn't go smoothly, the team's bickering prompts a hilarious shot of the priest slowly and sadly shaking his head. But they still reach the Pit Stop, at the Sphinx, at 11:27 A.M., three hours before their earliest competition even arrives in Egypt.

All the other teams proceed to the Roadblock at the Giza Plateau, where one team member will have to descend ladders 140 feet to the base of the Osiris Shaft. There they must retrieve a satchel filled with artifacts submerged in shallow water, return, and present it to an Egyptologist who will give them their next clue.

Predictably enough, Mirna protests claustrophobia and makes Charla climb down. Also predictably, Charla smokes the climb, even though the rungs are so far apart that her cousin would have been a more appropriate choice. When she emerges, the Egyptologist hands them a map of the Giza Plateau; the trick, which the teams must figure out for themselves, is to assemble the stone shards in the satchel over the map, and proceed to the next clue box in the area marked by a missing piece. Of all the teams, only The Clueless Barbies will not be able to figure this out. "We're clueless," they say, providing their nickname.

Detour: "Rock and Roll" or "Hump and Ride." In "Rock and Roll," teams use ancient techniques to transport 600-pound blocks 100 yards; in "Hump and Ride," which closes at 5:30 P.M., teams must use horses to guide camels laden with cargo to a carpet merchant. By running like hell, Team Habibi gets to "Hump and Ride" just as the camel wranglers are packing to leave. Everyone else has to schlep stone.

Night falls. Chip redeems himself in the eyes of the Barbies by providing direction at a crucial moment. Marshall's limp gets worse. And the Moms, arriving last, remain in the game but have all their money confiscated.

1. Colin and Christie (Team Extreme) 11:27 A.M.
2. Charla and Mirna (Team Habibi) 6:41 P.M.
3. Brandon and Nicole (Team Divine Intervention) 6:45 P.M.
4. Chip and Kim (The Enthusiastic Tourists) 6:46 P.M.
5. Marshall and Lance (The Pizza Brothers) 7:21 P.M.
6. Kami and Karli (The Clueless Barbies) 8:33 P.M.
7. Linda and Karen (The Bowling Moms) 10:09 P.M. BANKRUPTED

Leg #6: Beware the Bad Goat

All teams except for the Moms receive sixty-five dollars. All make their way to the entrance of the Great Pyramid and descend 350 feet to a chamber the ancient Egyptians held to be the center of all creation. The clue there directs them to take a domestic flight some 400 miles to Luxor, and find the Karnak Temple. Team Extreme, arriving at the shaft by midnight, finds most of their seven-hour lead disappears in light of a 6:00 A.M. opening time. That's gotta be annoying.

Among the other teams, Charla has the advantage descending the shaft, which is only a few feet high and requires everybody except her to stoop or crawl. Lance worries that Marshall will not be able to climb back up afterward, but Marshall actually finds the climb easier than walking on level ground. Kami of The Clueless Barbies notes that she and Karla are "just confused."

At the airport, Team Extreme instructs their cabbie to wait while they run inside to confirm that they've found the right terminal. It seems they haven't, and Team Habibi, which has been waiting inside, immediately claims the cab for themselves. Colin seems reasonable enough when he returns to explain that he hasn't relinquished the taxi, merely left it for a moment. He has a case; his team's luggage is still in the trunk, and the cabbie hasn't been paid. It should be a simple misunderstanding, easily resolved. But before it's over Colin raises his voice, Mirna calls him a "maniac," Christie calls her rude, and Mirna spits on the ground. The war escalates further, and pointlessly, since they are in fact in front of the correct terminal.

The Moms beg for money from tourists and manage to get enough to continue. But with less than an hour to catch the 11:30 A.M. charter flight, they're once again blessed with a cabbie who takes them to the wrong airport. The second time, in two consecutive legs, that this has happened to them. But the charter is delayed almost two hours, and they are able to catch up with everybody, including the profoundly frustrated Colin.

The clue box at the Karnak Temple provides a Detour: "Herd It" or "Haul It." In "Herd It," teams must travel five miles, load ten sheep and goats aboard a boat, cross the Nile, and deliver them to a shepherd who will provide them with their next clue. In "Haul It," teams travel three miles to draw water from the Nile and deliver it by donkey.

Chip remains ebullient about everything, crowing, "[We have to load] ten sheep or goats into a Faluka and take them with the Concerta across the Maloppa! I don't even understand any of these doggone words!"

Lance says, "Beautiful day." Marshall, who is just inching along, barely able to walk now, moans, "Fantastic."

For those who pick "Herd It," the goats and sheep prove resistant to being loaded, and keep jumping off the boat. Charla, who's smaller than many of them, is unnerved. "Watch out!" she cries. "That's the bad one!" Brilliant cut to a close-up of a goat, exuding sheer evil.

Across the Nile, a Roadblock requires one teammate to dig through a marked section of sand, in search of a scarab. Nobody knows what a scarab is. But teams keep finding them anyway. The Pizza Brothers arrive very late, thanks to Marshall's knees, and dig into the night until Lance, who knows they're last, declares continuing "a waste of [my] time."

1. Colin and Christie (Team Extreme) 5:33 P.M.
2. Chip and Kim (The Enthusiastic Tourists) 6:01 P.M.
3. Kami and Karli (The Clueless Barbies) 6:03 P.M.
4. Brandon and Nicole (Team Divine Intervention) 6:10 P.M.
5. Charla and Mirna (Team Habibi) 6:28 P.M.
6. Linda and Karen (The Bowling Moms) 6:33 P.M.
7. Marshall and Lance (The Pizza Brothers) ELIMINATED

This marks the only time, in the entire history of the show, that a team quits in the field. (Unless you count Team Cobbler, which simply took its time getting to the Pit Stop.) And one of only two times that Phil has had to travel to a team's location in order to eliminate them on-site.

Leg #7: Bad Eggs

Receiving seventy-five dollars, teams return to Cairo, and from there take the fastest available flight to Nairobi, Kenya, where a charter to a "mystery destination" is waiting.

The dumbfounding war between Team Habibi and Team Extreme, which Chip calls a "clash of titans," escalates still further at Cairo's New Airport. Christie blocks the doorway to prevent Team Habibi from entering before Colin can finish paying their driver. Charla slips by under Christie's arms. Mirna elbows her way in, snapping, "Get out of my way, bitch!" Later, Charla regales the Moms with tales about the evil woman who tried to "control the whole airport." She has a point, about this particular offense at least, but her team goes on about it for quite some time, calling Colin and Christie, "the scum of the earth [who] think they own the Earth." Fed up, Colin forms a temporary alliance with The Clueless Barbies, Team Divine Intervention, and The Enthusiastic Tourists, for the express purpose of excluding Team Habibi.

Only the Moms, who somehow think Team Habibi more formidable, join Charla and Mirna in an alliance that almost works when Colin's alliance buys Swissair tickets that go through Zurich. That would be the most ridiculously roundabout route since The Gutsy Grannies went from South America to South Africa through New York and London. Team Habibi and the Moms buy Gulf Air tickets through Bahrain that arrive in Nairobi at 6:30 A.M.: an itinerary that would get them to their destination a full day earlier. This becomes substantially less cool when Colin finds out what's going on, and Mirna tells the reservations clerk, in Arabic, that these other Americans are violent and should not be allowed to fly.

Yes, she really does that.

It all comes to naught as every team gets on the same Gulf Air flight, and an attempt to take an earlier connecting flight through Dubai puts Team Habibi and The Bowling Moms in last place.

Subsequent charter flights land in Kilimanjaro, Tanzania, where teams must bus seventy miles to the town of Mto Wa Bu. Team Extreme and The Enthusiastic Tourists pay the going rate of five dollars, while The Clueless Barbies and Team Divine Intervention encounter a physically threatening driver who jacks them for more than a hundred. It's a threatening, scary situation, in which the driver persists in demanding more money.

The Detour in Mto Wa Bu involves a choice between bee wrangling, which everybody avoids, and delivering two wooden chairs to a family in town. The coolest development here involves The Enthusiastic Tourists (see p. 421 "The Most Endearing Racer Moments").

The Roadblock in the nearby village of Kibaoni involves a visit to the Kavishe Hotel, where one team member must cook and eat an ostrich egg, the equivalent of two dozen chicken eggs. Front-runner Colin wisely concedes that he can't ask his girlfriend to take a second food challenge. Alas, he burns the egg into near-inedibility and has to eat it anyway, a task that involves serious gagging. Predictably, Chip inhales his egg, and Mirna makes Charla eat.

A zip line leads to the Pit Stop, at the Lake Manyara Lookout, where Charla's tearful farewell[31] makes Phil gulp.

1. Chip and Kim (The Enthusiastic Tourists) 2:42 P.M.
2. Colin and Christie (Team Extreme) 3:00 P.M.
3. Linda and Karen (The Bowling Moms) 3:06 P.M.
4. Brandon and Nicole (Team Divine Intervention) 3:10 P.M.
5. Kami and Karli (The Clueless Barbies) 3:12 P.M.
6. Charla and Mirna (Team Habibi) ELIMINATED

Leg #8: Tryouts for the Remake of *Midnight Express*

Receiving $200, teams have to take a 100-mile cab ride back to the Kilimanjaro airport, return via charter flight to Nairobi, and from there book passage to the city of Dubai, in the United Arab Emirates. They will find the clue box across the street from the posh Burj al Arab Hotel, an architectural showpiece that resembles a billowing sail.

Much of the episode is taken up by the ugliest international incident in the show's history, in which Colin elevates dissatisfaction with his cabbie into a major, pointless confrontation that almost lands him in jail (see p. 265 "Colin on the Care and Feeding of Tanzanian Cabbies" for details). The other teams are aghast. Chip arrives at the conclusion that will take his team the rest of the way: "The team that's gonna destroy Colin and Christie [is] Colin and Christie."

Most teams except for The Bowling Moms manage to get on a Kenya Airlines flight that lands in Dubai at 6:00 P.M. The Bowling Moms miss that flight and don't arrive until after midnight, but suffer only a few uneasy hours, as the clue across the street from the hotel directs teams to its rooftop heliport, which doesn't open until 8:00 A.M. So everybody's equal again.

Incidentally, what do the other teams do when they have more than fourteen hours to kill in an exotic foreign country with limited money and no place to stay? The extras on the show's Web site offer a partial answer. They go to McDonald's.

---

[31] "I just wanted to prove to the world what I can do…and it's not easy when there are so many people pointing down at you…always thinking that you can't do it, and you have to work extra hard to do it…maybe triple hard as regular people…'cause you have to do it…you have to work extra hard to accomplish your dreams.…"

Anyway. The next morning, a cab and water-taxi race leads to a Detour, "Off-Plane" versus "Off-Road." In "Off-Plane," teams must taxi to the Umm Al Quwain Aeroclub, and tandem skydive 10,000 feet to their next clue in the desert. In "Off Road" teams must drive a four-by-four through a marked six-mile course in heavy sand, without getting stuck. The skydiving is faster, but only for the first team to arrive there, as flights take off forty-five minutes apart.

Only Team Divine Intervention and The Clueless Barbies go for the skydiving. They're neck-and-neck until The Clueless Barbies see the *Amazing Race* marked flag and Kami reasons, for no particular reason, that it might not be the right marked flag. As a result, they drive on, Divine Intervention arrives first, and The Clueless Barbies are forced to wait.

The Enthusiastic Tourists, close to bankrupt because of Chip's generous tipping, have only sixteen dollars left, and are unable to pay their cabbie upon their arrival at the dunes. In a scene that plays like a counterpoint to Colin's behavior earlier in the leg, Chip apologizes, pleads poverty, hugs the driver, and is forgiven the debt. (Some viewers equate what Colin did to what Chip did, a conclusion that makes sense to the extent that both drivers were shorted. Chip could have ended up in serious trouble himself, had the driver been so inclined. But a good attitude takes you far.)

Teams finishing the Detour take a camel and a GPS navigational device to the site of this leg's Pit Stop, a Bedouin camp. Viewers still irritated at Colin are not happy when his team comes in first.

1. Colin and Christie (Team Extreme) 10:51 A.M.
2. Brandon and Nicole (Team Divine Intervention) 11:27 A.M.
3. Chip and Kim (The Enthusiastic Tourists) 11:41 A.M.
4. Linda and Karen (The Bowling Moms) 11:42 A.M.
5. Kami and Karli (The Clueless Barbies) 12:14 P.M. BANKRUPTED

Leg #9: Shave and a Haircut, No Thanks

All teams except for The Clueless Barbies, who beg enough money to continue, receive fifty-five dollars and instructions to drive thirty-five miles to the Dubai amusement park, Wild Wadi. The park's 8:00 A.M. opening time translates to another bunching point.

On the way, Nicole offers enlightened commentary. "They have those church things everywhere, don't they?... What is it called, a mosque or something? They're on every corner. It's like Starbucks, here." I'll have a Jihad Latte Venti, thank you.

The banter between Team Extreme and The Enthusiastic Tourists, outside Wild Wadi's gates, belies voice-over portents of future betrayal. Colin voice-overs, "I think we can trust Chip and Kim more than the other teams." Kim offers, "Chip and I want Colin and Christie to self-destruct." Chip says, "We want them to underestimate us. We have to make Colin overconfident so he'll try to impress the rest of the competitors and Christie so he'll make a mistake." In the meantime, Chip brags about having been a wheelman for the mob.

In the morning, a quick trip down the hundred-foot waterslide Jumeirah Sceirah yields instructions to fly 2,100 miles to Calcutta, India. Both The Enthusiastic Tourists and The Bowling Moms make serious errors on the way to the airport: the Tourists take a cab instead of driving their own car as instructed, and the Moms leave their bag and passports at the park.

In Calcutta, the real wild card is this leg's Fast Forward, which will reward the first team to shave their heads in a Hindu ritual.

The Roadblock at Garia's Globe Brick Factory requires one team member to make twenty mud bricks by hand. It looks like simple drudgery, but the task is an exacting one, as any bricks not properly made will fall apart or be rejected by the factory owner. Tempers run high. Most teams have trouble. Kami of The Clueless Barbies needs forty-five minutes just to make her first two. Brandon has so much trouble that he abandons brick making for the Fast Forward. This proves costly, when the team arrives at the temple and finds out that head shaving is involved. The horrified professional models return to the brick factory with locks intact, even though this leaves them far behind. Nicole blames herself and weeps. Brandon shows his best side, assuring her it's all right and doesn't matter.

Crowded commuter trains separate teams still further. The Moms are once again delayed by a confused cabbie. Colin threatens to bust the ass of a local who cops a feel off Christie's bum.

In Calcutta, all teams encountering the Detour choose the task that involves transporting a taxi half a mile to Panditji's Garage. They are not told until they arrive that the taxi has no engine, but that scarcely matters, as the locals are so amused by the antics of the silly Americans that they fall all over themselves helping to push.

In a post-leg interview, Kim can't believe Chip hopped in to steer while making her push. Chip says, "Aw, baby, I'll make it up to you." Then looks away and can't help laughing. He also voice-overs, "Colin will defeat himself, but [we] will facilitate that for him."

Separated by hours, the teams straggle into Calcutta's Victoria Memorial, where Team Divine Intervention is saved by a non-elimination point.

1. Colin and Christie (Team Extreme) 2:35 P.M.
2. Chip and Kim (The Enthusiastic Tourists) 2:37 P.M.
3. Linda and Karen (The Bowling Moms) 3:25 P.M.
4. Kami and Karli (The Clueless Barbies) 4:38 P.M.
5. Brandon and Nicole (Team Divine Intervention) 6:07 P.M.
   BANKRUPTED

Leg #10: And the Lord Doth Intervene

All teams except for the bankrupted Team Divine Intervention, which begs enough money to continue, receive forty-five dollars with their instructions to fly nearly 7,000 miles to Auckland, New Zealand. Once they land they will have to drive themselves 220 miles to the town of Rotorua, and find their next clue at the Rotorua Museum.

Every team gets on the same flight to Bangkok, but the wrangle over connecting flights to Auckland is so frenetic that The Clueless Barbies resort to lying to a ticket agent about reservations they don't have. This novel strategy does not work. One twin notes, "I totally hate airports," which makes sense given her choice of reality show to appear on.

At the Rotorua Museum, both Team Extreme and Team Divine Intervention virtuously refuse to use the Yield. Will no one take advantage of the new rule this Race? No one at all? So far, apparently not. The Detour, also provided there, is "Clean" versus "Dirty." In "Clean," teams drive thirteen miles and, with expert guidance, ride a sledge down a one-mile white-water rafting course. In "Dirty," teams drive ten miles to a place called Hell's Gate and search hot, bubbling mud for buried clues.

No Detour choice has ever been clearer than this. Seriously. Some choices have been as obvious, but none have ever been more obvious. After all, which option is fun, and designed to be completed quickly?

Which option is unpleasant stoop labor that might last hours? In all obviousness: to pick "Dirty," you must be Clueless or a believer in Divine Intervention. Feel free to guess which teams will pick it.

Team Divine Intervention starts mucking about in the goo. Nicole musters some early enthusiasm for the task, calling it, "kind of cool." But as time passes, without an envelope, the teams find themselves filthy and frustrated. Brandon asks if they're doing it right, which leads Nicole to ask, how else could it be done? At long last, they have no option but prayer. This, disconcertingly, works, as they find the clue immediately afterward.

Of all the teams that take "Clean," the Moms are the most apprehensive about the white-water sledging. While donning the safety equipment, Linda even notes, "They're screwing the helmet to my head. It can't be good."

Far behind, the two teams bringing up the rear have a footrace to the Yield sign. As Chip and Kim get there first, The Clueless Barbies are terrified of being yielded. Chip milks the moment: "We choose to yield...the...NEVER WILL WE YIELD YOU, BECAUSE WE LOVE YOU!" He demands, and receives, a grateful hug from the twins. But his voice-over reveals that he showed this mercy largely because he thought the Moms were still far behind. When he finds out a second later that the Moms are actually ahead, he realizes that he's put his team in the position of a footrace for last place. The Enthusiastic Tourists could be in trouble. Unless, of course, the Barbies do something cluelessly time-consuming, like pick "Dirty."

The Roadblock, at Matapara Farms, requires one Racer to inflate a big plastic ball called a zorb, and bounce around inside it as it rolls down a steep hill. It looks like great fun, even if the process of leaving this ball, through its narrow valve, is disconcertingly reminiscent of birth. I guess that makes this Brandon's third time.

1. Colin and Christie (Team Extreme) 4:56 P.M.
2. Linda and Karen (The Bowling Moms) 5:23 P.M.
3. Brandon and Nicole (Team Divine Intervention) 6:46 P.M.
4. Chip and Kim (The Enthusiastic Tourists) 7:02 P.M.
5. Kami and Karli (The Clueless Barbies) ELIMINATED

And what lesson has Chip learned? "Use the Yield!" he shouts.

Leg #11: "My Ox is Broken!"

Colin and Christie have established themselves as the most formidable team in the show's entire history, coming in first or second for eight legs in a row. They only came in second when a food challenge was involved. Can nothing slow them down? Let's see.

A Roadblock beneath the Auckland Harbor Bridge requires one team member to climb a seventy-five-foot rope ladder to the girders beneath the roadway, walk across a set of narrow spans, retrieve the clue, and then descend by elastic line to the boat waiting below. Adventurer Colin makes short work of this. More good news awaits when Christie and he arrive at the airport with instructions to fly 5,000 miles to the city of Manila, in the Philippines. The next available flight, connecting through Singapore, leaves at 10:10 A.M., long before any of the remaining teams can catch up. As long as the Singapore connection pans out, Team Extreme can arrive in Manila at 8:20 P.M.

The three remaining teams all perform the bridge task in various levels of white-knuckled panic. Bunched at the Auckland airport, they arrange the next fastest route to Manila, one that will require an overnight stay in Hong Kong, and not arrive in Manila until 10:00 A.M.

Looks like Team Extreme has it all sewn up. But they reach Singapore too late to catch the connecting flight to Manila. And the next available flight connects in Hong Kong.

Hours later, the remaining teams languish in a Hong Kong airport terminal, despairing about Team Extreme's insurmountable lead. And then Team Extreme ambles in, waiting for the same flight!

What an opportunity. Everybody knows that the next task, at Maluguena Motors, has a Yield. If the Moms, or the Tourists, or Team Divine Intervention can get there before Team Extreme, they can drive Colin and Christie to last place. But it's the Tourists who do it.

The Moms, the Tourists, and Divine Intervention all commence their task, which involves installing decorations on a local mass-transportation vehicle known as a jeepney. Team Extreme shows up and discovers that they've been "betrayed." Colin's head explodes. He is helpless to do anything but watch, as every other team finishes and moves on before his team is even permitted to start.

The leg's Detour awaits, forty-five miles away, in a field behind a statue of a giant duck. This leads to a memorable exchange as Team Divine

Intervention departs the garage. Colin asks Brandon, "Where are you going?" Brandon yells out the window, "Giant duck!"

Colin must have wondered about that for a while.

The Detour is "Plow" or "Fowl." Nobody is dumb enough to take "Fowl," which involves herding a thousand ducks from one pen to another. "Plow" requires teams to drive an ox-drawn plow across a muddy field, until the plow hooks a line attached to the clue. The trick with "Plow" is that it goes much faster if both team members guide the ox. But thanks to the Yield, the Moms, the Tourists, and Divine Intervention all finish this task before Team Extreme even shows up. And Colin, who attempts to guide the ox by himself, suffers from the whims of an animal that goes wherever the hell it wants to go. Before long, he's literally screaming, "I CAN'T MAKE HIM GO OVER THERE!" and, in a supremely anguished cry various entrepreneurs have appropriated for buttons, T-shirts, and book titles, "MY OX IS BROKEN!"

A low point for them. And yet canny juggling of buses and taxis on the way to the Pit Stop at Manila's Coconut Palace still makes the final dash an agonizingly near thing. Team Extreme won't go gently.

1. Chip and Kim (The Enthusiastic Tourists) 3:46 P.M.
2. Linda and Karen (The Bowling Moms) 3:54 P.M.
3. Brandon and Nicole (Team Divine Intervention) 3:57 P.M.
4. Colin and Christie (Team Extreme) 4:02 P.M. BANKRUPTED[32]

The Bowling Moms are the first all-female team to make it to the final four. Way to go, Linda and Karen!

Leg # 12: Karen Gives Her All

The final two legs are broadcast as a single two-hour episode.

At the Pit Stop, Colin and Christie are still seething over their "betrayal" by a team they had considered allies. Conceding that the Yield was a "good move," Colin nevertheless derides The Enthusiastic Tour-

---

[32] Bickering with Christie during the ox task, Colin says, "Oh, my God . . . I hate you." This has prompted extensive Internet debate over whether he was addressing Christie or the ox. He maintains it was the ox. The uncut footage available on CBS.com sure as hell looks like he was addressing Christie. In either case, may we please concede that it was spoken in the heat of the moment, when he was frustrated beyond all measure? And that he was not expressing his true feelings for the mammal in question?

ists as "not trustworthy," while Christie refuses one of Chip's concilia-tory hugs. It's a game, guys.

Chip says, "Chip time is over. Chip, the friendly, la, la, la, having fun time is over. Now it's Kim time. Go for the jugular." We'll see if he's right.

All teams except Team Extreme, which begs enough money to con-tinue, receive seventeen dollars for this leg. The next clue box, in Lu-neta Park, directs teams to catch one of two charter flights to the island of El Nido. The two planes, which can carry two teams apiece, leave forty-five minutes apart, so departure times are critical. The Enthusias-tic Tourists and Team Divine Intervention get on the earlier 10:45 A.M. flight, which is bad news for The Bowling Moms, who now have to fight the much stronger Team Extreme for last place.

Teams reaching El Nido must hop separate boats and find a buoy bearing clue envelopes instructing them to use binoculars to search the shorelines of three local islands. All three beaches are flying national flags next to clue boxes, but only the actual Philippine flag provides a clue. Picking the wrong flag can be costly, as the travel time between each island is twenty minutes, and their driver is forbidden to help. But no team knows the flag, so every team has to search the beaches one at a time.

Along the way, we are treated to a lovely shot of Brandon peering through binoculars with one lens cap still on. Dude!

Brandon and Nicole content themselves with following Chip and Kim, and hanging back as Chip runs ashore, to see how he fares. A miffed Kim notes, "[Brandon] needs to get off the boat and look for himself." So when Chip finds the clue at the second island, he feigns failure with his strongest expletive yet, "Shucks!" When Brandon calls out to him to ask if he's found the right clue, Chip lies that it's not. This second "betrayal," which is like the first, nothing more than good strat-egy, drives a wedge between the former allies. Brandon says, "I will not trust Chip again." It's a game, fella. But the bad feelings linger: when Ni-cole needs Brandon's assistance prying a subsequent clue from a giant clam on the ocean floor, and Chip paddles over in response to cries for help that sound like she's drowning, Brandon and Nicole suspect him of trying to snatch their clue and angrily tell him to go away.

Forty-five minutes behind them, The Bowling Moms search the three islands in a different order than Team Extreme, reasoning that their only hope of beating the younger and stronger team is to find the clue first instead of at the same time. This pans out for them, as they leave Colin and Christie trailing by forty minutes. Will it be enough?

Cue this leg's suspenseful, emotionally agonizing Roadblock. The clue reads, "Have vertigo? Don't go." Brandon says, "What's vertigo?" The Moms don't know, either. The task requires one team member to climb a 150-foot limestone cliff, using an ascender. Brandon easily beats Chip at this. Chip fights exhaustion and stalls, just as Karen begins the climb. Everybody nervously watches the horizon for signs of Team Extreme. Chip makes it to the top and returns with the clue. Poor Karen stalls in exhaustion. "If she can do this," Linda says, "she's Superwoman." But Karen just hangs at the midway point, managing only the jerkiest upward progress, until Team Extreme catches up. Once that happens, Colin suits up and ascends, overtaking her with no trouble at all.

At the Pit Stop, a short kayak ride away, Karen tries to take the blame for her team's defeat. Linda snaps, "Don't you dare say that." Everybody give 'em a great big hand.

1. Brandon and Nicole (Team Divine Intervention) 3:16 P.M.
2. Chip and Kim (The Enthusiastic Tourists) 3:40 P.M.
3. Colin and Christie (Team Extreme) 3:46 P.M.
4. Linda and Karen (The Bowling Moms) ELIMINATED

Leg #13: It's Kim Time!

Receiving $630, teams must fly 8,000 miles to wintry Calgary, Canada, taxi eighty miles to Lookout Mountain, don snowshoes, catch a gondola to the top of the mountain, and hike a thousand additional feet to the top of the Continental Divide. Oy, what a schlep.

Chip notes, "Colin and Christie [have been] making a lot of mistakes. The Yield Kim and I placed on them threw them into a tailspin that we doubt they will ever come out of." Let's see.

The demanding trek up Lookout Point proves a major obstacle, as five of the six remaining players (Colin being the major exception) wheeze and gasp their way to the summit. "Picture Jesus up there," Brandon tells an exhausted Nicole, "like he has his arms wide open, and you're running to him." Colin tows Christie up by her ski pole. Chip and Kim fall so far behind that Colin, passing them during his team's descent, does a little standing somersault for their benefit. Talk about rubbing it in.

The Detour at Calgary's Olympic Park is "Slide" or "Ride." In "Slide," teams must luge down the Olympic course in under thirty-four seconds, the accepted competitive speed for amateurs. In "Ride," teams must mountain-bike down a slalom course in less than three minutes. In both cases, teams must repeat the course until they meet the required time. Team Extreme nails the luge on the first attempt. Team Divine Intervention experiences so much difficulty on the mountain bikes that Nicole is driven to weepy hysteria. They don't move on until after they switch to luge. Both these teams receive their clues and move on to the airport, where they have to book flights for the final city, Dallas, Texas. The Enthusiastic Tourists don't arrive at the park until long after the other teams have departed, and fall still further behind wiping out on the luge.

It sure looks bad for the Tourists, especially since both the lead teams are able to get reservations for an early flight to Dallas. Colin, who's not satisfied with that advantage, even calls ahead for a taxi.

But then comes Kim time. She discovers that the direct flight reserved by the first two teams has been delayed by fog. It will not leave at 7:03 A.M., but at 9:50 A.M. And the other teams, who bought these tickets some time ago and have almost certainly settled in for the night, probably don't know this. Grinning, practically trembling with excitement, the team buys tickets for a flight connecting through Denver that will now arrive in Dallas first. Catching up with the other teams at a hotel lounge, they pretend innocence. "All that work," Brandon marvels, "and we're all...on the same flight." Nobody notices Chip's difficulty keeping a straight face. "[I'm] just chillin' like a villain," he says, unable to resist snickering.

The next morning, Team Extreme and Team Divine Intervention figure out what's going on and, after some rough moments, get on the same flight to Dallas. But they make the mistake of checking their bags first, and cannot switch airlines in Denver, since post-9/11 fliers must ride with their own luggage. As a result, the Tourists arrive in Dallas nursing a slim ten-minute lead. They're first to the final task, a maze at the Fort Worth Stockyards, completing it and hopping back into their taxi just as Team Extreme arrives. But it's not over. They get caught in traffic, and Team Extreme's driver has no problem zipping by on soft shoulders!

1. Chip and Kim (The Enthusiastic Tourists) WIN
2. Colin and Christie (Team Extreme) PLACE
3. Brandon and Nicole (Team Divine Intervention) SHOW

Colin on the
Care and Feeding
of Tanzanian Cabbies

OLIN, THE DESIGNATED "VILLAIN" OF Race 5, has been
among the most vocal complainers about editing. He has
pointed to any number of incidents where the more intense,
ego-driven elements of his personality were accentuated or
(as he's alleged) actually fabricated, in ways that were hurtful to him.

The thing is, you don't even need that to feel some sympathy for the
man. There's plenty of evidence, on-screen, that he's not all that bad a
guy.

I won't take the position that he's an ass.

But on that particular day, he certainly behaved like one.

The events played out like this....

Teams had spent the last mandatory rest period at a remote game
lodge. Handed $200 at the start of the leg, they were to take a taxi 100

miles through African wilderness, to Kilimanjaro Airport, where charter planes were waiting.

It turned out that the going rate for the cab ride, alone, was a flat fee of $100.[33]

The math here is absurdly easy: $100 for 100 miles equals one dollar per mile—a more than reasonable rate in a modern city awash in mass-transportation options, and one that is even more fair given the remoteness of this particular location.

Colin and Christie can be forgiven for trying to bargain the price down to fifty or sixty dollars, given that conserving funds is part of the game. But the driver wouldn't go below $100, and they did enter his cab agreeing to that price. Colin did say, "It better be fast for a hundred dollars, [because] that's a lot of money," just as Brandon later said, "You guys are nuts," but that did not constitute a separate, prior agreement linking the price to the quality of the service. It was just a grumpy complaint, of the sort that always endears tourists to locals.

Later, on the road, Colin saw the taxi bearing The Bowling Moms coming up fast, and said, "Okay, man, I'm not paying you if they pass us." This amounted to adding a condition to the verbal contract between himself and the driver. It was a condition that the driver had not agreed to, but which, by Colin's perspective at least, was breached when the cab was passed by not one but two other teams.

The driver did not acknowledge the irritable American, either in word or deed. But let's point out at least one thing he could have done, under the circumstances. He could have pulled over to the side of the road and said, "Okay, then: if you're not paying me, I have no obligation to take you any farther. The distance we've traveled so far is on the house. If you want to go the rest of the way, you can agree to pay me the proper fee at the completion of our journey, or you can get out here and take your chances with the wildlife." Colin might have raged, but he would have had to recognize that, in this situation, the cabbie held all the power.[34]

A few minutes later, one of the rear tires blew out, and the driver revealed, for the very first time, that he had no spare. He was, in fact, al-

---

[33] At least one of the cabbies tries to charge a lot more, but $100 seems to be the rock-bottom price.

[34] Standing up for himself, at that moment, would have saved that put-upon cabbie a lot of grief later on.

ready driving on a donut. Colin was incensed. And in this, he had a right to be. It is extremely irresponsible for any driver, let alone a professional cabbie providing transport for a fee, to embark upon any extended road trip without a functional spare. This we know. Without conducting the research (as Colin, at that moment, obviously could not have done), we do *not* know the conditions of this driver's daily employment, or the quality standards of the local service industry, how long that cab was in service without a spare, whether the driver was assigned that cab by a dispatcher earlier in the evening, or owned it himself—in short, any number of factors that would affect how much responsibility rested on the driver's own shoulders.[35]

Fortunately for Colin and Christie, the cab bearing Kami and Karli passed by and was able to give up its own spare.[36]

We skip now to the team's belated arrival at Kilimanjaro Airport. Colin handed the cabbie fifty dollars, saying, "You can take it, or you can not take it. It's up to you. You drove on a donut the whole way. That's not safe." The driver said he would not accept fifty dollars as payment in full. Colin told him again it was that or nothing. The driver refused. Colin turned his back on the man and entered the airport.

We understand where Colin was coming from, here. We really do. The driver provided subpar service. But he still drove the American— what to him must have been an unpleasant, abrasive American—100 miles in the middle of the night, an investment of time and effort that represented his own pursuit of an honest living. His performance was far less than ideal, but the service contracted for was fully rendered. Colin had no moral or legal right to arbitrarily reduce his fee like that—let alone to walk away, having contrived a situation in which he could feel justified in paying nothing.

The driver pursued Colin into the airport, demanding his money. Colin went on and on about teams leaving first, getting there third, and so on, issues we cannot possibly blame the driver for not giving a crap

---

[35] One tourist information site advises drivers to avoid traveling at night, and always to carry *two* spares.

[36] The ladies correctly noted that Colin was less than perfectly gracious toward them in abruptly demanding their help, but we can give him the benefit of the doubt here, and observe that he may have been too busy restraining his anger and frustration to obey all the proper social niceties. His actions, once his own cab reached the airport, were sufficiently bad in and of themselves. We don't need to imply or invent any further villainy.

about. The man wanted to be paid. And he didn't want to be paid fifty dollars. Indeed, he said, "I don't want it," which was only proper, as taking any smaller sum would have probably indicated acceptance of the altered terms. Whatever you think of the driver's job performance, he knew enough not to compromise.

Christie was still fully complicit in Colin's determination to pressure the driver into accepting half. She even urged him to put fifty dollars on a nearby lounge and walk away. If Colin was being arrogant, then so was she. This is an issue only because she later proved capable of seeing the handwriting on the wall in a way that Colin did not.

The driver went away and returned with a police officer, pursuing Colin further into the departure area. Now, clearly, things had gotten more serious. A lady airport employee urged Colin to settle this, by which she clearly meant: *Are you out of your mind? This isn't worth getting arrested over.* (Every Racer shown on-screen was flashing Colin looks of resigned horror. They couldn't believe what they were seeing either.) Colin responded, "I'm not paying $100. You can bring any policeman you want down here. You can bring the *president of your country* down here, and I'll be glad to talk to him."

And that's where it left the realm of the seriously uncool and became something significantly worse. Colin failed to see it, but everything he'd done up to now was merely preamble to the further offense he had just caused. Before, he was just an irate customer, showing his dissatisfaction with a cab driver. Now, whether he knew it or not—and it's pretty clear not—he had made this about himself as an American, and about the locals as representatives of a second-rate power whose concerns did not matter a whit next to his. He was, in short, defying the entire power structure of the land where he was now behaving like a very ungracious guest.

He was in trouble before. He was in worse trouble now.

The officer invited Colin to discuss this at the local police station, which was a short walk from the terminal. Colin went. It was such a small outpost that they had to open the gates, and turn on the lights, just to deal with him—which for him should have been another clue that things had spiraled out of his control.[37] He asked the officer be-

---

[37] By now, the other Racers all looked like they were watching a slow-motion car wreck. This is, by the way, where Chip uttered his prediction, "The team that's gonna destroy Colin and Christie [is] Colin and Christie."

hind the desk if he spoke English. The man said yes and asked him if he spoke Swahili. And again, Colin failed to recognize the serious undercurrent there. The officer could probably guess that Colin didn't speak Swahili. He was *reminding Colin where he was.*

Christie began to have second thoughts about the wisdom of this course of action. The woman who not long ago had suggested that Colin just put the money down on a bench and walk away now became the voice of reason. Unbelievably, he told her she was making things worse. "This would be so much easier," he told her, "if you weren't making this so difficult." It was not hard to feel for her when she asked him just what he thought she'd done.

The officer in charge, one Sam Mahalwa, showed up, radiating a sort of weary authority. (In the highly unlikely event that these words ever get to him: Sam, I salute you. You're a mensch.) For a moment, Mahalwa seemed perfectly prepared to negotiate a price somewhere between the fifty Colin was prepared to pay and the $100 the driver demanded. But then, impossibly, Colin racheted up the tension yet another notch. Declaring that he was late for his flight, he turned away from Mahalwa and walked out of the police station.

Mahalwa followed him outside and, still the voice of reason, put the matter in terms so simple that a 5-year-old would be able to discern their intended import. "I'm a police officer. This is a police station. You see?" In other words: *This doesn't have to be a serious matter. I don't want the headaches that come with arresting a foreign national for a stupid, petty, and avoidable crime. But you're making this happen. Please understand the forces you're dealing with here, before this goes further than it has to.*

Mahalwa was, in short, behaving like a peace officer in the purest sense of the word. He saw that Colin had a point, but no case, and was giving him a chance to comply with the law while he still had a chance. There are a number of small-town sheriffs in the United States who would have already kicked Colin's ass inside a cell. Mahalwa only wanted to be reasonable with what was, for the moment, an unreasonable person.

Christie was now begging Colin to pay the $100 so they could leave.

Colin, who still didn't see what trouble he was in, snapped at the man: *"There's NO contract! We've got a flight to make!"*

Mahalwa now made the threat specific, telling Colin that the cabbie wanted to press charges. He ordered Colin back inside. Colin failed to respond. Mahalwa ordered him inside again. At what must be the most unbelievable moment in a long morning of unbelievable moments, Colin said, "No, no, I'm not going inside."

Think of that. Colin may still have thought that this was only an argument, but he'd just defied a direct order from a police officer. Mahalwa was actually showing a significant degree of restraint in simply repeating the order, multiple times, rather than engaging in a show of physical force. There's no way of telling how much of this was his own professional demeanor and how much was due to the obvious presence of a TV crew, but either way the man was showing a degree of forbearance that only reflects well on him.

Colin now began to realize the kind of trouble he was in. He even said, "I'm being thrown in jail," though that seemed to be a voice-over and there's no way of telling when he spoke those words and just how accurately they reflected his current state of mind. But he was still arguing when Mahalwa, who looked frustrated beyond all measure, told him, "We are suppose[38] to send both of you all before the court of law... you are right. You have to see, [the cab driver] is right also. But who is gonna give him his right?"

Prompted in part by Christie's urging, Colin took out the $100, flung it at the desk, and stormed out, with the indignation of a man who had spent hours dealing with stupid, unreasonable people.

It is worth noting, here, that he was still lucky they didn't come after him. The fact of the matter is that the damages here now outweighed the $100 under contention. For however long the dispute lasted, the cab driver was off the road and prevented from earning his living. The airport itself suffered a disruptive disturbance. The police had to spend their own valuable time dealing with him, when their services might have been put to better use elsewhere. Finally, flinging money at people is in and of itself a hostile act, perhaps not one serious enough to merit an arrest all by itself, but one serious enough to count as the last straw when tallying the actions of an individual who has been a pain in the ass.

Had Colin been arrested, the producers would have bailed him out, paid his fine, and done whatever they had to do to get his butt on a plane back home.

---

[38] (sic).

And he would have had to live the rest of his life as the man who gave up his shot at a million dollars by starting a fight over fifty.

The incident continued as Colin returned to his fellow Racers, relating the events in a manner that aggrandized his own sense of self-importance, blaming Christie's lack of support for his failure to win over the police, and ultimately obtaining a tearful apology from her.

None of that was pleasant, but the further we go into the aftermath, the further we get from the incident itself.

So let's talk, a little bit, about the assumptions that informed that behavior.

Again, we're not claiming any great insight into his character, only analyzing his actions on this particular day.[39]

But the fact remains that the assumptions on display are common ones, not only among Racers, but also among American tourists traveling in distant parts of the world.

Assumption the First: My inconvenience is more important than your daily life.

Many tourists are used to spending their vacations in luxury resorts, where they're waited on hand and foot. They come to expect the same level of service once they leave those unnatural cocoons and venture into areas where people actually work and live. But the real world is not a perfectly controlled environment. The real world is messy. And the real world is populated by fallible people who are just doing their best, just like the rest of us. Sometimes, you have to make adjustments for them. In your daily life, this means that if you enter a chain store and encounter a teenage sales clerk who has been left in charge of his department, with no training, no answers, and no idea where anything is, you do not scream at him at length for being incompetent. You show patience and understand that the world won't end if your transaction takes fifteen minutes instead of five. You deal with the problem as he deals with the problem. Apply this lesson to your world travels; balance standing up for your own rights with a little understanding for the person standing before you, and the day becomes more pleasant for everybody.

Assumption the Second: Everybody's interested in what I'm doing.

Irate tourists often fling the phrase, "I'm on vacation!" as if every-

---

[39] *We don't know these people.*

body they encounter has a reason to care about their good time. They fling it the same way Racers fling the phrase, "I'm on a Race!" But that doesn't mean anybody they confront in this manner is at all obligated to care. Remember the police officer Race 2's Wil confronted about the million-dollar prize, who simply responded that he wouldn't be getting any? Colin's arguments in the police station included the declaration, vital to his team but irrelevant to everybody around him, that the cabs had not arrived at the airport in the same order that they had left the Pit Stop, 100 miles earlier. The weight this carries with the cops is, quite rightly, a big fat zero. All inconvenience aside, the cab delivered its passengers well before flight time. Any other agenda the Americans have is entirely beside the point. Demanding special consideration for being "on a *Race*" is just obnoxious. This is not the same thing as saying that locals *can't* be interested. The show is filled with incidents where more congenial Americans make enthusiastic allies of cabbies, guides, and service people who become emotionally invested in helping "their" team. But that happens when Racers give their local allies reason to like them. Using the Race as a cudgel does nobody any good.

Assumption the Third: I can rewrite the rules.

No, you can't. The rules were set before you got here, and will still be in place after you leave. This doesn't stop tourists from taking pictures in areas where photography is prohibited, wandering into areas where they're not welcome, and flouting any local regulations that they believe interfere with the purity of their own experience. Nor did it stop Colin from deciding he could alter the terms of the taxi fare based on the time of its arrival at the airport.

Assumption the Fourth: Arrogance is more influential than humility.

By divine coincidence, so helpful as a case in point that it would be too contrived for mere fiction, Colin and Christie were not the only Racers to suffer a serious fare dispute with their taxi driver during this leg. It also happened, later on in the hour, and in another country, to Chip and Kim. Now in Dubai, Chip, who had depleted his team's funds by overtipping, found himself running out of money before his team's cab reached its destination. Upon their arrival, he could only appeal to the cabbie to forgive the difference. The man was not happy, but let Chip get away with it (thus earning himself a relieved hug). Now, the two situations are far from identical. The cabbies are different people, with different personalities.

They live in different countries, under the influence of different cultures. Chip and Kim ran out of money by accident, whereas Colin withheld his on purpose. The amount under contention was considerably less, as was the cabbie's own investment of time. But the nature of the offense hasn't changed. Chip did short the man, after the fact, for services already rendered, and the cabbie was a wronged party who would have been perfectly justified in calling in local law enforcement. But Chip didn't say, "You have to let me get away with this. I'm in a *Race*." He related to the man as a human being. And that turned out to be enough.

The cabbie who dealt with Chip that day probably went home feeling the hole in his earnings and muttering about stupid American tourists.

Stupid American tourists.

Not *arrogant, abusive, unreasonable* American tourists.

And that, finally, is the ultimate nature of Colin's offense here.

He complains about editing. But what editors do to the behavior of reality TV contestants too many American visitors do to the countries they visit abroad: in other words, they create impressions based on slivers of select experience.

There's a reason so many see us as shallow, complacent fools, wearing loud shirts and sunglasses as we demand to be waited on hand and foot: because for all too many, that's all we are, and all we ever will be. And for some, the very worst impression is the lasting one. As slipshod as that cabbie's services may have been, and as much as he may have been at fault for the dispute, all the people dragged into this imbroglio did not go home thinking, *What an ass that driver was.*

Nor did they go home thinking, *What an ass that passenger was.*

They went home thinking, *What an ass that American was.*

Which is not far from thinking: *All Americans are asses.*

Nobody's saying that travelers should allow themselves to be stepped on. The Race is filled with incidents where Racers run afoul of predatory service people (indeed, it had happened to Brandon and Nicole, just one leg earlier). Like all travelers, Racers are correct to stand up for themselves, when necessary.

But it's also incumbent upon us to recognize that we're guests in the places we visit, and that we owe a little patience toward those who will take us as typical representatives of our country.

And if that means swallowing our disapproval when things don't run as smoothly as we expect, and perhaps overlooking a small annoyance or two, for the sake of the big picture, that's what it means.

In the final analysis, we need to ask ourselves: *is this argument really worth having?*

Will this argument itself do more damage than whatever I'm arguing about?

At what point does principle trump perspective?

All evidence on-screen is that the dispute over the fare accomplished nothing but adding unpleasantness and discord to the fine African morning.

All evidence on-screen is that it could have gone a lot worse.

Sorry, Colin.

But that's an awfully stupid use of fifty dollars.

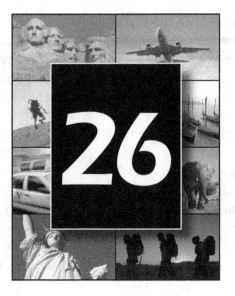

Marshall Fixes Us a Slice

MARSHALL HUDES, HALF OF THE team I dub The Pizza Brothers, shares three unhappy Race records with his brother Lance: the only team ever sidelined by physical impairment, the only team to quit in the field,[40] and (with Race 7's Mormon Girls) one of only two teams whose elimination required a special excursion on Phil's part. Together with his brother Lance, he runs the Dallas restaurant Café Nostra.

Q: *Let's talk a little bit about your experiences at the chocolate factory. How long were you there?*

MARSHALL: About an hour and a half. You know, those are the kind

---

[40] The journeys of Race 2's Team Cobbler and Race 3's Long-Distance Daters also ended with decisions that can be read as de facto resignations, but both of those teams took their time completing the leg in progress and hit the mat under their own power.

of challenges I don't like, and not just because I had to eat for an hour and a half. I'm saying that there's no skill involved. When Racers get to an event like that, like when they had to unroll a bale of hay to find the clue in the hay, it's just pure luck. Whichever one you run over to, if it happens to be in one of them, then you got lucky on your first try. Or you go to fifty... you're not trying to outthink anyone. There's no way [that] playing smarter or being more athletic could make a difference. I'm not saying that anyone has all of those skills, but it would be nice to look at an event and say that someone has an advantage because they outthought the other people, or they outhustled the other people, or something like that, but when it's a pure luck event, I'm just down on that. It's entertaining for the audience, and you have to keep that in mind, when you watch any of these reality shows, but I don't mind telling you, I've never been more frustrated in my life than standing at that table, biting into chocolates, and watching everyone come in behind me, bite into them, find [the right chocolate] in two seconds, while I'm there for an hour and a half and can't for the life of me come up with one.

Q: *How long did it take some of them to beat you?*

MARSHALL: Literally, three minutes. There were tons of them. We were the second or third team to arrive there, and of the teams that showed up while I was there, not one was there longer than ten minutes. And some of them were literally—the fifth or sixth chocolate in their mouths was the right one.

Q: *Was it physically sickening?*

MARSHALL: Yeah, but you didn't have to eat them. You couldn't have done it if you had to eat them. We figured out, afterward, based on how many chocolates were there, that I must have bitten into 3,000 chocolates during that time period....

Q: *Wow.*

MARSHALL: There's no way you could have eaten that amount. I was nauseous. Those chocolates had a soft center to them. So when you bit into them, the stuff in the middle, not quite a caramel but a liquidy soft chocolate, sticks to your teeth. So you are eating some of it and you are swallowing some of it, and [the production crew] wouldn't let you have any water. So you're getting to a point where your mouth was just coated in chocolate. So one of the things they edited out was me trying to spit out the chocolate, and clear my mouth and my throat. It was, uh, pretty disgusting.

Q: *I know you seemed pretty discouraged on-screen.*

MARSHALL: Yeah. It's just a devastating thing, knowing that you're doing so well, knowing that you're outthinking people, and then getting caught up on a task that is pure luck and no skill and watch everybody go by. You're just getting mad at yourself, because there's no one else to get mad at.

Q: *At the end of that leg, you make a mention in passing that, "My knees hurt." Was that the beginning of the problem?*

MARSHALL: I don't remember my knees hurting at that point. I'm assuming that was a valid edit. The first time I really remember my knees hurting was when we were on the plane to Russia.

Q: *I was wondering whether you got it when you landed on the hang glider.*

MARSHALL: No. It definitely had nothing to do with that. No, looking back on the thing, and based on what some doctors have said, afterward, that kind of pain is just inflammation, and really, what makes it worse was the flying. The up and down pressure changes in the airplanes. That's what started getting it worse. We'd been on so many hours of flights, with at least two connections, that it was really bad by the time we got to Russia.

Q: *Have you experienced that in any subsequent flights?*

MARSHALL: No, but I haven't been on that many flights in a row, in that short a period of time.

Q: *Skipping ahead to Egypt, you had to climb down the equivalent of thirty-five stories, down into the pyramid, when you had that kind of pain.*

MARSHALL: That was interesting, because going downhill did not hurt. The way that you bend your knees, and put the pressure on your knees, the way you had to crouch down and get down into that pyramid, it did not hurt at all.

Q: *What about coming back up?*

MARSHALL: Coming back up was not as good as going down. I think they show my brother saying, on top, "Go down a little bit and make sure you can come back up. If we got down into that pyramid, and then you tell me you can't come back up, I'm not carrying you back!" So he wanted to make sure I'd be able to make it. But, again, the angle of those stairs, and the way I had to bend my knee to do that, was not as bad as walking on a flat surface. The pain involved was not nearly as bad.

Q: *You were just barely shuffling on that day.*

MARSHALL: Oh, yeah. By that day, we had said in the morning that we weren't sure what we were going to do. Lance and I just said, "You know what? We're gonna give it a shot. We're gonna see how far we can go. If some event, or something, prevents me from going on, then we'll stop. Other than that, we'll just walk at a snail's pace and complete the leg and just get eliminated naturally."

Q: *Was that discussed during the Pit Stop, the possibility of you stopping for medical reasons?*

MARSHALL: No, they never put it in my head. They were always very nice in providing medical care, whatever I wanted and whatever I needed. They just waited to see what I was going to do. It was good. They let it come to a natural conclusion.

Q: *So we move on to the dig for the scarab, where it became clear that everybody was ahead of you.*

MARSHALL: I know we took some abuse, afterward. People were kind of down on the fact that we stopped at that point. But people don't really know what goes on. They don't get a feeling in the one-hour length of an episode just how much time passes in a typical leg of the Race. I said it in a ton of interviews, afterward. After commercials, you see about forty minutes of a television show that occurred over two to three days, sometimes. You don't see the marathon. Most people think the Race is a sprint, but it's really not. It's a marathon. It's about maintaining a lead, keeping the pace, and doing it the right way. And we could tell [where we were]. There's some legs where you can. And that happened to be a very explicit one, where there were literally squares marked off. We could tell how many squares had been dug and how many teams had already been there.

Q: *How behind were you, at that point?*

MARSHALL: A few hours. That leg of the Race was a very defined leg. Probably because of security reasons, they didn't want us straying too far. We were watching. We had seen all the teams running by us. So we got the idea. When you're in a situation like that and you see everyone pass by you, you can start gauging how far behind you are. So when we got to the sand we knew we were a couple of hours behind, already. And we knew it was the last event before the Pit Stop.

Q: *Even if I disagree with anything you did during the Race, quitting at that moment given your condition seems the most reasonable thing to do. I really find it hard to believe that anybody gives you a hard time about it. I think it was Lance who made the decision. Am I correct?*

MARSHALL: Yeah, he did. Especially since he was doing the digging, and I was the reason that we were going to be eliminated, whether it was that leg, or the one after that. It didn't matter. We knew we were getting eliminated. And that's the other thing everyone has to realize. It's not like we thought we had the ability to win the Race at that point. A few legs earlier, we did have the ability to win the Race. Once I got hurt, and once Lance saw it was just getting worse, that was it. You know, the only thing that's not covered in the show is what I was trying to do to make my legs better, when nothing was working. In Russia, I was given an oral anti-inflammatory. In Egypt, I saw a doctor during the Pit Stop and got an injection. And basically all the doctors told me the same thing. "Anti-inflammatories are going to help you maybe sleep through the night, but if you go out and start running again, it's gonna come right back. You need a couple of weeks of rest." (*laughs*) And everybody would laugh every time they said that, because the doctors weren't aware of what was going on and what the Race was all about. A couple of weeks of rest wasn't an option. So I took the anti-inflammatories and slept through the night, and woke up in the morning and stand up and bend my knees and say, "Ohhh! It feels a lot better!" And then, fifteen minutes into the Race, they'd be killing me again. It was just gonna keep building. And at the end of the day, Lance had spent an hour and a half, maybe two hours digging in that sand, and he couldn't find the scarab. It was dark. It was really cold. We were just kind of sitting there. And he just looked up and said, "I'm done." We knew we were done. He knew I couldn't walk. So there was no value in continuing it.

Q: *One of the things I say in the book is that I'm only writing about the people as they appear on the show, because it's very dangerous to make personal judgments based on these very short excerpts we see on reality TV. I also say I'm not interested in inter-team conflict, except as it bears on the Race. But in your particular case I have to talk about Charla and Mirna.*

MARSHALL: (*laughing*) Because it did happen on the Race.

Q: *Right. And I'm saying this as a viewer. I was very interested in seeing your season again, while researching this book, because the first time I watched it, I had a completely different perception. To me it looked like Charla and Mirna were getting the bum's rush from you. And now that I watch it again, it seems that they did just as much to start the feud.*

MARSHALL: Oh, yeah.

Q: *I didn't perceive that the first time I watched it. I felt such sympathy for Charla—*

MARSHALL: And that was very common. You're in the majority, not the minority, of how that happens. It's really bad when your own mother calls and says, "I feel bad for her! I'm kinda rooting for her!" And I'm like, "Ma! Are you listening!? Are you watching the show?" I think people had a hard time getting over that. I think that was a common reaction to Charla.

Q: *When they didn't want anybody to speak to you in the airport, was that the very beginning of the problems between you two?*

MARSHALL: Yeah, that was the beginning of the problems. We started out having no issue with them. We talked to them. We were actually very concerned about them as competitors, because they got the rumors out very quickly that they spoke eight languages. They were looking for allies and friends, and we were like, no problem. And then it all broke down at the airport. And, umm-mm...honestly, my brother is the much more difficult person to get along with. A lot of times, when Charla and Mirna were interviewed, they said, "Oh, Marshall's the nice one. Lance is the bad one." And once he makes a decision on whether he likes you or dislikes you, then it's all over. He will not hide his feelings. So once they told the other people not to talk to us, that was it. That flipped the switch. And it was all over at that point. That's where I made the comment, before, that there were things edited out that were said in the airport that day. He was really flipping out.

Q: *Remind me: was that you or Lance who walked away saying, "I hate them"?*

MARSHALL: That was me. The problem is, most of the things my brother said that day couldn't be aired on television. So his stuff all got edited out. I was trying to calm *him* down during that whole process, so that became the most shocking edit for me. I was expecting to hear one line my brother said that everybody expected to become the line of the episode, but I guess it was too over-the-top for CBS.

Q: *Let's talk about one of your team's more controversial moments: some comments you made about Russia being a miserable country.*

MARSHALL: If you look at all the interviews we gave after the Race, my favorite place that we went to was Russia. The quote was, "All of the people here seem so miserable." All of the intelligent people I've spoken to say people can only understand that if they've been to Russia. When you've walked around, and sat on the train, and looked at these people, it looks like these people are being transported to jail.

Q: *Very dour expressions.*

MARSHALL: It's a very weird, eerie feeling. I've taken trains in every part of the world, in all different countries, and I've met people from all over, and I've never experienced what I experienced on that train. When you look at the people, and there was no expression, and they just sat there staring forward, and they look miserable. It's very funny. People who have been to Russia tell me, "I knew exactly what you were talking about." And unfortunately, most people in America have never been to Russia. So they looked at it as an arrogant, nasty American comment. And it wasn't, at all. It was just what I was seeing at that moment. That's the thing about the show. I don't know if or when I ever would have made it to St. Petersburg, and now that I've gone there, a) I can't wait to go back, but b) it was really amazing to have this experience and see what these people are going through.[41]

Q: *When the Race aired, you showed it at your restaurant. You did some landmark business, I understand.*

MARSHALL: It's truly unbelievable, how dedicated the fans are. From the very first preview CBS put on the air, they heard on the preview that we were from Dallas, they figured out what restaurant my brother and I owned. They figured it out from seeing the street number on the door, and then they saw one word on our shirts, and they Googled us, and started calling the restaurant, and quizzing the people who were answering the phone whether the owners of the restaurant had been gone for a month, or had been on a show. . . . It was unbelievable from the get-go. So that was entertaining, and that gave us an indication that people really care a lot. So we decided, you know what, let's have viewing parties. The restaurant's not that big. It only sits about sixty people. We knew that just us and our friends would probably take up twenty, twenty-five of those seats.

---

[41] Marshall goes on to wonder if this has anything to do with their years of oppression under the U.S.S.R., but the explanation for this common perception among Western visitors is somewhat more basic (see p. 53 "Through Strangers' Eyes").

Q: *I guess this explains why I initially had so much trouble reaching you, until I went to e-mail.*

MARSHALL: It's still funny. Everybody that contacts you is usually very positive, bar one or two. There were one or two e-mails we got at the restaurant address that were really, really nasty. You know Alison from *Big Brother* (Team *Big Brother*)? I had watched her on *Big Brother* and wasn't very fond of her on that show. Once I got to meet her and talk to her, I said, "You obviously weren't a very popular person on that show. You were the villain. How do people treat you when you're out and about and doing things?" And she said, "It's so funny. People are so positive. Even people that probably hated me on the show will come up to me in public and act like they're my best friends. It's almost nonexistent for people to come up to me and start saying negative things." And she's absolutely correct. A lot of people have come up to me, when I'm traveling for business, and people come up to every airport, and I'm sure not all those people approve of things I did on the show. But everybody was very positive. That's the nice thing. People showed up [at the restaurant], they were great, they came back every week, we had a great time.

Q: *What was the reaction among your friends to some of the moments when you didn't come off all that well?*

MARSHALL: Well, our friends obviously know us. They knew our relationship from the get-go. They also saw, early on, that we were going to be feuding with Charla and Mirna. To be honest? A lot of folks said we got a bad edit. I think we got a good edit. (*laughs*) There were some nastier things said that didn't hit the air. Bottom line: we are who we are. We have our friends. We didn't go on this show—I'm gonna be careful what I say here—but there are teams who went on the show who were very cognizant about how it was edited, and we were not one of those. We had no aspirations of getting into Hollywood. We're not models, or former movie stars. We were not concerned about that. There were other people who were concerned about their regular career, so that when they were on the show, and they were running around, one would say something, and the other would smack 'em and say, "Watch that."

They were cognizant that they were being taped, and we couldn't care less. The only thing I kept saying to Lance was, "If you don't stop cursing, they'll never use anything you say on television."

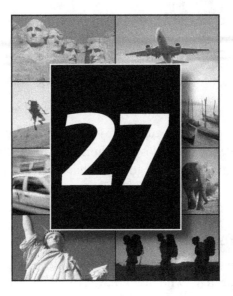

Race 6,
Dysfunctional Follies

RACE 6 FOCUSED ON THE ANTICS of some of the loudest, most dysfunctional, and abrasive teams in the show's history, a factor brought into sharp relief when many of the more congenial teams found themselves eliminated early on. Ugly incidents at the midpoint ratcheted up the controversy still further, angering, alienating, and—it must be said—further hooking audiences.

There was also one welcome rules change: from here on in, no individual player can complete more than six of the Roadblocks. Remember all those ladies who merely tagged along and watched from the sidelines as their alpha-male partners did everything risky, unpleasant, or difficult? Well, no more. From now on, everybody plays. Everybody has to step up to the plate, as frequently as they can stand it, lest they find themselves the ones stuck with the bungee-jump belly flop into raw sewage in Leg #11. This provision, alone, would have doomed some previous teams to an early defeat. And its addition to the competition adds a critical new strategy element to the competition.

DRAMATIS PERSONAE

1. Team Spry

Married couple Donald, 69, and Mary Jean St. Claire, 65. The oldest team so far has a tendency to get lost and fumble some tasks that require intricate concentration, but is far tougher than you might guess: especially Mary Jean, whose strength and resilience is at one point enough to make locals applaud and make hubby Don weep. Don't count them out.

2. The Queens Girls

Meredith Tufaro, 26, and Maria Sampogna, 26. A close-knit pair from the New York borough, who might have gotten farther had they thought of learning how to operate a stick shift.

3. The Brooklyn Boys

Composers and performers of the improvised Leg #1 ditty "New York Jews in Iceland," friends Avi Schneier, 32, a high school teacher, and Joe Rashbaum, 32, an ad executive, are among the (intentionally) funnier teams this time out, providing an entertaining commentary track for as long as their adventures last. Their biggest weaknesses: killer overconfidence, choosing travel routes, and selecting Detours.

4. This Year's Models

Couple Freddy Holliday, 35, and Kendra Bentley, 25, both models, make a young, energetic team whose greatest weaknesses include regular bickering and Kendra's vocal distaste for local conditions in third-world countries. **SEASON SUPERSTARS**

5. The Long-Distance Smileys

Kris Perkins, 30, a student, and Jon Buehler, 29, a bar owner, are long-distance daters, and one of the strongest and most persistently cheerful teams in this Race, who react to even the darkest moments on-screen with giggles and broader smiles. But are they ruthless enough to win? **SEASON SUPERSTARS**

6. Team Hellboy

Adam Malis, 27, a personal trainer, and Rebecca Cardon, 29, a model and gym employee, are an ex-couple using the Race to determine if they still have a future together. Quickly dubbed "Hellboy" because of Adam's pair of hair horns (easily the show's dumbest hairstyle, ever), the team proves a milder, gender-reversed replay of Flo and Zach, reaching heights of absurdity as Rebecca finds herself driven to distraction by her "drama king" partner's regular threats to throw himself off ferries and bridges. Can Rebecca keep her own sanity long enough to drag Hellboy over the finish line? **SEASON SUPERSTARS**

7. The Rampaging Hulks

Married professional wrestlers Bolo Dar'tainian, 38, and Lori Chestnut Harvey, 32, the most imposing team in this Race, have their share of weaknesses: short tempers, inattention to detail, and (at one point) a crucial counting error on Bolo's part. They're still a memorable pair, whose status as Season Superstars would have been assured were this particular Race not already overflowing with extreme characters. Let's just say they're a team to beat.

8. The Mormon Girls

Lena Jensen, 23, a devout mother and model, and Kristy Jensen, 26, "naughty" sister and "former striptease instructor," are an affectionate, formidable team who take well to adversity. Will their persistence overcome luck that enters the realm of the disastrous?

9. The Determined Actors

Actor-models Hayden Kristianson, 25, and Aaron Crumbaugh, 25, are strong competitors hampered by Hayden's complaining and Aaron's short temper. And Aaron is just no damn good on roller skates. Still a team to watch out for, especially given the surprise Aaron has up his sleeve.

10. Team CIA

At first, daddy and daughter Gus McLeod, 49, a pilot and ex-CIA operative, and Hera McLeod, 23, a special-ed teacher, seem doomed to early defeat. After all, Gus is one of the heaviest, and (it initially seems) laziest Racers in the show's history, a man whose greatest complaint, at the onset, is that his daughter insists on running everywhere. Go figure. And it's awfully hard to pry him away from free beer, even with the clock ticking. But put him on a glacier, or ask him to throw something at a target, and you learn what that CIA training is good for. Another team that barely misses Season Superstar status.

11. Team Explosive

Described by Phil as "the loudest contestant in the show's history," whose volume stymied sound crews across the world, Jonathan Baker, 42, an entrepreneur, entered the Race intending to become this season's villain, and subsequently spent much of his time on-screen screeching at his wife, *Playboy* model and artist 31-year-old Victoria Fuller. His rants and tantrums, which he now describes as heightened for the show's benefit, clearly horrify some of the other teams, even before the ugly incident in Berlin. **SEASON SUPERSTARS**

THE GAME PLAY

Leg #1: "New York Jews in Iceland!"

This leg airs as a single two-hour episode.

Receiving $175.28, teams starting in Chicago must make their way to Iceland via one of three available flights (all scheduled to arrive within five minutes of each other). Even before teams get as far as the subway to O'Hare, we establish the very first Racer to complain about his aching legs, and the weight of his backpack. That's—gasp—Bolo, the professional wrestler.

The very first player to get on the nerves of his fellow players is Jonathan of Team Explosive. Even before all the other teams know his name, Gus of Team CIA is calling for an alliance against "yellow shirt," who he already considers "a pain in the ass."

As for Bolo, he nods politely when Jonathan tries to bond with him by pointing out that they're both wearing primary colors and therefore qualify as superheroes. It's Jonathan's first superhero reference. Expect many.

Meanwhile, Freddy says that as models, he and Kendra know all the nuances of airports. He then tries to get information on flights to Iceland from a clerk whose airline only flies to Canada. Nice going.

In Reykjavik, teams grab marked cars and drive 130 miles along a rural highway, keeping their eyes out to Seljalandsfoss Waterfall, which is visible from the road. A path behind the waterfall leads to the next route marker.

Rebecca waxes poetic about the beautiful landscape, comparing it to Scotland. Hellboy scolds her for sitting in the backseat with her head up her ass, talking about Scotland, when she should be looking at signs. They also argue about whether he should be wearing his sunglasses or not. Remember those sunglasses.

Avi sings his soon-to-be Top 40 song, "New York Jews in Iceland."

Team Spry asks for directions in a town where, according to Don at least, everybody seems to be "blitzed."

The Mormon Girls and This Year's Models are first to the waterfall, but both worry that it's not the waterfall they want, and both return to the road and keep driving. Whoops. The Queens Girls also drive right past it. Double whoops. The Determined Actors delay The Queens Girls still further by giving them bad advice at a crucial moment (see p. 414 "The Smartest Moves Ever Made by Racers" for details). Triple whoops.

The clue box behind the falls sends teams 260 miles to the base of Europe's biggest glacier, Vatnajokull, where teams will be spending the night in tents, their departure times the next morning determined by tickets inside the tents.

Along the way there, Jonathan tells Victoria she needs to figure out what her boundaries are. And Mary Jean, tired by the long drive, becomes the first contestant this Race to threaten to toss herself off a bridge. It will happen again. Stay tuned.

At Vatnajokull, teams take shuttle buses to the route marker and then snowmobile two and a half miles onto the glacier proper, where tents are waiting.

Lori and Bolo amuse everyone at the glacier with a display of pro-wrestling techniques. But the real display of toughness comes from a guy who, up until this point, seemed just another Nervous Nellie out-of-shape dad, scolding his daughter for driving too fast. In the morning, he crawls shirtless from his tent, and bathes himself by dabbing snow under his armpits. "That'll wake you up," he says somberly.

Lori complains, "Ah'm so cold my implants are frozen!"

The Detour offers a choice between ice climbing with pitons, and a search through a glacial lake for clues hidden on buoys. Despite the effort involved, the ice climb is by far the preferable choice, with teams that take the boats slowed down by the sheer enormity of the task. The Brooklyn Boys take forever and add bad planning to bad judgment by deciding to take local roads, instead of the highway, all the way to the Pit Stop at the Blue Lagoon.

Meanwhile, Bolo calls Lori a redneck, Rebecca reminds us of Races past by putting regular gas in her diesel auto, and Mary Jean declares that she doesn't care if she dies as long as she isn't eliminated. I think it's six of one, half a dozen of the other, frankly.

1. Hayden and Aaron (The Determined Actors) 4:57 P.M.
2. Kris and Jon (The Long-Distance Smileys) 5:42 P.M.
3. Lena and Kristy (The Mormon Girls) 5:44 P.M.
4. Freddy and Kendra (This Year's Models) 5:46 P.M.
5. Jonathan and Victoria (Team Explosive) 5:48 P.M.
6. Lori and Bolo (The Rampaging Hulks) 5:50 P.M.
7. Adam and Rebecca (Team Hellboy) 6:33 P.M.
8. Meredith and Maria (The Queens Girls) 6:34 P.M.
9. Don and Mary Jean (Team Spry) 6:38 P.M.
10. Gus and Hera (Team CIA) 6:56 P.M.
11. Avi and Joe (The Brooklyn Boys) ELIMINATED

Leg #2: Hellboy's Sunglasses

Teams receive $181 and instructions to fly to Oslo, Norway.

On the way, Bolo provides the most unnerving teammate testimonial ever when he declares that before Lori straightened him out he was always getting arrested and beating people up. Ummm. So Lori provided a public service, then. And as they board the plane we get a fine taste of their relationship, as she playfully bangs his head against the bulkhead. It's like one of the sex scenes in *Body Heat*.

All teams arrive in Oslo on the same flight. But the thirty-five miles to the Holmenkollen Ski Jump proves an ordeal for many. Team Spry and the Models get lost. Team Explosive fights. The Queens Girls can't drive a stick.

The Roadblock at the ski jump turns out to be a 1,000-foot ride down a zip line. As usual, several players struggle with their fear of heights. Kristy is among the most nervous, but the funniest reaction belongs to Hellboy, who shrieks, "Mom, I love you!"

Jonathan, whose team is third to arrive at the Viking Village where teams spend the night, promptly horrifies The Mormon Girls by telling Victoria, "You owe me an apology. You owe me a big apology.... You need to look inside yourself and do something different!...I am so *proud* of myself!" Lena and Kristy look like they don't whether to laugh or run for the nearest exit.

The next morning, teams paddle across the fjord in a pair of Viking longboats. The seeds of further angst are planted when Hellboy lets Rebecca talk him into taking off his sunglasses. Critically, Freddy and Kendra lose the clue envelope they receive on the other side, and return to the clue box for another one.

On the road to the Honefoss train station, Hellboy realizes he left his sunglasses in the boat. For this, he loudly and angrily blames Rebecca. But when she tells him, at the train station, that their relationship is bad all the time, and "is going to be so over, very soon, because I can't do this," he realizes he's gone too far and offers to throw himself on the tracks, thus initiating a team theme for the Race.

After a 200-mile train trip to Voss, teams face the Detour: "Endurance" or "Accuracy." In the first, teams must roller-ski down a one-and-three-quarter-mile course. In "Accuracy," teams must complete three Viking games of skill. This is where Lori notes that, "In 'Accuracy,' you've got to be accurate." (Obvious statement. Take a drink.) Gus proves supernaturally gifted at "Accuracy." Aaron suffers more than anyone else roller-skiing, wiping out multiple times and even taking one fall onto a curb that looks like he's fortunate to still possess a functional spine.[42]

The fifteen-mile drive to the 1,000-year-old farm, Nesheimstunet, offers angst aplenty. Team Spry accidentally drives off with Team Hellboy's car, and must return. This Year's Models must wait out a half-hour penalty they receive for taking more than one envelope from the clue box. The Mormon Girls make a disastrous wrong turn. But it's The Queens Girls who show up last.

---

[42] I'm not kidding, either. That could have been serious.

1. Kris and Jon (The Long-Distance Smileys) 2:47 P.M.
2. Jonathan and Victoria (Team Explosive) 2:53 P.M.
3. Gus and Hera (Team CIA) 2:54 P.M.
4. Hayden and Aaron (The Determined Actors) 3:06 P.M.
5. Lori and Bolo (The Rampaging Hulks) 3:07 P.M.
6. Adam and Rebecca (Team Hellboy) 3:20 P.M.
7. Don and Mary Jean (Team Spry) 3:24 P.M.
8. Freddy and Kendra (This Year's Models) 3:46 P.M.
9. Lena and Kristy (The Mormon Girls) 4:05 P.M.
10. Meredith and Maria (The Queens Girls) ELIMINATED

Leg #3: Mormon Hayride

Team Spry receives a half-hour penalty for taking Hellboy's car in the last leg.

Receiving $363, teams must now travel 500 miles to Stockholm, Sweden, where a minor challenge involves sliding shot glasses across the bar in a nightclub made of ice. Any angst here proves entirely irrelevant as teams then bunch up outside the world's largest IKEA store, which doesn't open until 10:00 A.M. the next morning.

The IKEA Detour asks teams to complete one of two tasks that might be assigned to a store employee. "Count It" requires teams to count every pot, pan, or stuffed animal in three big bins, the trick being that some of these items are wrapped in multiples, and thus require teams to figure out whether they count as one, two, or three. The correct number of items for each team is 2,304. In "Build It" teams must build a computer desk from a kit.

"Build It" seems the preferred choice. And indeed, the first three teams to finish, the Smileys, the Actors, and Team CIA, are all folks who construct the desk. But many teams torture themselves at the pots and pans anyway. Bolo sounds off with a breathless, "66...68...80... 82 . . ." destined to cause him trouble later. The Mormon Girls come up with 1,891. This Year's Models come up with 1,572. The Mormon Girls counter with 3,168. This Year's Models venture 2,222, which is nice and symmetrical. Team Spry guesses 1,805. This is all very painful to watch—especially when Don, breathing too heavily to gasp out his latest count, asks the pretty young supervisor to give him a pass on account of his age—but none of it is even remotely as frustrating as the leg is about to become for The Mormon Girls, first to succeed in coming up with the correct figure.

Successful teams must now travel eighteen miles by train to Häggvik Station and ride a tandem bike to a farm with an ominously large number of cylindrical hay bales.

This, my friends, is the site of this leg's truly tragic Roadblock. One team member must unroll hay bales to find the clue envelopes hidden inside twenty of them. There are 270 bales and twenty envelopes, so each participating Racer should have to unroll an average of 13.5, before finding the clue. Once that's done, it's a fairly straight line to the Stockholm Pit Stop, aboard a famous ship known as the *Af Chapman*. But it doesn't work out that way for Lena and Kristy, who arrive in third place. In the hours after Lena commences unrolling bales, all the teams behind hers catch up, find the clue, and move on, while she's still plugging away. Even after the wrestlers and old folks leave, she still continues, into the night, in the hopes that a non-elimination, or a serious navigation error on the part of another team, might keep her team in the game. But 'tis not to be.

For only the second time in the history of the show, Phil must venture from the mat to relieve a team in the field. By then the sun has set, and Lena has spent eight hours battling pain and exhaustion to unroll 100 hay bales in search of that elusive clue envelope.

Unbelievably, Lena says, "I didn't want to be the one to ruin it."

Kristy can only respond, "You didn't."

Dammit, but this just ain't fair.

1. Hayden and Aaron (The Determined Actors) 2:04 P.M.
2. Kris and Jon (The Long-Distance Smileys) 2:05 P.M.
3. Gus and Hera (Team CIA) 3:06 P.M.
4. Jonathan and Victoria (Team Explosive) 3:10 P.M.
5. Adam and Rebecca (Team Hellboy) 5:37 P.M.
6. Freddy and Kendra (This Year's Models) 6:09 P.M.
7. Lori and Bolo (The Rampaging Hulks) 7:52 P.M.
8. Don and Mary Jean (Team Spry) 7:53 P.M.
9. Lena and Kristy (The Mormon Girls) ELIMINATED

Leg #4: Any Racer Worth His Salt

In a statement we can put in the "too much information" category, Rebecca says that when she started dating Adam, his mother was still cutting his toenails. It's pretty fair to say that this counts as one of the top five things you least want your ex telling a national television audience. There have been no further updates on this subject since the airdate.

Bolo uses the interesting construction, "You're better than me are."

Confusion over the correct opening hours for Stockholm's Town Hall Tower, where the next route marker awaits, causes some teams to oversleep, but the error matters little. Everybody makes it to Dakar, Senegal, by 8:00 P.M.

In this Race, Senegal takes the role India often plays on this show: a poverty-stricken country where conditions horrify Racers who have grown accustomed to the relative comforts of Europe. Hellboy, who's lived a sheltered life, calls the taxi the most nightmarish place he's ever been to. Hayden calls hers "gross." Kendra, sickened by the local smells, wonders if they're driving through sewage and endears herself to viewers with her first contemptuous use of the phrase "ghetto Africa." There's more to come.

Tonight's task requires teams to identify a poem by renowned literary figure, and one-time Senegalese president, Léopold Sédar Senghor. And if you think this is easy, consider how hard it might be, landing in Baltimore, to find an American capable of identifying a few lines by Edgar Allan Poe. Upon identifying the poem, Racers must find Senghor's grave, which offers its own challenges. Indeed, Jonathan has one of his own funniest moments, rarely cited in articles about the show, as he tries to mime "dead" for the locals. And Jon of the Smileys asks for directions to the cemetery where the author "resides right now." I think you're missing the big picture, Jon.

In any event, the 7:30 A.M. hours of operation cause a bunching the next morning.

At the cemetery, Kendra suffers heebie-jeebies from walking on dead people. Well, girl, how do you think they feel?

The fishing village of Kayar is site of this leg's Detour. Both options involve ways of dealing with fish. "Stack 'Em Up" requires teams to cover a drying table with the little buggers, whereas "Pull 'Em In" requires teams to board boats, ride out into heavy surf, and pull up four fish. The latter option depends on the fish, who don't reward Team CIA and Team Spry until seasickness leads Hera and Don to attract marine life by adding a little of their own last meals to the roiling waters. Nice of them to add to the local biodiversity.

The Roadblock awaits twenty miles away at a pink—that's right, pink—lake called Lac Rose, which locals mine for salt. One member of each team must pull up enough salt to fill a twenty-five-gallon basket on shore. A crowd deeply enjoys watching Americans do this. But the ladies really shine here, with Kris looking hot, Lori looking like an Amazon, and Mary Jean earning the tears of her husband and the enthused applause of onlookers. Hellboy's more whiny behavior leads Rebecca to call him a "girl." Naturally, on the ferry to Ile de Gorée, site of this leg's Pit Stop, he threatens to pitch himself over the side. Rebecca tells him that would be awesome.

1. Kris and Jon (The Long-Distance Smileys) 12:52 P.M.
2. Jonathan and Victoria (Team Explosive) 2:18 P.M.
3. Lori and Bolo (The Rampaging Hulks) 2:19 P.M.
4. Hayden and Aaron (The Determined Actors) 2:20 P.M.
5. Freddy and Kendra (This Year's Models) 2:21 P.M.
6. Adam and Rebecca (Team Hellboy) 2:22 P.M.
7. Gus and Hera (Team CIA) 2:45 P.M.
8. Don and Mary Jean (Team Spry) 4:28 P.M. BANKRUPTED

Leg #5: The Shove

Jonathan has already come off as one of the most abrasive Racers ever. His reputation as something worse rests on his actions here.

With all teams except Team Spry receiving eighty dollars, Racers must now pay their respects at the Slave House, where generations were loaded aboard ships to the New World. On the way, the usually sharp Rebecca says one of the dumbest things any Racer ever said. "I'd love to get out of Africa. I can see why so many people escaped." That's right, Rebecca. For centuries, all those people were in on the *cunning plan.* Sheesh. At least Gus redeems the occasion (see p. 423 "The Most Endearing Racer Moments"), the sheer beauty of his response so resonant in its depth of human feeling that Kendra takes emergency action to dispel any pesky aura of cultural sensitivity. "This city is wretched and disgusting," she rants. "And they just keep breeding and breeding." This while sitting behind an English-speaking cabbie. Seriously uncool.

Berlin, Germany, provides the Detour, "Beer" or "Brats." "Beer" sends teams to a Brauhaus, where they deliver the local brew to the patrons whose coasters bear their team photo. Teams have to deliver two steins per coaster and collect five coasters in all before receiving their next clue. In "Brats," teams travel to a place called the Citadel, and use a hand-operated sausage maker to make five links seven inches long.

Gus is hilarious at "Beer" (see p. 423 "The Most Endearing Racer Moments," again).

Of the Racers who take "Brats," Bolo is the least appetizing in extreme close-up as he seizes the opportunity to suck down sausage parts. A clowning Hellboy calls Jonathan "the biggest weiner of them all." Mary Jean interviews, "Oh my God, seven inches is really big." And local sausage workers become the latest onlookers to enjoy laughing at silly Americans.

The soapbox derby Roadblock is fun, but it pales next to the leg's emotional climax. That happens as Jonathan and Victoria head for the leg's Pit Stop at the Brandenburg Gate. Jonathan, who's been even louder than usual this leg, shrieks: "If another team beats us, Victoria, I'm going to lose it. I'm going to lose it on *you BECAUSE YOU CAN'T GET IT RIGHT ON THE GROUND!*"

The last moments become downright painful, as This Year's Models join in the scramble through streets narrowed by concrete barriers. As the models have the physical advantage in any footrace, Jonathan wants to jettison his team's backpacks. He dumps his by the gate to an open construction site. Terrified that it won't be safe there, Victoria scoops it up and runs behind him, sobbing and wailing, "I can't do it!" as she struggles to carry her backpack and his.

He does not take kindly to this, screeching, *"Why did you pick up my bag? WHY!?"* Nor is he happy when the Models come in first as a result. The punch he lands on Victoria's backpack sends her reeling.

Jonathan tells a less than sympathetic Phil, "She's gonna live with her choices." Showing admirable restraint, Phil tells the man he should "probably" talk to his distraught wife right about now.

And so he does, with a shrieked: "This is a *Race*. This is not about *compassion!*"

This book compiles no list of worst Racer moments, but again: seriously uncool.

1. Freddy and Kendra (This Year's Models) 2:55 P.M.
2. Jonathan and Victoria (Team Explosive) 2:56 P.M.
3. Hayden and Aaron (The Determined Actors) 3:11 P.M.
4. Kris and Jon (The Long-Distance Smileys) 3:12 P.M.
5. Gus and Hera (Team CIA) 3:13 P.M.
6. Adam and Rebecca (Team Hellboy) 3:33 P.M.
7. Lori and Bolo (The Rampaging Hulks) 4:30 P.M.
8. Don and Mary Jean (Team Spry) ELIMINATED

Leg #6a: Of Cannonballs and Lemons

Teams receive $408 and instructions to find their next route marker at Checkpoint Charlie, the guard post at what used to be the Berlin Wall. Kendra immediately wants to return to the hotel and do research. The clue box sends teams to the 1936 Olympic Stadium to put their names on a sign-up board. When This Year's Models sign up, two hours before the stadium even opens in the morning, Kendra again proposes returning to the hotel to do some research. Freddy wonders what the heck she wants to research. She just finds research, indoors, preferable to waiting around on the street.

Jonathan asks Victoria when she's gonna start carrying her own weight. That's a good question, if by that he means *only* her own weight, and not, let's say, also the weight of his backpack.

Kris ventures, "They should get some counseling."

The Roadblock turns out to be not just bungee but "hot rocket bungee," which slingshots riders 200 feet skyward from a standing position on the ground. All the women insist on doing this. Jonathan calls Victoria a superhero before and afterward.

Teams now have to fly 450 miles to Budapest, Hungary. The earliest teams jockey for a 9:45 A.M. flight on Malev. Team CIA goes to a travel agent and snags the last set of tickets just in time for Team Explosive, standing at another counter, to see the vacancies vanish off the screen.

Jonathan's head explodes.

In Budapest, teams claim notoriously unreliable local cars known as Trabants for the purpose of the sixty-two-mile drive to Eger. Some might have less trouble traveling that distance hopping on one foot. The Actors get a lemon with a dead battery. The Smileys and Hulks break down. Kris has her own best moment, laughing merrily at her team's useless car.

The castle at Eger hosts the Detour: "Catapult Crash" or "Cannon-ball Run." The first requires teams to hurl a watermelon with a catapult, smashing a wooden target 150 feet away. In "Cannonball Run" teams push a cannon into the castle courtyard, then take as many trips as they need to deliver fifty-five four-pound cannonballs, finally stacking them in a pyramid.

Gus and Hera attempt the catapult, but give it up quickly, seeing that this idiocy could take all day. But they then have to deal with Jonathan, who keeps demanding to know how they managed to get "his" airline reservations. (Gus can only mutter "little bastard.")

As for the man himself, he engages in his most bizarre behavior of the Race, wrapping the team's tarp around his neck and calling himself, you got it, a superhero, as he runs to and fro.

Victoria is not amused.

To obtain the next clue, teams have to return to Budapest and log onto AOL at the Net Klub Internet Café. A 10:00 P.M. opening hour virtually guarantees a mass bunching. But even as every other team files in, the Hulks languish on a rain-swept train platform, many miles away, having missed the last train back to town.

To be continued....

Huh? *To be continued?* That's never happened before!

INTERMISSION:

Clip Episode

The suspense stalls as the show treats viewers to an episode-long re-cap, complete with clips that didn't quite make it to the air the first time around. Some of these are moments the various Racers might have pre-ferred to keep under wraps. Among those: Bolo faking cerebral palsy to be hurried past a long line at the airport, Rebecca upsetting Adam by flirting with a stranger for the price of a sandwich, and Jonathan repeat-edly mispronouncing Senegal as "synagogue." But we also get:

- Hayden and Aaron singing with their cabbie in Senegal
- Kris and Jon frolicking with kids at the beach
- Jonathan being diplomatic (no sarcasm here; I mean it) to a local who wants the rich American to look at his screenplay
- Bolo and Hellboy making one hell of a comedy team, at the hot rocket bungee, asking Rebecca whether she's made out a living will and whether they can have her PowerBars
- Kris laughing uncontrollably at the absurd awfulness of the Trabant
- Hayden not making her team's vehicle woes any easier to take

But aside from all this: no new developments.
So: onward.

Leg #6b: Kendra Speaks Up

Houston, we have an explanation. The cliff-hanger heralds an innovation new to this Race: the double-length leg, with any number of opportunities for dramatic twists of fate. Among them: the Hulks get their ride and are able to catch up with every other team at the front gate of the Heritage Rail Museum.

There's some drama when the museum's steel gate bounces back down on the Racers attempting to dash inside. Freddy and Hera are the most seriously conked, but Freddy is the most enraged. "Who pulled the gate down?" he demands. "I want to know it now! *When I find out who pulled the gate down, it's somebody's ass! . . . One of you I'm gonna break in half!*" Well, let's be fair: getting slammed on the noggin by iron bars have never been a tonic for anybody's rationality.

The Racer most frequently maligned for explosive behavior, Jonathan, is the most visible peacemaker: an important point, given that he doesn't exactly distinguish himself with grace later on.

The Hulks claim the Fast Forward at the Budavári Labirintus, a labyrinth where they salute Hungary's vampiric legends by quaffing a goblet of yummy pig's blood. (Ahhh, the wrestlers of the night. What bruises they make.) They head from there to the Pit Stop at the Fisherman's Bastion.

We skip the Detour, a choice between scoring a goal against a local water polo player, and paddling across the Danube on an inflatable raft, to examine the most harrowing Roadblock in Race history.

At the 100-year-old Gundel Restaurant, all participating players must eat a twenty-four-ounce bowl of spicy soup, while a jovial Hungarian band provides musical accompaniment. First to arrive, Jon and Aaron, seem game enough.

Hayden offers to cheer Aaron on. He tells her flatly that if she even starts with that, he will stop eating. So that's one disaster averted. She does assure him that he's going to have the runs for a few days after this, which seems tremendously helpful.

When Jonathan and Victoria arrive, she gets elected eater. As she digs in, clearly revolted by the meal, Jonathan starts haranguing her for not eating quickly enough, and complaining that she's a "lightweight." Victoria gets sicker and calls out for a receptacle to hurl in.

Rebecca arrives and starts eating. "Yum," she says. Aaron tells her, "That's what I said, in the beginning."

Victoria screams that she's found a hair in her soup.

More eating. Victoria retches. Aaron retches from the power of suggestion. Victoria pukes and sobs. Rebecca doesn't even slow down. Jonathan tells Victoria she has to hurry. The retching sounds from Victoria's side of the table get even louder, though I'll be generous and assume it's still the food. The band falters. Aaron and Hellboy call for more music to drown out the sound.

Rebecca announces she's finished and exits with the clue in hand, though she does stop to feed the plants once she's safely out of view of the others.

Victoria's now heaving and sobbing in misery. Jonathan doesn't help by telling her repeatedly that they're gonna lose, by ordering the band to be quiet, or by calling her "drama queen" when she pukes again. Aaron retches again because of her.

The band starts reeling from the smell.

Victoria and Aaron finish. Freddy, who's not far behind, seems to be racing along until Kendra helpfully points out all the puddles of barf on the floor. And Freddy regurgitates back into his own bowl.

Ewww.

Late-arriving Team CIA has its own final moment of glory, when fat ol' Gus devours the bowl with gusto. But it's too little, too late. One iron stomach does not a Race make.

1. Lori and Bolo (The Rampaging Hulks) 11:12 A.M.
2. Kris and Jon (The Long-Distance Smileys) 12:01 P.M.
3. Jonathan and Victoria (Team Explosive) 12:02 P.M.
4. Hayden and Aaron (The Determined Actors) 12:06 P.M.
5. Adam and Rebecca (Team Hellboy) 12:07 P.M.
6. Freddy and Kendra (This Year's Models) 12:19 P.M.[43]
7. Gus and Hera (Team CIA) ELIMINATED

Leg #7: The Amazing Inflatable Hellboy

Receiving thirty-one dollars, teams emerge from a night bunched on the streets of a local neighborhood called Budafok (pronounced in a manner that evokes, for lack of a better phrase, Zen pornography) to discover their next destination, the town of Ajaccio on the island of Corsica.

One game of airport shuffle and 1,300 miles of air travel later, they're bunched again courtesy of the hours of operation at Napoleon's birthplace.

That's two bunchings in the first fifteen minutes for us, two nights in a row for them, and they haven't even done anything yet. Nothing of any real consequence happens until the tired Americans shuffle in to take their clues from the guy in the Napoleon suit.[44]

Team Hellboy is first to the Fast Forward, which requires both players to don old-fashioned diving suits, descend to the harbor bottom, and retrieve the clue from a lobster trap. Hellboy does not take well to this prospect, and once again says good-bye to his mom. But the slapstick doesn't begin until after he takes to the water. For whatever reason, he is unable to operate the helmet valve that reduces suit buoyancy by venting excess air and as a result floats helplessly on top of the water, as inflated as an aquatic Michelin Man. When Rebecca returns to the surface, clue in hand, he hasn't even gone down yet. He does try again, and this time makes it, but only—it seems—because by now he's more terrified of disappointing her than he is of the water. (He actually says, "She's gonna kill me.") In any event, the team wins the Fast Forward and gets a Cessna ride to Calvi, where they can then drive themselves to the Pit Stop at La Pietra.

---

[43] As Freddy points out, it has not been a great day for him. He began it by being slammed on the head with an iron bar. He ended it by eating his own puke. Not the glamor folks apply for.

[44] And that's *another* sentence it's been a privilege to write.

The next route marker awaits at Camp Rafalli, a fortress housing a boot camp for the French foreign legion. There, Racers find the Detour: "Climb Up" or "Fly Behind." In "Climb Up," team members use a mechanical ascender to climb a forty-five-foot rock wall. Once there, they must locate a marked terrace and receive a medal from a French legionnaire. Once they have the medal, they have to rappel seventy-five feet down another wall in order to claim their clue. In "Fly Behind," one team member is towed behind a Zodiac boat on an inflatable raft, while the other sits inside the Zodiac directing their driver to search a series of twenty-five buoys for one of only twelve with an attached clue. Everybody except Team Explosive takes "Climb Up," a test of physical strength at which, oddly enough, the wrestlers prove among the weakest. Go figure.

The Roadblock, ten miles away at a winery in the village of Zilia, requires each participating player to fill five wine bottles by stomping fifty-five pounds of grapes. Frazzled teams snap at each other a bit more than usual here (the major role reversal being Victoria's screaming at Jonathan). The familiar role of the native laughing at silly Americans is, in this scene, taken by a friendly black dog, who we get to see recoil from all the yelling. Poor thing.

The Determined Actors, who have had a hell of a day thanks to Aaron's getting lost and Hayden's constant griping, are saved by a non-elimination.

1. Adam and Rebecca (Team Hellboy) 12:12 P.M.
2. Freddy and Kendra (This Year's Models) 2:03 P.M.
3. Lori and Bolo (The Rampaging Hulks) 2:13 P.M.
4. Kris and Jon (The Long-Distance Smileys) 2:14 P.M.
5. Jonathan and Victoria (Team Explosive) 2:18 P.M.[45]
6. Hayden and Aaron (The Determined Actors) 2:51 P.M.
   BANKRUPTED

---

[45] Phil's online diaries report that he took great pleasure in allowing Jonathan to tell the Corsican greeter, at length, how much he liked Italy.

Leg #8: Last Straws, and Sharp Ones

Everybody but the Actors receives $143 with their instructions to take a ferry to Nice.

Bolo pronounces "Nice" like the value judgment, but don't judge him too harshly: teams have a field day mispronouncing their next major destination, Addis Ababa, Ethiopia.

Kendra complains, "We just *went* to a third-world country," rolling her eyes for emphasis.

Oh, boy.

The rocky relationship of Hellboy and Rebecca deteriorates still further after she shares vital flight information with the Smileys. For Rebecca, his anger is another last straw. "I'm so over it," she weeps. "I love the game...I love doing this. But...I hate being with you. You make me so miserable all the time." She says they're finished. She's been saying much the same thing, on and off, for several legs now, but this seems definitive. He has no ready answer, as there's no nearby bridge.

Flying over Ethiopia, a country TV coverage of famines past have led them to believe was all blighted desert, teams are surprised by the lush green landscape. After a subsequent charter flight to Lalibela, Kendra says, "It's a different kind of poverty. It's like these people choose to be this way. I think it's actually refreshing."

Oh, boy.

Tiny Lewz Village, home of many sweet children delighted by the antics of these odd Americans—it seems to be the most exciting thing to happen in this town in quite some time—provides the Detour: "Raise the Roof" or "Mud the Hut." The first requires teams to help a group of locals carry a thatched roof two-thirds of a mile, and place it atop a small Ethiopian house. They finish out the job by climbing a ladder to place a small jug on the roof. (Hellboy tells Rebecca, "Be quiet. I've never placed a jug on a roof before.") In "Mud," teams use a plaster made of dirt, straw, and water to cover the exterior wall of another house. Many teams take the latter choice, unaware that the straw has sharp edges that can slice open their hands. Freddy is first wounded. Kendra worries: "You have a cut and you're sticking your hands in crap." He philosophizes: "Well, maybe it's holy crap."

Not long afterward, Victoria shrieks as her own hand is sliced open. A distracted Jonathan fails to respond with enough alacrity for Kendra, who screams at him, "*Jonathan, help her!*" Kendra remains pissed at him as she continues to slap mud against the wall: "He...didn't...even... help...her!"[46]

Teams now collect two donkeys and take them three miles to St. George's Church, an 850-year-old house of worship carved out of solid rock (and site of the Roadblock, which requires one player to match a pendant provided by the priest with one of many different ones worn by the congregation). Along the way, there's much hilarity involving recalcitrant donkeys and the word "ass."[47] Kendra suffers an asthma attack. Hayden is befriended by a cute little boy named Balai. Team Hellboy Yields the Models, only to fall behind as Hellboy allows himself to be led to the wrong church. But Team Explosive makes the most critical error by taking only one donkey, thus forcing them to return for the other. They are last to the Pit Stop at Lalibela Lookout.

1. Hayden and Aaron (The Determined Actors) 1:16 P.M.
2. Lori and Bolo (The Rampaging Hulks) 1:31 P.M.
3. Kris and Jon (The Long-Distance Smileys) 1:48 P.M.
4. Freddy and Kendra (This Year's Models) 2:13 P.M.
5. Adam and Rebecca (Team Hellboy) 2:30 P.M.
6. Jonathan and Victoria (Team Explosive) ELIMINATED

Leg #9: Scratch the Hulks

As teams receive $171 and instructions to return to Addis Ababa, we learn that the much maligned continent of Africa has taken revenge on Kendra, in the form of stomach upset that leaves her making frequent and noisy visits to the porcelain God. Never has a model vomited so much for so long without weighing herself afterwards. Freddy, who had to *eat* his, just a few legs ago, doesn't ask her if she wants to save some for later.

Players arrive at the Addis Ababa Stadium, where they have to complete a four-person relay with local runners. Bolo mentions his days of fleeing the police on foot. He's got an interesting past, that one, even if his gait doesn't look like any big threat to Starskys and Hutches.

---

[46] Based only on what we see on the air, Jonathan doesn't always show Victoria a hell of a lot of sympathy when she's in distress during the Race, thus adding to the overall impression that so infuriated Kendra. But let's be fair about this particular incident. It's pretty clear he just didn't know what the hell his wife was going on about.

[47] Aaron says he's talented at guiding asses, and surreptitiously points at Hayden, a moment that must have gone over well when the two of them later watched the episode together.

From here everybody flies to Sri Lanka, mere weeks before its devastation by the Asian tsunami. The Racers travel through some of the areas destined to suffer the worst devastation, rendering it difficult to watch some of these scenes now without wondering how many of the background people survived.

Adam throws a memorable snit at the train station (see p. 406 "The Most Jaw-Dropping Errors Ever Made by Racers").

Galle is site of the Detour: "Tree Trunks" or "Elephant Trunks." The first requires teams to navigate ropes strung between coconut trees; the second to score a goal in elephant polo. Freddy has one of the best reasons for picking a task, ever: even if it turns out to be slower, Lord alone knows when they might have another chance to ride an elephant. Might as well enjoy the journey, I say. Certainly he enjoys the elephant a lot more than panicky Hayden enjoys the tightrope walk. He laughs, and she *screams*.

From there, all teams proceed to the city of Kandy, buy an offering at the local art association, and deliver it to a priest at the Temple of the Tooth. (I'm not kidding. The Temple of the Tooth is in the city called Kandy. That's irony for you.) The hours of operation, from 4:00 P.M. to 8:00 P.M., guarantee an overnight bunching that allows Team Hellboy to catch up: third bunching this leg, if I count correctly.

The next morning, upon receiving their clues from the priest, teams move on to Dambulla, where the Roadblock requires each participating player to climb 1,000 steps to the summit of Lion Rock. Once there, they use binoculars to search the surrounding rain forest for the *Amazing Race* flag, which marks where teams will have to go to find this leg's Pit Stop. Just reaching the summit requires the purchase of tickets, and—unfortunately for those who neglect to bring theirs along—one of the ticket takers is on the penultimate landing. Lori, who takes the Roadblock for her team, has to climb all the way up and then all the way down and then all the way up again, an ordeal that does little for her disposition. When she storms back down, she is *pissed*. And will remain pissed as the error leads to elimination (see p. 407 "The Most Jaw-Dropping Errors Ever Made by Racers").

Meanwhile, there's a truly classic edit. Bolo scratches himself absently. Cut to one of the local monkeys doing the same thing. Unfair, I know. But a great found moment.

Teams 2 through 4 have one of the closest finishes ever, separated by seconds as they swim to Phil across the length of a hotel swimming pool.

1. Kris and Jon (The Long-Distance Smileys) 11:59 A.M.
2. Hayden and Aaron (The Determined Actors) 12:04 P.M.
3. Freddy and Kendra (This Year's Models) 12:05 P.M.
4. Adam and Rebecca (Team Hellboy) 12:06 P.M.
5. Lori and Bolo (The Rampaging Hulks) ELIMINATED

Leg #10: Kris Is Mildly Peeved

Receiving $142, teams move on to Shanghai, China, where Rebecca has wanted to go since she saw Madonna and Sean Penn in *Shanghai Surprise*. Of course, that movie was set in the 1930s, and the place is bound to have changed a little in the last seventy years. The film was also a notorious bomb, leading us to wonder if it takes a movie that bad to influence her travel decisions. I can just see her booking passage to Ishtar or Inchon.

Hayden, who has promised not to nag Aaron quite so much, is in rare form at the start of this leg. Whenever she finds something to complain about, she not only makes her point, but makes it again, and again, and again, and... hey, I'm acting like her.

An early-morning bunch at Yu Yuan Garden leads to a scramble for taxis to the Huaneng Union Tower. But—go figure—no taxis want to take them. Drivers keep slowing down to say, "I can't take you." Why is not clear. Maybe they've been watching previous episodes, somehow.

Eventually, teams converge on the Huaneng Tower, where This Year's Models waste no time Yielding Team Hellboy, as payback for the latter team's Yielding of them in Ethiopia. They then move on to the Roadblock, which requires participating Racers to reach the top of a forty-story skyscraper, sit on a window washer's chair, and lower themselves to a marked window that, when washed, reveals a written message, "Tai Chi," on the other side of the glass. Lowering themselves the rest of the way, they then report the message to a supervisor, who hands them their next clue.

The Smileys get the worst cab of the bunch and arrive last, passing Team Hellboy only because that team is still waiting out its Yield. Kris is sufficiently irritated by the poor service to leave her cabbie with an aggravated, "Dude, you suck!" Hellboy, who hears her, marvels that it's the first time he's ever seen her upset at anything. So, hmmm. It's not just a sweetheart edit. She really is that way.

By contrast, Team Hellboy gets so involved with bickering that for several seconds they fail to notice that their hourglass has run out, freeing them to move on. Hellboy himself shows smarts by hailing a taxi while Rebecca is still completing her descent.

Teams move on to the Monument to the People's Heroes, where they must find one of four Masters among a large group of people practicing Tai Chi. That worthy personage hands them another clue which includes a map they must use to reach the end of Jiang Pu Road.

The Smileys get another crappy driver who takes them blocks out of the way. Crap.

The Detour is "Bricks" or "Ice." The first requires them to transport 300 bricks off a barge and onto a nearby pallet. The second requires teams to load two 220-pound blocks of ice onto the back of flatbed tricycles and deliver them to a fish market four blocks away. Everybody takes "Bricks," a task especially hard on Hayden (who bends under the load) and Rebecca (who drops hers in the water).

The Smileys are almost creamed by a taxi, and one second later by a bus, on their way to the Pit Stop at the Peace Hotel South. Jeez. Look both ways, kids.

Adam has the best reaction of any Racer ever bankrupted at the end of a leg. "See? We should have stopped for dinner!"

1. Hayden and Aaron (The Determined Actors) 11:20 A.M.
2. Freddy and Kendra (This Year's Models) 11:30 A.M.
3. Kris and Jon (The Long-Distance Smileys) 11:44 A.M.
4. Adam and Rebecca (Team Hellboy) 12:44 P.M. BANKRUPTED

Leg #11: Aaron Saves the Day

This leg, and the final one, air together as a two-hour season finale.

Phil's recap cites Adam's fear of "almost everything he encountered." That's in the freakin' *narration of the show.* So don't get on my case for making fun of him now.

Chatting on the train to Xi'an, which endures a number of eccentric pronunciations, Kris laughs that Jon's big fear for the trip was that she would turn out to be a real raging bitch. Hellboy says that sounds like

Rebecca on a really nice day. Rebecca looks less than amused. Note to Hellboy: when you should be walking on eggs, don't hop.

Yet another bunching, in Xi'an, leads to a Detour. Everybody takes the option that involves spray-painting automobiles. There's little additional complication at the subsequent hunt for the next clue box among the 7,000 ancient clay statues on display at the Terra-Cotta Warriors Museum.

But Hayden's starting to kvetch. She kvetches about their cab not going fast enough. She kvetches about their cabbie not knowing where he's going. This is all stuff Racers should be worried about—and which she's right to be worried about, as their cabbie *is* lost—but it's like the kvetch switch has been switched to eleven, and then broken off.

Things get worse after the team finds the clue at the museum and sets out for the next destination, the north peak of Mount Hua. Unbelievably, they hire the same cab driver a second time, knowing that he got them lost before...and he gets them lost again.

The Roadblock itself derives from the custom, popular among local couples, of stringing padlocks atop the mountain as a symbol of eternal love. Participating Racers must use the unique key included with their clue to unlock one of 3,000 padlocks. The luck-based challenge, which every team assigns to the ladies, is harrowing, especially when Kendra somehow misses the right lock and has to start over. But the continuing travails of the Actors, who have reached the mountain but cannot pierce the language barrier separating them from the correct shuttle bus, are worse. Hayden's reduced to yelling at the locals. Aaron says he hates China, and flings his backpack to the ground.

By the time the Actors ascend on the cable car, only Team Hellboy remains. Both teams face off, in the fading light, aware that the last gondola down leaves soon. Both ladies bleed from blistered fingers.

With less than half an hour left to go, the Actors quit the task, contenting themselves with a mere four-hour penalty. But no sooner do they turn their backs on Team Hellboy...than Rebecca finds the right lock at last.

Aaron winds up and comes *this* close to flinging his backpack off the mountain before some last vestige of sanity keeps him from letting go.

The Actors can only take the penalty and follow Team Hellboy, hoping that Adam and Rebecca manage to get themselves lost for four hours. That's unlikely. And Hayden's thoroughly disgusted with herself: "I lost this for us...I didn't know how to turn a key in a lock." She's not yet ready to hear otherwise. It's been a bad day.

At the Pit Stop on the South Gate of the Xi'an City Wall, Hayden says again that she feels she let Aaron down. Aaron assures her she didn't...then says he has a question to ask her, which he'd been hoping to save for the finish line. What question? Well, it involves getting down on one knee.

"Screw everything else," he says. "Because I have you."

So, in the end, it turns out to be a pretty good day after all.

1. Kris and Jon (The Long-Distance Smileys) 5:27 P.M.
2. Freddy and Kendra (This Year's Models) 6:46 P.M.
3. Adam and Rebecca (Team Hellboy) 11:20 P.M.
4. Hayden and Aaron (The Determined Actors) ELIMINATED

Leg #12: Pizza?

Receiving $200, teams now head for Puu Ualakaa State Park in Hawaii. There is no airport shuffle, as teams must make reservations before they reach the airport, but the scramble leaves the Models with a slight arrival time advantage over the Smileys, and a ninety-minute arrival time advantage over Team Hellboy.

Enjoying the language barrier one last time before leaving China, Rebecca tells the smiling cabbie that Hellboy has three testicles. That's three more than I thought he...oh, stop it. That's just cheap.

All three teams try to arrange earlier connecting flights during their respective layovers in Japan. All three fail, even though Kendra sobs about a sick child they need to get to right away, and Hellboy tells the helpless gate agent she's really, really mean.

I'm sure it bothers her to this very day.

The clue box at Puu Ualakaa is "Outfits," another luck-based challenge requiring teams to go to a clothing distributor and search racks containing 165,000 items of clothing for the garments that match the Hawaiian patterns on a selected mannequin. Not only that, but they get to keep the outfits. Kewl. The other, "Outrigger," requires them to join a steersperson in paddling an outrigger canoe down a course two and a half miles long.

The Smileys take "Outfits" and, unbelievably, complete their search before either of the two remaining two teams can finish the outrigging task. They're first to the Roadblock at Kamaka Air, which requires each participating Racer to tandem skydive from 11,000 feet up, to a clue box standing on a sandbar in waist-deep ocean waters.

This one goes to the guys. And it must be said that Hellboy makes the jump without invoking his mom.

Teams now head for the destination city, Chicago, where the next clue box awaits at the Water Tower.

A potentially crucial moment occurs at the Honolulu Airport. The Smileys believe their ticket clerk, who assures them that the flight landing at 5:43 A.M. is the fastest possible route. But the Models get a flight that lands half an hour earlier, at 5:15 A.M. That's a significant lead, entering the final city this late in the final leg. A minor miracle results in the first flight landing ten minutes late and the second landing fifteen minutes early, reducing the Model lead to only five minutes. (Team Hellboy is still in the air, significantly behind both.) Both make it aboard the same commuter train into the city, but the Models are first to the clue box and first to the next destination, Gino's East Pizzeria.

Yes, it all comes down to requiring each team to share a deep-dish pizza at 7:00 A.M. And though Kendra has a little trouble completing her portion, the Models do manage to complete their meal even before the Smileys arrive.

The final clue directs teams to Ping Tom Memorial Park. There's a jaw-dropping moment as Freddy asks a police officer to lead his team to the park, claiming an "emergency." (The cop is instantly all business, leading Kendra to quite rightly warn Freddy over his choice of words.) And there's some last-minute suspense as the cabbie carrying the Models has trouble finding out just where Ping Tom Memorial Park is (by contrast, the one carrying the Smileys recognizes the address at once). Will this stroke of luck slow down the Models and allow the Smileys to catch up?

Meanwhile, Hellboy stares at his pizza, complaining that he doesn't eat tomatoes.

1. Freddy and Kendra (This Year's Models) WIN
2. Kris and Jon (The Long-Distance Smileys) PLACE
3. Adam and Rebecca (Team Hellboy) SHOW

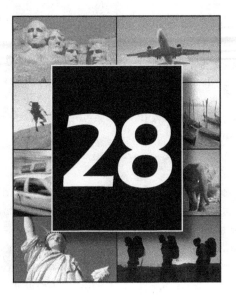

A Dear Jon Letter

EAR JONATHAN:
     I've got to tell you this much.
     I appreciate the interview.
     I also appreciate your constant offers of help, your willingness to discuss events that don't show you in the best possible light, and all the time you took out of your busy day.

All of that struck me as tremendously generous.

The best thing I can say about you is that you were much easier to deal with over the phone than writing about you has been on the printed page.

Because, I've got to tell you, you're the most problematic Racer in the history of the show.

I recognize many of the explanations you give for your actions. You set out to be the villain. Your behavior was heightened. You were on medication. You were victimized by selective editing.

I also note that your fellow Racers defend you with a passion that speaks well of your character off-screen. Your very name brings out the observation that you're one heck of a nice guy. I heard this from people who raced with you, and I heard this from Racers from other seasons.

In a couple of pages, I let you speak for yourself. I can't say I buy everything you say, but once you start saying it, I'll refrain from any further editorial comment.

But I've got to be true to myself, too, so I have to insert a little context.

First: Setting out to be the villain is one thing. So did Rob Mariano, one Race after you. He was cocky to the point of arrogance, conniving to the point where he skirted the boundaries of fair play, and so unflappable in his determination to win that many of his competitors made fools of themselves obsessing over him. But whatever else you can say of him, he never shrieked at anybody: not at Amber, and not at any other players. He never once made anybody cry, except possibly out of frustration that they couldn't wipe that knowing smirk off his face. Your behavior toward Victoria, and on a couple of occasions toward other players, came off as upsetting to them and to us as viewers. I still remember Meredith, of The Queens Girls, sniffing, "I'm not his wife. He doesn't have to scream at me." All right, so maybe she was being overly fragile. I'll buy that. But I'll also buy that you had yelled at her.

Second: Maybe your behavior was heightened in part because of showmanship and in part because of the pressures of the Race. I recognize that stress and hunger and sleep deprivation and constant frustration cause some Racers to do things that they would never do in their everyday lives. Flo is, of course, the poster child for that phenomenon. But she's not alone. No doubt, even Phil must be somewhat easier to get along with at home with his family than when he's hopping flight after flight to stay ahead of you guys. (Though I don't know how you'd measure that—maybe by measuring the arch of those eyebrows.) But, you know, even with all that heightened behavior going on, all that bickering and name-calling and petulance and tears, you're still the only guy, in the history of the show, who ever screamed at that volume, at that length, and that easily. Let alone the only one who ever shoved his wife hard enough to almost knock her over.

Let me put it this way, recognizing in advance that I'm about to offer a spectacularly inexact comparison. In real life, if you're the only guy on the delayed flight who calls the stewardess the "c"-word, then you can't excuse your outburst by saying that "everybody" was on edge that day. Sure they were. But don't drag them into your excuses for taking that obnoxious next step. They didn't go where you went.

There's also the fact that "heightened behavior" works both ways. Your season's Kris and Jon may not have been quite as unflappably cheery as they appeared to be on-screen, but no doubt their heightened behavior included being a little happier to be enjoying this once-in-a-lifetime opportunity for round-the-world adventure. No doubt they smiled a bit more than they would have were they back home doing things like sitting on uncomfortable chairs waiting for their oil to be changed. No doubt that folks who know Kris well can pick out the occasional day when she's downright cranky. But we all pick what behavior we choose to heighten.

I'm not qualified to discuss the medical issue, so I'll skip ahead to the editing explanation. And yes, I absolutely agree that editing creates an incomplete picture. I know, for instance, that the cabbie who ejected you from the cab did so only after a fender bender that is not shown on-screen; in the show, it looks like he just had all he could take of you. In the absence of any hard evidence to the contrary, I'm also willing to believe you when you tell me that an earlier shot, which looked like you were winding up to hit Victoria, came off looking worse than it was, because you were merely gesturing. I'll believe that, even if some others won't, because there's no reason to stampede to the worst possible interpretation of every moment. Finally, I'll believe that the couple of incidents where you seemed to have no sympathy for injuries suffered by your wife also came off as worse than they really were: there's no reason for me to believe you didn't show concern, perhaps a few seconds late, but well within the statute of limitations. After all, my own home life is in part a series of moments when I'm nose-deep in a project and my own wife comes storming into the room with an incensed, "Didn't you hear me saying, 'Ow'?"

We know that editing can create a lot of sins. It can, for instance, omit the cause of an argument and make an excitable guy look like he's flying off the handle for no reason. But, you know, that's not what happens in many of the scenes that show you at your worst. In many of those, we see Victoria say something in a conversational tone of voice, and you respond by screaming. On another occasion, we see you scream at Team Hellboy, for following you in the train station. The clip clearly shows that you're the one who turned around and started yelling, proceeding directly from zero to sixty without so much as a single cross word as provocation.

Race 5's Colin also complains about editing, pointing to specific cases where he believes moments were altered to create a nastier impression of him. But watching his season after yours, instead of the other way around, the Tanzanian incident discussed elsewhere is his only really bad moment. Let's talk for a moment about one of his good ones: the Roadblock involving the consumption of two pounds of caviar. Christie takes that one, and perseveres, despite a revulsion that makes her physically ill. Colin doesn't call her a lightweight or a drama queen. He sees that she's genuinely suffering, and treats her with compassion and support throughout. Contrast this to some of what you did, during a very similar incident in Budapest. Victoria's no less ill, forcing herself to eat that spicy soup. You call her a lightweight and a drama queen. Okay, so granted, you apologize later. But editing didn't put those words in your mouth.

The fact is, Jonathan, that there's only so much editing can do. Editing cannot make somebody scream when he didn't scream, it cannot change the words we physically see come out of someone's mouth, and it cannot completely mitigate moments like Colin taunting the law or you shoving Victoria. We saw enough of both incidents to get the gist. And there are no camera angles, or better edits, sufficient to make either of you look virtuous in either of those situations.

You said that there were several possible cuts. Well, I buy that. But let's be honest here. As I'm certain you acknowledge, there's no magic cut which shows Hera screaming at her dad for being lame. There's no magic cut where Jon hauls off and shoves a sobbing Kris hard enough to almost knock her over. There's no magic cut where Lena harangues Kristy about this being a Race, with no room for compassion. And there's a reason: because none of those things ever happened.

You provided the material.

You may not believe this, Jonathan, but I say all of these things with significant respect. Like I said, I appreciate all you've done for this book, and have no reason to demonize you. I'm willing to heed the word of all those other Racers who say you're usually a nice guy. I'm also willing to give Victoria credit for knowing you better than I do, because she's married to you and I only know you from a TV show or two. You certainly know what happened on the Race. But I know enough to be able to judge explanations for what I saw. And your explanations do not entirely satisfy.

I appreciate your giving me the opportunity to get these things off my chest, and, in all honesty, wish you the best of health and the best of luck in your future endeavors.

Sincerely,

—Adam-Troy Castro

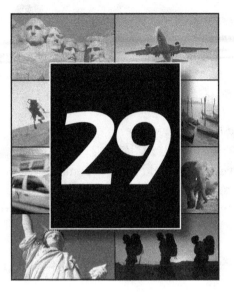

Jonathan Speaks.
Doesn't Yell. Speaks.

ENTREPRENEUR JONATHAN BAKER (TEAM EXPLOSIVE), the most controversial Racer in the show's history, dominated his entire season with his various eruptions. His on-screen antics reached their peak with an incident in Berlin so extreme that producers were moved to tell fans and press alike that he'd been given a stern talking-to. After the show aired, he and wife, former *Playboy* model Victoria Fuller, became among the most visible ex-Racers, appearing on multiple other reality shows, most recently including an (at press time, unaired) episode of *Fear Factor*, which has just reported another Jonathan and Victoria incident destined to make reality show history.

Q: *Am I speaking to Victoria, right now, or are you the only one there?*

JONATHAN: No, I'm the only one here, but if you need to speak with Victoria, we can arrange that for later. We've been doing interviews since five o'clock this morning, so she had to go.

Q: *Okay, I understand that. I thank you for the time you're able to give. If I get a chance to speak with her later, I'd enjoy that.*

JONATHAN: Absolutely. I want you to get it from both sides.[48] I do a lot of interviews, so I want people to know the television version of Jonathan and Victoria versus the real version of Jonathan and Victoria.

Q: *I understand that when you're on a show like this, you're getting the hothouse version of your personality.*

JONATHAN: I've always said that CBS could have cut three versions of the exact same Race. The good version, the bad version, the ugly version, and the nonexistent version,[49] like, you know, the Jon and Kris version.

Q: *Are you saying that there (could have been) a bad version with them as well?*

JONATHAN: Well, I think they have different versions of everybody. They know, going in, who they're going to pick to play what roles, but they definitely have different versions. If they wanted to pick Jon and Kris as the bickering team, they could obviously do that. After all, they're only showing about three percent of 500 hours filmed.

Q: *Well, let's start with a few background questions about the filming. First, I'm aware that you travel with a cameraman and sound man, and must buy tickets for them whenever you're traveling anywhere. Obviously, on-screen, you're only shown negotiating tickets for two people, but you're actually buying tickets for four.*

JONATHAN: Correct.

Q: *So you film this twice?*

JONATHAN: No, you only film it once. But when you go up to the agent, you buy two tickets. Then when the cameras go off, you have to buy two more.

---

[48] That never happened, but not out of any refusal on Jonathan's part; I had a lot of interviews to conduct and just made do with his own words. This exchange is included here to establish that he wasn't deliberately keeping her out of the loop. Also to be fair, we spent a lot more time discussing the Race as a whole, compared to the controversial aspects of his appearance, than is shown here; we focus on that for space reasons.

[49] That's actually four, of course.

Q: *What happens if you buy two tickets and there are no tickets available for your crew?*

JONATHAN: You don't go. The good thing is, they frustrate everybody equally.

Q: *When you're dealing with long delays between exciting moments—*

JONATHAN: The travel points.

Q: *—yes. How did you occupy yourselves at such points?*

JONATHAN: Some people go into down mode. Some people sleep. Some people do nothing. I treated it as a chance to get information. I made contact with as many people as I could. I panhandled. I found people with cell phones and got their numbers, so that if we needed them once we got where we were going, they were available to us.

Q: *So you were still working to get an advantage.*

JONATHAN: I never put the game down. Other people did. And that kind of made me crazy, and you saw the craziness....I must say that the Race you saw on television is not the same Race I ran.

Q: *I will ask about personal hygiene issues. Some Racers have said that by the time they get where they're headed, they smell like derelicts....*

JONATHAN: Part of the cost of doing business. I don't know about anybody else, but when I got on an airplane, I used to strip myself down, in the bathroom, and literally take a bath. I took the position that everywhere I went was like my home, and I had to do whatever I needed to make sure my body got the rest it needed.

Q: *What about food and water deprivation?*

JONATHAN: There's sleep deprivation, food deprivation, you walk around in a bubble like you're in a time warp...but I always had more money than anybody, because I would professionally panhandle. I would sit down next to somebody, and I would talk to them. I would ask them who they were, what they were, and what was going on. Without telling them I was on *The Amazing Race*,

I would tell them I was on a global adventure around the world, and I would tell them that in my normal life I was like them, that I was a businessman, who did this and did that, and then I would ask them for a couple of hundred dollars. I was very bold about asking them for a couple of hundred.

Q: *Did anybody actually give you that amount?*

JONATHAN: Sometimes I got a couple of hundred, sometimes I got fifty, sometimes I got more than that. People were very generous if they had the money. People took me to their ATMs. In Sweden, I had a guy—you kinda saw him on television—he took me to his ATM and gave me $500.

Q: *I'll admit to being impressed.*

JONATHAN: In the end we had all this money, and we ended up giving it all to the children in Ethiopia. We had a thousand dollars. I no longer needed the money, and I wanted to do something great, and I wanted the trip to climax with something amazing. And, you know, to see these people's faces, these people making eighty dollars a year, and I'm giving away a thousand dollars, which is something like eight times that, if not a little bit more. This is what's going to help them throughout their entire year, and we gave it to the kids to bring back to their mothers and fathers, so they could be a little joyous about it. We gave them all the clothes in our backpacks, and everything off of our backs. And you know what? This is what you didn't see of Jonathan and Victoria. You just got all this ugly energy. And, you know, *The Amazing Race* is a family show, and it really was supposed to represent something great. [They had villains] Colin and Christie, Jonathan and Victoria, and Rob and Amber, and they really calmed down with Rob and Amber. They didn't calm down with me and Victoria, or with Colin and Christie. We could have been the villains without having that nasty, abusive energy. But, everybody fought like that. Aaron threw his backpack at Hayden in China.[50] Adam fought with Rebecca. And so on....

---

[50] No, he didn't, actually. He got pissed off at her, and tossed her backpack at her feet, telling her it was time to carry it. But point taken. It was done in anger.

Q: *So you're saying the Racers in general were all the same way, and that your [scenes] were edited worse than the others?*

JONATHAN: I'm saying that. I'm also saying my actions were probably over-the-top. I went there turning off the filters. I went in there as a heightened reality. I went in there making the conscious decision to play it up and make reality television a moment in time on *The Amazing Race*. I didn't think that it was towards Victoria that all of this energy was going to be coming out, and it was really sad to see that every time I would rev up and do these great things that I run over Victoria in the process.

Q: *So we get to the moment that caused all the hubbub. That was the shove in Berlin. That moment was very ugly, and it's hard to explain away entirely as editing. Victoria was very legitimately upset at that moment.*

JONATHAN: But wait a minute. I never told her to come in crying. I never did that to her. She did that to herself. Because she was so visibly upset, people think that was caused by me. But if you look what's happening there, that was a zone camera. CBS does not show zone cameras. They do not show technical people in the background. You'll never see cameras, gibs, directors, and producers in the background. If you stop that scene, you will see Freddy and Kendra on the mat. You'll see all the production people. That camera was a zone camera from a mile away. And what you don't understand is that Victoria and I were fighting at that point. We were both in this kind of huff of "Why did you pick up my bag?" She was shoving me, and I was shoving her. When I shoved her, I shoved her knapsack as to "be quiet," [because] I was having a kind of boo-boo fit, and she was in a walk, breathing hard, and she kind of tripped over herself. Again, it wasn't right what I did, but I turned off the filters coming in. I had a choice. I could either say, "Baby, what's going on?" and calm her down, or take that moment and push it over the top... you know what? She broke herself down. And I think that she learned a lot about herself in that moment. Because... people think that was me, that I did something to her. And I had nothing to do with that moment other than the fact that I had dropped my bag. I just turned off the filters, and played up the moment. And, you know, looking back, they could have left that push in there all day along. That wasn't what bothered me. It was the editing up to that point that bothered me.

Q: *Because it showed the increasing tension leading up to that point?*

JONATHAN: Because of the ugly energy leading up to that point. It was just about Jonathan abusing Victoria. I don't hit Victoria. I've never hit her in my life. And I'm a better person than they portrayed me. And I don't mind being the villain. I just hated being what they set me out to me. You've got murderers in this world, child molesters, and then spousal abusers. I'm not a spousal abuser. Am I aggressive? Yeah. Was I verbally aggressive? Yeah. Was I running a race for a million dollars? Yeah. Do people die on the streets for five dollars? Yeah. So, in my mind-set, I entered this Race like a boxer entering a ring. I had trained for six months; I was ready to go. Victoria was still ramping up on the second leg. It was my mistake that I didn't turn down the volume, so that she could catch up to me. You know, somebody wrote something online that strikes me as one of the most accurate things anybody ever wrote about us. (*searching*) "Jonathan and Victoria were not sympatico. Jonathan was playing a game, and Victoria was an unwilling participant. She couldn't hold her own, and Jonathan didn't let that faze him. He totally ignored her needs and pushed that aside. That's what happened to plenty of teams, but Jonathan never pulled back."

Q: *Bertram van Munster made reference, in the press, to talking to you after that incident.*

JONATHAN: Never happened. Not in relation to that shove. I had quit the Race because I was so upset. I was upset with Victoria because it was very important to me that we stay focused. I didn't want to run a Race for the sake of running a Race. If Victoria couldn't step up to the plate and we couldn't get on the same path, I didn't want to continue. What happened is Phil and Bertram basically took us for a drink and said, "You can quit, you can do anything you want, but you'll regret it for the rest of your life. You need to keep going, because you have a chance to win. You have a chance to be two of the all-time best Racers on the show." Everything he was telling us, tooting our horn left and right, telling us we'd accomplished things with panhandling and so on that he'd never seen before—that brought us back into the Race.

Q: *Following that, you had the situation in Budapest, with the spicy soup. . . .*

JONATHAN: The one thing I regret was not eating that soup.

Q: *I wanted some.*

JONATHAN: I don't think so. It was pure Tabasco.

Q: *Sounds good to me.*

JONATHAN: Well, that's why I regret not doing it, because I could have put it down. Victoria was gagging. She was gagging from her throat, not her stomach, which made everybody else throw up. Freddy was the only one who truly threw up. . . .

Q: *In his own bowl.*

JONATHAN: Yeah, that was disgusting.

Q: *I think that was the most harrowing food challenge in the show's history.*

JONATHAN: Oh, I don't think so. I think the caviar scene in Russia[51] was ten times worse. They just didn't show how much vomiting was involved.

Q: *Which brings up an interesting point. A lot of the stunt work you do on the show, the bungee jumps and rappeling and so on, are safety-tested up the wazoo, which is why amateurs can do it without automatically getting killed. But these volume-based food challenges really strike me as potentially dangerous to people's health.*

JONATHAN: I agree with you. The soup, not so much, but to put four pounds of meat into somebody's stomach . . . all they want to do is

---

[51] Race 5.

make people throw up all the time. My gut instinct[52] is that they'll get away from that in the future.

Q: *What was your reaction once the show aired and you saw how you looked?*

JONATHAN: I knew it was going to be ugly. I didn't know until the third episode how ugly it was going to be, because the coming attraction of them stopping the motion as I raised my hand to Victoria—it just didn't happen that way—it was me pulling a map out of her hand. And that point I kinda knew what was happening. I was in talks with CBS asking, "Why are you doing what you're doing?" And they were like, "This is about ratings, and this is the way it works, and you signed it away," and I knew I did, so that was fine. But I said, "You could have gone about it a different way and had the same results, because you would have had a champion of a villain, rather than something that just had this ugly energy." At the end of the day, they said this was great television, that this was the greatest thing that ever happened to the Race. It cost them twenty-seven million to film the Race. My energy, my shove, my going over the top made them 710 million, and made them become the well-known franchise that they are today. Then Rob and Amber came in and solidified that. So, between Rob and Amber and myself and Victoria, we resurrected a dying franchise.

Q: *Was it?*

JONATHAN: Let me give you a little background about the show. Races 1, 2, 3, and 4 were all about the *Fear Factor* elements: getting to a race car and racing it, putting on the tires, bungee jumping. The strategic part of the game was using the Yield was pulled out because CBS wanted them to cut the budget. When 5 came, the show was ready to be canceled. They gave it one last shot, and cut the budget by cutting down the Fast Forwards, which broke my heart. Pulling out the Fast Forward took away the game aspect of it. And that's when they decided to use the Colin and Christie edit, to make the show all about caricatures, as opposed to the Race.

---

[52] To coin a phrase.

Q: *Still, you followed the Race trying to reclaim your reputation, doing spin control on Dr. Phil....*

   JONATHAN: I wouldn't call it spin control. I wanted people to understand what the combustion of this moment was. If you go to my Web site and you look at the press statement that was put out there, you will get a sense of what really happened.

Q: *It got pretty ugly for you, personally.*

   JONATHAN: We've been together for nine years. We've been married for four and a half. We have a pretty good relationship. We're not abusive toward one another. I can't tell you how much of a misrepresentation that edit was. But that also becomes the dynamic and the magic of what's going on here... because whenever we go out in public, whenever we're out in big cities like Vegas or New York or Chicago, anywhere but L.A., people don't come up to us and say, "You're bad people." They come up and want to know who we are, what it was like.

Q: *You still appear on other shows. Have you changed anything because of the bad experience?*

   JONATHAN: It wasn't a bad experience. It was a bad edit. To me, reality television is like going to summer camp. If there's a million dollars attached to it, I just take it a little more seriously. But you're running their maze, their gauntlet, and inside of that maze, that's reality.

Race 7,
Chasing Rob and Amber

THE WILD CARD THIS TIME out was the presence of Amber Brkich and "Boston" Rob Mariano, veterans of the reality show *Survivor* who met and fell in love while filming *Survivor: All-Stars* (coming in first and second, respectively). Already recognized as intense competitors from that show, their appearance here aroused the wrath of several other teams, who felt that that this team had already had a chance to win a reality competition and didn't "deserve" to appear on this one. Some players were not interested in running their own Race as much as they wanted to beat Rob and Amber, in particular. Wave good-bye to most of them.

The Race was marked by a fresh innovation: from this point on, teams arriving last during non-elimination legs are not only stripped of their money, but also of all belongings other than the clothes they have on. That's gotta suck.

The other elements distinguishing the Race: the two most upsetting mishaps in the entire history of the series. We're talking physical injuries here. Potentially serious physical injuries. It was not funny.

DRAMATIS PERSONAE

1. Team POW

Ron Young, 28, a helicopter pilot and POW in the Second Iraq War, and off-and-on girlfriend Kelly McCorkle, 26, a legislative correspondent and former Miss South Carolina, make up this team. They're strong competitors, but their relationship issues dog them throughout, especially at the very end, when it all gets to be too much, already.

2. Team Enron

At first, Uchenna Agu, 40, an energy broker, and Joyce Agu, 44, a sales manager, who had their savings wiped out by the corporate collapses of Enron and WorldCom, seem a virtual reprise of Race 5's Chip and Kim. It's not just that he shaves his head, or that they're a level-headed, forty-something black couple running the Race hoping for a million-dollar solution to crippling money problems, or that they seem to enjoy themselves throughout, or that he appears to have a cast-iron stomach that serves him well during food-consumption challenges, or even that they make a habit of stopping to help weaker teams in trouble. It's *all* of that. Their greatest strength (and it's a doozy): not giving up when all seems lost. **SEASON SUPERSTARS**

3. The California Girls

California roommates Megan Baker, 26, a fashion designer, Heidi Heidel, 31, a full-time mom, are a nice, likeable, and attractive team, but aren't around long enough to leave any impression more substantial than that.

4. The Virginia Girls

Lifelong friends Debbie Cloyed, 25, a photographer, and Bianca Smith, 26, a high-school teacher, are smart, fast on their feet, and so insistently huggy, at least when things are going well, that some Internet posters (who really oughta get a life) presumed that they had to be hiding the true depths of their relationship. Ooooh. They show genuine talent for some aspects of the game. Alas, they're not exactly savants at llama handling, or finding the world's great mountain ranges.

5. Team Truman Show

Engaged couple Rob Mariano, 29, and Amber Brkich, 26, met and became engaged on one reality show, went on to appear on this one, and subsequently wed on another. Here dubbed "Team Truman Show," after the popular movie, because they seem destined to live all the major events of their lives on television, they prove one of the toughest, and hardest-to-beat, teams in the show's history. Their major strengths include their obvious cunning, endurance, and athletic ability, as well as a world filled with people who recognize them from *Survivor* and will fall all over themselves to help them win this competition too. Their major weakness: Rob's overconfidence, so extreme that at times he seems to regard actually winning as a tiresome formality. **SEASON SUPERSTARS**

6. The Bottom Feeders

Dating couple Ray Housteau, 44, a stockbroker, and Deana Shane, 27, a marketing executive, are not quite as unstoppable as Ray seems to think they are. His constant scary pronouncements about which teams do not deserve to be ranked with his, and his contempt for the weaker teams he considers "bottom feeders," make many audiences long for the dropping of the other shoe. It also earns him the name we use here.

7. The Gay Blades

Lovers Lynn Warren, 30, and Alex Ali, 22, both executive assistants, are among the teams obsessed with beating Rob and Amber. That is, truly obsessed with Rob and Amber: they don't appear to be concerned about the doings of any teams other than the pair from *Survivor*. It gets to be a bit much, to tell the truth. Their weaknesses include: dealing with local merchants. Their strengths: dealing with each other.

8. Team Energizer Bunny

This Race's dark horses, married Meredith Smith, 69, retired executive, and Gretchen Smith, 66, retired flight attendant/RN, are between them the oldest team in the show's history. They're also often lost, often in over their heads, and often certain that they're about to come in last. Gretchen spends much of her time whining, "Ohhhh, nooooo." It's no wonder Ray counts them among the bottom feeders. But watch a few legs and you'll discover something. They refuse to go down, even in the face of injury or bankruptcy. Watch for Gretchen and the elephant. **SEASON SUPERSTARS**

9. The New Stooges

Self-described "two ol' fat fellas from the hills of South Carolina," best friends Ryan Phillips, 31, a general contractor, and Chuck Horton, 32, a salesman, are funny fat guys with pronounced Southern accents who provide hilarious commentary from their very first step. As they're quick to point out, they can count on their accents to give people the false assumption that they're stupid. They're not. But can they prevail, when they also admit they're toast the first time it comes down to a footrace?

10. The Bouncer Brothers

Brothers Brian Smith, 27, an actor/bartender, and Greg Smith, 24, a bouncer, are a young, fit team, funniest when they point out that they don't need the Race to figure out their "relationship." Their greatest strength is coming from behind. Their weakness is often having to. If it comes down to a footrace, they'll likely win. But they do need to work on their map-reading skills and their driving.

11. Team Heckboy

Mother and gay son Susan Vaughn, 54, a director of judicial affairs, and Patrick Vaughn, 26, a writer, declare an early mission to defeat Rob and Amber, but run into trouble as Patrick turns snappy, resentful, and eager to quit—all qualities that make him seem a replay of Race 6's much more memorable Hellboy.

THE GAME PLAY

Leg #1: "If You Ain't the Lead Dawg...."

This leg airs as a two-hour premiere episode.

Starting out from Long Beach, California, teams receive $132 and are alerted to catch one of two available flights to Lima, Peru. As always, the first drive to the airport is marked by plenty of breathless yelling, lots of "go, go, go," and some iffy driving moments—notably one where Heidi almost smashes up her team's car. Just imagine how embarrassing that would be. The Gay Blades witness the near-wreck, thus establishing one of their team themes for the Race.

Along the way, Gretchen wonders why they're not at home in front of their fireplace, watching this, instead of actually being in it. For one thing, the shows you're in aren't on tonight, so you don't have to worry about missing anything. For another, televisions tend to burn up if you keep them in the fireplace. Thank you, I'll be here all week. No way are these old folks lasting past the first leg—especially since the extra scenes on the DVD reveal that their first crisis was trying to figure out how to open the trunk of their automobile. Naah, they ain't lasting. Not at all.

Though there are plenty of amiable scenes of the teams getting to know each other, the upshot is that the American Airlines flight, which lands in Lima approximately ninety minutes earlier, carries everybody but The Gay Blades, Team Truman Show, Team Energizer Bunny, and The Bouncer Brothers. The remaining teams get a head start to the clue box at Plaza de las Armas, which directs teams to take a bus thirty miles to the city of Ancon.

Team Truman Show meets the first of several locals who leap at the opportunity to help the famous Rob and Amber.

The Bouncer Brothers and Gay Blades hook up with a local who not only guides them to the right place, but performs somersaults while doing it. A dismayed dog watches from a rooftop.

Once in Ancon, teams take rickshaws to the beach known as Playa Hermosa. The New Stooges show smarts by recognizing that they're a bit hefty for their rickshaw driver and getting out to help him pull, thus circumventing the letter of the rules while honoring their intent. True, they tire themselves out and have to hop aboard again, but it's still a good move. I do hope these guys stick around.

At the beach, three sand piles hide airplane tickets to Cusco. 6:00 A.M., 7:00 A.M., and 7:40 A.M. tickets are available, each pile clearly marked by signs. Teams claiming one ticket cannot change their mind and claim another. So it's worth their time to make sure they're looking in the best possible pile. The California Girls blow this rule by proceeding directly to the

7:40 A.M. pile, when there are still 7:00 A.M. tickets available. So do The New Stooges, thus blowing their previous "good move" karma. And Team Energizer Bunny. By contrast, The Bouncer Brothers are happy to remember their childhood lessons to the effect that 7:00 A.M. is earlier than 7:40 A.M. And Team Enron, arriving last, benefits from the sloppiness of every team that claimed the slowest tickets for no good reason.

It shakes out like this. 6:00 A.M.: The Virginia Girls, Team Heckboy, Team Truman Show. 7:00 A.M.: The Bottom Feeders, The Gay Blades, Team Enron. 7:40 A.M.: The New Stooges, The California Girls, Team POW, Team Energizer Bunny. But wait. The next morning, that middle plane suffers a mechanical problem and is delayed until after the 7:40 A.M. flight. Everybody on it manages to switch tickets and join the 7:40 A.M. flight, so we end up with a mega-bunching that affects everybody but the first three teams.

Arriving in Cusco, 11,000 feet above sea level, teams all follow instructions and drink some coca tea before proceeding, as a hedge against altitude sickness. This doesn't go anywhere, but it's a nice safety tip. On the taxi ride into the mountains, Rob tells Amber how easy it would be for their car to go over the edge and, in his words, cry, "Sayonara!" She studiedly ignores him.

From there, clues lead teams to a zip line across a gorge, which leads only to another zip line to the bottom of the gorge, which means that every team will now provide us with not one, not two, but four opportunities to watch silly people saying, "Whooooooo." Which most do (though the Stooges endear by talking about being the first team to load-test the line, and Gretchen endears by invoking the word wedgie). So we move on.

Following the zip line, we get the Detour: "Rope a Llama" or "Rope a Basket." "Rope a Llama" requires teams to lead two llamas up a hill, into their pen. In "Rope a Basket" teams sling baskets carrying thirty-five pounds of alfalfa across their backs, and carry them two-thirds of a mile. The llamas are easy enough to handle as long as players realize that somebody has to prod them from behind, but damn few Racers realize that. Of the players who take this option, Heckboy gets spit on, The Virginia Girls fight bitterly, and Team Energizer Bunny knows just what to do. They must come from the age when wild llamas ruled the Earth.

The Gay Blades sing their own made-up ditty, "We are racing in Peru, we are racing in Peru," which is such an *homage* to "New York Jews in Iceland" that they should pay Avi and Joe royalties.

Any teams that complete the Detour have to go to the Huambatio police station and hop in a marked delivery truck—apparently the local means of mass transportation—to the town of Pisac, site of a crowded and chaotic marketplace that hides the route marker with directions to the Pit Stop.

The delivery truck schedule pans out like this. First truck: Team Truman Show, Team Heckboy. Second truck: The Virginia Girls. Third truck, some time later: The Bouncer Brothers and The Gay Blades. Fourth (avoiding The Bottom Feeders by seconds): Team Energizer Bunny. (Gretchen breaks an old lady's eggs and ends up paying her off.) Fifth: The Bottom Feeders and Team Enron. Sixth: The New Stooges, The California Girls, and Team POW.

On the way, the Stooges sing "She'll Be Coming 'Round the Mountain," not the last team to do so (see p. 357 "Race 8, Bringing the Kids").

After the marketplace, it's a cab ride to the Pit Stop at La Merced, a church in Cusco. Lynn hectors his cabbie: "*Muy, muy, muy . . .* wait, what am I saying? Very, very, very?" Hee. Team Truman Show gets stuck behind a disabled van, and hops out to move it out of the way.

It all comes down to a footrace between Team POW and the Stooges, with the Stooges losing by a few short steps. Chuck notes, "If you ain't the lead dawg, the view ahead never changes." Which are definitely words to live by.

1. Debbie and Bianca (The Virginia Girls) 10:54 A.M.
2. Susan and Patrick (Team Heckboy) 11:05 A.M.
3. Rob and Amber (Team Truman Show) 11:09 A.M.
4. Brian and Greg (The Bouncer Brothers) 11:59 A.M.
5. Lynn and Alex (The Gay Blades) 12:00 P.M.
6. Gretchen and Meredith (Team Energizer Bunny) 12:24 P.M.
7. Ray and Deana (The Bottom Feeders) 12:41 P.M.[53]
8. Uchenna and Joyce (Team Enron) 12:47 P.M.
9. Megan and Heidi (The California Girls) 12:55 P.M.

---

[53] By the time her team reaches Huambatio, Deana is already showing signs of the eye irritation that causes her to spend much of her remaining time on-screen squinting like Popeye. It's not the kind of thing you want happening to you during your fifteen minutes of fame.

10. Ron and Kelly (Team POW) 12:58 P.M.
11. Ryan and Chuck (The New Stooges) ELIMINATED

Leg #2: Lynn and the Fishmongers

Teams now receive $480 and instructions to take a bus approximately 400 miles to the city of Arequipa, where the next clue awaits at the local shoeshine union.

Rob-hating intensifies during the long night at the bus station, when everybody meekly waits in line for a 6:20 A.M. departure, while he goes to the trouble of, you know, actually investigating his options. It seems a 7:00 A.M. bus has fewer stops and will arrive first. Rob shares this information with The Bottom Feeders and Team Enron, with whom he has a kind of loose alliance, but not with anybody else. The Gay Blades and Virginia Girls are among the several teams incensed upon discovering the deception. "It makes me nauseous to have to deal with that kind of stuff," Debbie says. "Let's just say it's a good thing people can't be voted off," Lynn says. And Rob, who has been here before, merely winks at the camera, as if to say, *just playing the game, my man. Just playing the game.*

The end result? Everybody ends up on the same ten-hour bus trip, which The Bouncer Brothers spend making very good friends with The California Girls. Are we gonna get to see one of those complicating Race-long flirtations? Let's wait and see.

Meanwhile, on the way to Arequipa, Rob colludes with Team POW, Team Enron, and The Bottom Feeders on another evil scheme: bribing the bus driver to only open the front doors, and not those in the rear, once they reach their destination. BWAH-ha-ha-ha!!!

The clue box at the shoeshine union requires each participating player to hit the streets and shine five pairs of shoes for one Peruvian sol apiece. Ron performs the task with military precision. Gretchen and Susan prove excellent at smudging shoe polish on socks, and Joyce stands on a side street hollering, "I need to polish some shoes! Help me!" Ah, well.

All teams completing the task are awarded airplane tickets to Santiago, Chile, on one of two flights leaving forty-five minutes apart. The first flight carries Team POW, Team Truman Show, The Bottom Feeders, Team Heckboy, and Team Energizer Bunny. Everybody else gets the second.

In Santiago, a clue box near a giant statue of the Virgin Mary provides the Detour: "Shop" or "Schlep." The first gives teams a shopping list they must fulfill at a local market, and deliver to a local restaurant. The second requires teams to pick up 180 books, of their choice, at a local bookstore, delivering them via hand truck to the Library of Congress, some five blocks away. Rob's skill at stacking books allows his team an early finish at "Schlep." Of the teams that pick "Shop," Team Heckboy runs out of money, Gretchen of Team Energizer Bunny screeches so much she disturbs stray animals, and The Gay Blades foment an international incident. Jeez.

In the end, The Bouncer Brothers spot The California Girls in the next cab over, and hop out to complete the Race to the Pit Stop at Cerro Santa Lucia on foot. It's a thrilling last-minute scramble, lent pathos when the Brothers realize that they now have to say good-bye to the girls. So, no Race-long flirtation. Sorry.

1. Rob and Amber (Team Truman Show) 12:34 P.M.
2. Ron and Kelly (Team POW) 1:24 P.M.
3. Ray and Deana (The Bottom Feeders) 2:17 P.M.
4. Uchenna and Joyce (Team Enron) 3:16 P.M.
5. Lynn and Alex (The Gay Blades) 3:19 P.M.
6. Debbie and Bianca (The Virginia Girls) 3:20 P.M.
7. Gretchen and Meredith (Team Energizer Bunny) 3:24 P.M.
8. Susan and Patrick (Team Heckboy) 3:35 P.M.
9. Brian and Greg (The Bouncer Brothers) 3:46 P.M.
10. Megan and Heidi (The California Girls) ELIMINATED

Leg #3: A Trip to the Beach

Receiving eighty dollars, teams must now pick up cars and drive 150 miles through the Andes Mountains, entering Argentina, where the next clue awaits at a bridge called Puente Viejo.

Forget some early intrigue involving purloined taxis, The Gay Blades scheming to oust Team Truman Show, and Meredith's hair sticking straight up in a way that resembles an old man mohawk. The parking garage where their cars await doesn't even open until 5:00 A.M., so everybody enters the building then, accompanied by a friendly street dog who looks like he knows where he's going.

As a result, teams end up traversing the switchbacks of one of the world's great mountain ranges in what amounts to a caravan, complete with aerial footage.

That is, every team but two. The Virginia Girls miss the crucial exit off the main highway and continue north long after they should have veered to the east. Team Heckboy is still puttering around Santiago looking for the highway long after every other team but the Girls have already crossed into Argentina. Serious yowch here.

Team Truman Show is first to the bridge at Puente Viejo, site of the Detour: "Paddle" or "Pedal." In "Paddle" teams join three professional rowers in paddling an inflatable raft seven miles downriver. "Pedal" requires teams to mountain-bike the same distance, along train tracks.

Far behind them, Team Heckboy is still climbing the Andes. Wow. That was some delay. Can't imagine anything that bad.

Like, for instance, Debbie and Bianca, enjoying a beachfront drive. They both go wow. But, ummm, guys, you weren't supposed to find the beach. You were supposed to find the *Andes*. Even as it occurs to them that they're in trouble, they have driven two hours past the necessary exit, adding four hours to their total time. Can they recover?

That depends on developments at Camping Suizo, seventy miles past Puente Viejo in the city of Mendoza. The Roadblock requires each participating player to complete a "traditional Argentinean meal," comprising four pounds of cow ribs, pork sausage, blood sausage, cow intestine, cow udder, a kidney, and part of a saliva gland. Four friggin' *pounds*.[54] When Team Truman Show arrives (second, after the Blades), Rob elects to eat.

Far behind them, Team Heckboy completes white-water rafting. And, behind *them*, The Virginia Girls finally arrive at the bridge. Debbie, who almost died in a rafting accident only two months earlier, agrees to face her fears and enter the water again.

At Camping Suizo, Rob realizes he can't finish. He also realizes that the penalty for refusing to continue, four hours, might still put him ahead of late-arriving teams that elect to eat. Persuading three other teams to quit *after* he does ensures his team's survival for the leg. Given

---

[54] Significantly, Ron, the former POW, goes on the record as calling this the "worst eating experience that I've ever had in my entire life. And, mind you, I lost twenty-five pounds in about eighteen days in an Iraqi prison. Not to say that the food in the Iraqi prison wasn't worse, but I didn't have to eat *four pounds* of it."

that he also had serious problems during an eating challenge on *Survivor*, it may be the smartest move any Racer ever made.

Cut to Team Heckboy. Mom's eating a protein bar. Heckboy's hoping his team can snag some cheap eats. Heh. But once they reach the Roadblock, Heckboy turns moody and resentful, and lingers over his feast just long enough for The Virginia Girls to catch up. Debbie tears into the meal with such gusto that the contest becomes a contest again. But the Girls are still last to the Pit Stop at Estancio San Isidro.

1. Lynn and Alex (The Gay Blades) 3:49 P.M.
2. Uchenna and Joyce (Team Enron) 4:07 P.M.
3. Brian and Greg (The Bouncer Brothers) 4:52 P.M.
4. Ron and Kelly (Team POW) 4:52 P.M.
5. Rob and Amber (Team Truman Show) 6:59 P.M.
6. Ray and Deana (The Bottom Feeders) 8:34 P.M.
7. Gretchen and Meredith (Team Energizer Bunny) 8:44 P.M.
8. Susan and Patrick (Team Heckboy) 8:56 P.M.
9. Debbie and Bianca (The Virginia Girls) ELIMINATED

Leg #4: Farewell to Heckboy

Receiving forty-five dollars, teams now travel twenty-five miles to a ranch called Cabaña La Guatana. The ranch doesn't even open until 6:30 A.M. A quick look at the last leg's departure times reveals that everybody who arrived early and ate the meat should arrive by then. In fact, it takes Team Enron, The Bouncer Brothers, and Team POW considerably longer. Why? I dunno!

Anyhoo, the Roadblock is a gaucho challenge, requiring each participating player to ride a horse around a series of barrels, and, using a stick, spear a ring hanging from a wire, in forty seconds or less. One early participant, Joyce, requests a "nice" horse and gets one that dumps her twice. It's all relative, dear.

Teams completing the Roadblock now drive themselves to Mendoza Airport, where one of two charter flights will take them to Buenos Aires. For once, the two flights are not a token interval apart. One's at 9:30 P.M., and one's at 2:30 A.M.

Leaving the Pit Stop with Deana after some teams have already completed the Roadblock and secured seats on the first plane, Ray uses his favorite phrase for the first time. "We're stuck at the back of the pack with the bottom feeders, and I don't want to be associated with teams of that caliber." He's especially embarrassed by Gretchen and Meredith. "We've got to beat the old people." It's no "I'm so serious, we've got to beat the midget," but it will do. There's a lot more of it in the deleted scenes. But wait.

The Gay Blades, Team Enron, Team POW, and The Bouncer Brothers—all of whom ate the meat—all secure seats on the 9:30 P.M. flight, and crow about this opportunity to leave Team Truman Show far behind. Lynn even takes great satisfaction in saying, "Survive *that*." They're all less than happy when Team Truman Show slips aboard just before the door closes.

Rob cracks, "Ron, how's your stomach?"

(Wait 'til the finale. Wait.)

Far behind them, The Bottom Feeders make it to the ranch, where Deana elects to ride. She fails several attempts. Ray's idea of support is telling her the horse isn't broken (unlike some oxen). He is not pleased when the oldsters show up and Meredith beats the competitive time on his first try. Hee hee.

Teams arriving in Buenos Aires must then travel twenty miles by train to the city of Tigre. This is the site of the Detour: two water searches called "Shipwreck" and "Island." "Shipwreck" requires teams to search a seven-square-mile area, filled with many abandoned vessels, for one particular wreck they can only identify from a photo taken when the boat was new. In "Island" teams must find the inlet to the San Antonio River and use a map to find a small island bearing their next route marker.

Despite the usual traumas, the first five teams all make it to the Pit Stop at La Martina (Argentina's most prestigious polo club) before the last three even arrive in Buenos Aires. Of those final three: Ray continues to obsess over beating the old people (declaring that he refuses to lose to them, "even [at] checkers"), Gretchen and Meredith muddle through, and a fed-up Heckboy, who's entered defeatist mode, wonders why his mom would even *want* to stay in. In the end, he's the one who gets what he wants.

1. Rob and Amber (Team Truman Show) 3:00 P.M.
2. Brian and Greg (The Bouncer Brothers) 3:38 P.M.

3. Uchenna and Joyce (Team Enron) 5:49 P.M.
4. Ron and Kelly (Team POW) 6:05 P.M.
5. Lynn and Alex (The Gay Blades) 6:11 P.M.
6. Ray and Deana (The Bottom Feeders) 9:20 P.M.
7. Gretchen and Meredith (Team Energizer Bunny) 9:35 P.M.
8. Susan and Patrick (Team Heckboy) ELIMINATED

Leg #5: Divested in South Africa

This leg, and the one after it, air as a two-hour special episode. Together, they document the two most serious accidents in the entire history of the show. It ain't funny. As my Grandma used to say, there's only so much running around you can do before somebody gets seriously hurt.

Receiving $217, teams bunch aboard the same flight to Johannesburg, South Africa.

The Bottom Feeders pull off a minor slick move on the plane, negotiating a free move to first class, where they stretch out, looking comfortably smug.

The Detour is "Tunnels" or "Tribes." The first sends teams fifty miles to rappel into some caves, crawl through the pitch-black labyrinth, and grab the clue before climbing back up. "Tribes" sends teams forty miles to a cultural center, where they find "traditional items" representing five tribes that must be delivered to the five respective chiefs. "Tribes" requires a lot of running around, as well as dealing with comic lunges from colorfully clad natives who enjoy spooking silly Americans.

Team Truman Show and The Bottom Feeders both head for the Fast Forward, a scary walk across a rickety rope bridge strung across the top of one of the towers at the Orlando Cooling Station—perhaps the most festively decorated power plant any of us has ever wanted to see. It's the China *Pattern* Syndrome. The Bottom Feeders get there first, claim the prize, and move on to the Pit Stop, at Soweto Overlook in Nelson Mandela's old neighborhood. Left behind, Team Truman Show can only move on to their Detour choice, "Tribes."

They do stop at a local hospital for information, and there discover something they hadn't known—that they're big celebrities in South Africa. (Their *Survivor* has just aired there.) This will turn out to be pivotal later in the leg.

Meanwhile, at "Tunnels," Gretchen slips and smashes her forehead against the rocks. But a face covered with blood is not enough to make her want to quit (see p. 424 "The Most Endearing Racer Moments").

The Roadblock requires one player from each team to head into a local crowded and confusing marketplace to negotiate the purchases of a backpack, diapers, a shirt, a blanket, and a toy, all of which they must deliver to a local orphanage. It's not made clear during the episode, but the DVD episode commentary by Teams Truman Show and Enron establishes that bargaining was a critical skill in this particular marketplace, and that teams blindly accepting the sticker price for everything risked running out of funds before they were done. Here, Team Truman Show benefits from their prior fifteen minutes of fame, as a local woman thrilled to meet Amber and Boston Rob drops all her other plans for the day to help Amber shop, and guide the team for the rest of the leg.[55]

All teams are emotionally affected by their subsequent visits to the Orlando Children's Home, where they're greeted by cheering, adorable kids. All regret having to rush off to the Pit Stop, but childless Uchenna and Joyce (who have said they want the prize money for in vitro treatments) take it most personally.

Saved by a non-elimination leg, walking wounded Gretchen and Meredith are divested of not only their cash, but also all their possessions save for their passports and the clothes they have on.[56]

Well, at least that's the worst thing that can possibly happen....

1. Ray and Deana (The Bottom Feeders) 10:41 A.M.
2. Ron and Kelly (Team POW) 12:39 P.M.
3. Brian and Greg (The Bouncer Brothers) 1:03 P.M.
4. Lynn and Alex (The Gay Blades) 1:24 P.M.
5. Rob and Amber (Team Truman Show) 1:33 P.M.
6. Uchenna and Joyce (Team Enron) 2:20 P.M.
7. Gretchen and Meredith (Team Energizer Bunny) 3:51 P.M.
   MUGGED

---

[55] Her name is Silindile Manyone. She spotted and recognized the *Amazing Race* clue box before she spotted and recognized Rob and Amber. She later told her family how she'd spent her day, but her brother didn't believe her until the show aired locally. The incident earned her a low level of local fame.

[56] Phil reports on the DVD that the local greeter standing at the mat with him was shocked by how mean this was: taking all the money and clothing from an old lady with a bandaged head. Well, yeah. It couldn't have been a great introduction to the show's moral aesthetic.

Leg #6: The Moral Parable of Boston Rob

As the leg begins, Brian of The Bouncer Brothers opens the clue envelope and reads in jest, "Make your way home and give Mom a big hug, then eat all her chicken enchiladas until you enter a food coma." Heh. Brian also notes that his driving has really sucked lately. Uh-oh.

Team Truman Show notes again that they're less than popular among their fellow Racers. Rob says, "I don't think we're getting any Christmas cards from these people." More foreshadowing.

All teams but Energizer Bunny receive $118 before a brief visit to the lion and rhino nature preserve, where teams nervously feed the lions from an open jeep.

Gretchen and Meredith, who have already been given a pity package containing spare clothing, beg spare funds from those teams willing to part with any. Ray, one of several who don't, even says he wants to put them out of their misery. He's only thinking of them, he says. Hee. Wait.

Highway confusion delays some teams as they return to the Johannesburg airport (and leaves The Gay Blades straying into inner-city neighborhoods that bring out their inner frightened white man). It matters little, as all teams arriving in Gabarone, Botswana, are destined for a massive bunching aboard a subsequent 9:00 P.M. train.

A taxi dispute with The Gay Blades leads Rob to say he's through being nice to any of these people. "I'm not even sure [Gretchen] fell down," he says. "[Meredith] may have pushed her just for effect, so people would feel bad for her." Now, I'm generally sympathetic toward him, and I know he meant it to be funny, but, oy, did that fall flat. And given what's coming up, the last thing he needs this leg is more bad vibes.

An additional 440 miles by train and bus leads teams to a statue of a giant aardvark, which must be a great source of local pride.[57]

There, buzzed by a crop duster a la *North by Northwest,* they receive directions to a spear-throwing Roadblock, requiring one player from each team to impale a burlap sack swinging to and fro at the end of a rope. There's much hilarity over the Bushmen, who remind several players of Yoda and the occupant of the White House, but it's not nearly as important as what happens next.

---

[57] Oh, grow up. That's not racism. As the next Race establishes, we have giant office chairs.

Teams now board Land Rovers and travel dirt roads to the site of the Detour. Unseen on the episode: they first receive safety briefings on vehicle handling in the often deceptively treacherous desert roads.[58] Very much seen: Brian has so much trouble navigating past the slippery patches that he flips the vehicle. It's not funny: their camera guy is injured in the wreck. The team's plight provides others passing by in the next few minutes with a little moral quandary about the propriety of continuing to place the Race above human considerations. Rob and Amber, who don't stop, cement their places on The Gay Blades shit list, and are surprised when even Phil brings it up at the Pit Stop (see p. 408 "The Most Jaw-Dropping Errors Ever Made by Racers").

The Detour is "Food" versus "Water." In "Food," teams wear themselves out grinding corn; in "Water," teams use reed straws to suck enough water from an underground spring to fill twelve ostrich eggs. "Water" is so much easier than "Food" that The Bouncer Boys, who have received a replacement vehicle, are able to catch up with The Bottom Feeders, who are bickering over who's the more depressing partner (see p. 415 "The Smartest Moves Ever Made by Racers"). The Boys chase them all the way to the Pit Stop in the desert, pull up alongside them just as they're parking, and beat them in a thrilling footrace to the mat.

Understandably, the Boys are so emotionally wrecked by now that they can barely speak. They weep as they find out their cameraman is going to be okay.

Pit Stop accommodations this time are army cots, lined up in the flat plain known as the Makgadikgadi Pans. (It's the largest salt pan in the world, says Phil.) The show fails to note that weather conditions prevented teams from actually staying there. But oooh, that was scary.

1. Ron and Kelly (Team POW) 5:29 P.M.
2. Rob and Amber (Team Truman Show) 5:43 P.M.
3. Uchenna and Joyce (Team Enron) 5:51 P.M.
4. Lynn and Alex (The Gay Blades) 5:52 P.M.
5. Gretchen and Meredith (Team Energizer Bunny) 6:12 P.M.
6. Brian and Greg (The Bouncer Brothers) 6:22 P.M.
7. Ray and Deana (The Bottom Feeders) ELIMINATED

---

[58] Gretchen, on the bumpy road: "I don't want to go home tonight, but I don't want to have my bladder up in my chest cavity either."

Leg #7: Brian and Greg, Fashion Gurus

Receiving eighty-five dollars, teams must now return to their Land Rovers and drive 141 miles, past the city of Maun, and then an additional forty-eight miles to Sankuyo Village, where the next clue awaits beside a water tower.

The Brothers waste time at another structure (which may or may not be a grain silo), going so far as to climb the ladder on its side. It's a fatal wrong turn.

The Detour at Sankuyo Village is "Carry It" or "Milk It." In "Carry It," both players have to transport three items, including a plate of corn, a bucket of water, and a bundle of sticks, on the top of their heads, to a cooking area seventy yards away. They can take three trips, but they can't use their hands. It's not a job for people who like to hop. "Milk It" sends teams to a corral, where they must catch and milk enough goats to fill a ten-ounce cup.

Ron thinks Kelly should be able to do the balancing act. After all, he says, she's the ballet girl. She gripes, "I don't balance buckets on my head while doing pirouettes." They switch to milking, putting Ron in a bad mood vis-à-vis her for the rest of the day.

Team Truman Show switches too.

On the road, Uchenna says, "We are definitely in Africa." So he knows what continent he's on.

Both Rob and Amber call the goats they're milking "he."

Uchenna and Joyce arrive and take "Carry It," and balance the objects with little difficulty, walking at a downright jaunty clip. Lynn invites a thousand angry forum posts by saying, "Uchenna and Joyce were *born* to this!"[59]

The Bouncer Brothers show up just as the last teams are leaving.

Teams completing the Detour drive themselves twenty-one miles to the Khwai River (not to be confused with the River Kwai). On the way, Ron and Kelly bicker, the Land Rover driven by The Gay Blades has a breakdown before its replacement has a flat tire, and Uchenna oohs over zebras and gazelles and elephants. I know which car *I'd* like to be in.

The Roadblock requires one player from each team to drive their Land Rovers across a crocodile-infested river crossing, retrieve a flagged

---

[59] This is just the kind of dumb statement that sounds worse coming out of your mouth than it does taking form on your tongue. But it was tin-eared, that's for sure.

post marking the entrance to one of several obstacle courses, and then drive down a path which requires that player to tow two fallen logs out of the way before obtaining the next clue.

Ron tells Kelly to "chill," which she somehow hears as "shut the fuck up." Maybe she has a cold. In either case, it leads her to call him a "piece-of-trash redneck." Shades of Lori and Bolo.

More trouble ensues when Uchenna takes the flag by itself instead of the post, and Team Energizer Bunny finds the Pit Stop at Khwai River Lodge without finding the route marker they need to present there. Both teams must go back and correct their respective errors, without being told what they did wrong.

Imagining themselves last, in what may be a non-elimination leg, The Gay Blades don several layers of clothing. The Bouncer Brothers, suspecting the same, take the opposite tack, arriving half-naked in wooly hats, sunglasses, mufflers, and colorful swim trunks, in the theory that the show can't possibly leave them with only these to wear. Alas, this is an elimination leg, so the theory isn't tested. But it is fun to see Phil come close to losing it.

1. Rob and Amber (Team Truman Show) 12:45 P.M.
2. Ron and Kelly (Team POW) 12:46 P.M.
3. Uchenna and Joyce (Team Enron) 2:08 P.M.
4. Lynn and Alex (The Gay Blades) 3:00 P.M.
5. Gretchen and Meredith (Team Energizer Bunny) 3:45 P.M.
6. Brian and Greg (The Bouncer Brothers) ELIMINATED

INTERMISSION:

Clip Episode

At this point in the Race, the series airs a clip show, summarizing prior events complete with additional footage. Most of this is disposable, though Brian and Greg get the best moment, sending up the Race tradition of couples using the Race to determine if they have a romantic future. Brian says, "We already know where we are in our relationship. We're not out to decide if we should be brothers anymore."

There's also an installment of road games between Rob and Meredith, as the *Survivor* star screws with the old guy's head by changing lanes and pretending to take an exit before turning back at the last minute. Amber, to her credit, is less than amused.

Leg #8a: Who's the Bitch?

Receiving $125, teams now head for Lucknow, India, on a tortuous course that requires them to first sign up for arranged charter flights to Francistown, Botswana, then fly via already arranged tickets to Mumbai (Bombay), India, then travel via a self-arranged itinerary to Lucknow. None of the intrigue at Francistown Airport results in a serious difference in arrival times, so we'll just skip over it, if that's okay with you. The one real highlight is Meredith asking Lynn why he's being so helpful, and Lynn saying, "because we want you guys in the finals with us," which is *not actually a compliment*, if you stop to think about it.

The cut scenes on the DVD reveal Lynn and Alex being even more catty about the player they dub "Amberexia" than they are on the aired programs. "I have no problem with Amber," Lynn says. "I just think she's a silly, immature, anorexic bitch." Alex opines, "She's such a miserable person that she takes it out on everyone else, like a big old rain cloud."[60] Well, as long as you have no problem with her. Jeez. This obsession with the doings of another team is so excessive it might lead even Race 5's Charla and Mirna to say, "Enough with the tunnel vision, already."

Anyway. Lucknow. Where after the usual amount of taxi confusion and racing through crowded streets, teams locate the next clue at Bara Imambara Palace. That directs them to take a horse-drawn carriage known as a tonga to the Kohinoor Steel Emporium, site of this leg's Roadblock.

This one requires one player from each team to search 600 steel boxes for the ten that include clue envelopes. So it's a luck-based challenge, but no haystack challenge. Seriously: if Racers are willing to open one after another, as fast as they can, a search rate as glacial as two boxes per minute should find the clue envelope within an average search time of about thirty minutes. That is, as long as Racers actually look. Amber, Kelly, Alex, and Uchenna search with relative efficiency, and find their team clues fairly quickly. Gretchen, on the other hand, spins around in

---

[60] One can understand Rob's cockiness and often sneaky game play getting old with some of his fellow Racers real fast, but unless Amber had a venomous side that never made it to the programs as aired, there's nothing in her demeanor (on this series, at least) to suggest that she deserves this. The anorexia comments make some kind of vague sense, since she does keep saying she wants to lose weight before the wedding. But "bitch" is a genuine head-scratcher.

a state of fluttery panic, wandering aimlessly through the stacks while moaning, "Oh, noooo...." and, "I don't know what to do."

Teams now hire cycle rickshaws to Aishbagh, where the Detour is "Solid" or "Liquid." Nobody takes the first, which requires teams to break up and deliver 175 pounds of coal. Good move. In "Liquid," teams push a tea cart to a crowded three-story office building, and deliver five cups of tea to workers named on a manifest, in exchange for business cards which they must return to the tea vendor in exchange for a clue.

It's not long before all these teams find themselves trailed by mobs of curious locals, who have gathered from the cameras and commotion that these Americans are celebrities of some kind. Rob and Amber attract one throng all by themselves, but Gretchen and Meredith arrive after the word has gotten out and are greeted by a flash mob of well-wishers, cheering from sidewalks and windows and overpasses. What do you do in such a situation? You wave, blow kisses, and try to keep moving—unaware that when first team Rob and Amber finally catch up with Phil, atop the Charbaugh Multi Flats apartment complex, he just hands over the next clue envelope and tells them they're still racing.

That's right, folks. It's another mega-leg.

Leg #8b: The Lady on the Elephant

Nothing that happened in the previous half of the leg mattered, as teams board a 9:00 P.M. train, with no knowledge of their eventual destination. The next clue envelope comes only when they're all bedded down in their sleeper compartments. It turns out that they're headed for Jodhpur, and are expected to arrive at 10:00 P.M. or 11:00 P.M. the *next* day.

The next long day on the train, Lynn complains that he doesn't have his eye cream, skin cream, or any cream, and would drink some if he had it. Joyce has fun dressing Uchenna in scarves. Amber and Ron bond over Rob's wussy fear of horror films.

A late-night hours-of-operation bunching at the Sardar Market clock tower in Jodhpur (it doesn't open until 10:00 A.M.) gives teams an opportunity to check out local hotel accommodations. Rob arranges for one hotel employee, Sanjay, to spend the entire next day guiding the team around. Lynn and Alex join the festivities at a local street wedding, while Gretchen and Meredith cheer them from the balcony. It must be a refreshing break before the next day's all-out panic.

The morning's Detour is "Trunk" or "Dunk." Nobody takes the cloth-dying challenge, "Dunk." "Trunk" requires teams to push a 600-pound wheeled teak elephant half a mile through city streets. The task should not take long if teams get locals to help. Astonishingly, Gretchen not only fails to help her hubbie push...but she also goes along with a local's suggestion that she climb aboard. There was nothing in the instructions requiring anybody to ride, but she rides anyway, adding to the weight and screeching at locals to get out of the way. It's a jaw-dropping error all right—which nobody involved ever considered—but it's also one of the comic highlights of the entire Race. Especially when she moans, "We've got a bad elephant."

The Fast Forward, ten miles away at a Hindu temple, is a replay of the head-shaving ritual Brandon and Nicole refused to do in Race 5. Uchenna and Joyce go for this one, even though Joyce remembers Race 5 and suspects head-shaving might be involved. This is not a problem for Uchenna, with his already shiny dome, but is destined to be somewhat more traumatic for the wife. When they arrive, she angrily says she frickin' *knew* it. But there's no time to go back, and so she insists on being shorn, even though a distraught Uchenna tells her she doesn't have to. It's difficult to watch these scenes without tearing up in empathy for both of them. But guess what: as Uchenna puts it, she's beautiful any way she comes (see p. 424 "The Most Endearing Racer Moments").

The Roadblock at Deora Krishi Farm requires one player from each team to ride a camel cart two times around a marked course. Some camels prove indifferent to this procedure.

The Pit Stop is Jaswant Thada, a royal tomb in Jodhpur. Though it seems to be a near thing, Uchenna and Joyce do make it to the mat first—and don't even win a trip for their troubles. Boo! Gretchen's less happy when her team arrives. She complains that they were running behind every other team's dust. "We weren't running behind one team's dust," an ebullient Meredith responds. And the one team whose dust they weren't running behind? Alas: say good-bye to the Blades.[61]

---

[61] Who, according to cut scenes on the DVD, didn't leave without passing some more comments about "Amberexia." Guys, I like you. Honestly. But give it a rest.

1. Uchenna and Joyce (Team Enron) 11:24 P.M.
2. Ron and Kelly (Team POW) 11:26 P.M.
3. Rob and Amber (Team Truman Show) 11:26 P.M.
4. Gretchen and Meredith (Team Energizer Bunny) 11:33 P.M.
5. Lynn and Alex (The Gay Blades) ELIMINATED

Analyze those times. That Fast Forward didn't really help Uchenna and Joyce very much, did it?

Leg #9: Rob, Petard: Hoisted

Teams now receive eighty-two dollars, with instructions to fly to Istanbul, Turkey.

The leg's tasks prove not nearly as pivotal as Rob being a smartass.

What happens is this: all teams book itineraries through New Delhi that land at 8:45 A.M.

Then Rob asks Gretchen, "Did you get on the earlier flight to Turkey?" He says this not because he believes there's an earlier flight to Turkey, but because he wants to play with her head. Well, he's also hoping she'll give up info, if she has any. But mostly he's playing with her head.

Yock-a-rama.

But the joke backfires. Teams Enron and Energizer Bunny, who don't know Rob was joking, do find a faster flight. It leaves Delhi, connects through Dubai, and lands in Istanbul at 6:20 A.M., two and a half hours before Rob's.

So they book that flight, firmly believing that they're only catching up. They have no idea that they now enjoy a two-and-a-half hour advantage.

During the stopover in Delhi, as POW and Truman Show go to check out flights themselves, Ron and Kelly have a heart-to-heart about the future of their relationship. Kelly tells him that he never makes commitments. He says he committed to the Army. She tells him, "And you got out of that, too—by being a POW."

Yes, she actually says that. Honestly. Millions of viewers stare at their TV sets in disbelief.[62]

"Oh, yeah," he says, with unforced sarcasm. "What I did is I crashed myself. I went through hell and torture so I could get out of the Army

---

[62] As horrid as that statement sounds, let's concede, as we have before, that there's something about sleeplessness and hunger and the pressures of the Race that interferes with rational thought.

early. I almost died, but I knew I was getting out of the Army early if I survived it."

What a clever plan.

In any event, POW and Truman Show don't find out about the faster flight. And even as Rob amuses himself (and, for an entirely different reason, us) discoursing at length on how clueless Meredith and Uchenna are, Enron and Energizer are already in the air on their way to a substantial lead.

Reaching the island of Kiz Kulesi, in Istanbul, teams search for garden gnomes[63] they have to bring with them to Pit Stop. From there, they move on to Galata Kulesi Tower, where the route marker provides the Detour, "Columns" or "Kilos." In the first, teams make their way to Binbirdirek Sarnici, a well supported by 200 columns, where they have to use map coordinates to find the combination to a submerged padlock. In the latter, teams travel to a public square and weigh enough pedestrians to add up to 2,500 kilos.

Gretchen and Meredith take forever to find the route marker at the tower, looking everywhere up to and including a samovar, but manage to maintain their lead over Teams POW and Truman Show.

Who are just now arriving at Kiz Kulesi and finding out from their ferry captain that the "idiot" teams have been in-country for hours.

Rob's head explodes.

Hee hee hee.

The Roadblock at the castle Rumeli Hisari requires one team member to "storm the fortress," which involves climbing a twenty-five-foot rope ladder, climbing a circular stone staircase, grabbing a key, rappeling back down, opening a lockbox, and opening the gate. Uchenna smokes this one, bringing Enron to a first-place finish, but it's second-place Gretchen who emerges as the leg's star. Moaning, "Ohhhhh," and "Eyeeeuyuueeehhh,"[64] as she flops about on the rope ladder, declaring that she doesn't have the strength; she goes ahead and finds the strength anyway. Wonder how Ray, wherever he is, feels about that.

---

[63] The four gnome statues are actually "Travelocity Roaming Gnomes," one of the show's more ham-handed product placements. However, the team that finds the one with the airplane on its base—Ron and Kelly, as it turns out—does get $20,000 worth of credit on the Travelocity Web site and a luxury hotel to stay in during the Pit Stop. Which must prove quite the comfort, for the mugged.

[64] Your spelling may vary.

1. Uchenna and Joyce (Team Enron) 10:53 A.M.
2. Gretchen and Meredith (Team Energizer Bunny) 11:57 A.M.
3. Rob and Amber (Team Truman Show) 12:37 P.M.
4. Ron and Kelly (Team POW) 12:53 P.M. MUGGED

Leg #10: While My Guitar Gently Weeps

All teams except for POW receive $477 with their first clue, which sends them off to visit some whirling dervishes. (Rob pronounces this "deverish," as if to say, I'm more deverish than you are. Funny, he doesn't look deverish.)

Team POW begs for money on the streets of Istanbul.

The clue box by the dervishes directs teams to London, England, where they must find the crosswalk made famous by a Beatles album. An entire generation of viewers feels intensely old as teams Enron, Truman, and POW have to *guess* that Abbey Road's the answer. Rob even says his dad is gonna kill him for not knowing. Ouch. Gretchen provides a little comforting balm to aging baby boomers by wishing the clue had referenced Mel Torme instead.

At the airport, Kelly grosses out viewers by "borrowing" lipstick from the lady behind the counter. How exactly does she put it back in the tube, afterward?

Having learned nothing from the last leg, Teams Enron and Energizer Bunny book the earliest direct flight to London, without checking if any other itineraries arrive earlier. Teams Truman Show and POW risk a flight to Frankfurt, putting themselves on standby for the connecting flight to London—a gamble that works, as both of those teams land in London an hour and a half before their competition.

In London, Rob and Amber pick up a local guide named Stuart, who helps them find and complete the Detour.

The route marker at Abbey Road directs teams to the London Eye, the forty-story ferris wheel on the banks of the Thames. That provides teams with the vantage point they need to find the yellow-and-red flag hanging from a hotel window.

Alas for Ron and Kelly, they've started bickering again, and she refuses to help search the skyline until after she gets an apology. It's a fine time to stand on principle, I must say.

The Detour is "Brains" versus "Brawn." "Brains" is a sorta scavenger hunt, involving items related to Sherlock Holmes. "Brawn" sends teams to Battersea Park, where they must transport five 160-pound boats from the lake to a storage area 500 yards away.

Teams Truman Show and POW are both well into the Detour by the time the two remaining teams arrive in London. When those two teams stop at the info desk to ask for directions to Abbey Road, the lady at the info desk asks, "So you're in the competition too, then?" In this manner, they learn they're two hours behind. Yikes.

The last clue of the "Brains" task alert teams to take all the Holmesian items to the great detective's home at 221B Baker Street. Amber proudly struts down the block wearing the deerstalker cap, chomping on the pipe, and waving the magnifying glass. It may be her most likeable moment on the show, which is saying a lot, unless you're Lynn and Alex.

At the Detour, Enron and Energizer choose "Brawn"—a good choice for big Uchenna, but an unaccountable one for Gretchen and Meredith.

Up ahead, at the Millennium Dome, Team Truman Show turns on its erstwhile allies, Yielding Team POW[65] just before a Roadblock requiring each participating Racer to drive a double-decker bus through an obstacle course of rubber cones. This task is so difficult, requiring so many attempts, that it comes down to a hilarious montage of Kelly, Joyce, and Meredith pounding their respective steering wheels with frustration. As Uchenna says, "It's anybody's game at this point." But the old folks are last to the mat at Potter's Field Park.

1. Rob and Amber (Team Truman Show) 2:47 P.M.
2. Ron and Kelly (Team POW) 4:26 P.M.
3. Uchenna and Joyce (Team Enron) 4:41 P.M.
4. Gretchen and Meredith (Team Energizer Bunny) ELIMINATED

---

[65] A cut scene on the DVD reveals, in greater detail, that Rob and Amber agonized over the best possible team to Yield. Rob favored Team POW, whereas Amber favored Team Enron. As we know, Rob got his way. But Amber was right. Think about it: they had reason to believe that Ron and Kelly were right behind them, and that Team Enron and Team Energizer Bunny were bringing up the rear. Yielding Uchenna and Joyce might have knocked out that formidable team and brought the much weaker Gretchen and Meredith into the final three. This doesn't qualify as a jaw-dropping error, since they couldn't be certain where the other teams were. But this may have been the moment that cost Rob and Amber the game.

Leg #11: This Truly Blows

This leg, and the leg after it, air together as a two-part season finale. So much happens in the final leg that this one doesn't even last the full hour!

The three remaining teams receive $630 with their instructions to catch a flight to Kingston, Jamaica, which pretty much makes everybody say things like "mon" and "arree." From there they'll have to cab it an additional ninety miles to Frenchman's Cove, in Port Antonio.

During the inevitable airport bunching, there is yet another step downward in the sad saga of Ron and Kelly. She chooses this moment to press him further about marriage, and he remains unwilling to commit. Given the stresses of the Race, her timing could be better. This is almost as bad as discussing this while being strafed by Messerschmitts. The confrontation ends in tears, with two legs still left to go.

Arriving in Kingston sometime at night, teams hit Frenchman's Cove, where the Roadblock involves limbo dancing. Each rung corresponds to an earlier departure time, for the next morning. Fortunately for the guys, the ladies are still free to perform Roadblocks. Amber and Kelly earn their teams 8:15 A.M. departures, whereas Joyce manages a mere 8:30 A.M., starting her team with a fifteen-minute disadvantage.

Grant's Level, in the hills outside Port Antonio, is the site of the Roadblock, which features the two river activities, "Raft It" or "Build It." The first requires teams to ride a bamboo raft eight miles down the Rio Grande, using only a pole to steer. In "Build It," teams build their own raft, cross the river, then climb a hill to grab the clue on the other side. All teams choose "Build It" over a river journey of uncertain duration, and all teams labor mightily at a backbreaking task which amounts to a hell of a lot of work. Rob and Amber, who know raft building from *Survivor*, do pretty well. Uchenna and Joyce are so good at it that they make up for lost time and are the first to finish. But the increasing tension between Ron and Kelly leads to angry bickering throughout. You get the idea it won't be all happy times on that raft.

Teams completing this task must now taxi eighty miles to Montego Bay. Once there, they have to find a villa at Round Hill. For most of the distance, teams are neck-and-neck, watching each other grimly through the windows of their respective cabs. It's a tense ride. All three teams have to stop at the same gas station. Rob and Amber fall behind when their cab is stopped by police for a routine tourist check, but their driver, Tyson, is able to catch up with the pack again—at which point they join Ron and Kelly in noting that the left rear tire of Team Enron's cab is looking awfully flat.

And then it pops.

No pun intended, but for Uchenna and Joyce, this truly blows....

1. Ron and Kelly (Team POW) 2:37 P.M.
2. Rob and Amber (Team Truman Show) 2:38 P.M.
3. Uchenna and Joyce (Team Enron) 2:48 P.M. MUGGED

Leg #12: Enron Rises Again

This is it—in the humble author's opinion, the most thrilling finale in the history of the show.

Teams POW and Truman Show receive $445 with their instructions to take a taxi twenty-five miles toward the city of Lucea. On the way they need to participate in a minor task requiring them to chop fifty onions. Both arrive at the restaurant before sunrise.

Bankrupted Team Enron doesn't have enough money to begin, so they make their way to the airport and begin begging. It's dawn before they have forty dollars—which is only enough to begin the leg because they're lucky enough to find a cabbie who accepts their story and agrees to chauffer them all day for a fraction of his usual daily earnings.

By now Team POW and Team Truman Show have moved on to the Detour at Rose Hall, a former plantation, now golf resort, where they find the Detour: "Pony Up" or "Tee It Up." The first requires players to participate in the local sport of horseback swimming, which involves riding a horse into the surf, then sliding off and holding onto its tail as it swims around a course of buoys. Damn, but I want to try that someday. None of the Racers do, however—not now, anyway. "Tee It Up" sends teams to the driving range, where they must land a ball on the green from 140 yards away. Both finish golfing while Team Enron has only proceeded as far as the onions.

Disgusted by his poor golfing performance, Ron says, "I deserve a pickaxe right through the scalp." Yes, he actually says that.

The first two teams must now fly 800 miles to San Juan, Puerto Rico, where they have to claim marked cars and drive nine miles to the fortress known as the Castillo San Felipe del Morro. First to leave, Rob and Amber make a flight that leaves at 9:54 A.M., and are landing in San Juan before Team Enron makes it as far as the driving range. They also make good time to the clue box outside the fortress, which directs them to travel another eighty-seven miles to an abandoned sugar refinery in Aguadilla. But then they hit rush-hour traffic. Rob, who should be used to it from his hometown, notes that when he hits traffic in Boston, he's not trying to win a million dollars. Well, yeah. And this traffic may cost him just that, as the team arrives in Aguadilla after sunset only to find themselves outside a gate that closed at 4:00 P.M.

Leaving Jamaica eight hours after Team Truman Show, Team Enron finally pulls up at the Aguadilla sugar refinery late at night and discovers themselves the lucky recipients of a three-way bunching. Heh heh heh.

The Roadblock, which requires one player from each team to leap off a bridge into the ocean, is not nearly as critical as the subsequent rush for flights to the final destination city, Miami. Ron and Kelly are so busy bickering they miss a critical turnoff, and fade from the game. For the remaining two teams, a killer game of airport shuffle leaves Team Truman Show snagging a 10:00 A.M. flight just as it boards. The jetway retracts. Uchenna and Joyce beg, beg, and beg some more at the gate...prompting the agent to make an emergency phone call to the pilot, who allows the jetway to return to the plane and permits the boarding of these two late-arriving passengers. Rob says, "This sucks."[66]

Finally, in Miami, the two teams search for a cigar factory identified to them as The King of the Havanas, which they don't know is a translation for its actual Spanish name, El Rey de los Habanos. The search does not go well for Rob and Amber. Uchenna and Joyce, who are brought directly there by their Spanish-speaking cab driver, nevertheless have one final hurdle to cross: they run out of money on their way to the Pit Stop at Fort Lauderdale's Bonnet House, and find themselves caught a few short steps from their million-dollar prize, thanks to a cabbie who refuses to accept Uchenna's wedding ring as payment. And so, the last few minutes come down to an agonizing race between how well Team

---

[66] For some time after the show aired, Rob joined some suspicious fans in implying producer interference, a charge that Bertram van Munster vehemently denies. It is ridiculous to believe that *The Amazing Race* could have had delayed the departure of a commercial aircraft, at the very last minute—especially since such decisions are known to be up to pilot discretion, since the show as aired does indicate the phone call from the gate agent, and since Rob and Amber chortled so memorably when benefiting from exactly the same kind of indulgence during Leg #4.

Truman Show's cabbie can make up for lost time, and how quickly Team Enron can beg the shortfall from locals....[67]

1. Uchenna and Joyce (Team Enron) WIN
2. Rob and Amber (Team Truman Show) PLACE
3. Ron and Kelly (Team POW) SHOW

At the finish line, Kelly seizes the opportunity to further discuss Ron's failure to commit. His fixed smile is...complicated. The girl certainly has a great sense of timing.

---

[67] Some viewers take Uchenna's insistence on "[making] sure that man is covered!" as proof of his team's essential goodness. Well, no slight to Uchenna's integrity and ethical standards, but he honestly had no choice. A game provision (which may have been added after Race 5's Tanzanian incident) required him to settle the debt before moving on. As it is, the driver grumpily settled for a lower amount. That said, there is a postscript. After the finale aired, Uchenna and Joyce appeared on a local radio show and were delighted when that driver called in, asking if he could have the rest of his fare now. (He got it. AND an exceedingly generous tip.)

Race 8,
Bringing the Kids

MANY FANS, AND PREVIOUS RACERS, consider the Family Edition, which cast families of four in teams that often included minors and even preteens, a poor relation to the version from previous seasons. At least two Racers from previous seasons told me they stopped viewing after the first episode. And for the most part, they had the right idea. The old Race featured multiple highlights per episode; this one seemed to go entire legs without anything of interest happening. It was not entirely devoid of entertainment value, but it was a major disappointment.

Why didn't it work? In part, because of its very design. Cast teams of two, and their adventures function as snapshots of relationships. They may be healthy relationships, or funny relationships, or even appalling car-wreck relationships, but they're *dialogues*; they work as stories that can be followed. Cast families of four, and in all too many cases what we get instead are quartets of bickering people all trying to talk at the same time. It becomes harder to pick out individuals, let alone Season Superstars. In this Race, for instance, the Godlewski sisters were definitely characters, in both senses of the word—but for a while they just came across as a giggly, high-pitched pack of pink ladies, somehow managing to communicate even though nobody ever shut up. It took several legs before they calmed down enough to reveal, for instance, that Christine was the tearful one who so frequently got on everybody else's nerves. The Linzes were likeable as a group, but the boys seemed interchangeable twenty-somethings, who greeted each situation with more or less identical frat-boy humor. And the Aiellos, a trio of sons-in-law united in their affection for the older guy whose daughters they all married, were equally undistinguished; they seemed like nice folks, but as seen on TV there was really little reason to keep track of which son-in-law was which.

The show was also simplified, in part out of solicitousness toward the children involved. Oh, sure, there were still eliminations, and Yields, and even muggings for teams that arrive last during non-eliminations—but somehow these Racers never ended up sleeping on the street, and indeed spent a number of consecutive legs driving around in comfortably appointed campers. There were no exhausting foot sprints across town, no immersions in third-world conditions, and, indeed, damn little outside the U.S. Even within the United States, too much of what these Racers encountered was passive by design: they visited Bart the Bear, or a version of Buffalo Bill, or Old Faithful, and then moved on, having accomplished little but look. Again, much of this seemed to be out of concern for the kids, but, really: the show featured some kids who confronted adversity with more aplomb than the adults. If the show wasn't interested in testing them, then why cast them at all?

I would also say that there was no culture shock, but that's not entirely true. There was plenty. And it mostly took the form of the ongoing conflict between the evangelistic Christian Floridians known as the Weaver family and a number of their closest competitors in the Race. The conflict between Linda's brood and their (most prominent of several) enemies the Linzes and Godlewskis was not entirely the fault of the folks from the Sunshine State (as with many Race feuds, it seemed to begin with a misunderstanding, before escalating, much of its longevity due to differing standards of playing nice), but the Weavers did do their absolute best to keep it up, wrapping themselves in an unlovely self-righteousness that completely erased the substantial sympathy they invited at the onset. There's no doubt about it: this Red State/Blue State culture war did exhibit a strange fascination—but the show works best when such shenanigans play out against actual exotic locales, and not, let's say, Utah. (Though the Weavers had enough troubles dealing with that state.)

When producers announced that the next Race would return to the two-member team/global-Race format, fans heaved a sigh of relief.

A couple of words about the format of this particular group of summaries. First, I eschew team nicknames this time out; there are more than enough names to deal with, and the surnames function quite well as group labels, thank you. Second, I find myself forced to omit the Race completion times, as there are multiple indications that the departure times for the immediately subsequent leg (which have always been my source for this information), are, for the first time ever, not a consistently reliable indicator of when Racers arrived. In short, it's not always some multiple of twelve hours. I don't know whether this had to do with logistical considerations, or further concern for the well-being of the children. But we can cite it as further evidence that the Family Edition was not a great idea.

DRAMATIS PERSONAE

1. The Linz Family

Three brothers and a sister from Cincinnati. Tommy, 19; Megan, 21; Nick, 24; Alex, 22. Young, energetic siblings distinguished by a generous helping of bodily function humor, the longest-running Weaver feud, and (for a while) a seeming inability to finish any leg in first place.

2. The Bransen Family

A dad and three daughters from Park Ridge, Illinois. Walter, 51; Elizabeth, 25; Lauren, 22; Lindsay, 20. Mostly distinguished by fat ol' Wally, who complains multiple times per leg that he can't keep up with his daughters. He turns out to be somewhat more useful than he believes.

3. The Rogers Family

Parents and kids from Shreveport, Louisiana. Denny, 46; Renee, 42; Brock, 19; Britney, 22. The big question here is: when's the wrong time to listen to Dad, instead of Brock?

4. The Weaver Family

A widow and her three kids from Ormond Beach, Florida. Linda, 46; Rachel, 16; Rebecca, 19; Rolly, 14. The departed dad, who worked at the racetrack, was hit by a car when trying to clear debris from the road—a tragic backstory that resonates when the traumatized kids are twice expected to participate in racetrack tasks. It gives us reason to empathize, but doesn't excuse everything that follows, especially some of their comments regarding Utah. Linda is fierce as hell when she thinks she's protecting her kids; Rolly does most of the physically demanding stuff.

5. The Schroeder Family

Dad, step-mom, and kids from New Orleans, Louisiana. Mark, 40; Char, 39; Stassi, 16; Hunter, 14. Stassi's revulsion for the Weavers provides much of the early conflict. Hunter has one moment he probably lived to regret acting out within full view of TV cameras. The family suffered from the show's "hometown curse" in more ways than one—weeks after filming completed, they lost their home to Hurricane Katrina.[68]

6. The Aiello Family

Dad and three sons-in-law from Mansfield, Massachusetts. Tony, 57; David, 26; Matt, 31; Kevin, 31. Big ol' fat Tony is obviously the weak link, physically, but is also the clear emotional fulcrum: he loves these guys, and they love him. Don't expect them to be around for long.

7. The Paolo Family

Parents and sons from Carmel, New York. Immigrant dad Tony, 52 (another Tony); Marion, 52; D. J., 24; Brian, 16. The most contentious family of the Race, who can be tracked from orbit by the emotional shrapnel that surrounds any interaction between Mom and the boys. They can

---

[68] The Rogers family stepped up, hosting the family for some time in the wake of the disaster. It has been reported that all but one of the remaining teams offered financial support as well.

be hard to take, in the early legs, but they stick around long enough to provide some leavening context.

8. The Gaghan Family

Parents and kids from Glastonbury, Connecticut. Bill, 40; Tammy, 42; Billy, 12; Carissa, 9. Parents and kids are seasoned travelers and marathon runners who might have been dangerous were it not for a critical early mistake. The kids are more mature about the whole thing than many adult Racers we've seen.

9. The Godlewski Family

The maiden name of four sisters from Des Plaines, Illinois. Tricia, 26; Christine, 37; Sharon, 39; Michelle, 42. (See if you can spot the change-of-life baby.) A very giggly team of sisters, clad in pink, who work well together until they start to get on each other's nerves.

10. The Black Family

Parents and kids from Woodbridge, Virginia. Reggie, 42; Kim, 40; Kenneth, 11; Austin, 8. The surname of the Blacks, who are black, provided some risible sentence constructions, including on-screen captions identifying them as "The Black Family"—which they are, of course, but not just in the manner it seems to the casual channel surfer. Indeed, this reportedly backfired on Phil on one occasion when he innocently introduced them in public. During their short run, Austin, the youngest Racer of all time, seems a little overwhelmed and unprepared for the competition. They're likeable folks, who aren't around long enough to reveal any compensating strengths.

THE GAME PLAY

Leg #1: Coming 'Round the Mountain

Gathering beneath the Brooklyn Bridge, teams claim SUVs and hie forth to Soho, where they must pick up (if not actually buy—it's unclear) their camping equipment for later in the leg. There's plenty of confusion navigating around Manhattan, with the hometown curse going to the ever-bickering Paolos, a team that will spend much of its time on-screen yelling.

Pop Aiello notes that he's never been camping, a fact that astounds his three sons-in-law until the epiphany strikes them all at once: *three daughters.* Gee, the poor guy.

Every team has to stop and meet "Frank," i.e., a pair of hot dog vendors, i.e., the first Race's Kevin and Drew, who go unrecognized until Brian Paolo hoots with delight upon seeing them.

Carissa notes the graffiti on all the buildings. "Are you allowed to use spray paint?" she asks. Her amused dad says, "I think they discourage it, honey."

Several teams get lost on the way to Washington Crossing, Pennsylvania, where they have to paddle a boat across the Delaware, at the very spot once traveled by the nation's first George. Once on the other side they have to collect a thirteen-star American flag, bring it back, and be quietly respectful during the folding ceremony. Char Schroeder warns her kids, "Don't let [the flag] touch the water. It's disrespectful, or something." Or something. Mom Paolo asks the guy to hurry it up a little bit, and one of her sons calls her retarded. There's gonna be a lot of this.

At Belmont Plateau, in Philadelphia's Fairmont Park, teams pitch their tents and earn their departure times for the next morning. The first three teams to manage this trick get to leave at 10:00 A.M., with the next three drawing 10:30 A.M., and the final three trailing at 11:00 A.M.

So here's where we stand. 10:00 A.M.: Gaghans, Weavers, Aiellos; 10:30 A.M.: Schroeders, Rogers, Bransens; 11:00 A.M.: everybody else.

The morning's Detour is ninety-two miles away at the Brubaker Family Farms: "Build It" or "Buggy It." In the former, teams build a working water mill from a kit. In "Buggy It," two members of the team must drag or push a 500-pound Amish buggy one and a half miles. "Buggy It" seems an obvious choice for strong parents with small kids, so the Gaghans take that, overtaking the Aiellos while Billy and Carissa sing "She'll Be Coming 'Round the Mountain." The Weavers lose control of their buggy on an incline, terrifying the kids (who are still recovering from the loss of their dad) when it runs over Mom. Give her credit for being no-nonsense, at least at this stage of the game: when the kids get weepy, she snaps that it's over, and she's fine. It's not the first time she'll have to be the family's icon of strength, or the last.

The search for the Pit Stop, at the Rohrer Family Farm, leads one of the Aiello boys to note, "We're looking for a farm, so it's probably in farm country." Well, yeah.

The Black family is last to arrive, and, dammit, it is tough to watch Phil break the news to 8-year-old Austin....

1. The Godlewski family
2. The Gaghan family
3. The Weaver family
4. The Rogers family
5. The Schroeder family
6. The Paolo family
7. The Bransen family
8. The Aiello family
9. The Linz family
10. The Black family ELIMINATED

Leg #2: Great Pink Ladies of the Civil War

Teams now drive a whopping fifteen miles to York, Pennsylvania, home of a house that looks like a shoe. The old lady inside pokes her head out the window and asks them if they're interested in taking away a kid or two. No, not really.

Now headed for Washington, D.C., where the next clue awaits at the Capitol Reflecting Pool, the Rogers family goes astray. Dad blames son Brock until the family points out that he's the one who made them drive in the wrong direction. Dad grumps, "I can't do everything." Brock stews. We get a glimpse of some real teen resentment, there. Rebel without a Fast Forward.

The big problem for some teams reaching Washington is recognizing that the Capitol Reflecting Pool is the oval one at the Capitol, not the famous rectangular one at the Mall. The Gaghans, who started the Race strongly, fall to the rear of the pack, circling the wrong reflecting pool again and again until an aggravated Billy complains, "Let's ask." The teams that manage to find the right reflecting pool also find the Roadblock, a search for "spies" at the Tidal Basin.

Elsewhere, there's plenty of two-fisted Paolo action. Mom receives abuse from her sons for noting that the gas gauge is running awfully low, and later (when the shortage becomes critical) exults in having been right. "You're going to hear it for the next 500 miles!" she yells. "Do you understand that a car needs gas? Does anything compute in your brain?...None of you ever EVER, EVER listen to me!" Well, if you have the moral high ground, might as well seize the day.

The Detour, forty-nine miles away at Welbourne Manor in Middleburg, Virginia, is "Heat of the Battle" versus "Heat of the Night." In "Battle," teams run into a full-scale Civil War battle reenactment and use stretchers to transport five "wounded" soldiers to the surgeon's tent. In "Night," teams fill twenty oil lamps from a barrel, bring them to the quartermaster, and light all twenty. In either case, teams that complete the task need only run to a nearby meadow to find the Pit Stop.

Everybody in the first wave of arriving teams takes "Battle" except for the Weavers and Schroeders. And, I gotta say, it kinda blows the verisimilitude of this impressive battle reenactment to have folks in touristy T-shirts running around in the center of it. The Godlewski sisters, in their pink T-shirts, are perhaps the most jarring. It's, like, the oddest secret weapon Robert E. Lee ever unleashed on the field of battle.

Only after all the other teams make it to the Pit Stop do the Rogers and Paolo families arrive to duke it out for last place. Both go for the stretchers, but Mom Rogers is so exhausted after "rescuing" the first soldier that she makes her family switch to the oil lamps in mid-task. It turns out to be a very bad mistake for a team that was already running behind. It comes down to a footrace between the Rogers and Paolo families, with Marion Paolo already walking very badly....

1. The Weaver family
2. The Linz family
3. The Godlewski family
4. The Schroeder family
5. The Aiello family
6. The Bransen family
7. The Gaghan family
8. The Paolo family
9. The Rogers family ELIMINATED

Leg #3: The Bransens Have Gas

Families must board a van with a professional driver, and accept a stress-free ride to the airport, where they must book flights to Charleston, South Carolina.

The Linz sense of humor comes into play as they find themselves stuck behind a truck labeled "WIDE LOAD." Wackiness ensues. Ahhh, those Linzes.

The epidemic of Weaver-hating, soon to become the theme of the Race, is first visible to viewers at the airport, when Stassi Schroeder sees them evilly consorting with a reservations clerk. The fiends. Also, the Aiellos ask them what's up, and the Weavers either don't hear them or don't respond. David of the Aiellos (whose last name is not Aiello, of course) becomes the first to actually come out and say, "I hate them." But stay tuned.

Palling around with Rolly, Hunter Schroeder confides that his step-mom Char is a "bitch." Which, really, ain't as bad as it looks; it's just the kind of grumpy, irritated thing a kid his age would say, out of hearing range, when *literally millions and millions* of people aren't hearing him say it. Bet the family loves having the moment saved for posterity.

Skip the airport shuffle, and move on to Charleston, site of the Detour, "Forrest Gump" or "Muddy Waters." "Forrest Gump" sends teams out on a shrimping boat, where they must behead 200 pounds of shrimp. "Muddy Waters," an off-road challenge, requires teams to drive a four-by-four across a 400-foot gully filled with mud. The latter requires multiple attempts. The Aiellos, who fail *thirteen* times, are wryly amused midway through their ordeal when the Gaghans show up and nail the task on the first try, this time not singing any songs about mountains.

Charter buses take teams on an eight-hour journey to a "mystery destination," the U.S. Space and Rocket Center, where the Roadblock requires two members of each team to ride the centrifuge at three Gs. (One of the Linzes riding remarks that the pressure makes him want to fart, which is notable only as it's the third fart comment this team has made since the premiere. If I was making team nicknames for this Race, I would definitely call them Team Fart. So it's a good thing that's not happening.) From there, it's just a quick dash to the nearby space museum, and from there to the Space Shuttle Pathfinder, where Phil awaits.

The Bransens arrive first, and win the best prize any team has ever,

ever won for a first-place showing before the finale: for each licensed driver, which means all of them, credit cards good for free gasoline for life at every BP and ARCO station within the United States. Even with the fine-print limitations not mentioned on the air (fifty dollars per card, per week), the value calculated against life expectancy works out to quite the hefty sum, second only to the million-dollar prize awarded for first place. (Taken over decades, as opposed to one lump sum subject to taxes, the real value might even be more.)

As for the second group: the long bus trip is hard on the Weaver girls, who suffer a little emotional collapse that does little to endear them to their fellow passengers (see p. 415 "The Smartest Moves Ever Made by Racers." Yeah. Really. I'm serious).

1. The Bransen family
2. The Linz family
3. The Schroeder family
4. The Godlewski family
5. The Weaver family
6. The Paolo family
7. The Gaghan family
8. The Aiello family ELIMINATED

Leg #4: A Huge Secretary with Poor Bladder Control

Receiving fifty-one dollars, teams head off for Anniston, Alabama, and the world's largest office chair, which is so covered with puddles from a recent rainfall that you get the impression the world's largest secretary forgot to don her Depends.

We get more mysterious Weaver-hatred, this time from the Schroeder kids. Hunter calls them "white trash," an odd turnaround for a kid who was palling around with Rolly just one leg ago. Stassi calls Linda "The Wicked Witch." I dunno where any of this comes from. The Weaver-hating that makes some modicum of sense later seems to erupt out of nowhere here. We can only shrug and move on.

Brian Paolo asks his mom to repeat the name of the town again. She shrieks, "ANNISTON!" and hits him on the back of the neck with the clue envelope, an act of extreme brutality that causes him to cry in agony from his paper cut. I just report the facts, people.

Carissa Gaghan gets to climb the ladder leading to the office chair, which is a good thing, as she will soon need a reason to remember being useful.

Anyway, the Race now moves on to the Motor Sports Hall of Fame in Talladega, Alabama, a site that the Bransens note will not sit extremely well with the Weavers. (It doesn't. The girls have another panic attack. Mom has to remind them that their dad loved racing and that they should just get through this.) It turns out that the task at the Talladega Super Speedway does not involve cars at all, but rather a "party bike," one of those ridiculous deals where everybody sits around in a circle and gives each other thigh strain. When the Gaghans arrive, Carissa is not quite big enough to reach the pedals, but at least she has the memories of her performance at the office chair to warm her.

Everybody completing the orbit on the party bike now rushes off to Hattiesburg, Mississippi, where they must search out the Southern Colonel. They're not told it's a trailer dealership. Woo-hoo. Once there, they have to search the various trailers for the ones with the best morning departure times.

On the drive there, the Bransen girls see the Linzes one lane over and decide that it would be really cool to moon the other team. Which one of the girls does. With her father in the car. It's an interesting moment.

The Schroeders manufacture their own difficulty finding the place (see p. 409 "The Most Jaw-Dropping Errors Ever Made by Racers"), a genuine downturn that makes Stassi cry.

Carissa thinks the trailers are "eeeeeevil."

In a terrific example of why this Race is less than thrilling, the morning's first task turns out to be finding a BP station and asking for Les. Whoo. Can't wait for the uncut scenes on that DVD, people. I can't get enough of asking for Les. Things get a little more interesting as teams make it to Fairview-Riverside State Park, where the Detour is either "Work," which involves using a two-person saw to cut four slices off a log, or "Play," which requires teams to paddle out to a riverboat and beat a dealer at blackjack. Still less than thrilling, but okay.

The Pit Stop turns out to be in the French Quarter of New Orleans, resulting in a journey that gives Linda Weaver a fine chance to tell her home-schooled kids that Pontchartrain is one of the five Great Lakes. But it's the Schroeders who succumb to the hometown curse, and hit the mat last. A few weeks later, Hurricane Katrina hits and destroys their home. It's not the best of all possible years.

1. The Bransen family
2. The Paolo family
3. The Linz family
4. The Godlewski family
5. The Weaver family
6. The Gaghan family
7. The Schroeder family ELIMINATED

Leg #5: Oh. A Different Country. Joy.

At long freakin' last, the Racers leave the United States, heading for that bisected country, Panama, home of the paper cut of the Americas. Once there they've got to find the Smithsonian Tropical Research Institute, board boats, and cross to the island where one Ricardo Diaz will be lying around in a hammock with a handful of clue envelopes. Great work if you can get it.

Turns out that there are two flights to Panama City, both of which are provided to the Racers, making us long for the days when teams got dumped off at some foreign airport and had to scramble like rabid dogs trying to arrange their flights. That was fine television. But the way this little simplified game of airport shuffle works out, the plane arriving at 6:40 P.M. carries the Bransens, the Linzes, and the Paolos, while the one arriving at 9:10 P.M. carries the Godlewskis, the Gaghans, and the Weavers. On arrival, all six teams naturally find out that the Institute doesn't open until 7:00 A.M. the next morning, so we're once again faced with one massive bunching, just in case any of the teams might, you know, actually do something that would give one of them an advantage.

Sigh.

The boat trip goes badly for the Gaghans, whose driver thinks it will be a fine idea to head off in the wrong direction to pick up some other passengers. Yow.

Anyhow, Ricardo Diaz stirs himself from his nap to hand teams the Detour, which is "Rhythm" or "Coos." The first sends teams to four locations to pick up musical instruments that must be delivered to the

Take Five jazz and wine club. In the second, teams bus to a local park and use binoculars to search for wooden replicas of local birds.

Anybody remember walking with tigers? Climbing mountains? Mining for salt? Going on safari? No? Must have dreamt it. Anyway.

The Paolos and Gaghans both try to make the Fast Forward, which Phil explains is the only Fast Forward on this entire Race. (Boo! Bring back the Fast Forward! We miss the most advantageous time to go for it!) This turns out to require tandem bungee jumping. The main reason the Gaghans go for it, it seems, is that Carissa has been eager to bungee jump ever since she learned she was going to be on this show, which is about as good a reason as anything else, I suppose. The most dramatic moment here involves the bungee jump not at all, but rather a spectacular trip and fall that propels Tammy Gaghan slamming headfirst into a parked taxi. Now, if THAT were the Fast Forward, and Racers who failed to collide with sufficient impact had to do it again and again until they got it right, we might have something.

The Paolos grab the Fast Forward when D. J. overcomes his fear of heights to jump with Mom.

Elsewhere, the Bransens discover that the local they drafted to guide them to the Detour has actually instructed their bus driver to take her to work. (Hee.)

The Roadblock at the baseball stadium requires one player to make a base hit off a local Little League pitcher. Also about as exciting as it sounds, though the war between the Weavers, Godlewskis, and Linzes intensifies over the propriety of saying, "Suh-wing, batta-batta-batta."

Last to the Pit Stop at the Miraflores Locks, the Godlewskis suspect they're last and show up wearing multiple layers of clothing in the Panamanian heat.

1. The Paolo family
2. The Weaver family
3. The Bransen family
4. The Linz family
5. The Gaghan family
6. The Godlewski family MUGGED

Leg #6: Bean There, Done That

All teams except for the Godlewskis receive seventy-four dollars with their instructions to toodle off for the bus station and sign up for one of three charter buses to San Jose, Costa Rica. They leave half an hour apart, the next day, but it doesn't matter a dang what bus teams get on, as the 200-mile trip to San Jose comes complete with a guaranteed bunching point at the other end. The fourteen hours between the Pit Stop and the bus departures gives the Godlewskis ample opportunity for begging. The excitement level fails to rise above comatose.

Arriving in San Jose, teams claim vans from an all-night car park and drive thirty-five miles to Volcan Poas, a 1,000-foot-deep active volcano. The overlook they need is, of course, locked behind a gate until the next morning. It's about as blatant a planned bunching as we've had since Race 6. My eyelid flutters, then sinks back down.

In the morning, everybody is goggled by the caldera. The only exception is one of the Weaver girls, who complains, "That was the dumbest volcano I've ever been to." I examine this sentence and slowly walk around it, tilting my head as I try to discern its species.

In any event, the clue directs teams to the Doka Estate, a coffee plantation seventeen miles away. Teams are also informed that there's a Yield ahead. We get a nice montage of several teams, including the Linzes, Paolos, and Godlewskis, all discussing how to use the Yield, which is by far the most interesting thing they've been asked to do this trip. Hilariously, *everybody* on these three teams wants the pleasure of Yielding the Weavers, though it's the Paolos who win that particular privilege.

The Weavers devote their time in limbo to a) declaring their moral superiority to teams evil enough to do such a thing, and b) making fun of the team photographs aligned on the Yield box. They think it's hilarious that Tony Paolo has a garbage truck, and deride the Godlewskis as bottle blondes with chest implants. The Weaver-hate becomes a little less of an enigma.

The Roadblock requires the participating player to search a mound containing 800 pounds of coffee beans for the one bean painted red. It's a haystack task, and it goes no more happily, as all teams (including the resentful Weavers) find their respective beans and hit the road while Tammy Gaghan follows in the footsteps of Lena and Kristy.

After Megan Linz completes the Roadblock, her brothers congratulate her on her balls. She snaps back, "Twenty-one years I was looking forward to getting my balls." One of her best moments.

The Detour up ahead is "Relic" or "Ripe." "Relic" is a search through a rainforest preserve for four relics of varying sizes. "Ripe" sends teams to load fifteen bushels of bananas aboard pulleys. The bushels weigh about a zillion pounds, which is why it's so great to see Tony Paolo wow his sons with his physical strength, and for the sons to admit that they're wowed.

In the end, it comes down to a race between the Weavers and the Gaghans. And the Pit Stop, a beach in Quepos, becomes the site of what may be the saddest elimination ever, as Carissa tries really, really, really, really, really hard not to cry. Dang it all to heck and back.

1. The Paolo family
2. The Linz family
3. The Bransen family
4. The Godlewski family
5. The Weaver family
6. The Gaghan family ELIMINATED

Leg #7: Oh, Buoy

This leg, and the next one, air together as part of a two-hour episode.

Teams receive $310 and directions to the first Roadblock at a beach known as Playa Maracas, where one Racer must grab the clue from an offshore buoy. Tony Paolo elects to swim for his team, and starts to flounder, requiring the intervention of a rescue crew. High and dry, D. J. rolls his eyes, asking, "Why did he say he could do it if he couldn't do it?" Yeah, that's right. You can't take Dad anywhere. He just annoys the emergency crews.

The clue directs teams to take a taxi to Grecia and find the Iglesia de Metal, an entirely metal church where, it turns out, a funeral is now in progress. This is a stroke of luck for the mourners. A parade of reality show contestants is, of course, exactly what you want to deal with when you're burying somebody.

The Detour is "Brush" or "Barrel." In "Brush," teams taxi ten miles to an oxcart factory, where they must hand-paint wagon wheels; in "Barrel," they travel the same distance to a sugar-cane plantation, where they must load a flatbed trailer with a ton of sugar cane. That latter option also requires some diddling around at a barrel factory.

A few (televised) moments later, when the clue found in the barrel factory reveals the next destination as Phoenix, Marion speaks for disappointed Race fans everywhere: "What are we going to Phoenix, Arizona, for? I wanna go to New Zealand!" It may be the only time a Racer ever nails the major problem with a Race while it's still filming.

As teams trickle into the San Jose airport and begin booking itineraries to Phoenix, the Weavers corner D. J. to give him crap over last leg's Yield. They wanna know why he would do such a thing. After all, they *like* him. They've been nothing but *nice* to him. Looking nervous—*who are these people, and why are they surrounding me?*—he tells them, honestly enough, that he was trying to knock their team out. The Weavers gasp in such overplayed shock that their mouths become little O's. "Well," Linda says, suddenly all Clint Eastwood, "you don't have any Yields left, and we do, *sweets.*"

You kinda wonder if these folks ever get that mad playing Scrabble. *Why would you use that Triple Word Score? I've been nothing but nice to you. And I have the Q...Sweets.*

There's a crisis as some of the teams arrive at JFK International for their layover in New York City. The airline has lost all records of the Godlewskis' connecting flight to Phoenix, and there are no further seats available. Their chances now rest on a manic rush to Newark Airport, to take another flight from another airline. The punch line is that this one gets them to Phoenix forty-five minutes ahead of anybody else.

The Roadblock at the Bondurant SuperKart School requires one team member to do fifty laps on a go-kart. The racing task is not exactly easy on the Weavers, who once again get the family tragedy shoved in their faces. Linda, who elects to ride, erupts in scorn about being passed by Tommy Linz. "Oh, you're going to write *that* one in a book," she says. "A 20-year-old guy passes a 46-year-old woman!"[69] To which, all sympathy aside, I can only say, shut up. It's a Race. A race *within* a Race. What did you expect? Polite following?

---

[69] She's absolutely right. This is a book. And I'm officially reiterating, a 20-year-old guy passed a 46-year-old woman.

Last to the Pit Stop, thirty-two miles away at Fort McDowell, are the Bransens, who benefit from some last-minute intervention from the Paolos (see p. 425 "The Most Endearing Racer Moments").

1. The Godlewski family
2. The Weaver family
3. The Linz family
4. The Paolo family
5. The Bransen family MUGGED

Leg #8: The Apple Core from Heaven

The Bransen girls beg for money as every other team receives seventy-three dollars with their instructions to an airport in Mesa, Arizona, where they must look for an outfit known as Fighter Combat International.

The next morning turns out to be the Roadblock, which requires one participating Racer from each team to go up in a fighter plane and execute a loop under the pilot's guidance. Looks real cool, perhaps the most exciting thing the players have had the opportunity to do this entire Race. There are no vomit incidents, fortunately, though we do get D. J., on the ground, showering his brother Brian with scorn for not getting it on the first try. This Roadblock would be even more enjoyable if it allowed strafing.

The next route marker is seventy-seven miles away, at Lipan Point, an overlook on the edge of the Grand Canyon. On the way, Rebecca Weaver sees the Godlewski vehicle pull up alongside them, and reacts by throwing garbage. No, really. It seems to have been an apple core. She actually throws food at a competing car.

Not long afterward, as they pull up to the booth at the entrance to Lipan Point, this time directly ahead of the Linzes, Linda Weaver tells the guard to give the car behind them a "nice long history" of the area. The guard is not fooled by this brilliant ploy, and indeed merely tells the Linzes, "Boy, they were talking a lot of smack about the vehicle behind them." The Linzes are neither surprised nor bothered, though they do start looking forward to that next Yield. The Weaver-hating is even less mysterious.

The clue, which amounts to a "Sorry, wrong canyon," merely directs

Racers another 137 miles to the Glen Canyon Dam in Page, Arizona. Teams take their one and only look at one of the great natural wonders of the world before sadly leaving it behind.

The Detour at Glen Canyon is "Bearing" or "Bailing." "Bearing" requires Racers to follow compass coordinates from clue box to clue box until they have three. "Bailing" sends teams deep into the canyon to pump out a half-submerged rowboat and drag it ashore. The trick in that latter option is to bail out enough water to flip the rowboat over, thus emptying it in one big swoosh.

The Paolos, who arrive last (once again, because nobody listened to Marion), have their last major fight of their time on the show, and danged if they haven't grown on us, because this time the mutual abuse is actually endearing. Marion warns D. J., "I'll take your frickin' head off." And D. J. says, "Ma, this is a big river. I can drown you here and no one would find your body." She responds, "Just try, buddy." Which is, you know, perversely lovely. No sarcasm here. I'm totally serious. It's lovely, like the Sopranos doing Cosby.

The Pit Stop involves a drive to Lake Powell and a boat trip up the river, which may qualify as the third canyon of the leg. The boat race hoses the first-place Linzes as the Godlewski vehicle turns out to be faster.

At the Pit Stop, the Weavers hold forth on their distaste for the other teams. "Those people are, like, classless," says Rachel. "What it is is we don't cuss, and it's just hard to, like, deal with people like that and then have them group up against you and be the only family that's trying to live a Christian life." Throwing garbage at moving vehicles, making fun of sanitation workers, and mocking ladies with chest implants is, on the other hand, the epitome of admirable behavior. I include a dotted line so readers can insert their own commentary.

As for the Paolos, they bicker all the way to the mat, but then own up to pride in one another. So it's a tearful farewell for them, now.

1. The Godlewski family
2. The Linz family
3. The Weaver family

4. The Bransen family
5. The Paolo family ELIMINATED

Leg #9: Revigorating, Injuvenating

Now equipped with big campers to lug behind their respective SUVs, teams head for Monument Valley, site of many John Ford westerns. Along the way, we get updates on the Godlewskis (who think Christine talks too much), the Linzes (who are sick of being beaten to the mat at the last minute), the Weavers (who are still upset at being treated so rudely), and the Bransens (who are staying out of the who's-ruder fight, in the hopes that the controversy will slow down everybody else.)

Neither camper-handling woes or the helicopter ride to the top of Elephant Butte amounts to much. But the Godlewskis and Linzes plot to Yield the Weavers if either team gets the opportunity. This far from the Yield, the pact has precious little to do with "most advantageous" and everything to do with payback for nasty looks and apple cores. But, hey, anything to keep them entertained.

Next we get a 180-mile drive to Moab, Utah, site of the rock formation Gemini Bridges. On the way, the Weaver kids go on at length about the notorious ugliness of the Utahan desert. Rolly says, "God must have spent a little less time on this state." He further notes that he's never heard one thing about Utah, which prompts Mom to note that the Mormons live here, and Rachel to gasp, "No wonder." I insert another dotted line.

The Detour at Gemini Bridges is a choice between "Drop Down" and "Ride Down." In "Drop Down," teams rappel 270 feet into the canyon, one team member at a time. In "Ride Down," teams mountain bike six miles to the same location. All teams but the Weavers take the rappeling task, a fact that has nothing but good things to say about Wally Bransen, who is less than enthused but goes along for the sake of his daughters. The Weavers bike down still complaining about how much they hate Utah.

The Godlewskis arrive late because their crew drained their car battery charging up the camera equipment. They receive no time-credit. Well, at least nothing that spectacularly unfair could possibly happen again.

All any of this gets anybody is a night in their campers at Green River State Park, and their departure times the next morning are a mere fifteen minutes apart. The next morning they drive off to a private home in Heber City to meet "Bart," who turns out to be the famous Bart the Bear, who they of course don't actually meet so much as look at. Bart waddles out with the clue envelope and gives it to his trainer, who promptly hands it to the Racers, bear spit and all.[70]

This clue sends Racers to the Olympic Park at Park City, Utah. All teams but the Weavers take the best route, 40 North; the Weavers take a scenic loop and are delayed by hours, dragging their big fat camper on a narrow road from which they cannot turn off. They stop for some ice cream, believing that it "revigorates" and "injuvenates" you. When they arrive at the Roadblock, which requires one player from each team to ski jump into a swimming pool, they are grimly satisfied to find themselves Yielded by the Linzes. And they're so sick of the whole thing that they look forward to elimination, and are completely unenthused when they find themselves merely mugged. They thus become the first team ever to be mugged twice.

The Pit Stop is the Salt Lake City Public Library. Honestly. The Taj Mahal. Ancient rat temples. The Sahara. The Eiffel Tower. Icelandic glaciers. Versus... the Salt Lake City Public Library? How profoundly embarrassing.

1. The Linz family
2. The Bransen family
3. The Godlewski family
4. The Weaver family MUGGED

Leg #10a: Where the 'Rhoids Are

Receiving eighty-seven dollars, teams now head for the parking lot of the Park City High School, which is about as exciting as any other parking lot. They get to enjoy a comfortable night's sleep, thanks to the

---

[70] This was actually the second Bart the Bear. The original Bart the Bear starred in movies as varied as *Clan of the Cave Bear, The Bear, The Edge*, and *Legends of the Fall*, always playing a character known as "The Bear." He was actually a presenter at the Oscars one year. Bart the Bear II, whom the Racers "met," appeared in *Dr. Doolittle 2* and *Without a Paddle*. None of the Racers seemed to realize that they were in the presence of a bona fide celebrity, but to be fair, he didn't seem all that impressed with reality show personalities either.

campers they're still lugging around. This really has become the very first *Amazing Race* where the goal seems to be making sure the Racers don't get elevated heart rates.

The Weavers, who have begged enough money to continue, once again react to the Yield by angrily confronting the folks who Yielded them. Linda demands, "Are you sorry?" Alex can only offer a bland, "No." Megan mutters a somewhat more emphatic, "Hell, no."

Onward to hot air balloons. The necessity of inflating them first gives the Godlewskis one of their own all-time best moments, as someone counts off to three, "One! Two! Three! Four!" and Michelle repeats, "Four!?!?" It doesn't translate to the printed page, but you gotta trust me—in practice, it's hilarious.

The Bransen and Linz balloons suffer a midair collision, which amounts to what always happens when two balloons bounce into one another, which is nothing, though the show tries to play the event for high drama.

Upon landing, teams are driven back to their campers (sigh), and must make their own way to the Heber Valley Railway, site of the Detour, "Spike It" or "Steam It." In "Spike It," teams lay a twenty-foot section of rail, using sledgehammers and spikes and that kind of whatnot. In "Steam It," teams use wheelbarrows to transport 400 pounds of coal to a train engine. Again, the Weavers take the option not chosen by the other teams, but this time it works out for them, as they complete the task in very short order. As for Wally Bransen, who worries a lot about being a drag on his team, he totally rocks the rail option, doing the hard labor while his daughters goggle at their dad actually leading a task. It's his best moment on the Race.

Christine Godlewski, who says she cries easily and has in fact demonstrated it in previous legs, cries again when her sisters are mean to her.

Teams now head for the Tree of Utah, a sculpture out in the middle of the Bonneville Salt Flats, which was designed to bring life and color to the stark landscape but which one of the Bransen girls accurately derides as more like the "tree of hemorrhoids." (It's about as dumb as roadside attractions can get without involving big balls of string.)

Then we have another night in a campground, with the next morning's departure order a reflection of respective arrivals. This time it's the hopping-mad Linzes arriving last. Seems their crew drained their car battery by juicing up the cameras. They receive no time-credit. That's the kind of spectacularly unfair thing that could never...oh. Wait.[71]

The next morning, the Weavers, who have had one too many race-track moments, are rewarded with a cattle-herding Roadblock that highlights Rebecca's equestrian skills. So she gets to be terrific at something.

Teams completing the task need to head for Yellowstone and sit around waiting for Old Faithful to erupt, before being handed directions to the ranch where Phil awaits. That's right. They sit round waiting for Old Faithful. And next they do something even lamer. This is the Muzak of *Amazing Race* seasons.

When the Bransens and Weavers footrace to the mat in a seeming competition for first place, Phil doesn't help matters much by announcing that this is not the Pit Stop.

It's another uber-leg.

And yawn.

Leg #10b: Getting on Christine's Back

One by one, teams receive the bad news that the Race is still on and that they must now travel forty-nine miles to Turtle Ranch in Dubois, Wyoming. The trailing Godlewskis have the best reaction to this, as Michelle complains, "You're just torturing us!" and Phil happily agrees, "I know, I'm torturing you." He doesn't seem all too sorry.

Everybody wonders if Turtle Ranch will involve eating turtles, or something, but no: it's just another all-night hours-of-operation bunching, obliging everybody to sack out in their campers as they wait for something of consequence to happen in the morning. So, again, somebody please tell me: what, exactly, is the point of having these uber-legs if the second half always begins with the Racers on an equal footing again?

The Weavers share more feelings of persecution, which I skip.

The Detour at Turtle Ranch turns out to be "Pioneer Spirit" or "Native Tradition." The first requires teams to construct a wagon, hook it up to a team of horses, and ride it a quarter-mile. "Native Tradition" involves the construction of a teepee, which a Native American chief will

---

[71] The anger is not shown on-screen, but both the Linzes, and the other teams who witnessed it, report that it was significant.

have to judge. I skip over some of the woo-woo-woo type cartoon Indian behavior in the presence of the chief, which is about as painful as the most culturally insensitive thing any Racers ever did in any country not their own. I do report, however, that the teepee-building is Christine Godlewski's finest hour, as (with what appears to be considerable pain) she supports Sharon on her back for however long it takes the adjustments on the tent to be completed.

Next, teams drive 221 miles to Cody, Wyoming, where they must find the hotel named after Buffalo Bill's daughter. Cultural illiteracy rises its ugly head as several Racers wonder if Buffalo Bill was a mythical figure (no), maybe the guy with the big axe (no) or whether his daughter was Calamity Jane (also no). The task at the Irma Hotel turns out to be nothing more than dressing up in period costume and getting their pictures taken with some dude whose full-time job happens to be calling himself Buffalo Bill and getting his picture taken with tourists. This would be worthy of extreme derision as the lamest "task" in a Race filled with lame tasks, were it not for the amusing aftermath, as most of the females still left in the competition look at their family's perfectly presentable souvenir photographs and complain about how bad they look. Wally Bransen horrifies his daughters by proposing the photo as the family picture card, and Rolly Weaver smiles knowingly as his mother and sisters compete in the I'm-ugly-you-look-better-than-I-do sweepstakes. (It's one of his more endearing moments.)

The final task, seventy-three miles away at the Red Lodge Mountain Golf Course, is a Roadblock, requiring two Racers from each team to pile into luxury golf carts designed to look like Buick Lucernes, pick a colored flag, and search the course for four golf balls of the same color. It's a luck-based task, to some extent, but one that can only go better with sufficient focus. The Godlewskis, arriving last, do not quite manage to muster that focus (see p. 409 "The Most Jaw-Dropping Errors Ever Made by Racers").

The Pit Stop is forty-three miles away at Green Meadow Ranch. The Weavers are stopped by a cop for speeding, and rapidly approach "E" on their fuel gauge, but no last-minute Godlewski surge materializes. The Pink Ladies are out and the contentious Floridians in.

Down to the final three.

1. The Bransen family
2. The Linz family
3. The Weaver family
4. The Godlewski family ELIMINATED

Leg #11: To the Falls

This leg airs as a two-hour season finale.

Teams have been provided tickets to Montreal, Canada, which would be a real hoot if the next location were actually Jamaica. There's some airport shuffle as teams look for better flights, but that's not nearly as interesting as the last of the Race's misunderstanding-fueled conflicts. Alex Linz and Rolly Weaver collide while running, and go down in a pile. Alex gives Rolly a pat on the back, the kind not too difficult to interpret as *that's okay, no harm done, we're both fine.* Mama cries, "No! Don't touch him!" Which is fine as a moment of maternal panic, less so as an accurate interpretation of what actually happened.

In any event, once airport shuffle is done, the Linzes and Weavers book passage that lands at 4:10 P.M.; the Bransens are scheduled to land at 5:00 P.M. Although that flight gets delayed by an additional half-hour. Yowch.

We skip a search through an underground tunnel[72] complex for the next clue. By the time teams get to the Detour, at the CDP Capital Building, the Weavers are substantially ahead. It's "Slide It" or "Roll It." "Slide It" is a curling challenge, by which I mean the Canadian sport, not anything to do with hairstyling. "Roll It" requires teams to travel to an arboretum and use traditional lumberjack tools to move four logs along a track. The Weavers rock the curling, as do the Linzes; while the Bransens rush off to deal with big honking logs.

Later, in the American Pavillion, teams face the Roadblock, where one team member has to learn how to complete a manuever on the flying trapeze. The Weavers are still ahead as Rolly completes that clue.

Later, at the Stade Olympic, teams have to compete in what may the most aggravating needle-in-a-haystack challenge since Lena and Kristy went down in flames. Somewhere, in this stadium with 56,000 seats, are

---

[72] Incidentally, I have never understood the phrase "underground tunnel." What's an above-ground tunnel? Are human habitrails, looping in and out of city skylines, at all common in real life?

three departure times for three early-morning charter flights to a "mystery destination." (The departure times are only five minutes apart, so it doesn't matter all that much, but teams will drive themselves crazy looking for any flights at all.) The immensity of the search gives the Linz and Bransen families time to catch up. It also starts to wear on the elder generation. Wally says, "[This] is gonna take all frickin' night. I'm going to kick somebody's ass." Linda Weaver and the Weaver sisters just want to give up, with Rebecca calling the whole thing "stupid" and Mom curling up on a cot to catch some sleep. Rolly is less than happy (see p. 409 "The Most Jaw-Dropping Errors Ever Made by Racers"). They do take a last stab at searching, once Mama wakes up, and do half-heartedly find the last clue.

The next morning, the "mystery destination" is Toronto, where the view from the CN Tower offers teams a chance to spot the next route marker. This leads to the leg's second Detour, "Ship" or "Shoe." In "Ship," teams sail across the harbor to a sailing ship, where one player climbs 100 feet to retrieve the clue. In "Shoe," teams race to the Shoe Museum—yes, the Shoe Museum—where they have to pick a pair of shoes and search 100 milling women for the one wearing an identical pair.

None of this is incredibly thrilling.

Still further up ahead, a buoy bobbing in the Niagara Whirlpool leads teams to the final destination city, Lewiston, New York, where a final Roadblock requires each participating player to complete an oversized seventy-one-piece jigsaw puzzle of North America. As the Weavers have fallen behind due to navigation errors, this final competition comes down to the Linzes and Bransens. It would have been interesting to see the geographically challenged Weavers compete in this challenge, but that will wait until after the million dollars is awarded. And the recipients of that are no big surprise, as—despite considerable strengths that do include the much-maligned Wally—there's no way the Bransens can beat the Linzes in a footrace.

1. The Linz family WIN
2. The Bransen family PLACE
3. The Weaver family SHOW

The Race 8 That Would Have Pleased Us

EPILOGUE:

The Amazing Race Web site reveals that the second- and third-place teams competed in one final challenge to win SUVs identical to those they drove around during the show. The challenge was another geography puzzle, requiring teams to match icons representing objects and places they had encountered to their respective places on the jigsaw-puzzle map already completed. In the end, it's the Bransens who win the car, which is appropriate enough, as they don't particularly need to worry about the price of gasoline.

FIRST LEG

Eleven teams, including The Blind Guys, The Escaped Felons, The Obsessive-Compulsives, The Passive-Aggressives, The Restaurant Critics, The Pirates, The Chartered Accountants, The Contract Attorneys, The

Mall Santas, The Dog Lovers, and Carissa Gaghan all by herself, are flown by helicopter to the top of a 300-foot-tall mesa and told that they must make their way to Big Ben in London. Every team has trouble climbing down except for Carissa Gaghan, who has brought her own bungee cord. She takes the Fast Forward, a bungee-jumping challenge, and proceeds directly to the first leg's Pit Stop, Stonehenge, where she wins a lifetime supply of bungee cords. All other teams have to deal with that leg's Detour ("Paper" or "Plastic") and Roadblock ("Dentist Appointment"), but they all make it within forty-eight hours of Carissa, with the exception of The Passive-Aggressives, who remain atop the mesa waiting for each other to do it. They are eliminated by an aggrieved Phil, who had flown all the way to London to welcome Carissa and then had to fly all the way back to Arizona to eliminate the Passive-Aggressives. They tell him that they'll be happy to leave the Race, if that's what he really wants.

SECOND LEG

The ten remaining teams receive instructions to cross the English Channel by any means possible, as long as that doesn't include a boat, a car, a plane, or a train. The Contract Attorneys fall behind when they spend twenty hours searching the clue envelope for subsidiary clauses. Of the teams that attempt to swim, only Carissa Gaghan storms Omaha Beach without serious delay; she is first to the Detour ("Nap" or "Jump Up and Down Excitedly") and first to the Roadblock ("Paint Every Building in Portugal"). The Pit Stop, atop a nearby roller coaster, stymies her at first when she doesn't reach the minimum height requirement, but the other teams take so long to arrive that she is able to grow the required three inches an hour before the second team (The Mall Santas) arrive, driving a bevy of exhausted and resentful reindeer. She wins the dog Guido, which upsets Joe and Bill, as they don't learn about this until six months later when they watch the episode at home, and the guy with the pet carrier shows up at their door. The Contract Attorneys never do cross the English Channel and are therefore eliminated, though they charge their hourly rate and are able to claim a million-dollar check anyway.

THIRD LEG

The nine remaining teams receive instructions to fly to Tunisia and count every grain of sand in the Sahara Desert. The Restaurant Critics take the Fast Forward but demur when they find out it involves using ketchup. Everybody else sits beneath the broiling North African sun, trying to make their limited supply of bottled water last between them, and in serious danger of mass dehydration until Carissa Gaghan develops an advanced artificial-intelligence paradigm that immediately nails down the number, within five. The producers, who don't know the correct answer themselves, throw up their hands and provide the latest in a cruel series of ostrich egg Roadblocks, all the more impossible because this time Racers are actually required to lay it. We draw a kind curtain over how they actually accomplish this. Carissa Gaghan is first to the Pit Stop, where Phil just sighs and hands her the keys to his car. Everybody else, walking funny, straggles in a few hours later, except for The Restaurant Critics, who are still at the Fast Forward waiting for the ketchup to emerge from the bottle.

FOURTH LEG

Teams now make their way back to the very same field where Lena and Kristy, the Mormon sisters, have spent the last few years gamely unrolling hay bales. It seems that the producers have been providing them with hundreds of additional hay bales on a regular basis, in the hopes that they'll eventually find that elusive clue envelope. Every team shows up, finds a clue envelope, and departs, leaving Lena and Kristy behind, still refusing to give up. The Roadblock ("Abdominal Surgery") and Detour ("Continue Racing" or "Go Home") leave teams neck and neck. They descend into the Paris sewers, expecting to emerge a few blocks later, but learning to their dismay that this actually is the Pit Stop and the site of their mandatory twelve-hour rest period. Carissa Gaghan wins, of course. The Chartered Accountants are eliminated.

FIFTH LEG

Teams proceed to the Great Wall of China, where the Roadblock requires one member of each team to build another one just like it. Carissa Gaghan is the first one to realize she can just take a four-hour penalty instead, although by then she's halfway through Manchuria.

From there, players fly to Thailand, where they must locate and repair Colin's ox. It turns out that he was right all along and that it actually was broken, but the farmer who owns it neglected to buy a service contract and there's no place to get spare parts this time of year. Carissa Gaghan improvises a solution using a Pez dispenser and a bungee cord, and propels the beast well past the confines of its rice paddy, and into Bangkok proper, where its landing nearly crushes Phil. Carissa wins more bungee cords. The other teams limp in without oxen of their own, but find out that this is the first of two predetermined non-elimination legs, and that they're still in the Race, though they'll all be stripped of their money, their luggage, and all their clothes, INCLUDING (in a new twist) everything they have on them. This is not a happy development for anybody, as the Pit Stop is a traffic circle in Bangkok, and they all have to stand around miserable and naked while Carissa has dinner with the producers. Everybody quits in a huff, except for Carissa, who bungee jumps one more time before being handed the million-dollar check.

Visiting the Gaghans

THE EIGHTH EDITION OF *THE Amazing Race* was far from a series highlight, as even the Racers acknowledge, but it did give viewers the chance to meet some remarkable people, among them the inexhaustible Gaghans. We caught up with Bill, Tammy, Billy, and Carissa (along with younger daughter, Kelly) in Orlando, where they were all running Disney marathons. The overwhelming impression, from the kids at least, was that their first[73] fifteen minutes of fame were fast becoming old news, less a once-in-a-lifetime adventure than one in a series, which has already receded into the past. Check out, for instance, their "favorite part" of their adventure! Also check out the family reaction when the Race's inter-team conflict comes up....

---

[73] I say their "first" fifteen minutes of fame because I ain't counting them out of the game, yet.

Q: *Let's talk a little bit about how you became involved with the show. I know that you, Tammy, were the first one to apply.*

TAMMY: Yeah, a bunch of times. I started to catch it around season two. It was the same as *Survivor*: I missed the first season and started to catch it around the second season. I didn't start applying until my younger daughter was about four, so that she'd understand that I'd be coming back. Earlier than that, I thought she'd be too needy without me. I wanted [Bill] to apply with me, every time a season would come around, but it was almost like he'd hide from me, because I was the one who was always checking the Internet, finding out when the new application would be coming out. I asked him numerous times, but he's much more practical than I am, so he's the one who kept saying, "I've got a job," and "Who's going to watch three children when we're away?"

Q: *Easy questions like that.*

TAMMY: He would say, "If you can get your mother to watch the kids." And I'd say, "Oh, you're no fun to play with. Just fill out the application and the video!" So I [applied with] my dad. He did it with me twice. And then a friend of mine who I met on the Internet, on one of the message boards—I've done that for years now—we found out we both enjoy running, we're both moms, and we're going to be The Internet Buddies or The Marathon Moms, and nothing happened with that, either. And then I guess one of these guys (*indicating Billy and Carissa*) caught their attention.

BILLY: I wouldn't blame them, you know.

Q: *So you guys starting watching it too?*

CARISSA: I think we started watching it around season six. Because it was on around nine o'clock, our mom taped it for us. We watched it the next day. It was a good show. We liked it.

Q: *I know you guys have traveled a lot before the Race. You didn't do all the stuff you did on the Race, but a lot of people on the Race are not practiced travelers like you are. You've been to a lot of places. Where have you been?*

BILLY: I forget.

CARISSA: There have been so many.

BILL: Well, what's your favorite trip?

BILLY: When we went to Bali.

CARISSA: Yeah, Bali.

BILL: We went to Bali for Thanksgiving in 2004, so.

CARISSA: Nice trip.

BILLY: It liked because it was so warm. The climate was nice. It was in the rainy season. When we went to the monkey village, it was raining, and the monkeys were mean.

Q: *How were they mean?*

BILLY: They were like little humans.

TAMMY: It's a temple, and there's a monkey god. He helped save the people. So they don't hurt the monkeys, and they allow the monkeys to roam free at these temples. So people have to go on tour and visit the monkeys. But monkeys are very smart, and some actually steal things. They'll take your glasses, and there just happens to be a person who can get the monkeys to come off the tree.

Q: *With your glasses.*

TAMMY: With your glasses.

BILL: For five dollars.

(*Laughter*)

TAMMY: They've got a good racket there.

CARISSA: There was one little monkey that climbed on top of me and tried to check out my pockets.

Q: *Anywhere else?*

BILL: We lived in Korea.

TAMMY: We watch the [Race 4 Korean episodes] and find them so funny, because we know that Korea is one of those Asian cultures where people like to save face. And [cab drivers] won't tell you that they don't know where they're going, because they're just negative. So they'll just figure it out. And Koreans are accustomed to that.

BILL: We love to travel. We love to be out of our element and love to be... cautiously uncomfortable. We're certainly not out trekking.

I'm sure there are families even more extreme than ours, but we're comfortable sleeping in twenty-dollar hotel rooms, and sleeping on the floor…the kind of things that are not so typical when you're staying in a beautiful hotel like this.

TAMMY: So we thought the Race was way easier than [we'd expected]. We thought for sure we had an advantage over the other people. We didn't know that we were going to be in a SUV, where we then had a disadvantage, because we only had one driver and one navigator. But the other teams had three people in the back who could navigate.

BILLY: The Weavers were really good navigators.

TAMMY: People ask what was toughest. Was it the physical challenges, was it this, or that—no, it was the driving! Sometimes, when we had to make a quick decision over which way we were going, he had three maps, trying to figure it out, and we'd drive by the Linzes, and they'd have maps, and—

BILL: I helped.

Q: *I saw!*

CARISSA: And I helped find the arrows.

BILL: Yes, you did.

Q: *From what I've seen on the show, a lot of Races were lost by missing a highway exit—as I in fact did, on my way to this interview,[74] trying to find highway entrances and exits.*

TAMMY: I'm sure the other Racers will tell you that, even normally, trying to find directions is difficult. When you're on the Race, something's not clicking right in your brain. The adrenaline's pumping and you just don't think sometimes.

Q: *From speaking to other Racers, I know that the interview process requires days of sequestration in a hotel. It occurs to me that this must be even more difficult for a family with energetic kids than it is for a couple.*

---

[74] There's something perversely wonderful, albeit only in retrospect, about driving to meet an *Amazing Race* team, passing a clearly marked turnoff, and then traveling several miles out of your way looking for the next exit while your wife yells at you for not LISTENING to her.

BILL: That week, when you're doing the final interviews, is intensely more traumatic than all of the Race. Because you've gone so far and you can see the goal of getting on the show, and you realize that only half the people who are there on those interviews are going to make it. You've got to be yourself, and you've got to be comfortable with what you're saying during the interviews. But on the other hand, you don't want to screw up and say something stupid. And then, maybe what they're *looking for* is you screwing up and saying something stupid. Maybe it was tougher having the kids along, but we knew in advance that we were going to be locked in a cage for a period of time, so we had to bring something to keep them entertained.

CARISSA: It was nice. We had a TV.

TAMMY: The very simple things keep them happy. [During the Race] we were on a bus trip, and there were some people having issues with being on buses...which I can't blame them for, as we were expecting to have airplanes. And they're complaining about the bus, and the kids are like, "Why don't they like the bus? Look! It's got a cup holder!"

CARISSA: There were bathrooms!

BILLY: There was a DVD player on the bus!

TAMMY:...on that one bus in Costa Rica. And even when we had to sleep in that bus station in Panama, we were like, "Are they really gonna make us sleep here?" But to them, it was like an adventure.

Q: *So you get all the interviews done, and you found out you were going to be on the Race. But you still had absolutely no idea that it was going to be largely domestic.*

TAMMY: We were never told anything. Every time we opened a clue, we thought we were going overseas.

BILL: They threw us a huge curveball and we all fell for it. It never clicked in our brains. (*laughing*) Okay, they sent us off to get camping gear, we're going to go camping. One family, the Paolos, almost didn't bring the gear. They thought they just had to go up to the counter, get their clue, and leave. Now, that would have been funny, if they'd started the whole Race off without their camping gear!

Q: *I would have liked to see the scene where they found out they'd needed it.*

BILL: (*laughing very hard*) Ohhhhhhhhh, no. "*Ma!* We've got to go back to New York!"

(*Giggling all around*)

BILL: It's just like Tam said. You just kept going, clue to clue, okay, we're in Virginia, we're going to D.C., soon we're going to Europe.

TAMMY: Each night, we spent... the two of us would get out the maps and figure out, how do we get to the nearest airport from here? So they really had us.

Q: *The critical error for you guys was in Washington, D.C.*

BILL: Oh, yeah.

TAMMY: That killed us.

Q: *How long were you stuck on the Mall?*

TAMMY: Less than two hours but pretty close to it.

Q: *And you're very aware, at this point, that other teams are passing you.*

TAMMY: The clue said, "Go to the Reflecting Pool at the U.S. Capitol." It didn't say "Capitol Building"; it said "U.S. Capitol." So we're assuming the U.S. Capitol is Washington, D.C. We were the first ones into D.C. We knew a way to go into D.C. quick.

BILLY: We were the first ones *in* Washington, D.C.!

TAMMY: I think the problem was, having watched some of the earlier seasons, is that they didn't always have the clue in a clue box. It could be on a bench, in a little box. It could be someone with the clue in their hand. You don't know it's gonna be this big box. It just said, "Around the Reflecting Pool." So we went around the reflecting pool, or as close as we could get to it, and then we said, "Okay, now let's go out another twenty feet." We went around the reflecting pool again. That's when we met up with the Schroeders. So we figured, okay, maybe it's around one of the memorials. So we checked out the Vietnam Memorial. 'Cause you don't know.

Q: *That's a long walk.*

BILL: It really is.

TAMMY: Our poor camera guy.

BILL: Yes.

TAMMY: So then we saw the Schroeders, and they said, we'll go check over here. Well, at that point, they realize they're in the wrong place. So they came back near us, and we said, "Did you find it?" They didn't want to tell us. So they said, "Oh yeah, we're going to check over here." And we didn't see them come back.

BILL: We never realized that they'd found it until we watched the show.

TAMMY: We started yelling, "You dogs!"

BILL: "You ditched us!"

TAMMY: And then we saw the Aiellos. The Bransens came pretty quickly, and we were with them for a while. We were in the Korean War Memorial, a bunch of places. Wally [Bransen] finally told us there was another reflecting pool.

Q: *I remember from watching the show. Billy was the one who said, "We should ask somebody."*

TAMMY: The thing was, we were like, "What are you going to ask them? Did you see a clue box?" Because they tell you you can't say you're on *The Amazing Race*. You can't say you're looking for a clue box.

BILL: It was just overconfidence. We're at the Reflecting Pool. We just don't see the clue.

Q: *(To the kids) I know that you had some long road trips.*

CARISSA: Sixteen hours on the bus in Panama.

Q: *Did you have any trouble keeping your excitement up? Not that I saw, on the show, but....*

BILLY: It was really cool [on that bus] because they had these huge cup holders, and the seats were like first-class recliners on an airplane, because they went all the way back. And these DVD players.

CARISSA: That was on the Panama one.

Q: *But in the car, there had to be times when you kept saying, "When are we gonna get someplace?" Were you still excited to be on the Race, or did you ever have any problems with that?*

BILLY: Me and Carissa fooled with each other, making jokes and stuff, talking about stuff, and then Dad would say, "Be quiet, we have to pay attention," or whatever. So we just looked out the window. Carissa fell asleep most of the time.

(*General laughter*)

Q: *They showed that a few times.*

TAMMY: They loved showing that.

BILL: We tried to involve them when we could. Obviously, sitting in the SUV for long periods of time, we had a disadvantage for that. We talked as a team and said, there are times when we have to be in Race mode, when everybody's got to be contributing. And then there's other times when we could be silly and foolish, when we knew where we were going, and were just trying to kill time.

Q: *On your Race, a couple of teams had conflict between them from a very early point. How much of that manifested in the Pit Stops, rather than on the air?*

TAMMY: (*honestly confused, perhaps misunderstanding the question*) On our Race, there were teams that had conflict with each other?

Q: (*a little taken aback myself*) *Um, yeah.*

BILLY: (*patiently explaining it to Mom*) The Weavers and the other people.

BILL: Did you see it?

TAMMY: Oh no, I just meant, like, with other shows, or was it just our show.

BILLY: You said, "Fear is like water."[75]

BILL: Do you want to answer the question then? Smarty boy?

(*General laughter*)

BILLY: I kind of forgot the question.

BILL: That's our team.

---

[75] And no, I don't know the relevance of this.

Q: *Just staying apart from it.*

BILL: That's it.

BILLY: I would say a little bit more on the Pit Stops than in the Race, because when you were in the Race, when you saw another team, you didn't give a thought about it and you just kept going. When you were in the Pit Stop, you interacted with the other teams. Like—was Virginia the one with the inn?

TAMMY: Yes.

BILLY: It was a thirty-six-hour Pit Stop. A nice little cozy inn. It was very nice. They had a TV in there—and board games. I don't think I saw the Weavers come down much, unless it was when I was upstairs.

CARISSA: Rolly came down for a while, and played chess.

BILL: The production people told us along the line that the Race had a much different feel to it than a lot of the other Races. It may be the premise that there were families there, and it was a gentler, nicer Race, at least amongst the teams. I think from the very first, when we got into Pennsylvania and started pitching tents, and all the teams started helping those that came after them—it was an easy way to show goodwill to the other teams, because you never know when you're gonna need a friend down the line.

TAMMY: We saw [bad] stuff, but having kids, people aren't really going to say stuff to us, in front of the children, and people were very friendly to us, because of the children. We can say that there was one team that wasn't very nice to us, and it wasn't the Weavers.

(*She isn't going to say who, but then—*)

CARISSA: Ohhh, the Godlewskis!

(*Very widespread laughter at this slip*)

Q: *Very political.*

BILL: I wish the Godlewskis were here....

TAMMY: I thought for sure they would show some of the things they said to us....

BILL: Before we went home, after the show was over, we had a little wrap, one of the sisters apologized to us: "I'm sorry about anything I might have said." So we went home thinking, "What the heck did she say?"

TAMMY: They would say they didn't really think kids should be on the Race, and say, I can't believe you brought your kids here....

BILL: Just one of the sisters, really.

Q: *During the buggy challenge, where the kids sang "Coming 'Round the Mountain," that was one of the best moments of the Race, as far as I was concerned.*

CARISSA: Yeah.

Q: *That had to really bug the Aiellos.*

BILL: One of those guys was in the Marines, and these other guys see themselves as sporty young guys, and here's this mom, dad, and two little kids breezing right by them. We did not stop. We stopped two times on that whole track, to shift positions, and otherwise we were going constantly. We see these other teams with their hands on their knees, and Tommy Linz puking—

TAMMY: We only saw that on the show. We were ahead of them.

BILL: Just having the strength and endurance from running, that challenge hit us perfectly.

TAMMY: They were surprised we did that challenge, because they catered the [mill construction] for people with younger children. So when we did the buggy, we could hear Bertram in the background—

BILLY: In his golf cart.

TAMMY: —screaming, "She's an animal! She's an animal!"

Q: *We can't have this discussion without bringing up the red bean.*

(*Carissa moans*)

BILL: That was yours.

TAMMY: That was mine. I have a big jar of beans on my kitchen counter.

CARISSA: With the red one glued to the inside . . .

TAMMY: So I can find it.

Q: *What was it like for you when the show aired? What kind of feedback did you get from your friends?*

BILLY: I don't think Dad has many friends.

(*General hilarity*)

BILL: I got you.

New Combinations

HALF THE FUN OF *THE Amazing Race* is the interactions between players, some of whom may be well-suited for competing with one another, or—sometimes more memorably—not. Were we of a demented frame of mind, and empowered to force players together at gunpoint, we would enjoy watching the following:

1. Race 8's Carissa AND Race 6's Hellboy

An actual little girl, competing alongside a player who sometimes merely acted like one. One can imagine her slapping him silly: "Will you please GROW UP?"

2. Race 6's Gus AND Race 5's Chip

As long as everything ahead of them consists of eating challenges, they have a direct route to the finish line.

3. Race 6's Kris AND Race 3's Jill

A team of perpetual smilers, who may cheer each other up until their respective heads explode.

4. Race 5's Colin AND Race 3's Flo

The extreme sportster who never wanted to slow down, chained to the Racer most afraid of heights who never wanted to speed up. The irresistible force, meeting the unmovable object.

5. Race 1's Amie AND Race 8's Christine

Two ladies who cry very easily at moments of emotional stress. Between them, they'd shed more salt than Race 6's teams had to haul out of that lake in Senegal.

The Most Jaw-Dropping
Errors Ever Made by Racers

ONE OF THE MAJOR FACTORS that renders *The Amazing Race* so unpredictable is human error—the simple avoidable mistake that can take even a strong team miles out of its way, or delay it beyond the possibility of recovery. Wrong turns, simple miscommunication over clues, and failure to notice street signs all qualify, and are inevitable. Stress, exhaustion, and the pressure to make a decision right now, even if that decision is dumbfounding, can all lead Racers to torpedo themselves in more imaginative ways. Some mistakes were so memorable that we can only wonder what the Racers in question were thinking. Asterisks denote those that led to the team's elimination in the same leg. I observe that anybody who takes these boners as reliable indicators of real-world intelligence should flash back to the last dumbass move they made on a road trip. That's right. I'm talking about you.

1. Lenny (Team Monument) Gets Random at the Eiffel Tower (Race 1, Leg #3)

When a Roadblock sends Lenny up the Eiffel Tower stairs to search the skyline for a flagged monument, he has no idea where to look and comes back down the stairs to report failure. When Karyn makes him go back up and try again, he asks locals for the names of monuments, and picks Notre Dame (which is a cathedral, not a monument) more or less at random, dragging Karyn all the way across Paris on what amounts to a wild guess. Her reaction to this is perfectly understandable, but not exactly a high point in their relationship. For future reference, Lenny: any city the size of Paris has several monuments, and you can't pick the right one by sticking pins in a map.

2. The Guidos Linger in Bangkok (Race 1, Leg #9)

Winners of a Fast Forward that allows them to proceed directly to the Pit Stop some 500 kilometers away, the Guidos inexplicably spend the day in a hotel, where they can "sip ice tea and sit in air-conditioned splendor." They chill out on their balcony, enjoying the view and assuring each other that they have "plenty of time," while every other team beats them to this leg's Pit Stop, the Tiger Cave Temple in Krabi. It's a stunning example of Racer hubris, biting them in their respective butts. Only the more serious error committed by Nancy and Emily saves the Guidos from elimination this leg, but the damage is done: previously a team to beat, they're no longer a serious threat.

3. Nancy and Emily (Team Oh, Mom) Get a Cab in Bangkok (Race 1, Leg #9)*

Believing themselves irretrievably far behind, and panicky after failing to find a private car parked on the city streets, Team Oh, Mom could take the other permitted option and book passage by bus instead. Had they done this, they would have made it into the final four, and quite possibly won a million dollars. But they're so eager to get out of their situation, and so certain of their inevitable defeat, that they hail a taxi again. Their twenty-four-hour penalty leads to their elimination. It's a shame, but as a result they become poster children for the Race maxim: *Don't ever give up, even if you think you're far behind, because somebody ahead of you might be making a really stupid mistake.*

4. Blake and Paige (The Smiley Siblings) in Rio de Janeiro (Race 2, Leg #2)

Forget fear of heights. With all other factors being equal, what option do you think would take less time? Hang gliding from the top of a mountain to a beach down below? Or searching a mile and a half of that same beach for a hidden clue, using metal detectors? Yeah, we thought so, too. But Blake believes "the sand thing will be so much faster." His clever plan is to somehow find a place to rent a metal detector in the middle of the night, search the beach before the task opens in the morning, find the place where the clue is buried, then return to take the metal detector provided by the producers and go straight to the treasure they've already found. The overcomplicated scheme turns out to be a nonstarter, and costs the team dearly, as they have to return to the hang gliders after losing their place in line.

5. Peggy and Claire (The Gutsy Grannies) Take a Flight to New York (Race 2, Leg #3)*

One of the most harrowing rounds of airport shuffle in the show's history requires teams to make their way from São Paulo, Brazil, to Cape Town, South Africa. There are no direct flights available, so just getting reservations becomes an all-day ordeal, which requires every team to book connecting flights through London, Milan, Lisbon, Frankfurt, or some combination thereof. One of the last teams to succeed in leaving São Paulo, The Gutsy Grannies virtually guarantee their own elimination by booking an extra leg through New York, an itinerary which takes them many hours, and thousands of miles, out of their way. (And even then, they miss their connecting flight in London.) We can't be all that hard on them, as we have no way of knowing if the other teams left any other seats available on their own tortuous itineraries. Maybe New York really was the only flight available. But this still marks the only time a team missed an interim destination by a full planetary hemisphere.[76]

------

[76] Further investigation reveals that had Peggy and Claire made their London connection, they would have arrived in South Africa ahead of some teams. Still, it's a jaw-dropping itinerary.

6. Wil (The Constant Snipers) Loses the Clue in the Last Leg (Race 2, Leg #13)

You've spent the last several weeks running a contentious Race around the world. It's now coming down to the wire. With a million dollars resting on what you do in the next day or so, all alliances have entered the realm of history...especially since you haven't exactly endeared yourself to your remaining competitors. This is not the best time to throw out your only copy of the clue with the maps you no longer need. Your rivals might not be inclined to help you, even if they liked you. It's also not a great idea to blame your partner, with whom you've been fighting on and off, for losing the clue envelope that the camera confirms to have been in your possession all along. It's a good way to make the implosion total. Wil does all of this. The results are not pretty. Remarkably, this jaw-dropping error is inextricably linked to a brilliant recovery: see p. 412 "The Smartest Moves Ever Made by Racers."

7. Heather and Eve (The Law Babes) Take a Cab in Lisbon (Race 3, Leg #4)*

The instructions tell Racers they must walk the one-and-a-half miles to the fortress Torre del Belem. The Law Babes can be forgiven for missing this provision in the heat of the moment, and taking a cab instead. They're not the only Racers to make that kid of mistake. Not by far. But they discover their error in the cab, tell their driver to turn around, talk themselves out of that, tell their driver to stop, talk themselves out of that, and finally—displaying a truly jaw-dropping grasp of logic, even for lawyers—decide the clue means that taking a cab there is okay as long as they then walk to the mat on their own two feet. (That must have been a relief to any cabbie afraid he'd have to navigate up that narrow stone stairway.) First to the mat, the ladies receive a thirty-seven-minute penalty that proves fatal in this leg, where every team arrives within a narrow thirty-one-minute spread. In the end, the two recent law school graduates fall to a simple matter of reading comprehension. You can blame stress and sleep deprivation, of course...but don't law students get that, too?

8. Andre and Damon (The First Responders) Bribe the Brothers in Portugal (Race 3, Leg #5)

Catching up with The Wonder Twins and Team Oh, Brother at the train station, The First Responders offer them thirty euros just to let them ride along. This gesture does little to establish the Responders as valuable allies capable of fending for themselves. As for the brother teams, they confer and say, essentially, yeah, well, why the hell not. Thirty euros to ride with us on a train we're all getting on anyway. Knock yourselves out. The moment marks a serious downturn in The First Responders' status as a team to watch.

9. Half the Remaining Teams Fill Their Cars with the Wrong Fuel in Spain (Race 3, Leg #5)*

Driving provided vehicles from Cabo de Roca in Portugal to Algeciras, Spain, Aaron and Arianne (The Twin Haters), Ian and Teri (Team Grumpy), Michael and Kathy (The Long-Distance Daters), and Flo and Zach (Team Albatross) all stop to pump a little unleaded into their diesel tanks. They are not the only teams ever to make this elementary error (see p. 290 Team Hellboy, Race 6), but rarely on the show have so many people screwed up the same way at the same time. Survival, for these stranded Racers, depends entirely on how they move on from here. Predictably, teams react with varying levels of aplomb. Aaron curls into a ball and weeps, saying, "I'm so humiliated right now." Fortunately, a cop pulls over to investigate and helps them contact the rental company's insurance agency. Flo makes the first of many suggestions to just quit the game as hopeless, but is so excited when a local garage succeeds in fixing the problem that she squeals and hugs the mechanic. Ian gets a siphon hose and drains out the offending gasoline himself, a solution that may not be the most environmentally sensitive in the world, but at least gets his team back on the road. The Long-Distance Daters, who never do figure out the nature of the problem, simply walk to a nearby hotel and spend the night there, figuring that they have plenty of time to get the car towed in the morning. In the end, Team Albatross and Team Grumpy recover admirably, catching a ferry that leaves only one hour after the one carrying the front-runners. The Twin Haters catch one a few hours later, and manage to stay in the game. The Long-Distance Daters arrive at the Pit Stop after dark and are eliminated.

10. David and Jeff (Team Strategic) Catch the Wrong Kind of Fish in Malaysia (Race 4, Leg #8)

This team will later lose the Race to a hell of a bad airport shuffle decision that any one of us could have made, but their true silliest moment is when, instructed to catch fifteen big fish from a pen, they go to the wrong part of the dock and laboriously catch fifteen teeny tiny minnows instead. The little 'uns are, of course, not acceptable, so they have to start over.

11. Many Teams Try to Fly from Cairo to Nairobi via Zurich (Race 5, Leg #5)

The several teams aligned with Colin book this wildly roundabout passage, through Swissair, that might have delayed their arrival in Nairobi by as much as a full day behind the Gulf Air flights booked by Team Habibi and The Bowling Moms. Lord alone knows why they believed this would be an efficient route. In the end, they realize their error in time to join the teams on the Gulf Air flight, but not before they realize that going along with Colin on this was "the stupidest decision any of us have ever made."

12. Mirna (Team Habibi) Tells the Airline that Colin Is Dangerous (Race 5, Leg #5)

Over the course of the show, many Racers have foolishly asked airline employees to help them hide vital information from their competitors. ("Don't sell that guy a ticket—I'm racing him!") It's a dumb thing to do, because it amounts to asking these busy people to suck at their jobs. But few Racers have gone as far over the line as Mirna does, when she tells a representative of Gulf Air that Colin is "violent." (We don't see this clearly, thanks to an incomplete on-screen translation, but this is her own proud retelling.) Ineffectual as the tactic turns out to be, just imagine the consequences, in this post-9/11 world, if her dire warning had been taken seriously. Sure, she might have benefited, at least in the short term, from having Colin detained, or placed on a no-fly list... but she also could have ended up in serious trouble herself for spreading a false alert. In the best possible scenario, which is to say getting the lie to stick and not suffering any repercussions during the Race, she would have left an internationally televised record of herself giving false information to impede a fellow traveler. Not cool. Colin and Christie aren't always the most likeable Racers in the show's history, but they would have been quite right to sue her ass off.

13. Colin (Team Extreme) Foments an International Incident in Tanzania (Race 5, Leg #6)

Discussed elsewhere, but dumb, dumb, dumb.

14. Lena and Kristy (The Mormon Girls), and Freddy and Kendra (This Year's Models) Decide the Waterfall Isn't Good Enough in Iceland (Race 6, Leg #1)

The Mormon Girls and This Year's Models are first to the Seljalandsfoss Waterfall, but both stay in their cars, deciding that it can't possibly be the place they're looking for. Lena and Kristy lose hours to this mistake. But that's not nearly as bad as what happens to The Queens Girls (see p. 414 "The Smartest Moves Ever Made by Racers").

15. Bolo (The Rampaging Hulks) Performs an Inventory in Stockholm, Sweden (Race 6, Leg #3)

Counting by twos during the inventory task in a Stockholm IKEA, Bolo gasps, "66…68…80…82…." This technique somehow fails to result in an accurate figure.

16. Kendra (This Year's Models) Offers a Helpful Observation in Budapest (Race 6, Leg #6b)

We've noted this before, but it deserves notation on this list. If a million dollars rides on your boyfriend's ability to scarf down spicy soup, it's an extremely poor idea to point out all the puddles of vomit left behind by other players. Kendra means to flatter Freddy by comparison, but the moment of vivid visual suggestion is enough to make him lose it himself. By his own estimate, he redeposits four ounces back in his own bowl. The sight is so horrible that Kendra retches, almost completing the cycle by adding to the general regurgitative ambience. Give her credit for feeling really, really, really, really, *really* bad about it.

406 • "MY OX IS BROKEN!"

17. Jonathan and Victoria (Team Explosive) Are One Ass Short in Lewz (Race 6, Leg #8)*

The bickering team has to deliver two donkeys to a farmer three miles away. They're so busy snapping at each other that they misread the clue and only take one. When they arrive, they find out they're one ass short. There has been much unkind commentary about how they miscalculated the number of asses on hand. This book won't sink to the obvious joke except to note that there is one. But in the end, it's simply their constant fighting that keeps them from seeing their mistake before it's too late. The error forces them to return to the donkey corral and come back with the donkey, a round-trip distance comprising an additional six miles.

18. Freddy (This Year's Models) Shows His Talent for Detail in Lewz (Race 6, Leg #8)

Freddy is elected to perform the Roadblock, which the clue prescribes for players with an eye for detail. Kendra advises him to think detailed. He promptly falls over, running into big ol' obvious fence post right in front of him. That could not have boded well.

19. Adam (Team Hellboy) Decides to Quit in Sri Lanka (Race 6, Leg #9)

Last to the train, the ever-melodramatic Adam decides that he's had enough of the game. He wants to return to the airport and book a flight back home. Yes, he actually says that. But no, that's not his long-term plan. That's just a snit, thrown by a guy with a tendency to stage dramas at moments of stress. Unlike Peach and Flo, who did want to quit at equivalent moments, he's just flinging his frustration in Rebecca's face, and daring her to deal with it. In what has got to be one of the great extended uses of sarcasm in Race history, Rebecca calls his bluff, declaring, "Okay. Let's get a cab." Stunned, because that was not the response he expected or wanted, Hellboy can only follow her outside as she goes through with this proposed plan and hails a cab for their proposed retreat to the airport. "Yay," she says. "Let's quit. I'm up for that!" What makes this especially funny—and, probably, galling for Hellboy—is that it puts him in the position of arguing that they shouldn't. The CBS Insider videos, available on the show's Web site, reveal that there's a lot more of this than ever got on the air: he also claimed that he wanted to track down their by now departed cabbie, wherever in the city he happened to be by then, and yell at him for making them late. Rebecca called that bluff as well, declaring it a *great* idea.

20. Bolo (The Rampaging Hulks) Doesn't Go after Lori in Dambulla (Race 6, Leg #9)*

The Roadblock requires each participating Racer to reach the summit of Lion Rock, an ascent involving some 1,000 steps. Bolo has neglected to give Lori the ticket she'll need to reach the top floor. He realizes this while she's still climbing. He reacts by continuing to sit on his ass, as he waits for her to come down and scream at him for being so stupid. Granted, he's in a pretty self-disgusted place right now (the big lug actually seems on the verge on tears), but he *has* the ticket. Why doesn't he take to the stairs and climb as fast as he can, in the theory that he'll save his team some valuable time if he intercepts her on her way down? Answer: he honestly doesn't think of it. The oversight contributes to his team's subsequent elimination.

21. Gretchen and Meredith (Team Energizer Bunny) Choose a Shopping Task in Santiago, Chile (Race 7, Leg #2)

Given a choice between lugging books and shopping with your own money, when you're already short of funds, what seems an advantageous choice to you? Yeah, me too. But the oldsters venture into the marketplace anyway, and have to rely on the kindness of locals. This is one of several moments where luck overrides bad decisions for this astonishingly long-lived team.

22. Lynn and Alex (The Gay Blades) Make a Scene in a Chilean Marketplace (Race 7, Leg #2)

When the fish they've bought for the shopping task turns out to be slightly underweight, the boys march right back into the marketplace and accuse the merchants of having rigged scales. Before long the merchants are meeting their hostility with added interest. "I just got totally hated," Lynn says. Well, yeah. And at the moment, you pretty much deserved it.

23. Debbie and Bianca (The Virginia Girls) Miss the Andes in Chile (Race 7, Leg #3)*

It's one thing to miss the crucial turnoff taking you to the Andes. It's another to miss several clues that you've made a disastrous error, and not realize what you've done until you find yourself toodling along beside the beach. The remarkable thing here is not that they make this mistake, which adds four hours to their journey...but that this incredible error leads to one of the most remarkable (if sadly incomplete) recoveries in Race history (see p. 423 "The Most Endearing Racer Moments").

24. Rob and Amber (Team Truman Show) Play Bad Samaritan in Botswana (Race 7, Leg #6)

When Brian and Greg flip their Land Rover, injuring their cameraman, most of the teams either get out to determine if there's anything they can do (Lynn and Alex), or at the very least slow down long enough to register that the boys are waving them on (everybody else). Rob and Amber do not. "There's no way we're stopping," Rob says. "This is still a competition. Let's not be crazy." Then he smiles with what can be interpreted as happiness at his good fortune. Exactly how much would it have handicapped his team had he slowed down, stuck his head out the window, and said, "Is everybody all right?" If not because he had any meaningful help to offer, then at least for the sake of establishing that he gave a damn about the well-being of these people he'd been traveling with? The answer is seconds, and it's not too high a price to show a little common humanity. Even Phil seems a little taken aback by this at the Pit Stop, with his deadpan, "I see. So you left them on the side of the road?"

25. Gretchen (Team Energizer Bunny) Gets on the Elephant in Jodhpur (Race 7, Leg #8b)

It's easy to see *why* she does this. A local offers her a lift, and she goes along with it, in the theory that he must know what he's doing. But the result is one of the more bizarre turns any Race has ever taken—as this loud, shrill-voiced old American lady sits atop the teak elephant her exhausted hubby must push through city streets, and screams at locals to get out of the way. The other teams, the production staff, and Phil are all astonished that she would choose to do such a thing. Oddly enough, the tactic may have helped—by making such a spectacle of herself, she helps gain the attention of locals who assist Meredith in pushing. But the comic highlight is when she moans, "We've got a bad elephant." A phrase that, like the one about the ox, could have been the title of this book.

26. The Schroeders Reject Local Advice Outside Hattiesburg (Race 8, Leg #4)

Looking for Southern Colonel, a mobile home dealership, the Schroeders solicit but fail to heed the advice of a cop who tells them it's a mobile home dealership. Both parents chuckle. "That wouldn't be [it]," says Mark. Wrong guess.

27. Sharon and Michelle Godlewski Melt Down at the Red Lodge Golf Course (Race 8, Leg #10b)*

Here's a question. You're one of four remaining teams in a race for one million dollars. You want to get into the final three. You're in last place right now, but not far behind your closest competition, competing in a task that requires you to search a golf course for brightly colored balls. Having gotten this far, with a million dollars at stake, would *you* throw a snit over your sister's handling of the golf cart, and virtuously insist on proceeding on foot? Would the two of you be willing to bleed precious time on bickering, when *completing this task as quickly as possible* is your one chance of staying in the game? No, I didn't think so either. We can't say for certain that this incident cost them a place in the final three—as there's no way of telling just how far behind they were—but with every second critical, it might have.

28. The Weaver Ladies Want to Quit in Montreal Olympic Stadium (Race 8, Leg #11)

Here's another question. You belong to a family that has suffered an unimaginable loss, and which has suffered tremendous financial hardships in the aftermath. You have wangled a spot on a hit reality show, with a first prize of one million dollars. By hook or by crook you have endured all the way to the final three. So, now you have a one-in-three chance of a life-altering infusion of cash. However exhausted you might be, when told to search a 56,000-seat stadium, would you now start complaining that you don't want to go on? Would you even for one instant say, as Rebecca does, "[I think this is] just stupid"? We can understand the impulse to take a nap, as Mom Weaver does, but any discussion of quitting, this close to the end, this close to a *million dollars*, is downright baffling.

The Smartest Moves
Ever Made by Racers

I T'S EASIER TO PICK OUT serious errors than it is to pick out examples of sterling competence, as Racers can proceed all the way to the finish line just by doing whatever's expected of them, without ever bringing their own ingenuity into play. The following incidents all showed remarkable creativity in keeping Racers in the game, or propelling them to the front of the pack. Asterisks indicate moves that contributed to victory in the leg.

1. Rob and Brennan (The Young Lawyers) Rent a Phone in Alaska (Race 1, Leg #12)

Having saved their money since the first leg, The Young Lawyers are able to offer a total stranger $300 for a temporary loan of her cell phone, promising to mail it back later. This doesn't prove all that critical to the outcome, as they still get on the same flight as their only serious competition, but it was a clever move, then within the rules, that could have proven decisive in other circumstances.

2. Chris and Alex (The Bouncers) on the Flight to Queenstown (Race 2, Leg #10)

The Siblings, Blake and Paige, have pulled a fast one by managing to bring their luggage aboard in defiance of official airline rules. This will give them an advantage of several minutes over teams who have to claim their baggage at the Queenstown Airport carousel. Against all odds, The Bouncers manage to enlist the stewardesses in their shenanigans and prevent anybody from leaving the plane until all the baggage has been off-loaded. This may be pretty obnoxious—all the passengers not involved in an international reality show competition must have appreciated it very much—but it does work. A telling shot of one stewardess, wearing a big broad smile, helps establish that TV cameras are the true international language.

3. Wil and Tara (The Constant Snipers) Recover from Losing the Clue (Race 2, Leg #13)

Following his team's loss of the all-important clue envelope in Maui (see p. 402 "The Most Jaw-Dropping Errors Ever Made by Racers" for details), even viewers who've come to dislike Wil might feel sorry for the man they see suffering on the first leg of a long flight to Anchorage, Alaska. He's alienated from his partner, will receive no help from any other teams, and has no idea what he's going to do. There's a telling shot of him sleeping with his hand pressed against his forehead, like a man who's afraid his brains are about to fall out. But his mind is working, even as his partner Tara changes seats to sit beside her favorite Race buddy, Alex. During the layover in San Francisco, the Snipers go straight to the airport bookstore, Simply Books, and pore through reference works on Alaska to find the name of a charter service that sounds familiar. (It's during this ordeal that Blake, not Wil's biggest fan, amuses Paige and The Bouncers by stuffing handwritten instructions in an official Race folder, explaining, "I feel bad because Wil lost his route info. So I made him some new route info. 'Fly to Siberia and find the most desolate place possible.'") Meanwhile, Tara comes up with the answer. Could it be Rust's Flying Service? That sounds right. Just to be sure, she calls from an airport phone and ask the folks at

Rust's if they're expecting three teams. The answer is yes. At Rust's, where players are supposed to give the pilot the destination, waiting for another team to take off and saying, "Follow that plane!" works just as well. The desperate improvisation puts Wil and Tara back in the game.

4. Ken and Gerard (Team Oh, Brother) Pull a Fast One in Ho Chi Minh City (Race 3, Leg #11)

Teams have to claim a cyclo bike and ride it on a flagged course down city streets, which includes a ferry trip across the Saigon River to a café on the other shore. Both teams involved in the so-called "brother alliance," The Wonder Twins and the Oh, Brothers, have been running around like decapitated chickens, looking for the route marker, with no success. This is critical. If it comes down to a footrace, The Wonder Twins win.

Then the Oh, Brothers spot Flo and Zach boarding the ferry, and rush to board. Flo immediately warns them they need to go back and get a bike. By Flo's own admission, this is not motivated by any desire to help them, but rather out of concern for staying ahead, and a need to get them off her team's ferry. This is a serious tactical error for her, as it doesn't delay the Oh, Brothers, but rather saves them time by helping them perform the task correctly.

Frankly astonished by the warning, the Oh, Brothers are able to leave the ferry before making a serious mistake. But even that's not the end of their good fortune. Even as the ferry leaves them behind, the Oh, Brothers encounter Derek and Drew, who are also sans clue and cyclo bike, and have also spotted Zach and Flo on the ferry.

Seizing the opportunity to knock out their strongest competition, the Oh, Brothers pretend they haven't seen anything, and rush off on what The Wonder Twins can only misinterpret as another clueless wild goose chase. The end result? The Wonder Twins board the next ferry on foot, and reach the Pit Stop only to be informed that they've made a critical error and have to go back. Ken and Gerard, arriving on the very next ferry, now have a bike and can tell the Twins what they've done wrong. They even urge the Twins to hurry, as the leg might be a non-elimination. But it isn't. The Oh, Brothers arrive at the Pit Stop in third place, and win a place in the finals. Their erstwhile allies, The Wonder Twins, just get a ride home.

Best of all, there are no hard feelings. It's a Race.

5. Zach Handles Flo During Her Collapse in Nam O, Da Nang, Vietnam (Race 3, Leg #12)

Never, before or since, has any Racer fallen apart as completely as Flo does during the penultimate leg, in Vietnam. And never has any Racer faced with a troublesome partner shown as much patience, or gentle persuasion, as Zach does getting Flo past this dark and scary place. His ultimate brainstorm—paying locals to help Flo paddle across the river—may have flouted the spirit of the rules, but it did get them to the end of the day…and turned out to be a great investment as well (see p. 179 "It's Her Party, and She'll Cry if She Wants To" for further discussion).

6. Zach's Desperate Airline Reservations Gamble in Da Nang, Vietnam (Race 3, Leg #13)*

Another brilliant move, by the best Racer of all time, in the travel agency where Racers must book their passage to Honolulu. With his partner falling apart again, and no economy seats available, Zach realizes he has to hurry up and get her on the road in order to stay in the game. So he bends the rules and buys business class tickets again, gambling that he can trade them in for economy seats at some point during the long seventeen-hour train ride to Hanoi. There has been extensive debate over whether he should have been allowed to do this, but nobody can argue with the results: he gets Flo on the train and stays in the game long enough to borrow another passenger's cell phone and make the necessary changes in their flight. "Zach has worked a small miracle," Flo admits, when their itinerary actually turns out superior to the one obtained by the other teams.

7. Aaron (The Determined Actors) Misdirects the Queens Girls in Iceland (Race 6, Leg #1)

The Queens Girls have missed the Seljalandsfoss Waterfall on their first drive-by, and have turned around to attempt another pass. When they pass The Determined Actors, who have already obtained the clue there, and are now on the way to Vatnajokull Glacier, Aaron gestures through the car window that the girls should just follow him. He does this knowing that they haven't found the waterfall yet and that he's leading them hundreds of miles out of their way. Hayden tells him he's being "rude," and he declares that he "doesn't care." The Queens Girls don't discover their error until the next gas stop, by which point they've driven an hour and a half out of their way. Now they have to go back. So, adding up: an hour and a half past the waterfall, an hour and a half retracing their steps back to the waterfall, and a hour and a half heading toward Vatnajokull again, just to reach the point where they first discovered their error. That's four and a half hours Aaron cost this other team, by simply lying to them at the right moment. We recognize that Hayden was right, and that lying to The Queens Girls was "rude." And we also recognize that the overnight bunching on the glacier puts the Girls back within reach of everybody else. Aaron had no way of knowing of what was up ahead, and delaying other teams by that many hours is a good move just on general principle.

8. Rob (Team Truman Show) Gets Three Other Teams to Quit the Meat-Eating Task in Mendoza, Argentina (Race 7, Leg #3)

As various Racers torment themselves over a Roadblock requiring the consumption of four pounds of meat, Rob realizes early that he cannot finish. Consulting with Amber, he establishes that the four-hour penalty for failing to complete the task will start counting down at the moment the next team arrives. He further realizes that if he talks other players into quitting *after* him, he can guarantee that they'll be still waiting out their penalties after he's freed to move on to the Pit Stop. Deana of The Bottom Feeders and Meredith of Team Energizer Bunny both follow his lead, providing a comfortable cushion between his team and elimination.

9. Brian and Greg (The Bouncer Brothers) Pick the "Water" Option in Botswana (Race 7, Leg #6)

Far behind due to their serious auto accident, The Bouncer Brothers arrive at a Detour where everybody still at the site has picked the "Food" option. Reasoning that they face elimination if they do the same thing as everybody else, they pick the "Water" task, hoping that it will prove easier. It's a critical choice that keeps the team alive for one more leg.

10. Linda Weaver Makes a Game Out of Cheering Up Her Daughters at the Waffle House (Race 8, Leg #3)

Yeah, I know: many fans were vocal about considering this very same moment one of the most annoying Racer moments ever, and the turning point that changed the general public perception of this team from a traumatized family in mourning to a bunch of yowling wack-jobs. After this incident, they were well on their way to becoming the perceived "villains" of this Race. But that's not the way I saw this moment. Sleep deprivation, the tensions of the day, and the uncertainties of an eight-hour bus ride to a "mystery destination" (actually, Space Camp) all prove too much for Rebecca, who becomes, in a single word, hysterical. She may really be that brittle. Or the demands of this particular reality show may not be an exact fit for her. But for the moment, at least, she falls apart. And Linda cannot calm her down, not even when the bus stops to permit Racers a roadside meal at The Waffle House. Linda tells her daughter not to let the other teams see her like this. Rebecca says she can't. And Linda says, "Then *lie*." At which point the entire Weaver clan rides a nigh-instantaneous mood swing to the other end of the emotional spectrum, dancing in the parking lot and, upon boarding the bus, tormenting their fellow passengers with their own version of that torture-the-driver staple, "The Song That Never Ends." Granted, this makes the other teams (and many viewers) think they're just a bunch of Fruit Loops. But look at it this way: the situation was a bad one. Linda needed to do something. And her suggestion, which turned being in a good mood into a defiant game, did effectively remove Rebecca from a dark and despairing place. Whatever else you say about her actions after this point—and we are pretty critical—"Then *lie*" was an inspired suggestion.

The Most Endearing
Racer Moments

1. Drew Leading Kevin (The Fat Bastards) on the Camel (Race 1, Leg #5)

Just about everything these guys do (but for a few rough patches) is endearing, but this may be their funniest moment ever.

2. Cyndi and Russell (The Pastors) in the Samba Club (Race 2, Leg #2)

Cyndi and Russell have never been to such a place before and have no idea what to expect. They're a little taken aback by all the scantily clad ladies, it being a little bit different from what they're used to at home. Afterward, Russell wears the big, broad grin of a man who just enjoyed himself a lot and isn't entirely sure he wants his wife to know how much.

3. Oswald and Danny (Team Fabulous) Hit the Mall in Hong Kong (Race 2, Leg #7)

Rather than rush to another bustling, overcrowded airport to book their flight to Sydney, Australia, Oswald and Danny find an upscale travel agent who tells them that obtaining their tickets will take no more than an hour. During that hour, they venture forth to buy Frappuccinos and cologne. "Oh my God," Danny gushes. "I feel like a real person again!" They go on to explain that visiting the mall is like going to church for them. There's nothing like a shopping center, Oswald says, to bring two friends together. The end result: they get to Sydney half an hour ahead of all the other teams.

4. Oswald and Danny (Team Fabulous) Tandem Bungee Jumping in New Zealand (Race 2, Leg #10)

The Race has seen any number of people do things they would rather crawl across shattered glass than do, with bungee jumping one of the most, or least, popular, depending on who you speak to. Few had a more photogenic reaction than this Miami pair. Thanks to a camera setup that allows us close-ups of their faces all the way down, we bear witness as acrophobe Oswald screams like a baby and buries his face against Danny's chest, begging, "No, Danny! No, Danny! No more!" Danny's no help, as he's too busy lighting up with uncontrollable laughter. Afterward, it's Oswald who says, "That was the best experience I've ever had in my life." Together they make you feel it.

5. Ken and Gerard (Team Oh, Brother) Punting in Cambridge (Race 3, Leg #3)

There's something about a team downright reveling in assaults upon its own dignity that deposits it in the plus column for all time. Ken and Gerard prove less than deft piloting their punt down the river, and each tumbles into the water, earning the cheers, applause, and enthusiastic laughter of the locals. Their big, broad smiles during all of this serve as eloquent rebukes to the Racers who complained about the same boats despite remaining high and dry.

6. Jill (The Sweetheart Smileys) Takes a Fall in Portugal (Race 3, Leg #5)

Racing to a clue box at Cabo de Roca, Jill trips, falls flat on her face, and is back up and running so quickly that she might as well have had bedsprings mounted on her nose. It's one of the best "Fall? What fall?" moments in Race history.

7. Ian (Team Grumpy) Returns to Vietnam (Race 3, Legs #11–12)

Ian's team is called the Grumpies for good reason. They don't engage in outright screaming matches, as some other teams have, but they do seem to conduct much of the Race in a kind of seething irritation, at each other as much as their surrounding circumstances. Which is why it's so touching to see Ian's demeanor change so completely for the duration of the Race's stay in Vietnam. At first apprehensive about his return to the country where he fought in a bloody and internationally traumatizing war, Ian's comments run to looking out the cab window and murmuring things like, "[There are probably] still landmines out there." A little later, he waxes philosophical, saying: "58,000 Americans died here, fighting a war to try to keep a people free. Hundreds of thousands of Vietnamese died. Those men didn't die in vain. It's sad...but it's over." And, "This is the first time I've been in Vietnam since the war ended, and I like it. I like the culture, I like the people. I felt confident. And if things change, times change, people change. They're embracing us, and over time, the wounds will heal." By the end of the eleventh leg, he actually seems to be glowing with delight, enjoying his status as the silly American being laughed at by the citizens of the country he and other soldiers bled for. There's a very real sense here that the man's putting some personal ghosts to rest, and you're not to going to find me making fun of it.[77]

---

[77] Some viewers perceive a degree of racial insensitivity, as well, when he reacts to positive developments by shouting things like "Numbah one!" But let's give the guy a break, for multiple reasons. First, he hasn't been there for thirty years and can be forgiven for falling into the speech patterns of a soldier who served there in his impressionable youth. Second, he's showing exuberance, not arrogance (i.e., he means well). Third, and most importantly—the Vietnamese who witness his antics don't seem to take any particular offense. Far from it. They laugh at the silly man, reacting to the feeling rather than the vocabulary. In life, understanding often arrives in small steps, not large ones. And that goes not just for Ian, but for those of us sitting in our living rooms watching him.

8. Flo (Team Albatross) Has a Moment of Self-Awareness in Seattle, Washington (Race 3, Leg #13)

Yes, Flo, clearly one of the five most irritating Racers in the entire history of the show, does deserve a place in "Most Endearing Moments," during her team's final scramble for the finish line. They're in the cab, proceeding straight to the mat. All the work, and all the angst, is now behind them. All that remains, now, is finding out how well they've done. Speaking honestly, she says, "I'm sorry that I've been a pain in the ass this whole trip." And then, turning to Zach, who has not been quick to reply, she cries:"*You're supposed to say I haven't been!*" Some viewers, long fed up with her behavior by now, take that little postscript as evidence that she's still living in denial, but just look at that hopeful smile on her face. The apology is genuine. The postscript is an attempt at humor, as she tests Zach to confirm that their friendship is still intact. When Zach replies, "You haven't been," it's just as clear that he understands what she's really asking. And then she weeps, apologizes a second time, and hugs him. At the risk of being incredibly corny, a friend is like a home, in that he's someplace you can return to even when you've been bad. Flo and Zach may not have ended up a couple, but that is very much what we're seeing here.

9. Jon and Kelly (The Mockingbirds) Plunge Down the Trampolino Olympico (Race 4, Leg #2)

In this task, teams have to board a rubber raft and slide it down the manmade ski slope known as the Trampolino Olympico. The problem for Jon and Kelly: they didn't realize they had to pick up their rubber raft first. Rather than hike all the way down, they slide down the slope on their butts. There's very real charm in Kelly's progression from realizing that she has to do this crazy thing, further realizing that she's actually gonna do this crazy thing, and then going ahead and actually doing this crazy thing, shrieking in mingled terror and exuberance all the way down. The Air-Traffic Controllers, who witness their descent, find the act a defining moment of reckless stupidity, which is also a legitimate interpretation. But dang. For moments that establish just what the more adventurous Racers are willing to do in order to win, you can't do much better than this.

10. Several Teams Brave the Pile of Manure Outside Amsterdam (Race 4, Leg #5)

The show's occasional ventures into gross-out territory run the risk of turning the series into an international *Fear Factor*, but triumph when they function as character-defining moments, establishing in the most vivid terms just what the players will or won't do to win. This leg's Detour offers an excellent case in point. In this task, players need to choose whether to load cheese aboard pallets, or search a fifteen-foot-tall pile of manure with their bare hands. A surprising number of teams brave the manure, perversely enjoying the experience despite a stench that causes several to mime gagging. The Clowns cry, "MANUUURRREEE!" and start pelting each other with the stuff. The NFL Wives make comments about changing diapers at home. The Mockingbirds find the clue envelope and give each other a high-five, making sure they're using their poo hands, before turning away from one another to gag in perfect unison. The most astonishing aspect of all this: nobody whines. Nobody backs down. Somehow, they all maintain their dignity in a profoundly undignified situation, distinguishing themselves with displays of truly heroic bravado. It's impossible to imagine some of the Racers from past and future Races (Flo? Hellboy?) not only going along with this exercise in competitive scatology, but even seeing the humor in it and having a good time despite themselves.

11. Chip and Kim (The Enthusiastic Tourists) Visit an African Family in Mto Wa Bu (Race 5, Leg #7)

In the kind of scene we wish we saw more of, The Enthusiastic Tourists take a few minutes off to enjoy some hospitality from a local family. Short as the visit is, Chip and Kim recognize how important this moment is to their local hosts, and understand that this few seconds of grace meant more than any advantage they might receive from pressing on. (They still came in first for the leg.)

12. Brandon (Team Divine Intervention) Fails to Take Off the Lens Cap in Thailand (Race 5, Leg #11)

Getting the lay of the land through binoculars that are still blocked by one lens cap, Brandon exemplifies the principle that certain manifestations of cluelessness are always loveable.

13. Avi (The Brooklyn Boys) Serenades the Fjords in Iceland (Race 6, Leg #1)

"New York Jews in Iceland" may have only one line, but it's still the best improvised song lyric of several to come out of *The Amazing Race*.

14. Gus (Team CIA) Takes a Bath on the Glacier (Race 6, Leg #1)

Up until now, the fattest Racer to date hasn't done all that much to distinguish himself. He's huffed and puffed on his way up stairs, complained when his daughter ran or drove too fast, and reacted to the sight of the waterfall with a sleepy, "Oh, yeah." He doesn't exactly seem overflowing with enthusiasm for the endeavor. One almost feels sorry for this couch potato, pressured by his daughter into taking such a strenuous trip. But then the Racers spend the night on Vatnajokull Glacier, where the air must be, let's say, a little nipply. Big ol' fat Gus emerges shirtless from his tent, grabs handfuls of ice and snow from the ground and scrubs his armpits, his only comment a heartfelt, "That'll wake you up." Never mind that some of the more vocal members of the Race viewership reacted to the sight of his beer belly and man boobs with aghast cries of, "Gaaaaah." More to the point: this guy's not the pushover he initially seems to be.

15. Kristy (The Mormon Girls) Pushes Over a Hundred Hay Bales (Race 6, Leg #3)

Third to the Roadblock, The Mormon Girls are dealt a bad hand by the law of averages, as Kristy labors for more than eight hours unrolling hay bales while the six teams after hers show up, find the clue, and move on. By then her hands are covered with cuts and, according to later interviews, her body is covered with ticks. But she's still plugging on, like the anti-Flo she is. Of all the teams ever screwed by luck-based challenges, hers may be the all-time most heartbreaking.

16. Don (Team Spry) Breaks Down Watching His Wife Kick Butt in Senegal (Race 6, Leg #4)

Overcome with emotion as he watches Mary Jean work like a pack mule hauling salt from Lac Rose, Don's voice breaks: "She's one hell of a woman. I'm so proud of her." This is another moment I'm not about to mock.

17. Gus (Team CIA) Weeps at the Slave House in Senegal (Race 6, Leg #5)

Big ol' fat Gus will be the only Racer to make the endearing list three times. The first time this leg is at the Slave House in Senegal, where Racers pause to pay their respects at the "Door of No Return," where slaves were loaded aboard ships to be taken to the New World. Hera wonders if the slaves had any idea what they were getting into. Her dad's answer is a stark, immediate, and articulate, "Why would there be any reason to tell 'em?" But his big moment is at the gate itself, where he breaks down and weeps unashamedly. Later, apologizing to Hera for "embarrassing" her (he didn't), he interviews, "I didn't cry at my mother's funeral. I didn't cry at my father's funeral. When I went through those doors, I saw myself. And then I started realizing that this is a connection with a part of [myself] that [I've]...never been able to fully connect with. I hope that the others can realize the magnitude of the human experience that is incorporated in this Race that we run."

18. Gus (Team CIA) Sneaks a Beer at the Brauhaus (Race 6, Leg #5)

Waiting tables at a beer house, as part of the Detour in Berlin, big ol' fat Gus seizes every opportunity to sample the wares, grossing out and exasperating his daughter Hera. His best moment comes when they've finished the task, and he drives her crazy by wanting to stay and have some more beer. His body language, as he tries to trick her into turning her back so he can snag another mug, is to die.

19. Debbie and Bianca (The Virginia Girls) Almost Catch Up in Argentina (Race 7, Leg #3)

The Virginia Girls have previously made one of the most disastrous navigation errors in Race history, somehow finding the beach when they were supposed to find the Andes. The error adds four hours to their travel time. They seem doomed, especially when the next task turns out to be white-water rafting, an activity that had almost drowned Debbie a couple of months earlier. But it may be too early to count them out. Not only does Debbie join the rafting despite her fears, but she also plunges into the subsequent meat-eating Roadblock with equal gusto, unbuckling the top button of her pants in preparation for what promises to be a belly-busting ordeal. All the players on the sidelines watch this with frank, unadulterated awe. "I think she's gonna eat it," says an admiring Rob, who had given up hours ago. "This chick's tough." And she is. So tough that she finishes the meal mere bites behind Heckboy, who started long before her. It would be nice if the toughness translated to survival in the leg, but 'tis not to be.

20. Gretchen (Team Energizer Bunny) Shrugs Off a Busted Noggin in South Africa (Race 7, Leg #5)

During the spelunking task, Gretchen slips, falls, and comes up smiling, despite a face covered with blood. She says, "Find the clue, honey. Don't worry. I've been wanting a face-lift for a long time." While safety workers clean and stitch the gash in her forehead, which like most head wounds bleeds well out of proportion to its size, her number one concern is making sure her husband (understandably a wreck about the whole thing) continues his search for the clue envelope. By the time they leave the cave, Gretchen looks like she's been through a war: she's wearing a gauze bandage turban, her face is bruised and covered with blood spots, and her white T-shirt is now a disconcerting shade of pink. Now she worries about her appearance: "I can't go to Soweto Market like this!" But she goes on. For the first time, we realize that Team Energizer Bunny might be tougher than it looks.

21. Joyce (Team Enron) Gets Her Head Shaved Outside Jodhpur (Race 7, Leg #8b)

She suspects it. She's afraid of it. She says the very idea freaks her out. But when her team arrives at the Fast Forward, where participating in a Hindu ritual will require team members to shave their heads, she bites back her tears, rolls over her husband's objections, and goes for it, weeping as her braided locks fall to the ground. The most wonderful thing about all this—next to Uchenna's deep empathy for her as she tearfully allows her head to be denuded—is that the procedure proves to be a cosmetic miracle. She was a good-looking lady before, but the shaved head makes her downright regal. As it happens, she's not quite ready to believe this, and keeps her scalp hidden under a bandanna even after other teams beg for a look. But it's not long before she's comfortable with it. In any event, it's next to impossible to watch these scenes without tearing up on her behalf, loving Uchenna a little bit for the support he shows her during the ordeal, or feeling vicarious happiness for her when the end result turns out so well. After this moment, an all-time Race highlight, many viewers were united in one thought. *They had better frickin' win.*

22. Carissa Gaghan Makes a Statement of Principles (Race 8, Leg #1)

The only player to get on this endearing list in the pre-Race interview segments, 9-year-old Carissa declares, "I might be small, but I am not sshhtupid." She has us from hello.

23. Carissa and Billy Gaghan Serenade the Aiellos in Amish Country (Race 8, Leg #1)

Riding the Amish buggy later in the same leg, the kids produce what amounts to a childhood version of the "Jaws" theme, in the form of that old ditty "She'll Be Coming 'Round the Mountain," as their team catches up with, and overtakes, the temporarily bogged-down Aiellos. The moment rides the line between hilarious and annoying as hell, with fans of all backgrounds landing on opposite ends of the fence. I think it's great.

24. The Paolo Family Helps Out the Bransens at Fort McDowell, Arizona (Race 8, Leg #7)

Believing themselves last to the Pit Stop, the Paolos don multiple layers of clothing, in case of a mugging. Then they see the Bransens arriving, and rush to the Pit Stop, wearing the usual array of underwear outside their pants. When the Bransens arrive seconds later, the Paolos turn on them and cry: "Don't step on the mat! It may be on a non-elimination! Go put all your clothes!" The stunned Bransens comply, return a few minutes later wearing multiple layers, and are indeed deprived of all belongings except for the clothes they have on. The Paolos, who turned off some viewers with their constant fighting, here act quickly and instinctively to help out the one team behind them. It may not be the *smartest* tactic ever (which is why it's not on the smartest-move list), but it says a lot about their sportsmanship. Because they really didn't have to do that.

Race 9,
"T-Tow, My Ass!"

THE LARGELY DOMESTIC EIGHTH RACE was such a disappointment, to viewers and Racers alike, that Phil Keoghan and producer Bertram van Munster hit the interview circuit, promising a return to form with new international locations, even more difficult challenges, and even more extreme personalities. Among the specific promises made in one *Entertainment Weekly* article: one player, Lake, would supposedly be abrasive enough to give Jonathan Baker a run for his money, and another player, Yolanda would have long legs (to hear him tell it) bedazzling to the happily married Phil.

The accuracy of these promises ran about fifty-fifty. Yes, Lake was abrasive, and did get on the nerves of several fellow Racers (as well as prompt much spectacularly unfounded Internet speculation about wifebeating), but, to be fair, he didn't even come close to evoking the loudest voice in Race 6. If we must oversimplify these people with forced comparisons, as it seems we must, he comes off like a Southern Ralph Kramden: in short, a hapless blowhard who makes a lot of noise about being in charge, but whose partner, in this case Michelle, charmingly sees right through him. (Wife-beating, my foot.) That said, Yolanda does indeed have spectacular legs.

We have named this Race after one reaction to its most often-repeated catch-phrase, "T-Tow!", which partners BJ and Tyler exclaim multiple times per episode, amusing themselves and annoying the hell out of viewers. We can only guess how many cries of "T-Tow!" were edited out, in comparison to the number left in, but if the real-time frequency echoed the frequency of T-Tows aired, we can only commend their fellow Racers for not resorting to murder. As for what the damn thing means, we can only speculate, since the boys have provided multiple conflicting explanations. At one point they seem to be implying an acronym. At another they say it references the circle of life in the universe. Most recently it's been described as a personal joke, filched from the logo on a T-shirt they spotted in some Asian country. The actual truth may exist at some undefined point between any and all of these explanations. In any event, the catch-phrase contributed to making them one of the most controversial teams in the show's history, adored beyond measure by the viewers who enjoyed their infectious sense of fun and loathed beyond measure by viewers who found them a pair of self-aggrandizing attention whores.[78]

Complaints over the number of bunchings in past seasons may have contributed to a couple of purely linear legs where teams who did everything right still had no real opportunity to catch up with one another, instead merely preserving something close to their original starting order.

DRAMATIS PERSONAE

1. The Fabulous Furry Freak Brothers

Best friends BJ Averell, a 26-year-old online tutor from Los Angeles, and Tyler Macniven, a 25-year-old filmmaker from San Francisco. These

---

[78] The Television Without Pity forum devoted to the pair provides some harrowing extremes in both directions, remarkable even for a venue where Racers have always been loved and hated in equal measure. Count me among the folks who rooted for them.

guys dress in garish colors, call each other "Dude," and cry "T-Tow!" to the point of distraction. We have rarely mentioned the prior globe-trotting adventures of Racers, except when they prove relevant to gameplay (as with previous Teams Survivor and POW), but that happens to be the case here: at the time this Race aired, Tyler has already achieved a low level of notoriety in Japan for traversing the entire length of the country on foot.[79] His knowledge of the country was a mixed blessing, in the later legs. This team's strengths included their energy, their high spirits, several extreme strokes of luck, and their refusal to give up; their weaknesses include a certain constitutional failure to recognize when they're being too abrasive (which fosters a totally unnecessary feud with another team), and nonlinear thinking that at one point leads BJ to snatch defeat out of the jaws of victory. **SEASON SUPERSTARS**

2. Team Fierstien

Lifelong Friends Scott Braginton-Smith (a 41-year-old working in sales in West Harwich, MA), and John Lowe (a 38-year-old wealth manager from Dorchester, MA). These gay men hasten to inform the camera that they're just (strong emphasis on *just*) good friends. Much is made of John's extreme fear of heights, which he memorably overcomes in the first leg. Good for him. Alas, he loses the same number of points for a degree of impatience that causes team friction almost out of the starting gate. The team is not around long enough to establish any compensating strengths.

3. Team Legs

Dating couple Yolanda Brown-Moore (27, a science teacher) and Ray Whitty (31, attorney); both from Chicago. This tightly knit, physically robust team has a sad habit of getting lost on the road, in more legs than we can count. And though they get along quite well, most of the time, they spend one memorable leg, an entire two days, bickering at length and almost without pause over, essentially, nothing. They, for the most

---

[79] His two missions during this Japan walk were to impress his Japanese girlfriend, and track down his father's then-unknown birthplace, armed with nothing but an old sketch of some coastline provided by his grandmother. He not only found the seaside town in question, and took the girl back to America, but met thousands of Japanese and became a minor national sensation. A remarkable sixty-seven-minute documentary of his journey, *Kintaro Walks Japan*, is available at: http://video.google.com/videosearch?q=%22Kintaro%22.

part, get over it. The poster children for teams that would benefit from a little more skill at making out street signs.

4. Team Mojo

Dating couple Monica Cayce, a 23-year-old student from Fayetteville, AR, and Joseph Meadows a 23-year-old homebuilder from Fort Smith, AR. They call themselves Mojo, after the first syllables of their respective names. Not a bad team, weakened by Monica's Flo-like, but by no means Flo-scale, tendency to weep and declare defeat at moments of adversity.[80]

5. Team Boricua

Mother and daughter Desiree Cifre (a 24-year-old writer from New York, NY), and Wanda Lopez-Rochford (a 44-year-old corporate trainer from Smyrna, GA). Desiree looks a little like Norah Jones, and Wanda looks a little like Lena Olin. They call themselves Team Boricua, because of their Puerto Rican heritage, and for a while they're so game for anything that they seem likely and deserving candidates for the final three. Their strengths include Desiree's ability to allay her mother's fears, a gift that proves worthless when she falls prey to her own. Their weaknesses include navigating in Germany, and Wanda's fear of deep water.

6. The Stepford Dentists

Married parents Michelle Garner (a 36-year-old homemaker) and Lake Garner (a 37-year-old dentist), both from Hattiesburg, MS. Their accents are so irresistible that previous winners Chip and Kim posted video of themselves gleefully imitating their every line of dialogue (see www.chipandkim.tv). Lake actually uses constructions like "Dad-Gum,"[81] and proclaims himself the boss, an illusion Michelle goes along with but effortlessly deflates at several amusing moments. Another team that might have gone further, and done better, were it not for difficulties with navigation.

---

[80] She unnerves Joseph, and viewers, by breaking into tears in the first airport, before the Race has even left the United States. Not even Flo did that.

[81] My dad's gum is Wrigley's Spearmint.

7. Team Pee

I truly apologize for this. Certainly it would be nicer to call them the Frosties, or the Glamazons, the names they promote for themselves. But sisters Joni Glaze, 44 (a children's minister from Katy, TX), and Lisa Hinds (a 48-year-old realtor/artist from Santa Rosa Beach, FL) are the ones who claim to have wet themselves with excitement at a key moment during the first leg. What else would you have me call them? Team Depends?

8. Team Vague

Barry Lazarus (a 63-year-old retired physician), and Fran Lazarus (a 61-year-old retired accountant), both from Silverthorne, Colorado, seem lost and confused during the first couple of legs, making critical errors in navigation and Detour choices that render them even more a pair of sacrificial lambs than their mere age would indicate. And then things change. They may be the most incompetent team, in the early legs, ever to hit a groove in subsequent racing, but Barry and Fran became the oldest team to ever finish a leg in first place, and came within one elimination of joining Race 7's Gretchen and Meredith as another "old" team to make it into the Final Four.

9. The Smutty Slackers

Friends Jeremy Ryan, 26, and Eric Sanchez, 27, both college dropouts working as waiters in Fort Lauderdale, FL, make an opening speech about how they only work as much as they need to live, and how they wouldn't mind being rich as long as they don't have to work for it. Oddly, the other teams come to call them "The Frat Boys," a nickname that they eventually admit doesn't make any sense. They're "Smutty," here, because their comments about women often cross the line from the appreciative into the realm of the piggish.[82] On the other hand, they're strong candidates for the strongest, fastest, smartest, luckiest, most confident, and most competent team of all time, racking up the most consistent series of first and second place finishes in the show's history (and only falling into the bottom two once).

---

[82] One of the more consistent Internet rumors about the team is that they were a pair of gay guys, overcompensating with forced sexist banter, which (though apparently not true) was provided additional grist when the site www.defamer.com posted apparently real photos of them cavorting in a hotel room with BJ and Tyler. The images, which approach the explicit but never get there, appear to have been a defiant attempt by both teams to play with the heads of their more rumor-mongering fans. We could have done without this.

10. The Affectionate Nerds

Dating Couple David Spiker (a 30-year-old musician) and Lori Willems (a 22-year-old Pizza Hut Manager), are by their own admission "the nerdiest people we know." Both are from Manhattan, KS, a fact which led production crews to try to pressure them into making a "We're not in Kansas anymore" comment on-camera. They were sufficiently un-nerdy to resist. A team so close and so affectionate that a spell of (very) mild irritation with one another leaves David weeping in shame, they're not the most physically fit but certainly among the most enthused. Unfortunately, their enthusiasm flutters badly when killer fatigue sets in. Too bad they didn't make it to the final challenge. They might have been good.

11. The Pink Ladies

Childhood friends Dani Torchio and Danielle Turner, both 22-year-old college graduates from Staten Island, NY, think leveraging their sex appeal will help them get help from locals. They have the sex appeal, but the plan proves to be a non-starter. Give them credit for recognizing that and moving on to no-nonsense gameplay. As Racers, they're middling. As people to write about, they're all too confusing, as they have pretty much the same name and each Dani is always calling the other Dani. Shudder.

THE GAME PLAY

Leg # 1: In Which Ladies Wet Themselves

The Race Starts at the Red Rocks Amphitheatre, outside Denver. Teams receive the usual opening speech and $140, with instructions to fly to São Paulo, Brazil, and find their clue box on the roof of the Hotel Unique.

Lake endears himself to viewers with his grudging admission that a critical misreading of the clue is "at least partially my fault." Big of him. Monica starts crying in the Denver airport, unnerving Joseph mightily; you can see him calculating how many Race legs he's still in for. In São Paulo, Team Pee expresses surprise that Portuguese isn't the exact same thing as Spanish.

Atop the Hotel Unique—which is—the clue box sends teams to the Viedisteo Santa Efigenia Bridge, a pedestrian bridge where the next clue box awaits.

The Detour is "Motorhead" or "Rotorhead." In the first, teams taxi one mile to a motorcycle shop, and construct an entire working motorcycle from a frame, using an intact model as their only guide. In the second, teams taxi three miles to a heliport, consult a guide for aerial photos of one of three buildings, and get a helicopter ride to the roof of that building, where they search the floor below for clue envelopes. Almost everybody will pick "Rotorhead," starting with Team Boricua, Team Mojo, and The Nerds. The Pink Ladies head for the motorcycles, reasoning: how hard can it be? Well, this is how hard: as soon as they get there, they start flirting with the guys in the shop. No dice. Nobody is interested in building a greasy motorcycle for them.

Back at the bridge, Team Vague walks right past the clue box—literally within inches of it—complaining that it doesn't seem to be anywhere. They do the same coming back in the opposite direction. When they finally find it, Fran says, "I don't think it was here last time." Naturally, they decide they're up to building a motorcycle, and just as naturally, their efforts amount to watching Lake do it and hoping he'll be inclined to help. Lake does tell them that the spark plugs go on top of the engine, leading Fran to moan that she doesn't know how to recognize an engine. Not an auspicious beginning.

Up ahead, the teams returning to the heliport after completing their flight over the city now have to take another taxi to Santa Cecilia, where they must light a candle at a religious celebration.

Team Pee, which has had awful luck with traffic, makes it to the Copters, but not before announcing that they've wet themselves. We can only hope they're kidding. (Wouldn't it be wonderful if that happened in a Non-Elimination Leg, to a team then obliged to keep the clothes they have on?)

Team Fierstein brings up the rear at the Copters, with John (who hates flying, and hasn't been on a plane in eight years) hoping he doesn't panic. Surprise: he doesn't. He actually loves the experience. The team moves on to the religious ceremony, where John hilariously freezes as he catches sight of the lady with the big snake.

The Soccer Stadium is the site of the first Pit Stop.

1. Eric and Jeremy (The Smutty Slackers) 5:34 P.M.
2. BJ and Tyler (The Fabulous Furry Freak Brothers) 5:36 P.M.
3. Wanda and Desiree (Team Boricua) 5:45 P.M.

4. Dave and Lori (The Nerds) 5:49 P.M.
5. Lake and Michelle (Stepford Dentists) 6:10 P.M.
6. Joseph and Monica (Team Mojo) 6:45 P.M.
7. Ray and Yolanda (Team Legs) 6:47 P.M.
8. Fran and Barry (Team Vague) 7:06 P.M.
9. Dani and Danielle (The Pink Ladies) 7:19 P.M.
10. Joni and Lisa (Team Pee) 7:28 P.M.
11. Scott and John (Team Fierstien) ELIMINATED

Leg #2: The Suavity of Slackers

Teams receive a mere twenty-three dollars with instructions to make their way to a São Paulo office building, the Edifício Copan, specifically Blaco F. The 8:00 A.M. opening time guarantees a mass bunching by all.

The Slackers, who have charmlessly referred to the Pink Ladies as bitches and hos, are now hoping to get some sex on the Race, and have appointed the Pink Ladies their designated receptacles. The joking is pretty piggish, and gets worse as the ep rolls on. The Slackers do think it's cool that they get to see hookers on the way to the building, though, when they call out the window of the cab they quickly decide that the streetwalkers are men and better-off avoided.

The task at the Edifício Copan is a Roadblock. The building has four circular stairwells as fire escapes. One team member must climb any one of those four stairwells, then upon reaching the top, rappel down. Jeremy goes for the Slackers, giving Eric the chance to chat away with Dani of the Pinks. "You have to make the girls happy," he notes in an interview, "if you want to get in their pants later." He actually says that.

The Detour, ninety miles away, is "Climb It" or "Press It." In "Climb It," teams travel to a waterfall at Usina Jacara, and make a ninety-foot rock climb using mechanical ascenders. In "Press It," teams go to a sugarcane farm, press cane through a grinder, and distill 500 milliliters of ethanol. Which they then use to gas their vehicles. So the choice here is really based on physical fitness versus the ability to perform a painstaking task.

The Freaks, Mojo, and Slackers, all first to the Detour, are athletic teams who naturally pick the climb. Monica says to Joseph, "I'm up against a bunch of men, but I will work my butt off to do this." And she does. Tyler calls the climb awesome, the same word he uses to describe everything else. Monica climbs. The Slackers go off at length about how they need some hot girls in bikinis around here. Sigh.

Meanwhile, Team Pee freaks out over their temperamental VW, which stalls and stalls and stalls.

BJ and Tyler can't get their VW into reverse, but no problem: they just get out and push it until it's facing the right way. Cool. As hippies, they know their Beetles.[83]

Now on their way to the Pit Stop, a hacienda called Primavera Di Serra, the Slackers hope the Pink Girls make it, because otherwise, who would they have sex with for the next month? The Hippies? Ten million women begin to hate these guys. As they run to the mat, they holler, "Where's the Damn Phil at? I'm gonna smack you, woman!" Make that twenty million.

It all comes down to Team Vague and Team Pee. And guess what. Everybody else hits the mat in broad daylight. We now cut to pitch black darkness. Team Vague's delight, when they find out that they're still in the game—albeit at the end of the pack, once again—is a great moment.

1. BJ and Tyler (The Fabulous Furry Freak Brothers) 4:48 P.M.
2. Eric and Jeremy (The Smutty Slackers) 5:01 P.M.
3. Joseph and Monica (Team Mojo) 5:18 P.M.
4. Dave and Lori (The Affectionate Nerds) 5:28 P.M.
5. Ray and Yolanda (Team Legs) 6:31 P.M.
6. Wanda and Desiree (Team Boricua) 6:32 P.M.
7. Lake and Michelle (The Stepford Dentists) 7:06 P.M.
8. Dani and Danielle (The Pink Ladies) 7:07 P.M.
9. Fran and Barry (Team Vague) 8:24 P.M.
10. Lisa and Joni (Team Pee) ELIMINATED

Leg #3a: Nudge, Nudge, Wink, Wink, Say No More

We are told that during the Pit Stop, The Smutty Slackers did indeed "hook up with" The Pink Ladies, a fact presented here as if it should be accompanied with leering and winking.

Teams receive $307 along with directions to an early morning zipline task. The Freak Brothers, who arrive first, amuse themselves by leap-

---

[83] One suspects that had they competed in Race 7, they would not have needed any local help identifying *Abbey Road*.

ing out of the bushes to scare the bejeezus out of everybody else. Those wacky fellas.

After the usual shots of folks sliding down a wire and yelling, "Wooooooo!!!", Racers get the clue envelope, instructing teams that they must now take a bus back to São Paulo, and from there arrange a flight 7,300 miles to Moscow, Russia. Lake says, "Dang, I was hoping we wouldn't have to go to Russia." His objection is based on Moscow's climate, leading to my fervent hope that the Race requires a lot of time spent on glaciers.

Arriving bunched in Moscow, teams taxi to the Chaika Bassein pool, a high-diving facility where the Soviet teams trained for the Olympics. On the way, Dani says that the only thing she knows about Russians is that they drink and smoke a lot. Ah, well.

The Roadblock clue reads, "Who Wants to Take the Plunge?" Yolanda volunteers and is not happy when the challenge turns out to require a high jump into a pool (an outdoor pool, in freezing weather). It turns out that she can't swim. She not only goes on the *Amazing Race* when she cannot swim, but she volunteers for a task inviting her to take a plunge. Nice move.

The Stepford Dentists arrive. Lake tells Michelle to do the task. She protests, "I might have to do it naked." Odd assumption. He says to his wife, "So what?" Better answer. But then he takes the task. Later, she wonders, "Would you really make me get in front of all those Russian people with a bathing suit on?" I don't know what that means.

Wanda is a bad swimmer who is terrified of going underwater. Naturally, she also volunteers to "take the plunge." Astonishing.[84] She manages to do the jump, but for a while cannot bring herself to put her head underwater to get the clue envelope. Hysteria ensues.

After the task, The Smutty Slackers plan to share a taxi with The Pink Ladies. First to the curb, they tell the uncomprehending driver to wait for the pretty girls with the big boobies. They actually say that.

The Pink Ladies are not happy to realize, in the taxi on the way to the next clue box, that they left the bag containing their passports and all their Race information in the locker room back at the pool facility. Of course, the second they head back, their new beaus call them stupid. Sigh.

---

[84] One gets the impression that both Team Legs and Team Boricua expected the Take-the-Plunge task to involve iced tea.

The Detour is "Scrub" or "Scour." In the first, teams travel to a trolley depot, where they are provided cleaning supplies they must use to clean a Moscow trolley car, inside and out. In "Scour," teams make their way to a local theatre, where they must search 1,500 Russian nested dolls for the little-itty-bitty clue hidden inside only ten of them. A loud band provides extra annoyance value.

The Slackers and Stepford Dentists are first to find Phil behind St. Basil's Cathedral, where they are handed another clue. "You're still Racing."

To be continued....

Yes. It's this season's Uber-leg.

Leg #3b: Even More Nudge, Nudge, Wink, Wink

As the exhausted Racers converge on the mat, Phil directs them to fly to Frankfurt, Germany. Once in Frankfurt, they have to take a train an additional 100 miles to Stuttgart, and find the Mercedes Benz factory.

BJ and Tyler are so pleased that they tip Phil a dollar. Before they leave, they claim it back, reasoning that they may need it. Indian givers.

Cut to the Moscow Airport. The Slackers arrive in time to claim a direct flight departing at 7:15 P.M. The Fabulous Furry Freak Brothers and The Stepford Dentists claim a 9:15 P.M. flight. For everybody else, a massive computer malfunction affecting reservations for the entire airport proves an insoluble barrier to making that second flight, or any of several other flights leaving that evening; they all have to wait until the system is repaired and a fresh flight leaves at 7:00 A.M. the next morning.

The task at Stuttgart, a stone plug for Mercedes (and not the only plug of the episode), sends teams riding along with a professional driver roaring around the test track, and the vertical-curve Wall of Death, at speeds exceeding 170 kpm.

Lots of folks say woo.

The Roadblock 200 miles away is a needle-in-a-haystack search, sending one member of each team around a field to look under markers shaped like Travelocity gnome hats and feet. The clear advantage here lies with those who arrive at the field first, when there are more gnomes to find.

The Smutty Slackers are first to find a gnome, and with it, directions to drive to a factory called Bavaria Film. They are on their way before any other teams arrive.

Far behind them, Team Boricua drives in precisely the wrong direction, which is bad news for the Pinks, who are counting on them to navigate. When the teams get lost in precisely the same way twice, a Danielle moans, "This is like *Groundhog Day*."

Bavaria Film is site of the episode's Detour; "Break It" or "Slap It." The first requires teams to smash each other over the head with stunt bottles, one at a time, until they find the word "Prosit" on the back of one of the labels. (The people who make up these Detours must be getting punchy.) The other option requires teams to join a dance troupe, learn and perform one of those complicated Bavarian dance numbers where folks slap their thighs and knees in celebration of nothing in particular.

The Slackers arrange for kisses from the pretty local ladies, so they can proudly wear the lipstick on their cheeks. When they hit the mat in Munich, Phil calls them the biggest Casanovas in the show's history. They respond by hoping that the Pinks arrive soon, so they can enjoy "a little more tongue wrestling."[85]

The Freak Brothers run up to the mat backwards, just to be contrary. Yes, they actually do that.

Lake tells Michelle to zip the negatism. She responds with a masterfully sarcastic array of happy talk.

The Pink Ladies and Team Boricua arrive at the Roadblock late, and still have the Detour to complete. Desiree, who not so long ago seemed so unflappably confident, succumbs to weeping and despair. In the end, it's Team Boricua versus The Pink Ladies, in a race for last place.

1. Eric and Jeremy (The Smutty Slackers) 2:15 P.M.
2. BJ and Tyler (The Fabulous Furry Freak Brothers) 3:04 P.M.
3. Lake and Michelle (The Stepford Dentists) 3:09 P.M.
4. Fran and Barry (Team Vague) 5:03 P.M.
5. Dave and Lori (The Affectionate Nerds) 5:28 P.M.
6. Monica and Joseph (Team Mojo) 5:32 P.M.
7. Ray and Yolanda (Team Legs) 6:48 P.M.
8. Dani and Danielle (The Pink Ladies) 7:28 P.M.
9. Wanda and Desiree (Team Boricua) ELIMINATED

---

[85] Seriously, my dear Readers: Ecch, ecch, ecch, ecch, ecch. And, need I add: ecch.

Leg #4: Dave, the Abusive, Unfeeling Brute

Teams now head for the central opera house in Palermo, Sicily.

Receiving early information of a 6:30 A.M. flight that lands in Palermo at 10:30 A.M., the Slackers and the Freak Brothers amuse themselves by commandeering airport wheelchairs and having slalom races around the line-control posts. No, really. They actually do that.

Monica wants us to know she's not a dumb blonde. She then pronounces Palermo "Paller Moe." Joseph is even worse; he confuses the hell out of one ticket clerk by requesting passage to "Palomino." Yes, he actually says that.

The first flight, carrying the Freak Brothers and the Smutty Slackers, takes off on schedule at 6:30 A.M., three hours ahead of the competition. What's more, the Freaks wangle a better connection ahead of the Slackers and get an additional half hour leg up.

First to the clue at the opera house, the Freak Brothers are also first to the next clue box forty-two miles away at the seaside fortress known as the Castellano Del Golfo. There they find the Detour. "Foundry" or "Laundry." In the first, teams must walk to a nearby metal works, collect a 110-pound church bell, carry it to a small vehicle, drive that across town, and then carry it across a piazza and up a flight of stairs, delivering it to the priest who will reward them with a clue envelope. "Laundry" requires a search through 2,400 pieces of laundry hanging from clotheslines for one of only sixteen adorned with the *Amazing Race* tag.

The Roadblock requires each participating Racer to build a model of an ancient statue from provided parts. *No* team is told that the kits have two extraneous parts, a fiendish touch which will cause some nasty confusion.

At "Laundry," Barry plays the role of crotchety old man, wondering if some of these younger teams even know what a clothespin *is*. Why, these young whippersnappers.

The Pit Stop is at the Tempio De Segesta, one of the most intact structures left over from the Roman Empire. The Slackers complete their statue and hit the mat second, saying, "Ooooh, hottie," at the beautiful local greeter standing beside Phil. Sigh.[86]

---

[86] You wanna know who these guys remind me of? I'll tell you who they remind me of. They remind me of the wild and crazy Czechoslovakian brothers Dan Aykroyd and Steve Martin used to play on *Saturday Night Live*: the guys who always went on and on about meeting those hot American girls with their big American breasts.

The Nerds arrive at the Roadblock. Lori complains that she's out of shape. Dave murmurs that he can do without hearing that again. She says she's thirsty. He murmurs he can do without hearing that, too. This is as upset with her as he gets. Note this.

Arriving late and fighting to stay in the game, The Stepford Dentists reluctantly Yield The Pink Ladies. And I say reluctantly because Michelle is most teary about it, addressing the camera: "It's NOT PERSONAL!" Which doesn't stop Dani and Danielle from being pissed. Why would they do this to us, one Danielle asks. The other Danielle says, "Because they're hicks from the South and they're jerkoffs."[87]

Lori of the Nerds doesn't know what's wrong. Every time she builds the statue, there are two pieces left over. She weeps, disassembles the statue, and starts again. It takes her forever to realize the secret other teams got right away. Not all the pieces have to fit. But by the time the team gets to the Pit Stop, Dave is the one crying.[88]

This time it comes down to a footrace between Team Legs and The Pink Ladies....

1. BJ and Tyler (Fabulous Furry Freak Brothers) 2:29 P.M.
2. Eric and Jeremy (The Smutty Slackers) 4:11 P.M.
3. Joseph and Monica (Team Mojo) 5:00 P.M.
4. Fran and Barry (Team Vague) 5:18 P.M.
5. Lake and Michelle (The Stepford Dentists) 6:06 P.M.
6. Dave and Lori (The Affectionate Nerds) 6:25 P.M.
7. Dani and Danielle (The Pink Ladies) ELIMINATED

Leg #5: "I'm gonna stab somebody"

Receiving sixty-one dollars, teams drive 135 miles to Catania, still in Sicily, where the next clue box awaits at the ancient ampitheatre known as the Theatre Romano.

The Freak Brothers, who have a healthy lead, pause to go boody-boody-boody-boody to a friendly stray dog who goes belly-up for them. Boody-boody-boody-boody.

---

[87] She's upset.

[88] He's deeply ashamed of being so hard on her. For this team, being hard on your partner amounts to being mildly irritated at her. It speaks well of Dave that this was so unheard-of, in their relationship, that he had to weep in shame. Take that, certain others.

When they arrive after a night drive, they discover that the site is closed til 8:30 A.M. They decide to pull a fast one and put up a "sign-in sheet" which will force Racers to enter in the order in which they arrive. When the Smutty Slackers arrive at the Ampitheatre, still in darkness, they suss out the fraud in one tenth of a second. Both teams share a laugh at the idiocy of the sign-up sheet, a tactic which is now forgotten as it worked not at all. What scamps.

At 8:30 A.M., a minor time-wasting task at the amphitheatre, involving a count of cast-iron heads, leads those first two teams to the Detour, "Big Fish" or "Little Fish." The first requires each team to find a nearby street vendor, who will give each player a thirty-two pound swordfish. They must carry their swordfish a third of a mile to a local fish market, finding a specific vendor who will hand them their clue. The second requires teams to go directly to the fish market and man a booth until they sell four kilos of little fish—I didn't get the species, but they're about the size of sardines.

Both the Freaks and the Slackers make short work of the Swordfish task and are soon back in their cars, driving the sixty kilometers to Siracusa.

Some distance behind them, Team Mojo collects their pair of swordfish. They do not carry them over their shoulders, as the Slackers and Freaks did, but at an appalled arm's length. Note that this is a perfect way to maximize your arm strain.

Team Vague's car is lost in narrow local streets. "Go through there," Fran instructs. Barry points out that it's an alley not wide enough for their car. She says, then don't. Like it's a major surrender.

Mojo's having troubles. Buckling under the stench and weight of her fish, she sobs through drippy Alice Cooper mascara eyes: "This is the worst thing I've ever done!" Joseph has so many problems getting the locals to direct him to the right fishmonger that he says, "I'm gonna stab one of these locals through the head." The fact that he is carrying a swordfish at the time gives the threat added, if somewhat surreal, weight. Later, Monica whines, "I'm gonna smell like fish ALL DAY!" Has she ever seen this show?

The Stepford Dentists arrive at the merchant in charge of handing out swordfish. Hilariously, Michelle worries, "What if this is not him and we're stealing his fish?" Lake grimaces and says, "He wouldn't LET us." Good point.

Up ahead, the Roadblock requires one member of each team to score a goal while playing with a professional kayak polo team. I didn't know there was such a thing, even in Sicily.[89] And truth to tell, I don't think the Sicilians try very hard.

Ray takes the Roadblock and becomes the only player to capsize his kayak. In addition, his first toss misses the net completely, which is downright shocking for a black guy. I kid because I love.

The Nerds approach the Roadblock. Lori says, "May the Force be with us."

It isn't.

1. Eric and Jeremy (The Smutty Slackers) 10:33 A.M.
2. BJ and Tyler (Fabulous Furry Freak Brothers) 10:38 A.M.
3. Monica and Joseph (Team Mojo) 11:40 A.M.
4. Barry and Fran (Team Vague) 11:53 A.M.
5. Lake and Michelle (The Stepford Dentists) 12:17 P.M.
6. Ray and Yolanda (Team Legs) 1:02 P.M.
7. Dave and Lori (The Affectionate Nerds) ELIMINATED[90]

Leg #6: Welcome to Rome. It's Time to Leave.

Monica says she's always wanted to go to Rome. Too bad the Racers visit here only long enough to perform a minor task that plugs the summer's blockbuster movie, *The Da Vinci Code*.

Lake takes a deep breath and says, "Ahhhhh. Yoga." Which you gotta see to appreciate. It's downright hilarious.

In Athens, Greece, Monica notes that it's great to be "where thinking began."[91]

Another all-night bunching before the Agora opens at 8:00 A.M. There's torrential rain, which continues on and off for the rest of the day. The Slackers are first to the clue box, which along with route instructions also includes directions to this leg's Fast Forward, a plate-smashing task at the Stamatopolons Taverna.

---

[89] Only a fool bets against a Sicilian when depth is on the line!

[90] If this order sounds at all familiar, that's because, with minor adjustments, it is very close to the order in which they started. In short, without the Fast Forwards that can give even a last-place team a shot at the lead, and without the mega-bunchings that can force a leading team to reclaim its position more than once in a leg, the tendency will be for the order to remain intact.

[91] There's sorta bouncy music over this, making a joke of her not-incredibly-deep commentary, but let's give her credit. On a show where most of the first bunch of people to hit Paris in Race 1 had no idea what the Arc de Triomphe was, even a vague awareness of local historical significance qualifies as cultural literacy.

Any teams that don't take the Fast Forward must travel seventy miles by train from the Anargini railway station to the city of Corinth.

To find their next clue they must get off at the Isthmos Station.

At the Isthmos Station. Note this.

Mojo and the Slackers arrive at the Taverna and start smashing plates. (Gee, I hope they're in the right restaurant.) Damnably, it is the Slackers who smash the right plate and receive directions to the Pit Stop at the Fortress of Rion, a fourteenth-century stronghold on the Greek Coast.

Three teams get off as soon as they hit Corinth, *before* the Isthmos station. All three realize their error and decide to take a bus the rest of the way. "I hope this doesn't screw us up," says Michelle. Lake snarls, "It's NAWT GONNA SCREW US UP, DAMMIT!"

The Roadblock requires each participating Racer to bungee jump 240 feet over the Corinth canal. We get the usual woos, from everybody but Fran, who is terrified.

The Detour is "Herculean Effort" or "It's All Greek to Me." Both require teams to take marked cars to the same 2,300-year-old stadium, in Nemea. In the first option, individual members of each team compete in the discus throw and the javelin toss before both combine their strength to force a Greek wrestler from a marked twenty-foot circle. In "It's All Greek to Me," teams search a marked area for nine pieces of pottery shard with Greek letters on them, translate the letters into their English equivalents, and use a local map to find a town that uses those letters. (It's "Dimitsana.")

The Freaks discover that they have driven an hour in the wrong direction. No longer goofy as desperation takes over, they become subdued as they turn their car around and head back.

Barry backs his car into a tree. It's a serious crunch, too, which completely shatters the rear window. Barry says, "I didn't see it," starting a flurry of Internet ridicule over his lack of driving skills.

Lost, Lake gets so hysterical that Michelle tells him to pull off the road and take a deep breath.[92]

---

[92] Lake and Michelle had to have gotten pretty dad-gum lost, to still hit the mat after the Hippies. How lost? Tyler had this to say during an interview on the tarflies site: "We were certain we were last. But lucky for us, Lake and Michelle made the ultimate sacrifice. They drove to the complete opposite end of the entire country. They were on the east coast of Greece and we were on . . . we were on the west coast." That's on the scale of going to the beach when you're looking for the Andes. Assuming that's accurate, that's pretty dad-blamed lost.

Team Legs arrives at the Pit Stop second, hours behind the Slackers. They also receive a fifteen-minute penalty and cannot check in until the timer counts down. Mojo arrives, with Monica bracing for the elimination she expects. Her expression, when told her team is second, is priceless. "What?" she says dazedly. "How is that even possible?" Well, it is, girl.

Night starts to fall. The Dentists, still lost, drive through unfamiliar territories in torrential rain.

Tyler gives BJ a piggyback ride to the mat. Tyler tells Phil to go ahead and eliminate them. Phil tells them they're the fifth to arrive. *But—But!!!!* They *also* took the bus to the Isthmos Station. So they, too, have to wait out the next fifteen minutes and hope they're not eliminated....[93]

1. Eric and Jeremy (The Smutty Slackers) 11:54 A.M.
2. Monica and Joseph (Team Mojo) 4:31 P.M.
3. Ray and Yolanda (Team Legs) 4:41 P.M.
4. Fran and Barry (Team Vague) 6:20 P.M.
5. BJ and Tyler (The Fabulous Furry Freak Brothers) 8:51 P.M.
6. Lake and Michelle (The Stepford Dentists) ELIMINATED

Leg #7: The Desert Ordeal of Mr. Happy Fun Man

Teams receive fifty-three dollars with their instructions to cross the nearby lengthy Rio Antino suspension bridge on foot, and sign up for charter buses at the visitor's center on the other side. These buses will take players to the airport, where they must book flights 2,300 miles to Muscat, Oman (an Arab nation on the South Arabian Peninsula). Once in Oman, they will find their next clue at a giant incense burner. No kidding. A giant incense burner.

Within minutes of setting out, Team Legs begins one of those silly couple arguments that begin with joking and segue into actual fighting without ever picking up an actual point. The tipping point is Ray saying, "Find the damn bridge." Would you believe that the bickering over this continues for the remaining two days of the leg? Yolanda gives him an especially hard time for cursing at her. Girl, he didn't curse at you. He damned the bridge.

---

[93] The suspenseful interlude, as they await the arrival of Lake and Michelle, amounts to pointless torture of a team that is perfectly safe, as The Stepford Dentists are subject to the same penalty.

Their mood is not helped when their navigational difficulties contin-ue in Oman. Ray calls the journey "just like driving across the desert." Ummm. It is "just like" driving across the desert because you *are* driving across the desert. Similes don't work if you compare something to itself. At one point, confronting a washed-out road, Tyler says, "Dude! Is this, like, the most awesome chocolate surprise you have ever had?" I know he's referring to the muddy water, which does indeed look like choco-late. But it remains unfortunate phrasing, given the photos that have shown up on Defamer.com.

The Detour at Baith al Battha is "Camel" or "Watchtower." In the first, teams take a ferry across the river and use a block and tackle to load a living camel onto the back of a pickup truck, then use a hand-drawn map to deliver the beast to a Bedouin camp one mile away. In "Watch-tower," teams take the same ferry and search three hilltop watchtowers for the one that holds a traditional local silver "message box," which must be delivered to the Al-Sayegh Gold and Silver shop, also one mile away.

The most interesting thing here is the sweet solicitousness the Racers (especially the ladies) show the camels, worriedly asking them if they're okay and assuring them that everything will be all right. The camels, be-ing camels, don't care.

The Freaks and Team Vague are first to the Roadblock in Al Hawi-yah. This requires all participating Racers to dig through 117 mounds of sand to find only one of six buried shuwas, a traditional Omani dish of spiced lamb that is wrapped in a palm leaf and steamed in an under-ground oven. Oh, and by the way, they must bring the shuwa with them to the Pit Stop, because it's tonight's dinner.[94]

BJ grins ear to ear as he gallops forth, first to start digging. But fate hands him the Lena and Kristy treatment. As every other team (includ-ing the once-again lost Team Legs), arrives, finds the shuwa, and moves on, the combination of backbreaking labor and broiling desert sun drives him close to the edge of collapse. He is no longer Mr. Happy Fun Man. Up ahead, at Jabreen Castle, Phil's mind is visibly blown as Team Vague ar-rives first. They are also the only team to arrive in daylight.

The Slackers, delayed by an ill-advised "shortcut," and the Freaks, de-

---

[94] The sixth Needle-In-a-Haystack task this Race, by my count.

layed by BJ's hellishly bad luck, end this leg not racing for first place, but for last.

1. Fran and Barry (Team Vague) 5:35 P.M.
2. Joseph and Monica (Team Mojo) 5:54 P.M.
3. Ray and Yolanda (Team Legs) 6:26 P.M.
4. Eric and Jeremy (The Smutty Slackers) 6:47 P.M.
5. BJ and Tyler (The Fabulous Furry Freak Brothers) 8:21 P.M.
   MUGGED

Leg #8: The Rottnest Leg

Team departure times usually reflect twelve hours since their respective arrivals, but the factors this leg seems closer to twenty-four. No explanation is given.

Every team but the Freaks receives $181 with instructions to fly 9,000 miles to Perth, Australia.

Sometime during the Pit Stop, BJ and Tyler approached their competitors and asked them to leave donations on the front seat of their automobile. This means of getting around the rules entirely depends on the goodwill of those other teams, and has mixed results. Teams Legs and Vague both leave the Freaks a few bucks, the Slackers demur, and Team Mojo leaves hating the Freaks and under the impression that they've been threatened with a Yield if they don't cooperate. A feud begins.

The Slackers explain that they think giving money away is stupid, in this competition, and then, once again say one thing too many. "It's like trying to get in a girl's pants. You know, lie, cheat, steal...you do whatever you can." How lovely.[95]

The Freaks pick up a hitchhiking Bedouin named Adbul Hamid who, like them, happens to be heading for Muscat. Abdul shows his appreciation by buying them gas and lots of junk food. Tyler hugs him. Abdul shows Tyler that the Bedouins express the same feeling by touching noses. Delighted, BJ points at his own nose and says, "Can I get some of this Bedouin lovin'?" Abdul complies.

---

[95] Though I never bought the theory that they were a couple of repressed gay guys overcompensating for the camera, I did think it was wonderful that this was the impression they left so many viewers. It was exactly the opposite of the impression they wanted to leave, which is what made it such a good thing.

Barely making the plane (to the obvious displeasure of all the other teams), the Freaks spend the hours between Mercat and Perth begging more than $300 from their fellow passengers. Must have been a pleasant flight.

The clue box at the State War Memorial in Perth directs teams to travel to Fremantle and take a ferry to Rottnest Island. The name is pronounced "Rottenest," which is a great name for an island. (Phil explains that it's one of Western Australia's most popular vacation spots.)

Obtaining a night's lodging in a backpacker's hotel, Barry says, "This Race has ruined our sex life, I'll tell you that."

Fran gives a fervent, "That's for damn sure." God bless 'em.

Next morning: 7:30 A.M. Everybody boards the Rottnest ferry.[96] The Detour, at Salmon Bay, is a choice between "Sand" or "Sea." In the first, teams pick a pile of forty large, leafy branches and drag it 126 yards to a large sand dune. This is known as brushing the beach and is a standard measure against erosion. The latter requires teams to don snorkeling gear and search fifty crayfish traps on the ocean floor. Only a few traps have crayfish in them. Each team member must retrieve one.

Team Mojo returns with only one crayfish and learns they have to get another. "We have the crappiest luck!" moans Joseph. Uh, no, dude. You *made* your luck crappy, there. Returning to the water, Joseph finds another crayfish in its trap, but the rules require each team member to retrieve one, and he has already gotten his. Alas, Monica has the skeevies and doesn't want to touch the damn thing.[97]

A few minutes later, in one of those splendid juxtapositions that makes life so entertaining, Joseph says, "We are the kings of not reading the clues right and stuff," simultaneously realizing that he has put his bike helmet on backward.

Returning to the mainland, teams rush to the Roadblock at Fremantle Prison, a search on the grounds and through underground tunnels, with the aid of a Duracell flashlight and Duracell Copper-Top batteries (Plug-ola. Cha-Ching), which directs teams to the breakwater at the Fremantle Sailing Club, only one mile away.

Taxi woes, more than anything else, doom the final team.

---

[96] A really downbeat children's book about an evil boat in the Thomas the Tank Engine universe. (Oh, shut up.)

[97] The crayfish, like the shuwa, evidently became dinner that night.

1. Eric and Jeremy (The Smutty Slackers) 11:47 A.M.
2. Monica and Joseph (Team Mojo) 11:48 A.M.
3. BJ and Tyler (The Fabulous Furry Freak Brothers) 11:56 A.M.
4. Ray and Yolanda (Team Legs) 12:23 P.M.
5. Fran and Barry (Team Vague) ELIMINATED

Leg #9: "T-Tow, My Ass!"

Early on, and throughout the leg, BJ and Tyler engage in one of the dumbest and most ineffective attempts at villainy in the entire history of the show, trying to rile Joseph with intimations about Monica's alleged attraction to Eric. It's like teasing Archie about Veronica, except that the guys doing it are not Reggie but a pair of Jugheads. Paging Mr. Weatherbee.

In any event, the four remaining teams receive seventy dollars with instructions to travel to the Swan Bells Tower, a six-story edifice fifteen miles away.

The 8:00 A.M. opening time guarantees an overnight bunching. Several teams call for taxis, so they'll have a ride when they exit. The Slackers call to cancel these cabs, a tactic that backfires as they also find themselves rideless.

When Team Mojo rides off with impunity, both the Freaks and Team Legs assume that they were the ones who pulled off this underhanded and (given the inevitability of an airport bunching) ultimately pointless sabotage. Bad feelings continue to build.

Teams now must fly 1,700 miles to Darwin, Australia, and find the reptile sanctuary Crocodylus Park, where the next clue awaits in the crocodile pit. Mojo tells the airport ticket agent that they want the fastest flight to Darwin, and they don't want this info shared with the folks behind them. The guy asks, "What's it worth to me?" Joseph offers to have Monica kiss him. The agent's totally unimpressed look is priceless. Freeze frame it.

Everybody snags the 12:15 P.M. Qantas flight to Darwin, guaranteeing another overnight bunching outside Crocodylus Park. Third bunching this leg, and David and Lori didn't even get one. Sniff.

Nobody loses any limbs in the crocodile pit.

Headed for the next task at an airfield in Batchelor, both the Freaks and Team Mojo plan to Yield the other.[98] The Freaks win out

---

[98] Which is understandable, given the current animus between them, but also stupid. The Slackers, who had a part in driving these two teams against one another, have come in first multiple times, and you don't Yield the team you dislike; you Yield the strongest team behind you.

by mere steps, leading Monica to whine, "It's so unfair. We were here first." Ummm, no. The very point of this exercise is that you weren't. Roadblock: one player must tandem skydive (with an instructor) from 12,000 feet up. BJ, survivor of the shuwa hunt, now gets to do something fun. He yells "T-Tow!"

Monica seethes. "T-Tow my ass." He yells "T-tow!" again from 12,000 feet, and again as he comes in for a landing. Yolanda, watching from the ground, remarks, "He's so corny." Yeah. That's fair.

As BJ reaches the ground, his team is handed the next clue, which is to search the magnetic termite mounds at Litchfield National Park.

Joseph has so much fun mocking Monica's whining that for several seconds both fail to notice that the Yield is over.

The Detour up ahead is "Wet" or "Dry." The first requires Racers to wade one mile down a river through woods infested with poisonous plants and spiders. No kidding. In "Dry," teams drive six miles to the Aida Creek Valley Lookout, claim a marked Didgerido, and try to follow the sounds made by the musical instrument to an Aborigine playing one with the same markings. Before leaving, both team members must learn how to play a note. Sounds a little luck based—but as the Freaks and Slackers find out when tackling the "Wet" task, "Dry" is much faster.

Monica's still burning. "If you're going to Yield someone, that's sleazy...and the hippies are sleazeballs." Umm, Monica...sleazeballs they may be, that being a matter for opinion, but the Yield is not sleazy. It is a game option, provided by the people who made up the rules. Calling it sleazy is like playing checkers and saying, "I'm too principled to use the Kings." Besides, weren't you going to do it? And wasn't that Joseph, laughing uproariously as the Slackers called the cab company? Yolanda chortles at the Didgeridoo's fart noises, but the team is first to the Pit Stop at the Lake Bennett Wilderness Resort. And the other three teams? Bunched seconds apart on the road, they now head for a three-way sprint to the mat. Though several yards ahead of Monica, BJ tries to bypass a footbridge by jumping the gully beside it. It's a critical error, that slows him down and leaves his team Mugged again—especially bad news, as he is barefoot in boxer shorts.

1. Ray and Yolanda (Team Legs) 1:13 P.M.
2. Eric and Jeremy (The Smutty Slackers) 1:20 P.M.

3. Monica and Joseph (Team Mojo) 1:21 P.M.
4. BJ and Tyler (The Fabulous Furry Freak Brothers) 1:21 P.M.
   MUGGED

Leg #10: Legs and Exoskeletons

The first three teams receive $203 with their instructions to a) fly to Bangkok, Thailand, b) taxi to the Moshi Bus Terminal, c) then take a bus ninety-seven miles to Lo Paree, where their next clue awaits at the Three Spire Pagoda Buddhist Temple.

The Freak Brothers receive nothing. BJ still has no pants or shoes.

Yolanda, who feels bad for BJ, leaves him a pair of her purple stretch pants, which may not enhance his masculinity, but will allow him to get around in public. The Slackers, who showed no such compassion the last time the Freaks were bankrupted, leave BJ a pair of flip-flops. We will give those two teams credit for sportsmanship, but…um…why? At this point in the game, why would any of the other teams help them catch the next plane?[99]

In Bangkok, Team Mojo makes their most critical error. Missing the midnight train caught by the Slackers and Team Legs, they believe the ticket clerk who tells them the next bus is at 5:30 A.M. The Freaks are given completely different information regarding a first bus that leaves at 4:30 A.M. The discrepancy, which has to do with competing bus companies, proves critical, delaying Mojo so much that they're too late to be equalized by the bunching point up ahead.

The Three Squire Pagoda is home to hundreds of indolent monkeys, leading Jeremy to admire their lifestyle. "If we win the million dollars," he says, "we'll be monkeys." The scene cries out for a helpful Wizard of Oz to tell him that he and Eric had this attribute all along. The Roadblock requires each participating Racer to prepare a buffet for the monkeys, as per the local custom.

The Freaks and Team Legs both go for the the Fast Forward, involving something called an "Afterschool Favorite." Yolanda wonders if

---

[99] In any event, the Freaks head for the nightclub district and beg sufficient funds, hitting the airport in time to catch a flight essentially equivalent to the one caught by the prior three teams. It's yet another case of the Mugging utterly failing to affect game play. Install an even more stringent Mugging, where bankrupted Racers are proscribed from receiving help from more fortunate teams, and the penalty might mean something. Preferably: if Racers aren't appreciably slowed down by being barefoot and penniless, end the tradition entirely.

it's a game of cricket. Well, close. It's a traditional afterschool snack of deep-fried crickets and grasshoppers. There's a fun scene involving both teams eyeing each other over their bowls, each waiting for the other to quit. In the end, Legs returns to the Roadblock, but because of volume, rather than distaste at eating bugs.

Only now does Mojo arrive at the Temple, where Monica once again opines that they've lost. Joseph starts building his buffet. Along the way, we get a great shot of monkeys eating fruit, combined with a direct cut of Monica also having a bite. That is deliberate and cold.

Cut to BJ throwing up. The Freaks are not sure they can do this. BJ finishes anyway and tells Tyler that once you get to the bottom of the bowl, it's all legs and exoskeletons.[100] Thanks for the advice, guy.

The Buddha Garden, at Koh-Kret Island, some ninety miles away, provides this episode's Detour: "Move It" or "Altar It." The first requires teams to transport seventy-two clay pots from the pottery factory to a boat on the other end of a crowded marketplace. They must carry the pots using the local method—i.e. all lined up on a plank. "Altar It" requires teams to construct a shrine, and goldleaf a statue of the Buddha.

Team Mojo is alone at "Move It," a choice that proves unfortunate when Monica drops and breaks most of her pottery. Once again, she weeps that this is the hardest thing she's ever had to do. So the Swordfish didn't hold that record for long.

1. BJ and Tyler (Fabulous Furry Freak Brothers) 11:18 A.M.
2. Eric and Jeremy (The Smutty Slackers) 1:21 P.M.
3. Ray and Yolanda (Team Legs) 1:28 P.M.
4. Monica and Joseph (Team Mojo) ELIMINATED

Team Legs wins the episode's prize and gets to spend the night in a luxury hotel room. Let us see if that helps.

Leg #11: A Spin on the Japanese Pizza

This leg and the next one both aired together, as halves of a two-hour finale.

Racers and viewers who can count know that nobody's gonna be eliminated at the end of this leg, but a Mugging is in the works.

---

[100] And those exoskeletons are sharp. The Freaks reported cutting the inside of their mouths to hell.

Receiving $388, teams taxi seventy-five miles to obtain their clue from one of the elephants at the Royal Kraal. A minor bunching ensues as the Kraal does not open until 4:00 A.M. Feh.

There's also some minor comedy as the Freaks and Legs step in "crap" and "doodoo," but really, all of this comes down to a noxious plug, as all teams receive T-Mobile Sidekicks containing their next clue: instructions to fly 7,000 miles to Tokyo, Japan, where their next clue awaits somewhere along the sea of neon that surrounds Shibuya Square. The Freaks are naturally ebullient. They have both been to Japan. And Tyler is a minor celebrity there, who speaks the language.

Reaching the airport, Slackers and Team Legs both go to a general-info desk and find a United Airlines itinerary that arrives in Japan at 2:15 P.M. The Freaks are not able to get on this flight and must settle for a Thai Airways flight that lands sometime after 4:00 P.M. They can only hope that the language barrier is kind.

The Slackers and Freaks are able to reach Shibuya while Team Legs still wanders around the roads, unable to get coherent directions because of the language barrier.

The Slackers are first to find the flashing message, "Find Hachiko." Hachiko is a dog famous in Japanese lore, and there is a statue of him near Shibuya. There is also a guy wearing a long muffler in the *Amazing Race* colors. Directed to Hachiko, all three teams will eventually find the guy in the muffler, miss the point, and think *he's* Hachiko. Nobody will get that it's the dog. It doesn't matter, as this guy is the one who's handing out the clue envelopes, but we can wonder if the Racers had to wait for the episode to air before realizing their error.

The Detour is "Maiden" and "Messenger." The first involves transporting a woman by palanquin, the second zipping around on bikes delivering messages to office buildings.

Both tasks lead to an overnight stay in a capsule hotel, one of those odd Japanese places where travelers are stacked in tiny cubbies. The mint on your pillow is a Tic-Tac. There are also assigned departure times. The Slackers leave at 9:00 A.M., the Freaks at 9:15 A.M., Team Legs (which would otherwise be hours behind) at 9:30 A.M. Jeremy shows his frustration at Tyler's advantage, this leg. "Those hippies, and their dang…language-knowing." Hee. The cameraman nails him picking his nose.

The Roadblock at the amusement park Fujikyu Highland requires one member of each team to ride three consecutive thrill rides, including two roller coasters and something called a Pizza, searching for a man holding a big sign on the ground. (If they don't see the sign, they have to ride all *three* rides again.) Once again, travel there is not kind to Ray and Yolanda, as they lose their ticket on the expressway and have to pay a fine. The biggest character moment occurs when Tyler tries to psych Jeremy out, reporting that he's seen the sign when he really hasn't.

For the first two teams, there's a neck-and-neck paddleboat race to the Pit Stop, a swan-shaped tour boat. The Freaks arrive first and win T-Mobile Sidekicks, once again showing excessive glee at the dinky prize they've been awarded.

Team Legs, which arrives last by some time, thanks to another round of navigation woes, is of course Mugged.

1. BJ and Tyler (Fabulous Furry Freak Brothers) 12:18 P.M.
2. Eric and Jeremy (The Smutty Slackers) 12:20 P.M.
3. Ray and Yolanda (Team Legs) 3:01 P.M. MUGGED

Leg #12: The Detour that Wasn't

Teams must now fly to Anchorage, Alaska, and find their next clue on their rental cars in the airport parking lot.

To their credit, the Freaks leave 2,000 yen for the bankrupt Ray and Yolanda. I still don't see the point of bailing out bankrupt teams in a tough competition, especially when the Race is down to three. However, the Freaks twice received help from Ray and Yolanda, so returning the favor is fair enough.

Yolanda stops at a restaurant and succeeds in begging money from awestruck drunken Japanese who seriously think she looks like Janet Jackson. She doesn't, not really. No slight on her. But the Japanese men dance around, do fake Jackson moves, and hand her the money. She says, "I'll tell Michael you said hi." You can't make that up.

All teams must first drop their cars off in the Hotel Nikko parking lot. Arriving first, the Freaks arrange their 6:10 A.M. shuttle to the airport, and ask if the hotel has an Internet connection. They are told that an Internet lounge is upstairs. They then sneakily ask the desk clerks to hide the existence of the Internet lounge. Now, I have complained about this before. You really *can't* ask service people to cheat on your behalf. They're *not gonna* cooperate.

Except that…when the Slackers arrive, and also ask for an Internet connection, the desk clerk does exactly what he's been asked to do. He tells the Slackers that the hotel has no Internet. All this with a big broad grin on his face. The Slackers fail to see this incredibly obvious chicanery. So they grump over the stupid hotel and its failure to provide an Internet connection, and promptly get a much better flight via phone than the Freaks have been able to get via Internet.

None of this matters, as by the time Airport Shuffle, different departure times, and a Taipei connection shake out, all three teams arrive in Anchorage at the same time.

Frigid weather. Snow on the ground and still falling. A white airport. All three teams make it to their autos and learn that they must now drive thirty miles to Mirror Lake.

Team Legs gets lost, of course.

The Detour is a choice between taking a 150-mile round-trip plane flight to deliver medical supplies to a remote village, or using an auger to dig ten ice-fishing holes in the frozen lake. Bad weather means the plane can't take off anyway—according to the pilot, maybe not for minutes, maybe not for days—so the choice is rendered moot.[101]

Teams must now drive twenty-six miles to Kincaid Park, find the chalet, don the provided snowshoes and, using a map, search a trail for their next clue. The Freaks can't find the snowshoes provided, despite running past them several times, in an inadvertent shout-out to Fran and Barry.

Another airport bunching and a little running around later, teams are directed to return to the very location where the Race started: the Red Rocks Amphitheatre, outside Denver, Colorado. The Slackers and Freaks arrive there minutes apart, with Team Legs inevitably still somewhere behind them, on the road. The final Roadblock turns out to be a geography and memory test. Faced with an array of national flags, including those of all the countries visited in the course of the competi-

---

[101] Though it would have been amusing to watch some team absorb this information, nod sagely, and declare that they wanted to wait for the weather to clear. At the end of the leg we'd get a nice cut from the first- and second-place teams, arriving at the finish line in Denver, to those clever third-place dawdlers, still standing in the Alaskan cold, like the Guidos of blessed memory. But who would have done this? Fran and Barry?

tion, each participating Racer must run out into the field, retrieve the national flags, and line the correct flags up in the order the countries were visited.

Head to head in a last-minute scramble for the million, both teams struggle with faulty memories and fuzzy exhaustion. BJ's unable to find the Russian flag for the Freaks, and Eric makes critical mistakes in flag order and identification. But in the end, it's BJ who pulls out the win. T-freakin'-Tow.

1. BJ and Tyler (The Fabulous Furry Freak Brothers) WIN
2. Eric and Jeremy (The Smutty Slackers) PLACE
3. Ray and Yolanda (Team Legs) SHOW

Further Viewing

FANS OF *THE AMAZING RACE* may want to check out the following films, which evoke the controlled chaos of this competition.

Around the World in Eighty Days (1956). Directed by Michael Anderson. Starring David Niven, Cantinflas, Shirley MacLaine, too many others to list. Based on the Jules Verne novel about the adventures of Phileas Fogg, a London eccentric who bets that he can circumnavigate the globe under the titular deadline. Remade (poorly) with Jackie Chan, in 2004.

It's A Mad, Mad, Mad, Mad World (1963). Directed by Stanley Kramer. Starring Milton Berle, Mickey Rooney, Jonathan Winters, Spencer Tracy, too many others to list. This cameo-filled farce details the riot that ensues when a dying gangster (Jimmy Durante) advises the motorists who witnessed his fatal car wreck of $350,000 in stolen money, buried 200 miles away under "a big W." Expect massive property damage.

The Great Race (1965). Directed by Blake Edwards. Starring Jack Lemmon, Tony Curtis, Natalie Wood, Peter Falk, too many others to list. Perhaps the closest of any films, title and all, to the *Amazing Race* experience, this one's a farce about an automobile race around the world, which quickly narrows to two teams as accidents (and sabotage) wipe out all the other competitors.

If It's Tuesday, This Must Be Belgium (1969). Directed by Mel Stuart. Starring Suzanne Pleshette, Michael Constantine, Norman Fell, too many others to list. Not a race, but a character-based farce centered on one of those hectic package tours that require Americans to race from one European site to another without ever actually absorbing anything. The very title evokes *The Amazing Race*, which is so frenetic that players have been known to forget what country they were in.

Rat Race (2001). Directed by Jerry Zucker. Starring Whoopi Goldberg, Rowan Atkinson, Jon Lovitz, John Cleese, too many others to list. Billionaire John Cleese advises a group of Vegas travelers that two million in cash awaits, a mere 563 miles away. An uncredited remake of *It's A Mad, Mad, Mad, Mad World*, with some funny moments, even though it's not nearly as good.

And for the Truly Obsessive

FROM AN OFFICIAL LIST OF SHOW LOCATIONS:

3 Dives Jerk Restaurant, Lucea, Jamaica

3rd Street, Washington, District of Columbia, USA

4 Track Adventures, Restal Road, Woodhill, Auckland, New Zealand

700 Lavalle, Tigre, Buenos Aires, Federal District, Argentina

8 Trolley Park, Moscow, Russia

Abbey Road Studios, Abbey Road, Hampstead, London, England, UK

Aberdeen, Aberdeenshire, Scotland, UK

Addis Ababa, Ethiopia

Aeropuerto Arequipa, Arequipa, Peru

Aeropuerto Internacional Jorge Chavez, Lima, Peru

Aeropuerto de Santiago, Santiago, Chile

Aguadilla, Puerto Rico

Aishbagh, Lucknow, Uttar Pradesh, India

Ajaccio, Corse-du-Sud, France

Al Norte, Mendoza, Argentina

Alaska, USA

Algeciras, Cádiz, Andalucía, Spain

Alleppey, Kerala, India

Amani Lodge, Namibia

Amber Fort, Jaipur, Rajasthan, India

Trapper Creek, Alaska, USA
Trushidup Palm Oil Plantation,
Malaysia
Tunis Airport, Tunis, Tunisia
United States of America (USA)
Umm Al Quwain Aeroclub, Al
Ittihad Street, Dubai, United Arab
Emirates
Underwater World, Mooloolaba,
Queensland, Australia
Usina Parque Jacaré, Brotas, São
Paulo, Brazil
Vatnajökull, Iceland
Venice, Veneto, Italy
Viaduct Harbour, Auckland, New
Zealand
Viaduto Santa Efigênia, São Paulo
City, São Paulo, Brazil
Viajes Flandria Travel Agency,
Tangier, Morocco
Victoria Falls, Zambia
Victoria Memorial, Calcutta, West
Bengal, India
Victoria Station, Mumbai,
Maharashtra, India
Victoria, Philippines
Vienna Train Station, Vienna, Austria
Vienna, Austria
Villa Catedral, San Carlos de
Bariloche, Argentina
Vincent Daniels Square, Queens,
New York City, New York, USA
Virgin Mary Statue, Cerro San
Cristóbal, Parque Metropolitano,
Santiago, Chile
Voss, Hordaland, Norway
Waitomo Caves, Waitomo, Waikato,
New Zealand

Wangetti Beach, Cairns, Queensland,
Australia
Washington Dulles International
Airport, 45020 Aviation Drive,
Sterling, Virginia, USA
Washington's Crossing, Pennsylvania,
USA
Washington, District of Columbia,
USA
Water Palace, Jaipur, Rajasthan, India
Water Tower Place, 835 N. Michigan
Ave., Near North Side, Chicago,
Illinois, USA
Wellington, New Zealand
Wentworth Station, Queenstown,
Otago, New Zealand
West Nile Ferry Port, Luxor, Egypt
Westhaven Marina, St Mary's Bay,
Auckland, New Zealand
Whitford, Auckland, New Zealand
Wild Wadi Water Park, Jumeira
Beach, Dubai, United Arab
Emirates
Wild World Tropical Zoo, Cairns,
Queensland, Australia
Xau Xarra, Botswana
Xi'an, China
Yellowstone National Park,
Wyoming, USA
Yeni Camii Square, Istanbul, Turkey
York, Pennsylvania, USA
Yu Yuan Gardens, Shanghai, China
Zambezi River, Zambia
Zilia, Haute-Corse, France
Zitadelle, Spandau, Berlin, Germany
Zocalo Square, Mexico City, México
D.F., Mexico

Adam-Troy Castro

About the Author

ADAM-TROY CASTRO's short stories have been nominated five times for the Nebula, two times for the Hugo, and once for the Stoker. He has contributed to previous Smart Pop volumes about King Kong, Hitchhiker's Guide, *Alias*, and Harry Potter, among others. He has been assured that the paperback version of his collection *Vossoff and Nimmitz* will be out sometime in 2007. He lives in Miami with his long-suffering wife Judi and a rotating assortment of cats that now includes Maggie, Ralphie, Uma Furman, and Meow Farrow.

For news of future publications, as well as rants, art, movie reviews, and various silliness, check out his Web site at www.sff.net/people/adam-troy.